Tuning In

Tuning In

Experiencing Music in Psychedelic States

STEVEN J. GELBERG

Foreword by
WILLIAM A. RICHARDS

Cover Credit: "Sonic Universe," by Hugo Orosz / Orosz Visual Labs - https://www.instagram.com/oroszvisuallabs/?hl=en

Published by State University of New York Press, Albany

© 2025 State University of New York

All rights reserved

Printed in the United States of America

No part of this book may be used or reproduced in any manner whatsoever without written permission. No part of this book may be stored in a retrieval system or transmitted in any form or by any means including electronic, electrostatic, magnetic tape, mechanical, photocopying, recording, or otherwise without the prior permission in writing of the publisher.

Links to third-party websites are provided as a convenience and for informational purposes only. They do not constitute an endorsement or an approval of any of the products, services, or opinions of the organization, companies, or individuals. SUNY Press bears no responsibility for the accuracy, legality, or content of a URL, the external website, or for that of subsequent websites.

EU GPSR Authorised Representative:
Logos Europe, 9 rue Nicolas Poussin, 17000, La Rochelle, France
contact@logoseurope.eu

For information, contact State University of New York Press, Albany, NY
www.sunypress.edu

Library of Congress Cataloging-in-Publication Data

Name: Gelberg, Steven J., author.
Title: Tuning in : experiencing music in psychedelic states / Steven J. Gelberg.
Description: Albany : State University of New York Press, [2025]. | Includes bibliographical references and index.
Identifiers: LCCN 2024025612 | ISBN 9798855801118 (pbk. : alk. paper) | ISBN 9798855801125 (ebook)
Subjects: LCSH: Music—Psychological aspects. | Hallucinogenic drugs—Therapeutic use.
Classification: LCC ML3838 .G3705 2024 | DDC 781.1/1—dc23/eng/20240815
LC record available at https://lccn.loc.gov/2024025612

Contents

Acknowledgments		vii
Foreword		ix
Preface: Autobiographical Reflections on Psychedelics		xi
Introduction: Music and Psychedelics: A Sacred Synergy		1
Chapter 1	What Is a "Psychedelic Experience"?	17
Chapter 2	Expressing the Inexpressible: Music as Mysticism	35
Chapter 3	Beginner's Mind and "Letting Go"	49
Chapter 4	Timelessness, Hypersensitivity, and "Becoming" the Music	65
Chapter 5	Music, Emotion, and Aesthetic Ecstasy	81
Chapter 6	Music, Creator of Worlds: Synesthesia and Eidetic Visions	99
Chapter 7	Music from "Nowhere": Hallucinating Music	111
Chapter 8	Music in Psychedelic Psychotherapy	129
Chapter 9	It's Subjective: Choosing Music	153

Chapter 10	Is Classical Music Still Relevant?	161
Chapter 11	Ambient Music for Psychedelic States	185
Chapter 12	"World Music" and the Collective Unconscious	191
Chapter 13	Sound Alternatives to Music: The Music of Nature and "White Noise"	207
Epilogue		215
Appendix I	Spotify Playlists for Psychedelic Sessions	227
Appendix II	Abbreviated Versions of Select Spotify Playlists	231
Notes		247
Bibliography		279
Index		293

Acknowledgments

I would like, first, to express my sincere gratitude to Prof. William (Bill) Richards, a truly inspiring figure in the modern study of psychedelics and their therapeutic uses. Early in the formation of this book I introduced him to the project, hoping for constructive feedback. As someone immersed in both psychedelic studies and a lifelong love of music, he was enthusiastic and encouraging, providing the psychic and spiritual fuel necessary for me to proceed with confidence in this labor of love. He read early drafts and provided helpful suggestions and advice, answered questions, and generally remained tuned in to my progress. Finally, he generously agreed to write his eloquent foreword. I cannot thank him enough.

I am deeply grateful to all the knowledgeable, informative, and inspired writers and thinkers, alive and departed, whose words I quote in these pages. Much of the labor involved in writing this book consisted in casting a wide net in search of luminous gems of knowledge, insight, and revelation. Assembled together, their light intermingled and collectively cast a wide illumination on an important subject that, until now, has been largely neglected. In particular I must mention Aldous Huxley and Alan Watts, whose respective works *The Doors of Perception* and *The Joyous Cosmology* set me, as a teenager, on a path of discovery that changed my life.

Sincere gratitude also to my editor at SUNY Press, Richard Carlin, who, from my first submission, understood the value of the work, lent his keen editor's eye to help shape it into a better version of itself, and then patiently guided it through the publication process.

Finally, my undying appreciation for my beloved wife, best friend, and guardian angel, Nilima Bhatia. She sustains me with her unconditional love, understanding, patience, and buoyant good humor. I am truly blessed.

Permission to use material from the following publications has been granted:

Chapter 3. Philip Glass, "Listening to Philip Glass—The Composer Speaks with Tricycle," *Tricycle—The Buddhist Review* IX, no. 1 (Fall 1999): 40–42. Used by permission of Philip Ryan, executive editor, *Tricycle—The Buddhist Review*.

Chapter 10. Albert Hoffman, "LSD: Quite Personal," in *Hofmann's Elixir: LSD and the New Eleusis*, ed. Amanda Feilding, trans. Jonathan Ott (Oxford: Beckley Foundation Press, 2008). Used by permission of the Beckley Foundation Press.

Chapter 10. *My Psychedelic Explorations* by Claudio Naranjo, MD. Published by Inner Traditions International and Bear & Company, ©2020. All rights reserved. http://www.Innertraditions.com. Reprinted with permission of publisher.

Foreword

As I welcome you into the fascinating and sacred spaces that await you in the pages ahead, I feel as though I stand at an awesome threshold—perhaps at the doors of a majestic Gothic cathedral or beneath the central dome of a great Hindu temple or Islamic mosque, or somewhere in the scenic natural world where the sun is beginning to rise or where the Milky Way is just becoming visible. In and through his profound spiritual and artistic explorations, coupled with exceptionally comprehensive and disciplined scholarship, Steven Gelberg has given us all a very wonderful gift. As you will discover, he also writes with balance, clarity, touches of playfulness, and rich expressiveness.

The timing of this book's publication is ideal, not only coinciding with the emergence of psychedelic substances into the mainstream of Western thought and life, but also offering words of wisdom and nurturance to those of us who are awakening to our interconnectedness as essentially spiritual beings—as Teilhard de Chardin noted, "spiritual beings who are having human experiences." Beyond the limits of rational cognition and diverse human languages is that flowing river of energies manifested in sound that we call *music*. As the author often reminds us, it offers more than entertaining support or distractions; it can lead us in through our human struggles and foibles to the discovery of true revelation, to wisdom and healing in experiential realms of meaningful suffering, of insight, love, and beauty—all often quite ineffable. At times, we can quite literally "become music" in and through its changing rhythms, its dissonances and harmonies, and its subtle nuances and ineffable climaxes.

The extensiveness and thoroughness of this author's research and thought are truly remarkable. He not only surveys different genres of music, all with openness and appreciation, but also guides us in and through the ongoing process of discerning how best to select music for excursions into consciousness, with and without the facilitation of psychedelics. How far within do you dare to go? How willing are you to explore totally new perspectives on "reality"? Under what circumstances can you summon the courage to choose to fully entrust yourself to ever-deeper strata of your own mind to experience insight, resolve traumas, and explore the mysteries of transcendence irrespective of the suffering or joy entailed? *Nada Brahman*, the "sound God," appears to dwell within us all, whatever our spiritual orientation, and perhaps enjoys offering wisely choreographed guidance that may feel ominous and strange at one moment, but profoundly familiar and comforting at another.

I encourage you to venture into the pages ahead with readiness to learn both from the well-articulated experiences of many psychedelic pioneers whom the author quotes—whose wisdom and fresh insights are sometimes lost amid much contemporary verbiage—but notably also from Steven himself as he presents the fruits of many years of careful listening, existential questing, and critical thinking. His creativity has culminated in his own carefully constructed playlists, which he invites us to explore in the context of our own unique meditative disciplines. Onward with gratitude!

William A. Richards, PhD
Center for Psychedelic and Consciousness Research
Psychiatry Department, Johns Hopkins University
School of Medicine
Author, *Sacred Knowledge: Psychedelics and Religious Experiences*

Preface

Autobiographical Reflections on Psychedelics

By luck, fate, or chance, my adolescence coincided with the flowering of the psychedelic counterculture of the mid- to late 1960s. What an extraordinary time to be waking up to the world. I had my first LSD trip at age fifteen, in 1967, but I'd already had some preparation. Reading the American Transcendentalists Emerson and Thoreau in high school, I'd been introduced to the wisdom of nonconformity, of rejecting received "wisdom" in favor of finding one's own authentic inner truth. From Hermann Hesse's novels I imbibed the impulse to turn one's back on bourgeois society and to embrace the nobility of the spiritual quest. From British psychiatrist R. D. Laing, I became convinced of the arbitrary, constructed, and confining nature of "consensual reality." From Allen Ginsberg, whom I idolized as a kind of guru figure, I was exposed to the idea of fearless spontaneity and, in *Howl*, to the presence of the miraculous in all things.[1] And at last, from Aldous Huxley (*The Doors of Perception*) and Alan Watts (*The Joyous Cosmology*), I learned of the power of certain magical substances capable of liberating our socially conditioned minds and opening portals to sublime, higher states of awareness. Though quite young, I was as ripe as one might be for psychedelics. A few years later, as a graduating high school senior, I chose, as did all my classmates, some words of wisdom to accompany my senior portrait in the school yearbook. Mine were from William Blake: "If the doors of perception were cleansed everything would appear to man as it is, infinite."

I'd been a devoted consumer of music since childhood. From around age nine I became deeply immersed in the music of the "folk revival" of the late 1950s and early 1960s, listening to Pete Seeger, Bob Dylan, Joan

Baez, Judy Collins, and numerous others. Much of that music was steeped in social idealism, political progressivism, and a heartfelt humanism, with occasional flashes of psychedelia (e.g., the Incredible String Band.) I was an acoustic-only folk purist who viewed pop music as superficial and commercial, lacking the earnest, social-justice messages of folk music and the blues.

That bias against commercial pop included the early Beatles, until one day, at age fourteen, I listened to my older sister's fresh new copy of *Rubber Soul*. When "Norwegian Wood" came on, I had an epiphany. The sound of George Harrison's sitar set off a kind of quiet explosion in my inner being. Out of nowhere, I was now hearing the most beautiful sound I ever could have imagined: a mysterious, magisterial, complexly beautiful sonic texture that seemed broadcast from some distant universe. Part of the wonder of that first hearing is that amid the utter strangeness of the sound there was an uncanny sense of familiarity, as if I'd heard this otherworldly sound not years but eons ago in some other, more rarefied existence. I couldn't believe how utterly *beautiful* it was. I had to find more of that beguiling sound. Checking the album's liner notes, I found the name of the instrument that Harrison was playing: "sitar." I immediately went to my favorite local record store at the Roosevelt Field shopping center in Garden City, Long Island; approached the manager; and slowly intoned the word "sitar" as if it were a magical incantation. He walked over to the "International" section and pulled out an early (1957) Ravi Shankar album, *The Sounds of India*, which I purchased, took home, and devoured in a kind of trance. This instinctual attraction to the sonic grandeur of the sitar was a harbinger of things to come.

I was quickly swept up into the optimistic psychedelic zeitgeist of those days (which was not yet burdened with decades of contentious, propagandistic public discourse and diatribe). As a sensitive, deep-thinking kid with an existential hunger, the hippie counterculture that appealed to me was admittedly an idealized one. I admired the prototypical hippie, conceived as a free spirit who'd been gifted with the innocence of a child, the heart of a bodhisattva, and the mind of a mystic. It was *their* rainbow circus I wanted to run away to.

I followed the underground press, mainly *The East Village Other* and occasional copies of the *San Francisco Oracle* that made their way to the opposite coast. Aside from Huxley and Watts, I also read *The Varieties of Psychedelic Experience*, *LSD—The Consciousness-Expanding Drug*, and other early academic studies on psychedelics. I tuned in deeply to psychedelic rock, adorned the walls of my bedroom with psychedelic posters, smoked pot with my friends on the weekends. I eagerly awaited my virgin psychedelic experience with all the anticipation (I imagine) of a devout Catholic child awaiting their First Communion. When the first tabs of acid reached our upper-middle-class suburban New York neighborhood, the tripping began, generally with a girlfriend or with a small group of friends. When tripping indoors, the accompanying music was usually psychedelically tinged rock: the Beatles, of course, and Jimi Hendrix, Led Zeppelin, Cream, Grateful Dead, Jefferson Airplane, Traffic, Procol Harum, and Donovan, to name a few, plus some Ravi Shankar (usually my contribution to the mix).

During my freshman year at Washington University, St. Louis, I was a conscientious student, getting good grades while often tripping on weekends with a small coterie of like-minded countercultural friends. Extracurricular reading centered on sociological and civilizational criticism (e.g., Erich Fromm), Eastern mysticism, and psychology—especially works focusing on liminal forms of consciousness under the rubric "madness," which I now assessed as a dangerous but heroic protest against standard-brand reality. Those readings, along with more-or-less weekly tripping, increasingly raised doubts in my mind about the ontological status of consensual reality, creating a deep longing for transcendent truth, existential authenticity, and enlightenment.

I was one of those young psychedelic pilgrims for whom the acid experience contained a compelling invitation to "integrate" it into one's inner being—even if that meant eventually devoting oneself to a demanding spiritual practice. If those ineffably profound awakening experiences on acid were reliable intimations of ultimate reality, genuine insights into transcendent truths, were they not worth taking seriously, come what may? As psychedelia cast a widening opalescent glow on my consciousness, and as the outer world increasingly appeared artificial and dystopian, the contrast between those opposing worlds fed an evolving inner turmoil. What was I to do?

The counterculture had already erected various bridges between psychedelia and Eastern spiritual paths: the writings of Alan Watts, Aldous Huxley, Ram Dass, Timothy Leary and Allen Ginsberg, among others; the Beatles and other band's songs hinting at enlightened states and mystical paradises, with their LP cover art (which played a huge role in our visual culture) showcasing Eastern (and generally surreal and otherworldly) images; the enchanting, hypnotic music of Ravi Shankar and other Indian virtuosos; and pictures of Hindu gods and goddesses for sale in college bookstores. LSD created the culture, and the culture spread the psychedelic spirit.

When posters appeared on campus announcing an upcoming Ram Dass lecture at a local synagogue with the intriguing title "Beyond Acid," there was no question of my not going. Ram Dass was now fully Hinduized, looking holy in white khadi cloth, ample beard, and chanting beads. Sitting on a stage in lotus position, he caressed the strings of a large tamboura (Indian drone instrument) lying horizontally across his lap. He spoke gently, slowly, meditatively, about the art of ego transcendence and the beauties of spiritual awakening. Representing a particularly attractive combination of the intellectual, the spiritual, and the soulfully authentic, he was a perfect lure to the structured spiritual life that beckoned. I might have simply followed him back to his ashram had I been fully ready.

One day, in the campus gift shop, I spotted a gorgeous, large Indian print of the Hindu god Krishna. I knew nothing of Krishna or even that it was Krishna depicted in the image. What I beheld was an androgynous youth, a beautiful blue boy wearing a peacock feather in his flowing dark hair, sitting with a flute in one hand and an arm tenderly embracing a calf. To me it was simply a hypnotically alluring piece of Indian art serving as a portal to some impossibly sublime, peaceful, transcendent world. The print took pride of place in my dorm room, becoming an object of contemplation and, on acid, aesthetic and spiritual awe.

Sometime late during that freshman year, I awoke one morning from an intense eidetic dream filled with archetypal images of long-haired, long-bearded yogis meditating in Himalayan caves. The silent but unambiguous message, as clear as if delivered telepathically, was: "If you are serious about enlightenment, this is what is required of you: renunciation of the ephemeral material world and total dedication to a spiritual path. Enlightenment is not a fantasy, not a dream, not make-believe. Human souls have been seeking and attaining sacred wisdom for millennia. Yes, my boy, it is real. So . . . do like the Indian yogis do." Years later I learned that George Harrison had had a very similar dream and had subsequently entered the same path, with the same guru and same mantra, that would soon draw me in. For many years Harrison and I shared a close common friend—one of a handful of intimates invited to be present at his deathbed—but I never had the opportunity to meet him myself.

Several years earlier, in 1962, Allen Ginsberg had returned from a long stay in India, bringing with him a popular Hindu mantra he'd learned from a female *sadhu* (holy woman): Hare Krishna Hare Krishna, Krishna Krishna Hare Hare / Hare Rama Hare Rama, Rama Rama Hare Hare.[2] From that point on, Ginsberg sang the Krishna mantra at numerous poetry readings and other countercultural venues, the words of the mantra punctuated with the delicate resonance of Indian brass finger cymbals. Later, in 1966, living on the Lower East Side of New York City, Ginsberg heard about a holy man from India who had recently established a small ashram in the neighborhood and was chanting that same magical mantra. The poet, excited to explore the matter, visited the ashram, where he found Swami Bhaktivedanta surrounded by a small coterie of mostly ex-hippie disciples. Ginsberg liked the Swami, and so he befriended and promoted his mission, attracting more ex-hippie followers to the cause. Gradually the movement grew and evolved into the International Society for Krishna Consciousness, the "Hare Krishna Movement."

The following year, a capacity-crowd fundraiser in San Francisco's Haight-Ashbury was organized by Ginsberg and the local Krishna devotees. Advertised as a "Mantra-Rock Dance" and held at the Avalon Ballroom, performers included the Grateful Dead, Jefferson Airplane, and several other major West Coast bands. Tim Leary, "Acid King" Owsley Stanley, and other counterculture luminaries attended, along with an auditorium full of tripping souls. Ginsberg first, then the Swami, led the crowd in chanting the Krishna mantra amid wild acid-fueled, celebratory dancing. Afterward, Ginsberg addressed the colorful congregation, to whom he issued an open invitation to visit the recently established Krishna temple on Frederick Street in the Haight. "I especially recommend the early-morning *kirtanas*," he said, "for those who, coming down from LSD, want to stabilize their consciousness on reentry."[3] Any who might visit the temple would be greeted by a colorful sign above the entrance reading, in part, "Stay High All the Time, Discover Eternal Bliss." As for Ginsberg, he remained a friend and sometimes promoter of the Krishna movement, later changing his personal spiritual trajectory to Buddhism, especially of the Tibetan variety.[4]

During these early years of the Krishnas, the young shaven-headed and sari-clad converts would go out into the streets and parks (first in New York, then the Haight-Ashbury, then other countercultural centers and college towns) chanting the Krishna mantra and selling their mimeographed magazine *Back to Godhead* mainly to hippies (referred to by Swami Bhaktivedanta as "our best customers"). Along with the magazine, they distributed a flyer declaring "Chant Hare Krishna and *Stay High*

Forever. No More Coming Down." During its first several years, the Krishna movement consisted almost entirely of ex–acid-heads, who'd go out into the streets to proselytize their not-yet-saved (or shaved) hippie brothers and sisters. Back in its (now long past) golden days, the Hare Krishnas were a destination for trippers who indeed longed to "stay high forever" by chanting and serving Krishna, as well as a haven for psychedelic burn-outs.[5] By the late 1960s, the Hare Krishna movement had become "one of the major forms of post-psychedelic spirituality."[6]

Not long after the end of the spring semester at Washington University, I found myself on the road, hitchhiking from New York to my intended target of San Francisco, completely undecided whether I'd be returning to school in the fall or finding a home somewhere in Hippiedom, perhaps landing at a commune. Picked up on the New Jersey Turnpike by a big blue converted school bus, now a mobile hippie commune, I ended up a few weeks later in Boulder, Colorado. After spending some days in the mountains above Boulder trying to meditate unto Enlightenment and falling far short, and also having missed the call to reboard the bus for its onward journey West, I hitchhiked down into Boulder proper, which served at the time as a way station for hordes of young people heading to the West Coast. There, after some wanderings and strange adventures, I ran into a Hare Krishna devotee chanting solo on a street corner near the University of Colorado campus. This taciturn monk invited me to the local ashram, a house on a side street accommodating about fifteen members, and I made my way there the following day:

> I was instantly captivated by the electric-blue, bejeweled, flute-playing form of Krishna; mesmerized by the Hare Krishna mantra sung to the gentle drone of the drum and sweet tintinnabulation of brass hand cymbals; seduced by the whole wheat and lentil aromas wafting from the ashram kitchen. Though at first a little put off by the ritualistic guru worship, the scriptural literalism and the rigid asceticism (no drugs! no sex! no fun!), I was intrigued by the devotees' intense purposefulness and their convincing displays of bliss.[7]

This is not the place to go into a detailed account of the following seventeen years spent as a full-time, fully committed devotee of Krishna. A brief summary will suffice: I lived as a celibate monk (*brahmacari*) for ten years (1970–1980), then entered the "householder" order as a married (but still monkish) fully committed member—my wife an Anglo-Irish fellow devotee of exceptional intelligence, beauty, and charisma. I spent those years fully immersed in Bhakti yoga as practitioner, scholar, and teacher, enjoying frequent pilgrimages and study trips to India. I also managed to enter academia through the back door, first by independently studying the history, sociology, and psychology of religion, then by speaking on Indian philosophy and religion at various colleges and universities, and finally by being invited to present papers about the Krishna movement at academic conferences attended by historians and sociologists of religion. This lead to the publication of a number of articles in academic books and journals.[8] In 1983 Grove Press published a volume of in-depth interviews I'd conducted with academic scholars discussing various aspects of the Krishna movement.[9] The book received a number of positive reviews in academic journals. During this period I also provided tactical assistance and an insider's critical perspective to various scholars working on books and dissertations on the Krishna movement.

I remained in the organization a total of seventeen years (ages eighteen to thirty-five), leaving when, especially in the years following the founder's death in 1977, the organization entered a prolonged period of political instability and spiritual disillusionment. I stayed on another ten years, witnessing the gradual exodus of most of the early joiners, those for whom psychedelics had played a significant role in their initial involvement.

Finally abandoning the ashram in 1987,[10] I spent three rich, productive years studying comparative religion and, whenever possible, mysticism at Harvard Divinity School. I also returned, after seventeen years of meditative sobriety, to psychedelic exploration. While immersed in my studies at HDS, on select weekends I tripped with friends, usually one at a time, my main tripping buddies being two wonderful women friends, artists and nature lovers both, involving daylong psychedelic wanderings through the fields and forests of the Arnold Arboretum in Jamaica Plain, as well as hours exploring the lush landscapes of Mt. Auburn Cemetery straddling Cambridge and Watertown (designed by the great Frederick Law Olmsted), along with various other nature excursions. Since I mostly tripped outdoors in natural surroundings, music didn't play a prominent role, and my immersion in the subject of psychedelics and music didn't begin until years later. However, between 1994 and 2015, while fully immersed in black-and-white fine-art photography,[11] I spent innumerable hours in my home darkroom with music of various kinds a constant companion.

In 2011, shortly before my sixtieth birthday, a prostate cancer diagnosis abruptly reminded me of my own mortality. One day I began mentally projecting into a future of decline and possible incapacitation.

Ruminating darkly on a worst-case scenario, I pictured myself in a helpless condition at home or—a horrible thought—in an institution. I wondered: in such a situation, possibly alone and incapacitated, bereft even of my beloved mate (I'd divorced and remarried after leaving the Krishnas), how would I pass the time? How would I escape being crushed by boredom or depression? The answer came easily: music. I knew I could at least keep my sanity if I had ready access to a choice selection of my music library. Losing myself in music comes easily. I reasoned I could put all my favorite music together in one easily accessible place (an MP3 player?). Right away I began systematically going through my prodigious CD collection to assemble the best of the best.

After a brief time the project began feeling a bit limited, self-centered, all about me, and I wondered if there were some way I might modify it so I might share it with others. Since my tastes in music tend largely to be shaped by a psyche drawn to sounds suggesting mystery, wonder, and inward journeys—sounds appealing to sensitized and altered states—I decided to expand the project by curating a more wide-ranging collection of music specifically intended for use in psychedelic sessions. I'd tentatively explored various psychedelic playlists but wondered if more could be done in that area. That seed idea lead to many years' (and continuing) immersion in the musical universe of Spotify in a focused but open search for music possessing qualities that might bring beauty, depth, and inspiration to psychedelic states. This evolved, over time, into the creation of numerous playlists, most of which relate directly to the intended curatorial project. Now, several years later, those playlists have attracted a combined listenership of more than ten thousand. These are not playlists in the usual sense: timed, planned excursions, engineered soundtracks with items to be heard in a particular order within a single trip. Rather, each playlist is a generous repository of items brought together under a particular category, the main types being (1) single genre ("Classical Music for Psychedelic States," "Psychedelic Ambient"); (2) subgenre themes ("Classical: Fantastic Journeys," "Ambient: Alien/Otherworldly"); (3) cross-genre independent themes ("Faerie Realms," "Tribal"); and (4) extra-musical recordings ("Nature Sounds," "White Noise").[12]

Within the first year of this curatorial project, I began to think about systematically researching the role and uses of music in psychedelic sessions, whether within formal psychotherapeutic settings or spontaneous independent excursions. As I dove in, my first discovery, and a source of some amazement—considering the key role music has always played in psychedelic therapy and exploration—was how little of substance had been written on the subject. Struck by this lacuna, I decided I'd attempt to fill it. I already had a fairly sizable personal library on psychedelics, which subsequently mushroomed over years of research. I found most references to music in the psychedelic literature (academic, historical, scientific, clinical, narrative, etc.) to be brief and ephemeral: a few lines here, a few paragraphs there, occasionally a few pages, rarely more. A relatively small handful of articles in the scientific literature, based on limited clinical studies, turned out to be disappointingly insubstantial and superficial. Yet spread across numerous books and journals one does encounter scattered bits and pieces of colorful description, reflection, and insight, the richest material often found in published "trip reports." I realized my task was to assemble as much of this material as possible and see whether it might be shaped into a cohesive, thematically organized book, something that might be of practical use to the wider psychedelic community. As the research progressed, distinct themes began to emerge and an overall structure took shape. I often reflected on, even agonized over, the purpose of the project, haunted by the risk of imposing too much of an intellectual or interpretive template on an experience that, in its essence, defies rational analysis: a fear of reducing the ineffable to the conventional, the sublime into the prosaic, experience to mere rhetoric.

The idealized notion of "psychedelic science" notwithstanding, the psychedelic experience is not a single, predictable phenomenon reducible to rational or quantifiable categories. It is profoundly personal and subjective. One can, of course, study and record what is happening within the physical brain during a trip (the hard core of psychedelic science). One can even propose theoretical models—psychodynamic, philosophical, or otherwise—in an attempt to define patterns or meanings within the experience. But the experience itself, that which is felt directly within personal consciousness, naturally eludes precise description, not to speak of definitive explication. To me, and to many or most who have undergone the journey, the psychedelic state represents sacred territory, an experience of the holy, privileged access to archetypal and transpersonal realms of being, and therefore resistant to reductive analysis.

Presented within a thematic structure suggested by the research, and quoting numerous and varied sources and approaches to the subject (while adding my own reflections), this book dives deeply into an experience that, while very difficult to articulate, has produced an accumulated wealth of rich descriptive insight, ranging from the straightforwardly didactic to the colorfully mythopoetic. It approaches the topic from two different but paradoxically intertwined directions: how music magnifies, deepens, and even guides the psychedelic experience, and how the psychedelic state itself magnifies and deepens the aesthetic and spiritual experience of music. It is about a particular and endlessly fascinating form of what I've come to think of as "sacred synergy." Listening to music on a psychedelic is like no other experience in the world, as you shall see and hear.

Introduction

Music and Psychedelics: A Sacred Synergy

> How strangely do we diminish a thing as soon as we try to express it in words! We believe we have dived down to the most unfathomable depths, and when we reappear on the surface, the drop of water that glistens on our trembling finger-tips no longer resembles the sea from which it came. We believe we have discovered a grotto that is stored with bewildering treasure; we come back to the light of day, and the gems we have brought are false—mere pieces of glass—and yet does the treasure shine on, unceasingly, in the darkness.
>
> —Maurice Maeterlinck, *The Treasure of the Humble*

How beautifully does Maurice Maeterlinck (1862–1949), Belgian playwright, poet, essayist, and Nobel Laureate, describe—without intending to—the experience of returning to terra firma after a deeply profound and poignant psychedelic journey, with little more than broken, fragmented words to describe the experience. Presuming that Maeterlinck did not explore the effects of opium or hashish (as did some of his literary contemporaries), we know for certain that he had strong mystical and occult interests, and thus we can sense the authenticity within him of a characteristic frustration: the unfulfilled desire to convey, to share with others, miraculous experiences that cannot be described with ordinary words and concepts: to "translate" the untranslatable. As William James wrote: "the keynote of the experience is the tremendously exciting sense of an intense metaphysical illumination. Truth lies open to the view in depth beneath depth of almost blinding evidence. . . . Only as sobriety returns, the feeling of insight fades, and one is left staring vacantly at a few disjointed words or phrases."[1]

In this volume you will find the testimonies of many who have "dived down to the most unfathomable depths" or who "have discovered a grotto stored with bewildering treasure" and have returned with verbal accounts of the experience—brief or extended, simple or elaborate. These testimonies and reflections come from a variety of sources: some from "ordinary" people whose words were recorded during their psychedelic sessions or written down later. Other "trip reports" and broader observations come to us from well-known figures whose facility with or mastery of language is better suited to the task. One can hardly speak of the psychedelic experience without using either mystical or mythopoetic language. As R. Gordon Wasson wrote,

> [We are] entering upon a discussion where the vocabulary of the English language is seriously deficient. . . . We are all, willy nilly, confined within the prison walls of our everyday vocabulary. With skill in our choice of words we may stretch accepted meanings to cover slightly new feelings and thoughts, but when a state of mind is utterly distinct, wholly novel, then all our old words fail. How do you tell a man born blind what seeing is like?[2]

Since mere formulations of words cannot convey the actual flavor and texture of the experience, one writes with humility and care. Among the many literary writers and eloquent authors quoted in these pages are Charles Baudelaire, William James, Aldous Huxley, R. Gordon Wasson, Robert Graves, Anaïs Nin, and Alan Watts.[3] Further insights are provided by people who may never have experienced psychedelics but who share wisdom and insights closely related to the underlying themes of the book: the phenomenology of music and the meaning of mystical experience. All join together in an attempt, if not fully to "make sense" of the experiences they describe, much less offer a consistent interpretive framework, then at least to paint a word picture providing a richly textured, multi-hued impression of sublime experiences that are simultaneously mystical and fundamentally human.

Our approach is unabashedly humanistic and experiential, focused on subjective experience rather than scientific measures and processes.

This approach mirrors that of Swedish psychologist and musicologist Alf Gabrielsson, author of *Strong Experiences with Music:*

> Today, with increasingly sophisticated methods of studying what happens in the body and brain, one might perhaps wonder whether it would be better to examine experiences of music through "objective" measurements—for example, of heart activity, breathing, muscle activity, or what happens in various parts of the brain. There are a number of such studies, and they can in themselves be of great value. But they can never provide more than rough indications of the person's own "subjective" experience. So they can complement, but never replace, the person's own description of the experience.[4]

Psychedelic pioneer Myron J. Stolaroff makes a similar point:

> Mainstream science, through the dictum "if it can't be measured, it's not science," by and large ignores subjective or interior experience in favor of the objective outside world. This leaves them living in, according to [Ken] Wilber, a "monological" world, or "flatland." In such a world, much of that which is of great value to humans is nonexistent, such as the very essence of consciousness and the nature of the human mind. It is precisely these latter elements that are so effectively revealed through appropriate use of psychedelics.[5]

The personal and subjective approach to understanding psychedelic experience is well expressed and demonstrated by Prof. G. William Barnard in his book *Liquid Light*, an intimate study of ayahuasca spirituality based on deeply participatory fieldwork in the Santo Daime Church:

> You can read scientific studies replete with colorful pictures of brain scans of other people who are taking psychedelics; you can read impeccable academic papers analyzing, with reams of statistical data, the social behavior and psychological fitness of those who have taken entheogens. All of this literature serves an important function in this world of ours in which it seems that nothing is taken seriously unless it comes blessed with the

mantle of scientific respectability and rigor. . . . But if all that you ever did was to read "objective" analyses of psychedelics, I think that it's safe to say that you wouldn't have a clue as to the depth and quality of the shifts in consciousness that can and often do take place when you drink [ayahuasca], or take any other classical psychedelic substance.[6]

To put the matter most succinctly, Jean-Jacques Rousseau wrote in 1754: "As long as we choose to consider sounds only through the commotion they stir in our nerves, we will never have the true principles of music and of its power over our hearts."[7]

In *The Archaic Revival*, Terence McKenna also argues for the centrality of the experiential dimension in the study of psychedelics:

What's always been lacking in psychedelic research is an examination of the content of the experience, so we need to give these compounds to . . . people who are willing to work with them in situations other than a clinical setting. . . . The early approach with psychedelics was the correct one. This is the notion that intelligent, thoughtful people should take psychedelics and try and understand what's going on. Mature, intelligent people need to share their experiences. It's too early for a science. What we need now are the diaries of explorers. We need many diaries of many explorers so we can begin to get a feeling for the territory.[8]

Yes, *a feeling for the territory*. If you want to deeply feel and comprehend, say, a motion picture, you can study film or digital technology and the physics of light and image projection, or you can give yourself over to the cinematic experience. If you wish to understand psychedelic experience, you can shine a light on molecular actions and reactions in the gray matter, or you can take a psychedelic. What McKenna calls "the early approach" to studying psychedelics—having intelligent, curious, observant people take a psychedelic and then write about their experiences—has given us much of the fruitful descriptive material that is available to contemporary researchers and writers, which is one reason why many of the best descriptions of musical experience on psychedelics come from "early" (1960s and 1970s—and even nineteenth-century) accounts.

This book's humanistic and experiential orientation notwithstanding, the themes and conclusions you'll find herein are supported by empiric studies on the subject. An important 2020 article from the *Journal of Music Therapy* surveyed a broad range of peer-reviewed scientific literature ("qualitative and quantitative journal articles in four major databases") dealing with music-centered psychedelic therapy. These were their principal "findings":

> Music was widely considered integral for meaningful emotional and imagery experiences and self-exploration during psychedelic therapy. . . . Music could convey love, carry listeners to other realms, be something to "hold," inspire, and elicit a deep sense of embodied transformation. Therapeutic influence was especially evident in music's dichotomous elicitations: Music could simultaneously anchor and propel. Participant openness to music and provision of participant-centered music were associated with optimal immediate and longer-term outcomes.[9]

The article further notes: "Many studies reported scarce details about the music used and incidental findings of music experienced." Fortunately, the trip reports and commentaries in this book include numerous references to and descriptions of "music experienced." In the same article, under the heading "Exclusion Criteria"[10] — that is, sources of information not consulted for the article — the authors mention having avoided references to a variety of non-empirical, non-clinical sources, including "psychedelic use in nonclinical settings (e.g., recreational psychedelic use [and] ethnographic fieldwork examining psychedelic rituals)"; "studies examining therapists' perception of participants' music experiences"; as well as letters, commentaries, and conference proceedings. Not being bound by such exclusion criteria, this book encompasses all those sources of relevant testimony and more.

Our humanity, that which makes us "human," lies at the center of that field of learning we call "the humanities": encompassing the intellectual, ethical, creative, philosophical, and spiritual outpourings of our most evolved thinkers and feelers, the higher angels of humankind from all ages and cultures. Concerned as it is with the subjective dimension of the human experience, the humanities are the natural intellectual home for the study of psychedelic experience (as distinct from neurological and pharmacological studies of psychedelic substances and their effects, dominated, as would be expected, by materialist and reductionistic views of human consciousness). It's a matter of interest that the nineteenth-century origins of experimentation with psychoactive substances were strongly tinged with humanistic ideals. Author Mike Jay explains that such early experimenters "felt they were engaged in a project with its roots essentially in the Enlightenment: a scientific mapping of the unexplored realms of the mind whose future outcome would be a more highly evolved understanding of what it means to be human . . . ."[11]

The organic connection between psychedelics and the humanities is described in personal terms by scholar and theorist Thomas B. Roberts, co-editor of *Psychedelic Medicine* and author of *The Psychedelic Future of the Mind* and *Psychedelics and Spirituality*:

> The educational topics, philosophical issues, intellectual questions, and personal insights which evolved from my LSD experiences and subsequent investigations are a continuing source of growth. They have piqued my curiosity about areas of literature, religion, anthropology, and philosophy that I underrated before. The sciences, social sciences, and arts have taken on additional coloration and deeper meanings. In a very real sense, LSD experiences resemble a liberal education.[12]

As it strives for scientific credibility, social cachet, and political clout, the burgeoning movement that calls itself psychedelic science has tended to neglect the psychedelic humanities, which naturally focus on subjective human experience, thought and imagination, and their implications for the human collective. This may be because focusing on psychedelic *experience* per se requires that one grapple with such dodgy intangibles as mysticism, spirituality, and ecstasy—all of which are critical elements in the psychedelic experience. To focus too closely on the importance of these experiential intangibles is to risk being seen as mushy-headed and unscientific and, far worse, some kind of human residue of hippiedom—an association anathema to public-facing neuroscience, pharmacology, and burgeoning psychotherapeutic enterprises. This pattern of avoidance of the phenomena of intense subjectivity and mysticism is reflected even in the current academic study of religion. In her book *Lost Ecstasy—Its Decline and Transformation in Religion*, religion scholar June McDaniel argues that within recent decades, even scholars of religion have been minimizing the study of religious *experience*, as such: "The study of mystical and ecstatic experience is out of fashion in the modern field of Religious Studies. . . . Today, it may be accurately characterized as a field which is 'experience-distant.' "[13] One can only hope that the psychedelic enterprise does not follow the same pattern of undervaluing the experiential realm in favor of either scientific reductionism or the intellectual reductionism represented by meta-critical analysis dependent on faddish sociological and political theories that ignore the essence of psychedelia: the intensification and transformation of human consciousness and experience. McDaniel quotes the Benedictine monk David Steindl-Rast, who notes that "Every religion seems to begin in mysticism and end in politics."[14] Though psychedelia is not a religion, it perpetually faces the same danger of being overwhelmed by contentious political, social, and organizational issues and agendas that, again, draw attention away from the central gift of psychedelics: enhanced human awareness and access to higher states. This is why I emphasize the humanities as the most congenial home for the study of psychedelics. It is within the wider world of the humanities where one finds a deep and perennial interest in the human experience as such: encompassing consciousness, explorations in enhanced consciousness, the powers of imagination, aesthetic experience, the existence of the spiritual, and the quest for the sublime.[15]

Tuning In: Experiencing Music in Psychedelic States takes deep dives to explore and get the feel of the extraordinary ways in which people experience music while in psychedelic states. Such heightened experience of music can seem as if multiple invisible filters normally obscuring true hearing are suddenly, miraculously lifted. Among other topics, we explore the quasi-mystical sense of timelessness, a common feature of psychedelic states, which allows for a microscopically deep immersion both in pure sound and in music itself, as well as entrance into the musical otherworld that envelops one when the barriers between perceiver and perceived, subject and object, dissolve. We also explore the unique role that music plays in facilitating, shaping, and enriching psychedelic sessions: how music not only provides an extraordinary aesthetic delight, but also serves as a friendly guide and minder on your journey, each piece of music a sonic blueprint for unique inner experiences. A carefully curated playlist can initiate and nourish a journey of indescribable beauty, wonder, and emotional profundity.

Most psychotherapeutic (and other) settings for psychedelic experience typically include the presence of music, which has long been considered an important if not essential part of the experience. As psychedelic pioneer

8 | Tuning In

Dr. James Fadiman explains: "Most cultures that use plants for healing, divination, or spiritual revivification use music to facilitate the transition from one level of awareness to another and to enhance the feeling of safety by providing nonverbal support. With or without the ingestion of psychedelics, drumming, chanting, dancing, and singing are used worldwide to guide changes in consciousness. Music proves to be invaluable in helping people travel beyond their usual thought patterns."[16]

In the widely used didactic term "set-and-setting," used to encourage optimal preconditions for a "good trip" (i.e., a prepared and positive mind-*set*,[17] plus a safe, friendly, pleasing and supportive physical *setting* for the event), the setting almost always includes recorded (or occasionally live) music. Though many individuals, groups, and institutions have created musical "playlists" (music recommended for psychedelic sessions), they generally have had little or nothing to say by way of information or guidance. This book does much to help fill that void.

Tuning In: Experiencing Music in Psychedelic States examines several aspects of how listening to music while using psychedelics creates a completely unique and different listening experience. As Stanislav Grof explains, "one of the most common" statements found in LSD trip reports is "the feeling that on the session day they *really* heard music for the first time in their life."[18] What could *they* possibly mean by that? We also explore, in some depth, the causes (in music itself, human psychology, and the nature of mysticism) for such breakthrough experiences. The diamond at the center of the study is how psychedelics and music form a dynamic and seemingly miraculous synergy: music having the unique capacity to open up, deepen, and guide the psychedelic experience on the one hand, and the psychedelic state itself providing a portal into the heart and soul of music on the other. Note that this is not a study of "psychedelic music," which usually refers to "trippy" rock, pop, or electronica. We might say that rather than "psychedelic music" appreciation, this book concerns *psychedelic music appreciation*—music appreciation elevated from a cliché, a cultural platitude, to the level of aesthetic ecstasy, wherein even familiar music sheds its outer crust of familiarity and becomes a fresh, new creation, timeless and miraculous—and where such aesthetic pleasures deepen and evolve into something more existentially profound.

What is it, then, about music that makes it such a valuable ally to psychedelic experience? It has been suggested that music and psychedelic consciousness share a similar "ontology"—a similarity in their basic nature, some shared essential characteristics.[19] In the most obvious sense, both involve inner experience, deep subjectively, a certain fluidity and sense of timelessness, a resistance to rational analysis, and a reaching toward beauty, meaning, and the sublime. Their essential nature remains somewhat mysterious, despite numerous competing attempts to define and explain them. It will be helpful now to introduce these points by offering an overview of these and other themes that emerged as I've been exploring the subject over a number of years: themes that collectively (and I want to say "organically") constitute a theoretical framework for the book.[20]

A Shared Ontology: What Is It about Music That Explains Its Natural Synergy with the Psychedelic State?

Music and psychedelics share four common attributes that help explain why each complements the other:

1. Like consciousness itself, music, as a subjective experience, is immaterial, invisible, non-quantifiable. It is material only in the sense that before it emerges in consciousness as experience, it consists of subtle vibrations of air that move through space, enter the inner ear, then are transmitted to the brain, where they are transformed into abstract aesthetic realities.[21] Being immaterial, music, as a subjective phenomenon, does not possess a static form, but rather takes the shape, so to speak, of the container it fills: the individual, receiving consciousness of the hearer. There, it exists within a unique psychological environment, joining and interacting with the inner flow of experience. In psychedelic states, that interaction between music and consciousness is intensified and transformed in various ways.

2. Though we may try to possess it and contain it within a scaffolding of constructed meanings, music exists independently of concepts and words, as do core psychedelic experiences. One may be as cerebral and analytical as one wishes in describing the externals: the history (or sociology or anthropology) of music, the life and times of a particular composer, the minutiae of music theory, performance technique, the

physics of sound, music-therapy, recording technology, and so on. But music itself, as disembodied sound—as energetic vibrations mysteriously transmuted into the stuff of aesthetic sensation—defies quantification and rational analysis.

3. As do psychedelics, music creates its own experiential atmosphere, a distinct world, as it were. Given full, undivided attention (which it always deserves), music lifts one above the noise, clatter, and confusion of the external world and consensual reality, offering a welcome and healthy escape from the ordinary. The world-creating power of music is dramatically accentuated in the psychedelic realm, where the normally esoteric phenomenon of synesthesia (e.g., "seeing" music) transforms music into a complex visual reality.

4. Music has the extraordinary capacity to distill, embody, and express human emotion in all its variety, complexity, and subtlety. It may be understood as a nonverbal but incredibly eloquent delineation of the vast range, variety, and nuances of human feeling and awareness, a kind of sonic "index" to human consciousness and experience. In psychedelic states, music may be felt to convey and evoke emotions in their primal, archetypal form, revealing their awesome depth, richness, and nuance.

These four separate elements of a comparative ontology of music and psychedelics clearly are not mutually exclusive, but rather blend together into a suggestive thesis, one that is borne out experientially during a psychedelic journey as these abstractions come alive as deeply poignant, felt realities. The next two sections clarify how this "shared ontology" manifests as a complex synergy whereby (1) music shapes or guides the psychedelic experience, and (2) the unique perceptual characteristics of the psychedelic state provide extraordinary access to the inner richness and profound mysteries of music.

Music in Service to the Psychedelic Experience

Music provides deeper access to and helps shape and enhance the psychedelic experience in a number of key ways.

Music Facilitates and Energizes the Initial Ascent

Music—because it is a non-rational, post-linguistic medium—helps to ease and facilitate the move from rational to non-rational states of consciousness. It serves as an effective transitional tool, a bridge from ordinary ego-bound, language-oriented consciousness to egoless, transpersonal states. In other words, music helps the experiencer get "out of their head." This function continues throughout the experience by helping one circumvent the unceasing "languaging" to which the mind is prone.

Music Provides Structure to the Experience

Music provides a sense of order, coherence, and continuity that helps ease psychic disorientation. As one's usual ego structures and defenses are muted or transcended, music can function as a "jungle gym" (in Marlene Dobkin de Dios's term[22]) within consciousness, a minimal structure of pathways and guideposts to assist the flow of awareness. One may, alternatively, think of music as a type of protective exoskeleton within which consciousness may freely circulate. Another analogy is Stanislav Grof's image of music as providing a "carrier wave" that helps one move through difficult experiences.

Music Touches Our Inner Emotional and Spiritual Core, Revealing the Subconscious

Because music speaks to our deepest selves, giving form, texture, and a kind of structure to the depths and subtleties of human emotion, psychedelic therapists describe music's power to create portals into the subconscious, providing access to repressed memory and emotion, critical in psychotherapeutic settings.

Music Serves as a Projection Screen for Consciousness

Relatedly, because music is abstract rather than containing a specific code of embedded meanings, it provides a neutral screen on which the inner flow of consciousness may project itself. Music becomes a kind of mirror, an articulate reflecting pool for inner states, thus providing a certain level of objectification or tangibility for inner ideation and emotion; the medium (sound) becomes the message (the contents of awareness).

Music Creates Experiential Worlds of Beauty and Sublimity

A major feature of psychedelic consciousness is the experience of synesthesia, the blending or merging of two or more sensory modes, whereby musical sounds engender within consciousness their own complex visual realities. The music seeds visualizations, visions, whole worlds of eidetic (virtual) reality, visionary realms of indescribable beauty, complexity, and profundity, providing vast spaces for the free play of imagination.

Music Conveys Meaning, Wisdom

In psychedelic states, music is often experienced as possessing intrinsic noetic import, a communicator of profound truths about the human condition, the universe, and what lies beyond: a portal to perennial wisdom. Whether those perceived truths literally inhere in the music (as some feel) or are a psychological projection (as others assert) hardly matters within the experiential realm.

Psychedelics and the Musical Sublime

Just as music enhances the psychedelic experience, the use of psychedelics deepens and expands our appreciation of music itself.

Psychedelics Deepen Sensory and Aesthetic Sensitivity

In psychedelic states, sensory perception and aesthetic sensitivity are dramatically enhanced, including heightened sensitivity to music (and to sound generally). Hearing music with increased receptivity, acuity, and a greater capacity for penetrating attention allows for an immersive experience that is aesthetically intense, psychologically powerful, and spiritually profound. A common reaction to the experience is "It's as if I've never heard music before!"

The Subjective Slowing of Time Allows for a Deeper Penetration into Sound and Music

A common psychedelic effect is a subjective slowing of time, a feeling of timelessness, of "having all the time in the world." In that essentially mystical state, experiencers report extraordinarily close, even microscopic attention to musical sound and form, such as the ability to isolate and follow one instrument among many in an orchestra, notice tiny deviations in pitch, anticipate melodic changes, and, some claim, gain insight into the intentions of the composer or performer.

THE DE-HABITUATION OF CONDITIONED OR DEFAULT CONSCIOUSNESS INCREASES AESTHETIC RECEPTIVITY

Also known as "de-automatization" and "de-familiarization," de-habituation temporarily blocks conditioned responses: the conceptual, linguistic, analytical, and other subjective filters through which we normally experience sensory phenomena. In a successful psychedelic session, these conditioned responses partially or fully dissolve, such that nothing stands between the experiencing consciousness and the sound phenomena itself, resulting in the sensation that one has become the music. The verbal formula "become the music" hardly does justice to what is, again, essentially a mystical experience that defies description.

Psychedelics, the Law, and Their Safe Use

Despite the open matter in which I am discussing this topic, we still live in an age of virtual psychedelic prohibition, initiated in the late 1960s when the US government essentially banned LSD, bringing to a halt legitimate, productive scientific research and breakthrough therapeutic applications. As cannabis prohibition (initiated in 1937) has all but ended in most US states, laws regarding scientific research into psychedelics have begun to loosen, and increasing numbers of universities are participating in what is being called a "psychedelic renaissance" involving both scientific research and the creation of academic study centers (most recently at Harvard University). Despite the continuing ban on use outside authorized institutional settings, we are faced with the extraordinary fact that more than thirty million Americans have used psychedelics.[23] In other words, use of these substances is widespread and an ongoing feature of contemporary life.

This book supports the principle of "harm reduction" in the use of psychedelics. While acknowledging the current illegal status of these psychoactive substances in most jurisdictions, it acknowledges that because their use is pervasive, whatever measures can be taken, or information made available, to render their use safer, to reduce any possible harm that may result from their use, is a positive and realistic contribution to public welfare. If, in spite of the legal risks, you are going to explore the use of LSD, psilocybin,[24] ayahuasca, or any other restricted psychoactive substance, there are sane and responsible ways to proceed: preparations and practices that will lessen the chance of a negative experience and help assure a more positive one.[25] Any substance, legal or illegal, can be abused.

Those of us concerned with psychedelics as potent tools for personal growth and healing look forward to a time in the near future when these unique medicines (as they're often called in acknowledgment of their proven healing properties) are made widely available. People will then likely look back on the current prohibition with the same jaundiced eye with which they view the prohibition against alcohol use in the early twentieth century: as a foolish, costly, counterproductive, anti-humane exercise in bad policy (driven in part by craven political and racist motives)—all the more so because the dangers and negative social effects of alcohol vastly outweigh those of the standard psychedelics.

One concern, however, is that as the psychedelic renaissance takes root in the coming years and decades—when the dreams of reformers are realized in the form of ubiquitous psychedelic therapy centers treating a wide range of patient populations—psychedelics will have largely become co-opted by doctors, psychiatrists, licensed "trip-guides," "integration counselors," and, of course, psychopharmacological entrepreneurs in pursuit of profits. The institutionalization and medicalization of psychedelic experience will certainly benefit some, but, short of a more general program of legalization (as is beginning to happen in a few locales), it will leave out in the cold the majority of psychedelic users. Whether their interests are primarily recreational, curiosity driven, or aim toward higher aspirations—personal psychological growth, aids to creativity, spiritual exploration—they should have the inalienable right to manage their own lives and psyches within a society that calls itself "free."

However these societal issues resolve themselves, on a practical level psychedelics have shown themselves to be powerful agents for psychological healing and spiritual growth, as well as for rich and transformative aesthetic experience—which I, and many others, view as inseparable benefits. Most of those who have commented on sensory-aesthetic issues within psychedelia have focused almost exclusively on the visual realm: how things *look* in psychedelic states and how that enhanced visuality opens up a greater awareness of the beauty and metaphysical profundity of the world in which we live. Indeed, more needs to be written, I would say, on the extraordinary experience of wandering through art (or other) museums on *a manageable dose* of a psychedelic.[26]

But this book offers something new: a close, patient, and in-depth look into the world of psychedelically enhanced *hearing*, of music in particular: an enhancement that many users claim changed forever their appreciation for the medium. As always, the real gift of psychedelics is not cheap or temporary thrills, or even enhanced aesthetic sensitivity, but a life lived with more depth, awareness, and humanity. Taking psychedelics is not a way of life, or a complete or self-sustaining spiritual practice. Like anything else, it can be overdone or become an obsessive, ego-inflating habit. It should be treated, I believe, as a precious gift. Some, including Aldous Huxley and Richard Alpert/Ram Dass, have used the theological term "gratuitous grace" to describe the effects of these substances, whether derived from Amazonian plants, mushrooms emerging from cow patties, or chemicals synthesized in Albert Hofmann's laboratory.[27] Hofmann, who gave the world both LSD and psilocybin, viewed these substances as spiritual gifts. Himself the personification of selfless "psychedelic science," Hofmann wrote that LSD, borne of a "peculiar presentiment," is "not a product of planned research. I did not look for it, it came to me. This means to me that a higher authority thought it was necessary now to provide mankind with an additional pharmacological aid for spiritual growth."[28] For me, the mere fact that the creator (or conduit) of these mind-changing, soul-enriching substances should be both a gifted scientist and a genuinely spiritual human being, acutely aware of the multi-dimensional nature of both consciousness and reality, is a matter of uncanny good fortune. Albert Einstein himself wrote: "I maintain that the cosmic, religious feeling is the strongest and noblest motive for scientific research."[29]

Though we live in dark, dangerous, and unpredictable times, it is a gift to be reminded that the universe is indeed vast, multi-dimensional, and full of undiscovered wonders. Though I am far from being an enlightened soul, many years ago psychedelics lit a small, golden light way in the back of my consciousness that continues to emit a gentle, reassuring glow. It reminds me that there are realms of beauty, goodness, wisdom, and holiness existing somewhere, in some dimension of this infinite universe—whether within the vastness of human consciousness or in Huxley's universal "Mind at Large"—and that it is never fully out of reach. As William James observed, "Even if all that remained of these experiences was the vague memory of something profound, they nevertheless [indicate] the existence in the mind of multiple states of consciousness, each awaiting its trigger."[30] Or, as pioneering psychedelic therapist Betty Grover Eisner wrote to colleague Humphry Osmond, coiner of the term "psychedelic": "One can never be content to live always in the valley at sea level when one has experienced the rarefied ozone of the higher altitude. So it serves as a map left in the intellect, as a warmth or remembered radiance in the emotions, and as a still small voice or an agonizing goad in the conscience and a longing in the heart."[31]

1

What Is a "Psychedelic Experience"?

Throughout this book I use the term "the psychedelic experience." There is, of course, no such thing as *the* psychedelic experience; each is different, depending on numerous variables. It is merely a matter of convenience to use one general term to cover a multitude of unique experiences, which, even when viewed collectively, have generated a miasma of differing definitions and interpretations. As Grinspoon and Bakalar write:

> The most important point to understand about the nature of psychedelic experience is its tremendous range and its dependence on individual set and social setting. All drug effects vary with the character and expectations of the user and the physical and social environment, but psychedelic effects vary far more than those other drugs. . . . As small a matter as opening or closing the eyes, changing the music, or slightly increasing the dose can transform the quality of the experience. . . . The narratives of psychedelic drug trips are as luxuriant and varied as myths, dreams, and psychoanalytical revelations. In a sense there is no "psychedelic effect" or "psychedelic state"; to say that someone has taken LSD tells little more about the content and import of his experience than to say that he has had a dream.[1]

Because the focus of this book is on psychedelic *experience* (rather than brain science or psychopharmacology), I present here a select handful of descriptive texts each proposing a coherent overview, within the limitations of language, of psychedelic experience. Collectively, I believe they provide a lucid overview of the subject.

Interpretive Approaches to the Psychedelic Experience

Aldous Huxley, writing in *The Doors of Perception*, gives the closest we'll come in the present discussion to a "scientific" explanation (one mentioning brain function) of psychedelic experience. He describes how psychedelics disable the "cerebral reducing valve" in our brains, allowing for a radically expanded experience of outer and inner reality. Huxley borrowed this term from French philosopher Henri Bergson (1859–1941), who, Michael Pollan explains, "believed that consciousness was not generated by human brains but rather exists in a field outside us, something like electromagnetic waves; our brains, which he likened to radio receivers, can tune in to different frequencies of consciousness."[2] Because the human brain cannot process the entire "field"—that infinite profusion of "transmissions"—it requires a limiting mechanism, a kind of internal filter or "reducing value" to limit our experiences to those that are necessary for biological and social functioning.

Nevertheless, one might still wonder why that limiting mechanism is such a critical necessity. Why must the fullness of consciousness be so radically constrained? After all, temporarily freed from that constraint, "the material world," writes Pollan, "revealed itself to [Huxley] in all its beauty, detail, profundity and 'Suchness' . . . Huxley spent hours (and pages) dilating on the 'is-ness' of a chair, a bouquet of flowers, and the folds of his gray flannel trousers, entranced by 'the miraculous fact of sheer existence.'" Pollan continues: "The question arises: why don't we see this way all the time? Huxley suggests ordinary consciousness evolved to keep this information from us for a good reason: to prevent us from being continuously astonished, so that we might get up from our chair now and again and go about the business of living. Huxley recognized the danger of being constantly thunderstruck by reality: 'For if one always saw like this, one would never want to do anything else.'"[3] R. E. L. Masters and Jean Houston, authors of the classic *The Varieties of Psychedelic Experience*, offer this description of the function of the reducing valve:

> The brain, sense organs, and central nervous system function essentially as organs of selection and elimination. This eliminative process . . . helps protect us from being overwhelmed and disoriented by the vast quantities of useless and irrelevant knowledge that would be ours were we able to perceive the multiplicity of phenomena within our sensory and cognitive field. By screening out the multiplicity and leaving only those

perceptions with pragmatic potential to survival, our awareness is organically inhibited and we perceive only a fraction of our world. As Huxley has put it: "Mind at large is funneled through the reducing valve of the brain and the nervous system" and what survives the journey through this funnel is only "a measly trickle of the kind of consciousness which will help us to stay alive on the surface of this planet."[4]

Following this model, what psychedelics do is to temporarily inhibit the action of the "reducing value," allowing a torrent of perceptual, cognitive, and imaginative material to flow into awareness. This creates the subjective feeling of being inundated by rivers of thought, worlds of visualization, varieties and intensities of emotion, along with a sense of vastness and multi-dimensionality. That inflow may sometimes be experienced as chaotic and at other times masterfully resolved or integrated into manageable, meaningful, profoundly affecting patterns of heightened perception and awareness. For Huxley, that unconstrained inward flow represents "Mind at Large" ("cosmic consciousness," if you will). He elaborates:

> That which, in the language of religion, is called "this world" is the universe of reduced awareness, expressed, and, as it were, petrified by language. The various "other worlds" with which human beings erratically make contact are so many elements in the totality of the awareness belonging to Mind at Large. Most people, most of the time, know only what comes through the reducing valve and is consecrated as genuinely real by the local language. Certain persons, however, seem to be born with a kind of by-pass that circumvents the reducing value. In others temporary by-passes may be acquired either spontaneously, or as the result of deliberate "spiritual exercises," or through hypnosis, or by means of drugs. Through these permanent or temporary by-passes there flows, not indeed the perception "of everything that is happening everywhere in the universe" . . . but something more than, and above all something different from, the carefully selected utilitarian material which our narrowed, individual minds regard as a complete, or at least sufficient, picture of reality.[5]

William James describes one such "by-pass" scenario whereby Mind at Large may "leak" into "normal" consciousness: "There is a continuum of cosmic consciousness, against which our individuality builds but accidental fences. . . . Our 'normal' consciousness is circumscribed for adaptation to our external earthly environment, but the fence is weak in spots, and fitful influences from beyond leak in."[6] Rather than await fortuitous leaks, Huxley advises we be proactive and cut holes in that fence: "Modes of consciousness different from normal waking consciousness are within the reach of anyone who knows how to apply the necessary stimuli. The universe in which a human being lives can be transfigured into a new creation. We have only to cut a hole in the fence and look around us with what the philosopher, Plotinus, describes as 'that other kind of seeing, which everyone has but few make use of.'"[7] Psychedelics cut holes in the fence, allowing consciousness to tune into other wavelengths. Terence McKenna describes the phenomenon as only he can: "I assume that psychedelics somehow change our channel from the evolutionarily important channel giving traffic, weather, and stock market reports to the one playing classical music of an alien civilization."[8]

The Uniqueness of Each Psychedelic Experience

Having been introduced to Huxley's temporarily malfunctioning reducing value and the resultant influx of what he calls Mind at Large, we now need to emphasize the uniqueness of each person's experience of that cosmic cornucopia: that is, our own distinctive psychedelic experience. Charles Tart, a psychologist and prolific author on a wide range of altered states of consciousness, explains the difference between common pharmaceutical "drugs" and those substances whose action is primarily psychological (*psychoactive*):

> Our common experience with many drugs inclines us to think along the line that "Drug *A* has effects *X*, *Y*, and *Z*." This is generally adequate for most drugs. Heavy doses of barbiturates make a person drowsy. Penicillin cures certain diseases. Amphetamines stimulate people. When it comes to drugs whose effects are primarily psychological, however, the tendency to think that drug *A* has effects *X*, *Y*, and *Z* can be very misleading and introduces confusion. That type of statement attributes certain sorts of invariant qualities to the chemical effect of the drug on the nervous system. When dealing with

psychoactive drugs such as marijuana or LSD, however, both scientific research and the experience of users have made it clear that there are very few "invariant" qualities that are somehow inherent in or "possessed by" the drug itself.[9] Rather, the particular effects of a drug are primarily a function of a *particular* person taking a *particular* drug in a *particular* way under *particular* conditions at a *particular* time.[10]

To that list of "particulars" must be added one additional critical one: *at a particular dose*. There is no "standard" dose for any psychedelic, though individual clinical studies may choose to adhere to a particular dose, or graduated doses, for research or therapeutic purposes. All other factors considered, the higher the dose, the more powerful, intense, multi-dimensional, or "cosmic" the experience. Keep that in mind when reading various accounts of experiencing music on psychedelics, where the effects may range from mild enhancement of aesthetic appreciation to feeling oneself projected out into distant realms of intensely absorbing visionary experience. In the most extreme cases, music no longer exists as something exterior to consciousness, a mere object of perception, but becomes the substance and fullness of reality itself.

This notion of psychedelic substances as being different from conventional pharmaceuticals that display predictable and repeatable effects is also stressed by Stanislav Grof in his preface to *LSD Psychotherapy*:

> The critical element here is the recognition that LSD and other psychedelics function more or less as nonspecific catalysts and amplifiers of the psyche.... In the dosages used in human experimentation, the classical psychedelics, such as LSD, psilocybin, and mescaline, do not have any specific pharmacological effects. They increase the energetic level in the psyche and the body which leads to manifestations of otherwise latent psychological processes.
>
> The content and nature of the experiences that these substances induce are thus not artificial products of their pharmacological interaction with the brain, but *authentic expressions of the psyche revealing its functioning on levels not ordinarily available for observation and study* [emphasis added]. A person who has taken LSD does not have an "LSD experience," but takes a journey into deep recesses of his or her own psyche.

> When this substance is given in the same dosage and under comparable circumstances to a large number of individuals, each of them will have a different experience reflecting the specificities of his or her psyche.[11]

This facilitated "journey into deep recesses" of the psyche has powerful implications for psychotherapy and is one reason for the current renaissance of psychedelic therapies. As Grof states: "It does not seem to be an exaggeration to say that psychedelics, used responsibly and with proper caution, would be for psychiatry what the microscope is for biology and medicine or the telescope is for astronomy. These tools make it possible to study important processes that under normal circumstances are not available for direct observation."[12]

Psychedelics and Their Effect on the Ego

It should be clear now that psychedelic experiences are highly personal, subjective, and assume a virtual infinity of forms. That said, there do exist certain commonalities and widely shared experiential aspects of psychedelic states. Perhaps the most fundamental action of psychedelics, writes Michael Pollan, author of the highly influential bestseller *How to Change Your Mind*, is that they "silence or at least muffle the voice of the ego." Summarizing the views of psychiatrist Jeffrey Guss, Pollan continues:

> In his view, which is informed by his psychoanalytic training, the ego is a mental construct that performs certain functions on behalf of the self. Chief among these are maintaining the boundary between the conscious and the unconscious realms of the mind and the boundary between self and other, or subject and object. It is only when these boundaries fade or disappear, as they seem to do under the influence of psychedelics, that we can "let go of rigid patterns of thought, allowing us to perceive new meanings with less fear."[13]

Despite its offhand tone, this statement carries a load of critical information. While active, psychedelics have the unique and extraordinary power to deprive the ego of its near-total control over personal consciousness. What do we mean by "ego"? Admittedly, definitions vary, but for our purposes, I'll venture to say that ego is that socially engineered but haphazardly constructed sense of identity that effectively divides consciousness into various separate functions that help us navigate life-in-the-world, but that simultaneously deadens our awareness of the multi-dimensionality, depths, and subtleties of existence. How does the ego manage all that? Referencing the above quote,

1. It builds a wall "between the conscious and unconscious realms of the mind" (effectively removing from view most of what constitutes our multi-layered inner life).
2. It creates a nearly impermeable membrane between self and other (if by "other" we mean "others," it provides ideal conditions for interpersonal misunderstanding and conflict), as well as between subject and object, perceiver and perceived, observer and observed—that is, between us and everything else in the world and the wider cosmos.

The ego thus fractures our awareness into manageable functional parts, while blinding us to the incredibly rich, multi-dimensional nature of existence. No wonder, then, that as psychedelics deconstruct the tyrannical ego, this abundance and intensity of experience flows into awareness. Pollan himself affirms the centrality of this dissolution of the ego to the psychedelic experience:

> Of all the phenomenological effects that people on psychedelics report, the dissolution of the ego seems to me by far the most important and the most therapeutic. I found little consensus on terminology among the researchers I interviewed, but when I unpack their metaphors and vocabularies—whether spiritual, humanistic, psychoanalytic, or neurological—it is finally the loss of ego or self . . . they're suggesting is the key psychological driver of the experience. . . .
>
> Consider the case of the mystical experience: the sense of transcendence, sacredness, unitive consciousness, infinitude, and blissfulness people report can all be explained as what it can feel like to a mind when its sense of being, or having, a separate self is suddenly no more. Is it any wonder we would

feel one with the universe when the boundaries between self and world that the ego patrols suddenly fall away?[14]

D. H. Lawrence provides an eloquent description of how the all-powerful ego (which he characterizes as "the great image or idol which dominates our civilization, and which we worship with mad blindness") interferes with the free, natural, spontaneous flow of consciousness: "Consciousness should be a flow from within outwards. The organic necessity of the human being should flow into spontaneous action and spontaneous awareness, consciousness. But the moment man became aware of himself he made a picture of himself, and began to live from the picture: that is, from without inwards. This is truly the reversal of life."[15] I find Lawrence's words compelling, even haunting: *The moment man became aware of himself he made a picture of himself, and began to live from the picture*—living, as it were, from the outside inward, as if forever beholden to a script, forced to renounce both spontaneity and authenticity.

Providing a very different but complementary perspective, Alan Watts deflates the ego into an airy nothingness, a bit of inconsequential fluff: "There isn't any substantial ego at all. The ego is a kind of flip, a knowing of knowing, a fearing of fearing. It's a curlicue, an extra jazz to experience, a sort of double-take or reverberation, a dithering of consciousness which is the same as anxiety."[16] No surprise that Watts would cut to the heart of the matter with a Zen laser of aphoristic insight. Our main challenge in life, according to Aldous Huxley, is to learn "the art of obtaining freedom from the fundamental human disability of egotism."[17]

For me, the definitive explanation of the relationship between ego loss and the experience of an expanded sense of cosmic consciousness, which lies at the heart of a full-blown psychedelic experience, is provided by Dr. Albert Hofmann, the discoverer of LSD and synthesizer of psilocybin. While some neuroscientists studying the effects of psychedelics interpret ego loss in negative terms—as a deficit in consciousness ("depersonalization"), or as a glitch in the normal operation of cognitive function, allowing for "magical thinking"[18]—Hofmann views it in more overtly metaphysical terms:

> We only see and experience a small fraction of the surrounding world . . . with our everyday consciousness; in a mystical emotional state—when the receiver is adjusted to maximum width of perception—we simultaneously become aware of an endlessly expanded outer and inner universe. The border

erected between our ego and the surrounding world by our intellect is dissolved, and the outer and inner space blend into each other. We now experience the endlessness of the outer space in the inner space as well. The unlimited space is now open to an unlimited number of images flowing in, as well as to images from the past, experiences that were collected during the course of a whole lifetime—old images that were stored in the subconscious due to the limited space in consciousness. All these inner images are awakened to new life and fuse with the new ones flowing in. This extremely intensive experiencing of innumerable new and old sensory perceptions and feelings merging inner and outer space creates a sensation of eternity and timelessness, of an everlasting here and now.[19]

How Psychedelics Affect Consciousness

Let's now take a deeper dive into the universal or quasi-universal manifestations of psychedelic experience—those effects held in common by most psychedelic experiencers.

Derived from data collected over an eight-year study of the effects of psychedelics on more than nine hundred subjects, including many artists, Dr. Oscar Janiger and his co-author, Marlene Dobkin de Rios, offered a useful inventory of ways in which psychedelics, broadly speaking, affect consciousness. To paraphrase: what psychedelics do is accelerate the thought process, stimulating creative ideation; enhance emotional excitement and a sense of significance; expand consciousness to encompass both broad cosmic ideas and miniscule perceptual details; provide greater accessibility to past experiences and buried memories; cause things to appear to compose themselves into harmonious patterns; intensify colors so that everything appears brilliantly illuminated from within; impart aesthetic value to apparently ordinary objects; free the individual from preconceptions (de-habituation); and finally dissolve the boundaries between perceiver and perceived.[20] Masters and Houston provide their own inventory of psychedelic effects:

> Changes in visual, auditory, tactile, olfactory, gustatory, and kinesthetic perception; changes in experiencing time and space; changes in the rate and content of thought; body image changes; hallucinations; . . . abrupt and frequent mood and affect

changes; . . . enhanced recall or memory; depersonalization and ego dissolution; . . . increased sensitivity to nonverbal cues; sense of capacity to communicate much better by nonverbal means, sometimes including the telepathic; . . . magnification of character traits and psychodynamic processes; . . . and, in general, apprehension of a world that has slipped the chains of normal categorical ordering, leading to an intensified interest in self and world and also to a range of responses moving from extremes of anxiety to extremes of pleasure.[21]

An important early study of nearly four hundred patients[22] sheds light on how psychedelics can impact human values and personality over time: "Based on test data, observer ratings, follow-up interviews, and subjective reports, the following were noted: 'greater spontaneity of emotional expression, more adequate ego resources, reduction in depression and anxiety, less distance in interpersonal relations, more openness to experience, increased aesthetic appreciation, deeper sense of meaning and purpose in life, and an enhanced sense of unity with nature and humanity.'"[23]

In his book *American Trip*, Ido Hartogsohn, while arguing "for the profound context dependency of psychedelic effects" based on the widely divergent mentalities and circumstances surrounding the use of psychedelics, also acknowledges "some of their underlying fundamental characteristics": "Among these elusive fundamentals is first and foremost the intensification, amplification, and dramatization of meaning and experience. The second . . . is a hyper associative tendency, which can manifest and be interpreted as either disorganized or particularly creative. A third . . . relates to the blurring or dissolving of boundaries that is often noted by psychedelic philosophers but is also present at the sensual level, through the flowing, sinuous, transforming forms common to psychedelic sight and sound."[24] Later Hartogsohn restates and elaborates on these three psychedelic fundamentals. On the first point, regarding intensification of experience, Hartogsohn states:

> The psychedelic experience induces a remarkable intensity of experience, regardless of context. In fact, its intensity is precisely what makes it psychedelic.
>
> . . . All the other common effects of psychedelics emanate from their intensity. Under the effect of psychedelics, colors are intensified, sounds resonate a thousand times more fully, spiritual revelations appear to be of miraculous proportions,

emotions and interpersonal relationships are augmented, and the relationship with nature is enhanced.

Ultimately, so much of the effect of psychedelics might be traced back to the enhancement of the perception of meaning. . . . By enhancing the meaningfulness of mental objects, psychedelics allow users to focus their attention on them more intensively, gleaning new perspectives by identifying the details and ramifications that formerly seemed inconsequential.[25]

On the second fundamental, "hyper associative tendency," he explains that these "can lead to a reenchantment of the world through the discovery of Jungian-type synchronicities, to experiences in synesthesia, to novel kinds of creativity and innovation" (but also to "magical thinking and pathological-type paranoid thought patterns").[26] Finally, on the "dissolving of boundaries," he adds ego dissolution, depersonalization, and experiences of cosmic unity.[27]

Another common theme uniting a wide range of psychedelic experiences rests in the notion that the psyche possesses a kind of intrinsic wisdom that aims at healing and self-understanding. As William Richards explains: "Although the range of experiences is broad, the responses reported by subjects do not appear random or capriciously unpredictable. Given adequate dosage and interpersonal grounding, the states of consciousness that present themselves often appear to be ingeniously designed by an intrinsic wisdom within the psyche to facilitate healing or unfolding self-actualization. Typically, the content that emerges seems more relevant and potentially beneficial than any experience the subject and guide could have imagined and designed in advance."[28]

In our quest for unifying factors that help to broadly define psychedelic experience, let us finally note that state we call "awe." Michael Pollan describes it this way: "The concept of awe, I realized, could help connect several of the dots I'd been collecting in the course of my journey through the landscape of psychedelic therapy. Whether awe is a cause or an effect of the mental changes psychedelics sponsor isn't entirely clear. But either way, awe figures in much of the phenomenology of psychedelic consciousness, including the mystical experience, the overview effect, self-transcendence, the enrichment of our inner environment, and even the generation of new meanings."[29]

A particularly rich and detailed description of what might be considered an ideal trip—or, to be more specific, a "peak" experience within a highly fruitful session—offers some perspective. Over the decades, Stanislav Grof has supervised and guided thousands of psychedelic sessions. His description of a psychedelic peak experience suggests that it lends itself to (or, one may say, uncovers within the deep psyche) certain healthy, positive attitudes and values—what may amount to a psychedelically inspired ethical orientation (a "psychedelic ethic") if not, more broadly, a psychedelic metaphysic. According to Grof, for a person experiencing a peak psychedelic state:

> The general atmosphere is that of liberation, redemption, salvation, love, and forgiveness. The individual feels cleansed and purged. . . . He experiences overwhelming love for his fellow men, appreciation of warm human relationships, solidarity, and friendship. Such feelings are accompanied by humility and [an aspiration] to engage in service and charitable activities. . . . The individual's appreciation of natural beauty is greatly enhanced, and a simple and uncomplicated way of life in close contact with nature appears to be the most desirable mode of existence. The depth and wisdom in systems of thought that advocate this orientation toward life—whether they be Rousseau's philosophy or the teachings of Taoism and Zen Buddhism—seem obvious and unquestionable.
>
> In this state, all the sensory pathways are wide open and there is an increased sensitivity and enjoyment of the perceptual nuances discovered in the external world. The perception of the environment has a certain primary quality; every sensory stimulus, be it visual, acoustic, olfactory, gustatory, or tactile, appears to be completely fresh and new, and, at the same time, unusually exciting and stimulating. Subjects talk about really seeing the world for the first time in their lives, about discovering entirely new ways of listening to music, and finding endless pleasure in smells and tastes.

Grof concludes,

> The individual tuned in to this experiential realm usually discovers in himself genuinely positive values, such as a sense of justice, appreciation of beauty, feelings of love, self-respect, and respect for others. These values, as well as motivations to

pursue them and act in accordance with them, seem to be, on this level, an intrinsic part of the human personality. . . . The individual experiences [these values] without any conflict, as a natural, logical, and integral part of *a higher universal order* [emphasis added]. It is interesting in this connection to point to the striking parallels with Abraham Maslow's concept of meta values and metamotivations, derived from observations of persons who had spontaneous "peak experiences" in their everyday life.[30]

On a superficial level, there may appear to be a contradiction between the Stanislav Grof of *Psychedelic Psychotherapy* (1980), and the Grof of *Realms of the Human Unconscious* (1975). In the former (chronologically later) work we read: "LSD and other psychedelics function more or less as nonspecific catalysts and amplifiers of the psyche. . . . A person who has taken LSD does not have an 'LSD experience,' but takes a journey into deep recesses of his or her own psyche. When this substance is given in the same dosage and under comparable circumstances to a large number of individuals, each of them will have a different experience reflecting the specificities of his or her psyche."[31] However, in *Realms*, we do get a sense of there being something one might conceivably call "an LSD experience," involving, in Grof's words, a "general atmosphere . . . of liberation, redemption, salvation, love, and forgiveness," along with a heightened "sense of justice . . . feelings of love, self-respect, and respect for others"; a greatly enhanced appreciation for natural beauty, a desire to live closer to nature, and so on.[32] Compare this description to the following passage from Richard Bucke's classic work *Cosmic Consciousness*:

> An infinite peace and joy filled my heart, worldly ambitions and cares died in the light of the glorious truth that was revealed to me—all anxiety and trouble about the future had utterly left me, and my life is one long song of love and peace.
> . . . The effects of this experience on my daily life have been many, chiefly, I think, after the deeply underlying joy and peace are a faith in the eternal rightness of all things; a ceasing to fret and worry over the problems of evil; a desire to live in the open air as much as possible and an ever-growing delight in the beauties of nature at all times and seasons of the year; a strong tendency towards simplicity of life and deepening sense of the equality and brotherhood of all men.[33]

With Grof's description of a peak LSD experience and Bucke's example of "cosmic consciousness" being so similar, might one then be justified in speaking of an identifiable "LSD experience"? How do we reconcile these two apparently divergent views (i.e., non-specificity vs. specificity of psychedelic effects)? First of all, Grof's initial emphasis on the non-specificity of LSD's effects is presented in the context of distinguishing it from standard pharmaceutical drugs that are designed to address a particular physical (e.g., diabetes) or mental (e.g., schizophrenia) pathology: drugs that aim to relieve symptoms or cure a condition. Rather than being designed for such localized ameliorative or curative effects, psychedelics act more broadly and deeply. They "increase the energetic level in the psyche and the body which leads to manifestations of otherwise latent psychological processes"—in other words, "the psyche revealing its functioning on levels not ordinarily available for observation and study." In Grof's schema, then, psychedelics do not impose a particular experience as such, but rather take us on a journey into the deep recesses of our own psyches: now more transparent, less defended, and available for therapeutic intervention and healing. The critical question is, once we enter those depths, what do we discover?

In the preface to his first book, *Realms of the Human Unconscious*, Grof describes it as "the first of a series of books which will summarize and condense in a systematic and comprehensive way my observations and experiences during seventeen years of research with LSD and other psychedelic drugs," exploring topics such as schizophrenia, art and religion, personality diagnostics, therapy for emotional disorders, and the experience of dying.[34] The preface concludes with a description of a proposed final volume, which "will focus on the philosophical and spiritual dimensions of the LSD experience, with special emphasis on ontological and cosmological issues. It will describe in detail *the surprisingly consistent metaphysical system* that seems to be emerging from the experimentation with psychedelic substances [emphasis added]."[35]

I cannot say for certain whether that hypothetical final volume has yet taken form—perhaps it is spread throughout the many books that followed *Realms of the Human Unconscious*—but what is clear is that Grof essentially views psychedelics as having not only psychotherapeutic value, but also importance as a tool for exploring what lies beyond the ego-self, the public self, the constructed and conditioned self, the "biographical" self, our default identity. What lies "beyond" it is what Grof describes (above) as a "surprisingly consistent metaphysical system" characterized by particular values (i.e., liberation, love, forgiveness, a sense of justice, appreciation of beauty, nature, etc.) that are at once "an intrinsic part of the human personality" as well as "a natural, integral part of a higher human order." In other words, dig deep enough down into the individual human psyche and one inevitably arrives at a numinous "transpersonal" realm that constitutes our common spiritual inheritance. I think Grof, as a founder of transpersonal psychology, would embrace Theodore Roszak's description of the hidden but essential relationship between psychiatry and the transpersonal, spiritual dimension:

> What therapy must yet learn from the spiritual traditions . . . is that the inner universe it studies is not *merely* psychological. It must recognize that the personal can serve as a point of entry into the transpersonal. And where that happens, our measure of normality must take on the new dimension of transcendence, becoming a higher sanity than psychiatry has yet contemplated.
> . . . I suspect that for some time to come, until an all-transforming synthesis is achieved, spiritual intelligence in our society will stem from imaginative fusions of psychotherapy and traditional wisdom. Therapy will universalize the traditions; the traditions will deepen therapy and provide its metaphysical foundation.[36]

Grof's frank acknowledgement of the spiritual dimension of human life was, at least in part, a natural outcome of having sat with thousands of patients, often on high doses of LSD, experiencing profoundly mystical, transpersonal states: encountering, to use his words, the "ontological," the "cosmological," the "metaphysical," and the "spiritual." For perspective, he divides his clinical work into two periods: In Czechoslovakia in the 1950s and 1960s, he practiced *psycholytic therapy*, using doses between 100 and 250 micrograms with repeated administration (15–100 sessions). Since 1967, at the Maryland Psychiatric Research Center, he practiced *psychedelic therapy*: "The dosages are high—between 300 and 600 micrograms—and the number of sessions limited to between 1 and 3. The experiences are almost totally internalized through the use of eyeshades, headphones, and stereophonic music. The aim of this work is to communicate a profound experience of a transcendental nature—death and rebirth, feelings of unity with humanity, the universe, and God, archetypal phenomena, etc."[37] In Grof's view, as it is with many psychedelic therapists, it is the ego-transcending, transpersonal stage of awareness that is the hallmark of a fully realized psychedelic experience—a state that, however otherworldly or esoteric it may appear from the ground level, is in fact "an intrinsic part of the human personality." For a quintessential summary of Grof's view on psychedelics, his own words more than suffice: "I believe that used responsibly and in a mature way, the entheogens mediate access to the numinous dimensions of existence, have a great healing and transformative potential, and represent a very important tool for spiritual development."[38]

Twenty years before *Realms of the Human Unconscious* was published in 1975, pioneers in the newly evolving field of psychedelic therapy were thinking in similar expansive terms. They hoped to help their patients view their personal struggles and challenges within a broader humanistic and even cosmic framework—a perspective made possible through psychedelics. In a personal letter written in February 1957, psychologist Betty Grover Eisner reported: "I feel, and I think that Sid [psychiatrist Sidney Cohen] does too, that the best possible therapeutic LSD experience is one in which a subject glimpses the unity of the cosmos and his own place in it, and then sees and tackles his problems in relationship. And it can be done and that is what we are going to be doing."[39] Elsewhere Eisner states, "LSD makes available, from the very first session, other levels of consciousness which might require months or years of conventional therapy to effect. . . . Perhaps the most unique aspect of LSD therapy is the impetus and accessibility it provides for the mystic or unitive experiences from the simplest feeling of deep empathy between two individuals . . . to the magnificence of multidimensional unity."[40]

All this considered, is it any wonder why psychedelics have catalyzed, for so many experiencers, a dramatically heightened sense of the spiritual, a new appreciation for the vastness and multidimensionality of "reality," a fresh fascination with notions as deep and broad as eternity and infinity? Faced with such expansive and transformative experiences, one grasps for words, for language that might do justice to this confounding immensity that puts everything into a new and different perspective. Such experiences, when of sufficient strength, confound even the most intellectually sophisticated and spiritually sensitive minds. One compelling example is Dr. Huston Smith (1919–2016), internationally acclaimed authority on the world's religions with a particular fascination with their mystical traditions. During his first psychedelic experience on New Year's Day 1961 at the home of Dr. Timothy Leary, Smith took two capsules of mescaline ("an average dose," Leary informs him), and finds himself launched into a different universe:

The world into which I was ushered was strange, weird, uncanny, significant, and terrifying beyond belief. Two things struck me especially. First, the mescaline acted as a psychological prism. It was as if the layers of the mind, most of whose contents our conscious screens out to smelt the remainder down into a single band we can cope with, were now revealed in their completeness—spread out as if by spectroscope into about five distinguishable layers. And the odd thing was that I could to some degree be aware of them all simultaneously, and could move back and forth among them at will, shifting my attention to now this one, now another one. . . .

I was experiencing the metaphysical theory known as emanationism, in which, beginning with the clear, unbroken Light of the Void, that light then fractures into multiple forms and declines in intensity as it devolves through descending levels of reality. My friends in the study [in the next room] were present in one band of this spectrum, but it was far more restricted than higher bands that were in view. Bergson's notion of the brain as a reducing valve struck me as accurate. . . . As in Plato's myth of the cave, what I was now seeing struck me with the force of the sun, in comparison with which everyday experience reveals only flickering shadows in a dim cavern.

How could these layers upon layers, these worlds within worlds, these paradoxes in which I could be both myself *and* my world[,] and an episode could be both momentary *and* eternal—how could such things be put into words? I realized how utterly impossible it would be for me to describe such things tomorrow, or even right then to Tim or Eleanor. There came the clearest realization I have ever had as to what literary genius consists of: a near-miraculous talent for using words to transport readers from the everyday world to things analogous to what I was now experiencing.[41]

Speaking elsewhere of this same initial psychedelic experience, Smith boiled it down to this: "The dominant effects of the experience were two: awe (which I had known conceptually as the distinctive religious emotion but had never before experienced so intensely) and certainty. There was no doubting that the Reality I experienced was ultimate. That conviction has remained."[42] Put even more succinctly, I might borrow from Smith's definition of the preeminent attribute of a "realized being," and thus characterize the essence of the psychedelic experience as *an acute sense of the astonishing mystery of everything.*[43]

Speaking personally, some years ago, while coming down from a powerful trip, descending from a fluid realm of wordlessness into the constructed, constrictive world defined by concepts and language, I tried to intuit a few words, something concise, mantra-like, that I might retain as a reminder of that ineffable, sublime realm: invoking Maeterlinck,[44] some broken piece of glass to symbolize the luminous gems discovered in a now-fading psychedelic grotto. The words that flowed into mind and quietly passed my lips were these: "*Profundity beyond profundity beyond profundity beyond profundity.*"

2

Expressing the Inexpressible

Music as Mysticism

What is it about music itself that makes it such an extraordinarily valuable ally in psychedelic exploration and healing? Before diving directly into the subject of music and psychedelics, we should understand something about music's innate power to reach us at a very deep level and to open portals to states of higher awareness. There is no need to resort to esoteric metaphysical teachings to argue for the innately mystical and transformative potencies of music. As music therapist David Aldridge writes, "The universal qualities of music elicit awareness of that which lies beyond physical existence and brings forward inspirations about infinity, boundlessness and timelessness."[1] These are not the words of some ancient metaphysician or modern esotericist, but rather those of a contemporary academic. For a more poetic rendering of the same idea, we turn to our reliable guide in matters mystical, Aldous Huxley, for whom the most profound concerns of human existence exist beyond the expressive power of words: "From pure sensation to the intuition of beauty, from pleasure and pain to love and mystical ecstasy and death—all the things that are fundamental, all the things that, to the human spirit, are most profoundly significant, can only be experienced, not expressed. The rest is always and everywhere silence." "After silence," however, Huxley adds, "that which comes nearest to expressing the inexpressible is music. . . . on another plane of being, music is the equivalent of some of man's most significant and most inexpressible experiences."[2]

In the first part of this chapter, we look at some perennial ideas about the inherent metaphysical and spiritual properties of music, their capacity to expand consciousness and put us in touch with post-rational states. Later we explore these same ideas as they're articulated in the writings and musings of psychedelic thinkers and practitioners. This helps form a foundation for our later explorations into the experiential fact of musical mysticism as experienced in the psychedelic realm.

Philosophical, aesthetic, and metaphysical ideas about the meaning and significance of music go back millennia, but for our purposes we begin with the aesthetic ideas of Romanticism:

> For the romantics, art, as a phenomenon that is not subject to reason or discursive thought, now becomes the realm in which the world of the super sensible is revealed. Thus the romantics, adopting the all-embracing term *Poesie*, exalt art to the highest level, where it becomes cognition. . . . In this context, it is not surprising that music, an art form that on account of its immaterial nature is particularly stubborn in its resistance to conceptual cognition, becomes especially important. The romantic philosophy of music . . . regards music as the shattering revelation of a higher world, a world that calls forth divine tremors in its listener and remains concealed from everything else.[3]

Philosopher Arthur Schopenhauer (1788–1860) was a central exponent of Romanticism's views on art, particularly those concerning music. For Schopenhauer, music, while existing beyond the limits of ordinary reason, is a repository of a different kind of knowledge: that of metaphysical insight. In particular, he emphasizes the concept of "genius," the artist as the natural conduit through which wisdom reveals itself. This does not exalt the artist as some kind of god or enlightened soul, but simply as a channel, even a naive channel, of higher truths. In Schopenhauer's words, "The composer reveals the inmost nature of the world and articulates the most profound wisdom in a language that his reason does not comprehend; as the somnambulist under the influence of Mesmerism gives insights into things of which, waking, she has no concept."[4] For Schopenhauer,

> Music is not a language like other languages. Instead, for Schopenhauer, it is a "completely general language." It speaks not of this and that but of all and everything, and in doing

so it reveals "the inmost essence of the world." . . . [T]he language of music is, on the one hand, immediately comprehensible and capable of moving every individual in the most profound way. But, on the other hand, the language of music eludes comprehension by reason. Thus, for music there can be no translation into other, particular languages. Moreover, music's insights do not derive from rational reflection by the composer, translated in an intentional way into the language of music. Rather, the presence of metaphysical insight in music is due to compositional genius and its unconscious cognitive and linguistic achievement. . . . Schopenhauer insists on the capacity of music to do in tones what philosophy does in concepts—to do metaphysics. . . . Schopenhauer . . . [characterizes] music as the unconscious exercise of metaphysics.[5]

Music as metaphysics? Contemporary British composer John Tavener, for one, claims as much: "I consider my music is liquid metaphysics. I clearly cannot demand belief in what I believe in, but I can ask for an openness, or certainly an acceptance that another level of reality exists beyond this commonplace one."[6]

Many gifted, sensitive minds in various intellectual and humanistic spheres have written about music with a passion and devotion that may seem overblown to modern, jaded ears. They describe music in glowing poetic or metaphysical terms, exalting it as if it had descended from some luminous, transcendent realm. We prosaic mortals naturally tend to take such effusions with a sizable grain of salt. It is easy to minimize or dismiss these beliefs either as being sentimental or merely well-intentioned contrivances to promote the noble cause of "music appreciation" to the masses.

But among our fellow humans there are some who indeed are endowed naturally with depths of sensitivity to music (or other sensory stimuli) that far exceed our own, via either innate aptitude, rigorous training, or a combination of both. These fortunate souls experience music with a kind of aural sensitivity and emotional responsiveness that is far from "normal" and happens to resemble in significant ways how music is experienced in psychedelic states. It is, indeed, an exceptional privilege to be granted, under psychedelics, if only for a few hours, access to such rarefied states of aesthetic receptivity and musical ecstasy. To me, that is one of psychedelia's greatest gifts, as it is for scholar Benny

Shanon writing of ayahuasca but speaking for all psychedelics: its "great gift . . . is its capacity to bestow on lay people, for a brief period of time, the grace of the muses."[7]

In this section we hear from a variety of authors (outside the context of psychedelics) who speak of those essential attributes of music that, under ideal circumstances, can move us to tears, heal psyche and soul, and even serve as a window to higher consciousness. They speak of music as

- inhabiting a realm beyond words and concepts
- expressive or symbolic of our inner lives or of the inner flow of consciousness
- embodying or transmitting wisdom
- a marriage between beauty and wisdom (aesthetics and gnosis)

Obviously, by "music" we do not mean *all* music, as if music were a single entity or that any music may serve this purpose. Clearly we're using the term in a very broad sense, an almost archetypal one, as a sonic force or energy that, in certain configurations and circumstances, may have very potent effects on human consciousness. Those who have spoken of music in these terms often see it as a link to higher realms of being, other worlds, heavenly paradises, and even the infinite. For German Romantic author, artist, and composer E. T. A. Hoffman (1776–1822), music expresses a certain inarticulate, inchoate longing for transcendence: "Music is the most romantic of all the arts—one might almost say, the only genuinely romantic one—for its sole subject is the infinite. Music discloses to man an unknown realm, a world in which he leaves behind him all definite feelings to surrender himself to an inexpressible longing."[8] Similarly, for Victorian cleric, author, and music-lover Hugh R. Haweis (1838–1901), music gives form to our inner experience and voice to our deepest instincts: "Music . . . represents those modulations and temperamental changes which escape all verbal analysis; it utters what must else remain forever unuttered and unutterable; it feeds that deep, ineradicable instinct within us of which all art is only the reverberated echo, that craving to express, through the medium of the senses, the spiritual and eternal realities which underlie them."[9]

Beyond Western traditions, Al-Gazzali (c. 1056–1111), the great Persian Islamic philosopher, theologian, and mystic, similarly wrote in spiritual terms of music's capacity to ignite an inner longing for "that higher world of beauty": "The heart of man has been so constituted by the Almighty that, like a flint, it contains a hidden fire which is evoked by music and harmony, and renders man beside himself with ecstasy. These harmonies are echoes of that higher world of beauty which we call the world of spirits, they remind man of his relationship to that world, and produce in him an emotion so deep and strange that he himself is powerless to explain it."[10]

For modern composer Jonathan Harvey (1939–2012), music communicates the sense of an ideal order, providing an escape from the banality of everyday life:

> For those who take the trouble to listen to it seriously . . . [music] is capable of communicating with humanity in the deepest possible way, transforming the normal world by providing a glimpse of another one, just out of reach. Music can communicate the sense of an ideal order, a vision of an existence untouched by the banality and ugliness of everyday life. . . . Several composers have used metaphors of ascension and flight in order to convey the idea that music gives mankind the ability to rise above everyday life and into a mysterious area above. . . . Many, whatever their other beliefs, have shared the view of Schumann that "Music is always the language in which one can converse with the beyond." . . . For such composers, the communication of a vision of paradise is the ultimate goal of music.[11]

For fellow British composer Michael Tippett (1905–1998), the flow of music is a mirror of the inner flow of life, an expression of our inner being. It provides a sense of wholeness and coherence, an antidote to our normally fractured, alienated consciousness. Listening to music, "we are as though entire again, despite all the insecurity, incoherence, incompleteness and relativity of our everyday life. The miracle is achieved by submitting to the power of its organized flow; a submission which gives us a special pleasure and finally enriches us. The pleasure and the enrichment arise from the fact that the flow is not merely the flow of the music itself, but a significant image of the inner flow of life."[12] Contemporary American composer Philip Glass describes music as a "code for a larger structure," which thus can be heard "multi-dimensionally":

> What I suspect now is that actually music is a shorthand for something else. I mean that a piece of music is actually a code. An architect's plan for a building is not the building. But it represents the building. I think that music may function in that way. That's what I meant when I said I suspect it's multi-dimensional. . . . If we think carefully about our experiencing of music, when we hear it as a sound event we're actually only hearing one layer of it. . . . Music is actually a kind of a symbol for a rounder, more complete reality.[13]

Philosophers also have spoken of music's power to evoke the spiritual. One of the acknowledged classics in the philosophy of mysticism, *The Idea of the Holy* (*Das Heilige*), was authored by German theologian, philosopher, and comparative religionist Rudolf Otto (1869–1937). Otto is perhaps best known for his concept of the *numinous*, the profound emotional or aesthetic quality that he felt defined the heart and soul of the human religious impulse. For him, music was an important part of the story because it is a non-rational force that arouses in us a feeling for the numinous, the holy. For Otto, music is a force that integrates the rational functions of consciousness with the non-rational. Music thus arouses emotions in us that are "wholly other":

> There is another kind of experience in which we may find an example of the way in which rational elements in our feeling-consciousness may be thus penetrated by quite non-rational ones . . . I refer to the state of mind induced in us by . . . music, purely as music. It releases a blissful rejoicing in us, and we are conscious of a glimmering, billowy agitation occupying our minds, without being able to express or explain in concepts what it really is that moves us so deeply. . . .
>
> Music, in short, arouses in us an experience and vibrations of mood that are quite specific in kind and must simply be called "musical" . . . The resultant complex mood is, as it were, a fabric, in which the general human feelings and emotional states constitute the warp, and the non-rational music-feelings the woof. . . . The real content of music is not drawn from the ordinary human emotions at all, and . . . is in no way merely a second language, alongside the usual one, by which

these emotions find expression. Musical feeling is rather (like numinous feeling) something "wholly other."[14]

Finally, some authors have described music's ability to communicate more deeply than language ever can. In his monumental work *Remembrance of Things Past*, the great French novelist Marcel Proust (1871–1922) offers a mythopoetic reverie on music as an ancient and now lost "means of communication between souls." In one episode of the novel, having experienced a great musical work in concert, his inner thoughts are interrupted by various members of the audience who approach him to chat during the intermission:

> But what were their words, which like every human and external word left me so indifferent, compared with the heavenly phrase of music with which I had just been communing? I was truly like an angel, who, fallen from the inebriating bliss of paradise, subsides into the most humdrum reality. And, just as certain creatures are the last surviving testimony to a form of life which nature has discarded, I wondered whether music might not be the unique example of what might have been—if the invention of language, the formation of words, the analysis of ideas had not intervened—the means of communication between souls. It is like a possibility that has come to nothing; humanity has developed along other lines, those of spoken and written language.[15]

Proust's description will reverberate with what many experience while being absorbed in music on psychedelics, only to have an interjection of words and concepts, coming from outside or from within, break the spell and fracture the flow of experience—a dynamic, living experience compared to which words are but weightless, withered, desiccated things.

Music Mysticism in Psychedelic States

We turn our attention now to the psychedelic realm, both theoretically and experientially. The extraordinary ways in which music is experienced in psychedelic states cannot be reduced to a simple matter of chemically induced perceptual distortion or aural hallucination. Rather, it is the natural result of a profound opening of the senses and of a hearer brought to a state not only of unguarded, unconditional receptivity, but of spiritual cognition. A sufficient dose of psychedelic, supported by positive set and setting, can induce a psychedelic state that is indistinguishable from a mystical one, defined in part by William James as "a state of knowledge": "Although so similar to states of feeling, mystical states seem to those who experience them to be also states of knowledge. They are states of insight into depth of truth unplumbed by the discursive intellect. They are illuminations, revelations, full of significance and importance, all inarticulate though they remain; and as a rule they carry with them a curious sense of authority for after-time."[16]

In psychedelic states, music is more than music, more than an artful configuration of tones and melodies. Though attention to the beauty of composed sound is one level of the experience, it is common for music to "speak"—in its own ineffable language—through eidetic imagery, profound emotion, and finally through experiential knowledge. These states of insight are illuminations and revelations of such intensity and immediacy that they are experienced as self-evident, intrinsically authoritative, self-revelatory, self-luminous. The key here is that aesthetic experience and transcendent knowledge form a continuum, music seeming to open up onto, or to express within itself, a realm of revealed wisdom. In the psychedelic realm, beauty and wisdom are not only intimately related, but often indistinguishable, two manifestations of one sublime state, intertwined aspects of the same human impulse toward wholeness and transcendence. As such, in psychedelic practice, music functions not as a mere sensory sideline, something to add to a "setting" checklist along with flowers and a comfortable couch, but as the very food and fuel of a rich and deeply satisfying psychedelic experience.

Benny Shanon, an emeritus professor of psychology at the Hebrew University of Jerusalem who has studied ayahuasca use extensively both in native and non-native settings, has described in precise terms the role of music in ayahuasca rituals, providing insights that apply more widely to psychedelic aesthetics in general. Here he explains, with admirable clarity, the role of the aesthetic in ayahuasca ceremonials:

> First, the brew highly enhances people's aesthetic sensitivity and appreciation. Second, the visions the brew induces are exceedingly beautiful and having them is a most powerful aesthetic

experience. Third . . . splendid works of art are prominent in the visions. Fourth, the Ayahuasca experience is intimately related to music and the intoxication often makes people sing and play on levels much higher than their performances exhibit under normal circumstances. Fifth, with Ayahuasca, people often feel that the aesthetic is the prime measure of things. . . . Under the Ayahuasca intoxication, people feel that an entirely new world of sublime magnificence is revealed to them. In it, the aesthetic reigns supreme and the common impression is that it is the embodiment of eternal truths and the manifestation of the Supreme Good.

Shanon concludes by invoking Plato:

In his dialogue *Phaedrus*, Plato expresses the view that Beauty is unique in that it is directly manifest to the senses. This is in contrast to the other forms (in the Platonic sense), which are comprehended only through the exercise of the faculties of reasoning, which are always imperfect. Furthermore, Beauty is unique in that it has the power to reveal to us humans the existence of an ideal world beyond the world of sense. This, in turn, is a prime source for happiness. Again, these feelings and insights are very common under the Ayahuasca intoxication.[17]

Elsewhere Shanon also describes music as a bridge between this world and higher realms: "Music is unique in that it pertains to both worlds—the ordinary physical one and whatever non-ordinary one(s) may be experienced with Ayahuasca. Thus, in a most concrete fashion, music can function as the *axis mundi*—that is, the axis that joins the worlds . . . *par excellence*."[18]

If the aesthetic is a gateway to eternal truths, and if in psychedelic states music has a revelatory function, then we might say that music conveys meaning: but not in the conventional sense of functioning as a language conveying ideas. Shanon explains:

I maintain that Ayahuasca works in the manner of works of art: it makes one feel and experience in a particular manner, involves one in powerful affective dynamics, and bestows spiritual states of mind. . . . In light of its non-denotational semantics, music is especially telling in this respect. Although music can be symbolic, and sometimes narrative, usually it is neither: yet, music does convey meaning. Its meaning pertains to the dynamics of the emotions and states of mind that it invokes. Music makes us experience joy and sadness, hopelessness and the regaining of hope, the open-endedness of possibilities, the quest for freedom and the allure of personal aspiration, solemnity and frivolity, the acceptance of one's lot in life and the tragic dimension of existence.[19]

William Richards, widely respected psychedelic pioneer and author of *Sacred Knowledge: Psychedelics and Religious Experiences,* feels that exalted music expresses "the deepest processes and ultimate truths within human consciousness" and that such music had to have arisen "in profoundly sacred alternative states of consciousness":

When listening to music during the action of entheogen, it is common to hear claims of "having become the music," of "entering into the mind of the composer," or of beholding the eternal truth that the composer was attempting to depict or express in his or her composition. Music is thus often understood to be a nonverbal language that seeks to express, and is indeed capable of expressing, the deepest processes and ultimate truths within human consciousness. . . .

Music we call "great," often classical, choral, or symphonic, is also repeatedly claimed by some to be "the language of the gods." There are alternative states of consciousness in which music is intuitively known to reflect and express spiritual truth far above and beyond the threshold where words falter and cease. . . . It is reasonable to hypothesize that music that reaches so deeply into the human soul arose in profoundly sacred alternative states of consciousness, regardless of how they may have been engendered.[20]

Richards's perspective clearly reflects Schopenhauer's view of the composer as a conduit of higher wisdom. Psychologist Claudio Naranjo underscores this idea: "I am convinced that the great composers of the West have been teachers of humanity whose spiritual influence is ignored; and whether this statement is true or not for the majority of people today, I believe it is still true for those who listen to great classical music in their psychedelic journeys."[21] To avail oneself of such numinous musical transmissions, Naranjo advises that one learn

> to listen to music not as a simple aesthetic phenomenon and to please the ear, but as a heart-to-heart communication from the composer who wrote it, so that contact with the great musicians of the past may reach us as a great spiritual communion. Above all, for this, we must learn to become the music, laying aside our personal thoughts and day-to-day emotions, identifying ourselves through this with the will of the music, moment to moment, which is but the reflection of the will of the creator of that texture of sounds.[22]

Anthropologist Claude Levi-Strauss expresses the same theme: "Since music is the only language with the contradictory attributes of being at once intelligible and untranslatable, the musical creator is a being comparable to the gods, and music itself the supreme mystery of the science of man."[23] We find a similar idea, minus the overt mystical overtones, in Leo Tolstoy's novella *The Kreutzer Sonata*, where his character states, "Music instantaneously transports me into that mental condition in which he who composed it found himself. I blend my soul with his, and with him I am transported from one mood to another."[24]

One of the clearest assertions that music is linked to divine revelation comes, unsurprisingly, from Aldous Huxley. Listening, on mescaline, to Bach's Fourth Brandenburg Concerto (one movement in particular, the Allegro), he describes it as "the knowledgeless understanding of everything . . . undifferentiated awareness broken up into notes and phrases and yet still all-comprehendingly itself."[25] On another occasion, listening to Bach's B-minor suite and the "Musical Offering" on a relatively modest dose (75 micrograms) of LSD, Huxley described his experience as deeply profound:

> The tempo of the pieces did not change; nevertheless they went on for centuries, and they were a manifestation, on the plane of art, of perpetual creation, a demonstration of the necessity of death and the self-evidence of immortality, an expression of the essential all-rightness of the universe—for the music was far beyond tragedy, but included death and suffering with everything else in the divine impartiality which is the One,

which is Love, which is Being or *Istigkeit*. Who on earth was John Sebastian? Certainly not the old gent with sixteen children in a stuffy Protestant environment. Rather, an enormous manifestation of the Other—but the Other canalized, controlled, made available through the intervention of the intellect and the senses and the emotions.[26]

For Michael Pollan, listening to what was for him a very familiar work by Bach (the Cello Suite in D Minor)—yet realizing that "until this moment I had never truly listened to it"—the music seemed to provide a glimpse into "the very meaning of life":

"Listen" doesn't begin to describe what transpired between me and the vibrations of air set in motion by the four strings of that cello. Never before has a piece of music pierced me as deeply as this one did now. Though even to call it "music" is to diminish what now began to flow, which was nothing less than the stream of human consciousness, something in which one might glean the very meaning of life and, if you could bear it, read life's last chapter.[27]

For another tripper, a simple immersive vision flowing from music apparently lead to a life-changing evolution of consciousness: "The music wove me into a cocoon, and I burst out as a butterfly. This banished for me the meaning of death and led me into a dynamic acceptance of life and freedom from the fear of [death]."[28] In another trip report, the guide (G) puts Tchaikovsky's Violin Concerto in D on the turntable and tells the subject (S), "Relax now . . . and let yourself be absorbed into the music":

S: (After listening silently with his eyes closed for about twenty minutes) "Ahhhhhhhhhhh."

G: "What is it?"

S: "I've never listened to music like this before. . . . I'm hearing so much more intensely with my outer ear . . . and yet . . . at the same time I'm listening with my inner ear . . . I hear melodies . . . and melodies in the melodies. I hear Tchaikovsky himself! And I can see it all too! The melody passes before my (closed) eyes . . . I see . . . I see centuries and all of the glory and the tragedy of man . . . *Everything* is in this music! . . . But especially the tragedy of man" [multiple ellipses in the original].[29]

Those who've had similar experiences can understand how a single piece of music can seem to contain *everything*, to be capable of providing an endless succession of visions and illuminations: in this case, an eidetic, panoramic view of the endless flow of human history, with both its glories and horrors.

Closely tied to this theme of the essential relation between the aesthetic and transcendent wisdom, between music and revelation, is what Ido Hartogsohn termed the "intensified ontology" of psychedelic experience: "the intensification, amplification, and dramatization of meaning and experience." This helps explain why music is perceived as having momentous import, far exceeding its "merely" sensory or aesthetic function. Hartogsohn relates this intensified ontology to the experience of "presence," whereby sound and music are experienced as "hyperreal":

> Under the effects of psychedelics, things seem to announce and manifest themselves more fully. In other words, they seem more present, as in Huxley's fascination with the flowers in the vase, which he felt were "what Adam had seen on the moment of creation—the miracle, moment by moment, of naked existence," or his repeated invocation of the concept of suchness, the rare and wondrous moment in which something, usually an object, is perceived and recognized clearly and lucidly in its full presence. Psychedelics often accentuate the contours of objects and expose them more fully. Such objects might include colors, sounds, thoughts, and emotions, which might seem so real as to be hyperreal.[30]

Claudio Naranjo also speaks of the intensity, the presence, and the ontological weight of music heard in psychedelic states:

> True as may be the description by Havelock Ellis . . . of his mescaline experience as "an orgy of vision," listening to music is at least as significant as attending to the visual world and is generally regarded as the best doorway to ecstatic experience.

At best, the experience of musical audition may lead the individual to echo the statement of classical India: "*Sabda Brahman: sound is God.*" Just as the visual world may convey (beyond the particulars of form, color, objects, and meanings) Beingness or *Istigkeit*, so sound in itself, beyond musical forms and psychological content, becomes suffused with Being, a Being with which the listener identifies as he dissolves in the music, becoming nothing and the music all at once.[31]

Having now explored the inherent metaphysical and spiritual properties of music, and how they are amplified and internalized in psychedelic states, we can now take a closer look at the psycho-spiritual processes by which the experience of music is radically transformed.

3

Beginner's Mind and "Letting Go"

> The problem with listening, of course, is that we don't. There's too much noise going on in our heads, so we never hear anything. The inner conversation simply never stops. It can be our voice or whatever voices we want to supply, but it's a constant racket. In the same way we don't see, and in the same way we don't feel, we don't touch, we don't taste. First we have to get to that point where we've entered a world where we can listen. . . . Let's say that we've got the crowd of ninety-five lunatics in our head to stop. Then the real activity of listening takes place. Then we come to the doorway of the world of listening.
>
> —Philip Glass

Beginner's Mind

As we prepare to dive into the phenomenology of psychedelic experience—dealing with such subjects as the experience of timelessness, sensory hypersensitivity, and the sense of merging with music—it will be helpful to grasp the foundational concept of *de-habituation* (or *de-automatization*, or *de-familiarization*), by which it's possible to hear music unencumbered by our own mental and perceptual presets, to hear with "innocent ears," as it were. One may think of de-habituation as a kind of self-initiated psychological decolonization, resulting in a temporary respite from the pervasive psychosocial conditioning within which we've been marinating since birth. In the simplest sense, it means to see or hear or experience things freshly, free from hardened perceptual habits and previous mindsets.

Such purity of perception is attained, in the words of English Romantic poet and philosopher Samuel Taylor Coleridge, "by awakening the mind's attention from the lethargy of custom, and directing it to the loveliness and the wonders of the world before us . . . but for which, in consequence of the film of familiarity and selfish solicitude we have eyes, yet see not, ears that hear not, and hearts that neither feel nor understand."[1]

As psychedelic pioneer Humphrey Osmond explains, ordinarily we view the world through our assumptions and conditioning:

> Our briefs, what we assume . . . greatly influence the world in which we live. That world is in part, at least, what we make of it. Once our mold for world making is formed it most strongly resists change. The psychedelics allow us, for a little while, to divest ourselves of these acquired assumptions and to see the universe again with an innocent eye. In T. H. Huxley's words, we may, if we wish, "sit down in front of the facts like a child" or as Thomas Traherne, a seventeenth-century English mystic, puts it, "to unlearn the dirty devices of the world and become as it were a little child again."[2]

Cultural anthropologist, psychotherapist, and psychedelics researcher Marlene Dobkin de Rios describes how we've internalized those "dirty devises" as our own psychological programming: "Under normal circumstances the exquisite complexity of the mind is fairly rigorously programmed, or habituated, to keep it from breaking through into another totally chaotic reality which the Freudians call the id. Thus the mind functions much like a straightjacket, presenting us with an illusory world of unalterable reality and employing extensive fail-safe mechanisms to enable us to function within homeostatic limits. Under the influence of LSD, the habituation pattern of the brain is overwhelmed."[3] As Alan Watts put it, "What we call self-consciousness is thus the sensation of the organism obstructing itself, of not being with itself, of driving, so to say, with accelerator and brake on at once."[4]

Ordinarily, every perception is colored or tainted by memories of similar past perceptions, which have accumulated and solidified into general impressions, prejudices, and expectations. In his book *Musicophilia: Tales of Music and the Brain*, neuroscientist Oliver Sacks explains, "Perception is never purely in the present—it has to draw on experience of the past. . . . We all have detailed memories of how things have previously looked and sounded, and these memories are recalled and admixed with every new perception."[5] When we listen to a familiar piece of music that has been burned into memory, the stored version of that music is activated and accompanies (and thus partially obscures) the "live feed." As Sacks explains: "We apprehend a piece of music as a whole. Whatever the initial processes of musical perception and memory may be, once a piece of music is known, it is retained not as an assemblage of individual elements but as a completed procedure or performance; music is performed by the mind/brain whenever it is recollected."[6] Excuse me, but is that not extraordinary? Sacks is saying that when we listen to a piece of music a second, tenth, or hundredth time, we're mostly hearing only an auditory shadow or simulacrum of the original, a pre-recorded cerebral replay. Such established, concretized musical perceptions, Sacks points out, "must be especially powerful in a strongly musical person."[7] But even such a musically experienced (or overexposed, or even jaded) person may receive the gift of "beginner's mind" in a psychedelic session and reexperience music as a fresh, pristine, new object of awareness.

Michael Pollan and psychiatrist and psychedelics researcher Julie Holland discuss de-habituation (vis-à-vis cannabis), describing it as a transcending of mental presets or, more simply, a temporary "forgetting" of our ingrained perceptual patterns:

> JULIE: There's no doubt that short-term memory is temporarily diminished when somebody gets high. But what I think is enjoyable to people is this idea of dehabituation, that they're seeing things with fresh eyes. Memory is the enemy of wonder. When people get high, everything is new and intense because of this forgetting . . .
>
> MICHAEL: It's a childlike way of looking at the world—Wordsworth's child. The child sees everything for the first time; and, of course, to see things for the first time, you have to have forgotten that you've seen them before. So forgetting is very important to the experience of awe or wonder.
>
> JULIE: It aestheticizes commonplace things. When something is sort of distanced or estranged, it somehow becomes more beautiful.

MICHAEL: It italicizes it, in a way. You set it apart, and you actually see it. It gives a freshness to things that we take for granted all the time. . . . putting them up on a pedestal.[8]

Eloquent as always, Allen Ginsberg offers his take on cannabis de-habituation (a process intensified under psychedelics): "The marijuana consciousness is one that, ever so gently, shifts the center of attention from habitual shallow purely verbal guidelines and repetitive second-hand ideological interpretations of experience to more direct, slower, absorbing, occasionally microscopically minute engagement with sensing phenomena."[9] This process of de-habituation or de-familiarization pushes the "reset" button in perceptual awareness, removing from any object of perception its habitual mental associations, its assigned meanings. With that re-set, perceptions are now "uncontaminated by personal needs or preoccupations . . . removed from the tyranny of hopes and fears, of desire, of personal striving"[10]—or, as Huxley put it, freed from viewing the outside world as an "emotionally charged ego."[11]

Masters and Houston define the heightened sense perception afforded by psychedelics similarly, as freedom from seeing things in terms of their external or imposed attributes, their "function, symbolism or label categorizations," or any other attributes "not accessible to sense perception alone," anything that might "dilute the immediacy of perception."[12] This purified or de-conditioned perception is sometimes referred to as "the aesthetic way of knowing" (a term originating with Schopenhauer). It is closely related to the phenomenological concept of perceptual or cognitive "bracketing," that is, observing an object in its singularity, set apart from its contextual background—seen now as a "thing-in-itself," allowing for direct, unmediated experience. Alan Watts describes this "unprogrammed mode of attention" as "looking *at* things without looking *for* things," a purified perception that "reveals the unbelievable beauty of the everyday world."[13] "The invariable mark of wisdom," observed Emerson in his essay "Nature," is to see the miraculous in the common."[14] "It is apparent," writes R. A. Durr in *Poetic Vision and the Psychedelic Experience*: "that many of our greatest writers have seen the world very much as it is described in the psychedelic reports, when 'the earth, and every common sight . . . did seem/ Apparelled in celestial light,/ The glory and the freshness of a dream'" (Wordsworth, "Intimations" Ode).[15] Here, as is often the case, elements of Romanticism, phenomenology, and Transcendentalism combine to lay an articulate philosophical foundation for psychedelic thought and practice.

In his enlightening book *Music and the Ineffable*, French philosopher Vladimir Jankelevitch describes how most of us listen to music superficially, backgrounding it behind endless mundane distractions, while even the professional music critic distracts himself from music's essence by focusing on external facts and analytical speculation:

> Most people demand from music nothing more than light intoxication, which they need as background accompaniment for their free associations, a rhyme to support their musings, a rocking cradle for their ruminations. . . . For them it has become home-furnishing music . . . melodious rumblings heard under the meal and the chitchat . . . musical background for busy people. So the listener says: let's think about something else. And the musicologist decides in turn: let's talk about something else. For instance, the composer's biography, or his erotic affairs, or his historical significance. . . .
>
> What is necessary is music itself, in itself . . . and not music in relation to something else, or circumscribed. Alas, music in itself is an unknowable something, as unable to be grasped as the mystery of artistic creation.[16]

Music itself, in itself—not in relation to anything else. That is how one hears when the mind is cleared of conventional, conditioned associations and egoic expectations. Krishnamurti seems to have this in mind when he states, "Listening has importance only when one is not projecting one's own desires through which one listens. Can one put aside all these screens through which we listen, and really listen?"[17] That is the effect of de-habituation, de-automatization, and de-familiarization: to hear sound in its *suchness*, to borrow a profound Buddhist concept.

This is one of many areas where we find uncanny correspondences between basic concepts in Eastern philosophies (Buddhism, Taoism, Hinduism) and psychedelic mysticism. In her eye- and ear-opening book *Deep Listeners: Music, Emotion, and Trancing*, musicologist and Southeast Asianist Judith Becker describes the concept of pure aesthetic perception, drawing upon ideas from the Hindu Tantric tradition:

> The idea of aesthetic appreciation in Tantric teachings has to do with a special kind of perception, of paying full attention to whatever is before one at the moment. The Tantrics of medieval India linked the study of perception and cognition with aesthet-

> ics. One is taught constantly to strive to be in the present, not mentally reliving the past nor rehearsing the future. One strives to be mindful of every moment and to see, hear, taste, smell, and touch without preconceptions, without the intervening overlay of the memory of past experiences. To see things as they are, to hear music as it is, without precognition or judgment, is to perceive aesthetically. Refinement of perception, according to Tantric philosophy, can lead to a refinement of cognition and a dissolution of the boundaries between oneself and the thing perceived. *Aesthetics as clarified perception becomes a cornerstone of spiritual practice* [emphasis added].[18]

It is hard to imagine a clearer, more crystalline explanation of pure perception or lucid hearing. Admittedly, since these ideas are coming to us, unavoidably, via concepts enshrouded in language, they may appear highly abstract, idealized, even esoteric. Nevertheless, we are still dealing with *experiences*, albeit particularly intense, rarefied experiences that happen to exist in a dimension beyond conventional understanding. Words are, at best, merely indicators, signs pointing in a vague general direction. To help clarify and solidify the matter, I offer the eloquence of Aldous Huxley, who transposes and transcribes his own ecstatic, unconditioned, non-dual experience of a particular piece of music into the main character of his final novel, *Island*. This character, named Will, is listening to Bach's Fourth Brandenburg Concerto while on a psychedelic (referred to in the novel as *moksha*-medicine—*moksha* being the Sanskrit term for spiritual emancipation):

> Tonight, for the first time, his awareness of a piece of music was completely unobstructed. Between mind and sound, mind and pattern, mind and significance, there was no longer any babel of biographical irrelevances to drown the music or make a senseless discord. Tonight's Fourth Brandenburg was a pure datum—no a blessed donum [gift]—uncorrupted by the personal history, the second-hand notions, the ingrained stupidities with which, like every self, the poor idiot, who wouldn't (and in art plainly couldn't) take yes for an answer, had overlaid the gifts of immediate experience.[19]

The Fourth Brandenburg Concerto was a particular favorite of Huxley's. He knew it intimately, particularly the Allegro—so intimately that it became, in effect, his "private property." Now, under LSD, unobstructed and uncorrupted by personal memory and conditioning, his character hears it afresh, as "an unowned Thing in Itself":

> It was the same, of course, as the Fourth Brandenburg he had listened to so often in the past—the same and yet completely different. This Allegro—he knew it by heart. Which meant that he was in the best possible position to realize that he had never really heard it before. . . . The Allegro was revealing itself as an element in the great present Event, a manifestation at one remove of the luminous bliss. Allegro was the luminous bliss; it was the knowledgeless understanding of everything apprehended through a particular piece of knowledge; it was undifferentiated awareness broken up into notes and phrases and yet still all-comprehendingly itself. And of course all this belonged to nobody. It was at once in here, out there, and nowhere. . . . Which was why he was now hearing it for the first time. Unowned, the Fourth Brandenburg had an intensity of beauty, a depth of intrinsic meaning, incomparably greater than anything he had ever found in the same music when it was his private property. . . .
>
> And tonight's Fourth Brandenburg was not merely an unowned Thing in Itself; it was also, in some impossible way, a Present Event with an infinite duration. Or rather (and still more impossibly, seeing that it had three movements and was being played at its usual speed) it was without duration. The metronome presides over each of its phrases; but the sum of its phrases was not a span of seconds and minutes. There was a tempo, but no time. So what was there?
>
> "Eternity," . . . He began to laugh.
>
> "What's so funny?" she asked.
>
> "Eternity," he answered. "Believe it or not, it's as real as shit."[20]

"Letting Go": Music and Trance

It is necessary to abandon yourself completely and let the music do as it will with you—to be a vessel through which it passes.

—Debussy

As psychedelics act to de-habituate consciousness, to disengage us from the burden of fixed patterns of thinking and being, we can help the process along through a simple, voluntary act of surrender. It is no surprise, then, that in their empirically based article "Psychedelics, Meditation, and Self-Consciousness," Millière et al. conclude that "Higher ratings of willingness to surrender are associated with stronger mystical type experience in both psychedelic experiences and meditation."[21] The key to entering into a full psychedelic experience, then, is that of "letting go," of relaxing the defensive ego and opening up fully to the experience. As we have it from the *Tibetan Book of the Dead* by way of the Beatles, "Turn off your mind, relax, and float downstream." It means, simply, that one lies back and allows the experience to wash over one without conscious resistance. William Richards describes it as "the conscious decision . . . to surrender . . . to the unfolding stream of experiences. An attitude of openness, honesty and curiosity, a spirit of adventure that supersedes normative desires of the ego to censor, be cautious, and exert control."[22]

Music assists and enriches the psychedelic experience in various ways, but serves a special function during the initial ascent: it draws one's attention away from the reactive, thinking mind via its powerful allure—music now transformed into a source of aesthetic wonder. Especially calm, gentle, meditative music can ease a mind that may be apprehensive, aware that it is about to undergo an experience that may be disorienting, emotionally challenging, even existentially overwhelming. Some gentle, positively affective music can make the ascent easier, assuage fear, and provide a sense of beneficent support. It helps one "let go" of brittle ego defenses, the fight-or-flight response: resistance that can, in and of itself, bring on anxiety, fear, and a negative experience. Quiet, calm, reassuring music can get a trip off to a positive start and help provide a measure of calm at any point thereafter.[23]

The advice to just "let go" is easy to offer but not necessarily easily followed. Why would we, why *do* we, resist? Essentially, because we're conditioned to hold onto that which is familiar and to fear the unknown. Unless we've attained an enlightened state of consciousness (sought by many, attained by few), our default, day-to-day consciousness is shaped and molded by our ego, that makeshift, provisional sense of self by which we define who and what we are, what "reality" is, and how to navigate it. A functionally healthy person is presumed to have a fairly stable sense of self, an "I" that presents itself to the world in a reasonably consistent manner and moves through the world with definable purposes and goals.

We may speak of that ego as being both interior and exterior. The "exterior" ego is that outwardly facing persona that, having absorbed the rules and regulations of life within a particular society, navigates day-to-day existence, interrelating with other selves and fulfilling needs and expectations. The "interior" ego is, let us say, a general sense of what it feels like to be "me," the overall flavor of subjective existence, my sense of what I am and what is real. The ego, functioning both externally and internally, seeks stasis, smooth predictability, and avoidance of disorienting shocks and surprises.

When we're beginning to feel the effects of a psychedelic, when our inner awareness begins to shift, to become aware of a certain "otherness," something strange or uncanny, our attachment to ego-centered stasis may feel threatened. It may try to hold on to the default, familiar sense of self while the mind attempts to "make sense" of the unfamiliar sensations. The best course, then, is simply to relax as best as one can (there are simple relaxation exercises one can easily learn, such as calm, measured deep breathing). However, if the resistance is too great, if one instinctually feels compelled to battle the inevitable, fear and anxiety rise up and may lead, at least temporarily, to a "bad trip." Speaking about this phenomenon, Ram Dass explains that, as the trip begins, "what may happen is that the person reaches a point where even the minimal structure needed for holding onto a sense of self is perceived to be in jeopardy. Some people who are not prepared for that push against it, and when you push against it, the whole paranoid process starts, [leading to] a user-generated hell realm."[24] In *The Varieties of Psychedelic Experience*, authors Masters and Houston elaborate:

> For many subjects the emergence or eruption of this wealth of primarily sensory phenomena may constitute the first experience of the "dark woods." If the subject here attempts to maintain his normative structures of time and relationship, if he attempts to play Procrustes and fit the psychedelic flood tides to the old predrug-state frame of reference, he may be in for some unpleasant moments. A sense of confusion and chaos are the usual results of the subject's insistence on trying to preserve his normal categorical orientation.[25]

Throughout the psychedelic literature, music is proposed as a powerful antidote to the resistance that can derail a meaningful and productive trip, not only at its inception, the "ascent," but at any point throughout the journey. This issue often arises within the therapeutic context. Stanislav Grof explains in *LSD Psychotherapy*, "LSD subjects frequently report that the flow of music helps them to let go of their psychological defenses and surrender fully to the experience."[26] James Fadiman similarly writes, "Music proves to be invaluable in helping people travel beyond their usual thought patterns."[27]

A number of other early pioneers in psychedelic psychotherapy discovered and established the importance of music as an indispensable asset in the therapeutic process, particularly with reference to its effectiveness in helping clients let go of defenses. In "The Use of Music in Psychedelic (LSD) Psychotherapy," Helen Bonny and Walter Pahnke explain that "music complements the therapeutic objectives . . . by helping the patient relinquish usual controls and enter more fully into her inner world of experience."[28] Another pioneer, Dr. Ruth Fox, elaborates:

> During the first hour or two of the reaction the patient may try desperately to hold onto his usual defenses, resisting the new consciousness brought about by the drug. . . . However, if helped to ride through these signs of resistance, the quality of feeling may change, and with surrender there often comes a feeling of peace and contentment. Music, classical or non-classical according to the patient's taste, can facilitate this change in mood and will often lead the patient into a transcendental or psychedelic experience.[29]

Chronicling an extended series of self-experiments with LSD, Christopher Bache writes that "the first time I was able to use the music in my sessions . . . [it] took the experience to a new level of intensity, underscoring the important role that music plays in helping us surrender more completely to the psychedelic state."[30]

However, music's role is far more than merely that of a calming salve or relaxant. Rather, music's almost magical transfiguration in the psychedelic state, whereby it transforms into a powerful, aesthetically compelling presence, allows it to effectively draw attention away from distracting thoughts and ego defenses. The most eloquent psychonaut would be at pains to articulate this potency of music more convincingly than does Scottish philosopher Adam Smith (1723–1790), for whom instrumental music "presents an object so agreeable, so great, so various, and so interesting, that alone, and without suggesting any other object, either by imitation or otherwise, it can occupy, and as it were fill up, completely the whole capacity of the mind, so as to leave no part of its attention vacant for thinking of anything else."[31] This is a point worth repeating: it is not just the inherent relaxing quality of a particular piece of music that helps the experiencer let go, but music newly transformed, infused with magic, now an intangible object of profound wonder that cannot but enchant and entrance.

It is worth our while to attempt a deeper, more comprehensive understanding of our psychologically inbred resistance against the act of "letting go"—one that involves not only the individual reactive psyche, but broader societal and cultural forces. To suggest such a wider field of influence on the experiencer, Betty Eisner notably added "matrix" to the standard dyad of "set and setting" that shape the psychedelic experience: "Set refers to the subject; setting is the environment of the session. Matrix is the environment from which the subject comes: the environment surrounding the subject before and after the session, and the larger environment to which the subject returns."[32] Eisner's "larger environment" refers mainly to a broader context encompassing family and lifestyle, the general "life situation" of the individual. This expands the notion of individual set from the immediate state of mind of the individual entering a psychedelic session to that person's wider psychological influences and resultant character. Neitzke-Spruill and Glasser state the matter a little differently, defining Eisner's "matrix" not as a separate, third category, but simply as an expanded definition of "set." Defining "set" as "an individual's disposition," they divide it into "long-range" and "immediate": "The long-range set is composed of a person's general personality characteristics and individual history [Eisner's matrix, more or less], while the immediate set refers to a person's expectations for using the drug and is heavily influenced by the motivating for using."[33]

I would suggest that Eisner's matrix concept, even in expanded form as suggested above, would be strengthened if enlarged to include the entire society, culture, and civilization that surrounds the individual. Why? Because all of those factors participate in molding the individual consciousness that is entering the psychedelic state. This is important because our learned resistance to "letting go," to surrendering the fortified ego-self, has broader societal implications than those apparent within the immediate psychedelic setting. These are worth examining, even if briefly, to help us understand the civilizational context in which we find ourselves consciously resisting states of deep absorption, also known as "trance states."

In his article "Music and Trance," John J. Pilch discusses our culturally determined inability to be fully absorbed in *any* activity, to surrender to the moment: in other words, our inability to enter *trance* states. Although "altered states of consciousness are universal human phenomena," the modern secular West "not only does not use altered states of consciousness but frequently vehemently denies that they are of any value."[34] Referencing the advent of modern science that "disrupted the bio-psycho-spiritual unity of human consciousness," he cites psychiatrist Arthur Kleinman, according to whom "we have developed an 'acquired consciousness,' whereby we dissociate self and look at self 'objectively.' Western culture socializes individuals to develop a metaself, a critical observer who monitors and comments on experience. The metaself does not allow the total absorption in lived experience, which is the very essence of highly focused altered states of consciousness. The metaself stands in the way of unreflected, unmediated experience, which now becomes distanced."[35]

As an aside, the idea of a meddling "metaself," whether ego or superego, is certainly not a recent invention. Nearly two centuries ago, in a literary essay on hashish, French writer Théophile Gautier (1811–1872), offers an apt characterization of the metaself. While describing his own interior journeys immersed in a beatitude only possible in the absence of such egoic surveillance, he refers to it as "that detestable witness ever dogging one's footsteps."[36] A century later, Aldous Huxley likewise rejoices in his own temporary liberation, via mescaline, from the egoic metaself: "That interfering neurotic who, in waking hours, tries to run the show, was blessedly out of the way."[37]

Pilch notes that the metaself doesn't develop fully until an individual reaches adulthood, stating that "infants and young children still possess the ability to become totally absorbed in every aspect of their lived experience."[38] To loosely paraphrase a renowned sage, one must become like a child, a trusting soul unburdened by excessive egotism, in order to enter transpersonal realms of consciousness.

In *Deep Listeners: Music, Emotion, and Trancing*, Judith Becker explores the subject of trancing in relation to music, employing the term "deep listening" as a prerequisite for entering a musically induced trance state. Affirming the views of Pilch and of Kleinman (above), Becker challenges the West's cultural and psychological aversion to trance, to surrendering to states of deep immersion in immediate experience: "The normative model for a post-Enlightenment Western 'self' can be antithetical to trancing. The trancer necessarily must surrender personal will and accept the penetration of her bodily boundaries. A Cartesian rational, disengaged self will resist trancing. . . . Trance in our society suffers from our unfamiliarity with it, our historical aversion to it, and from our deep antipathy to the idea of not being fully in conscious control of our behavior."[39] The particular contribution that music makes to trancing, as experienced by "deep listeners," is that it stops "inner languaging," the cerebral-linguistic noises the mind makes as it attempts to distance itself from, and avoid exposure to, the immediacy of lived experience.[40]

The relation between music and trance is made amply clear by the author of the classic study *Music and Trance*, Gilbert Rouget, who states, "The trance state, a phenomenon observed throughout the world, is associated most of the time with music. Why? people will no doubt ask. Quite simply, because it is music that throws people into a trance!"[41] That's a pretty unambiguous statement, which is supported by Marghanita Laski, author of the exhaustive, data-based study *Ecstasy*, who concludes: "I believe that of all the more common triggers to ecstasy, music would be the most rewarding to study in any attempt to find a relation between the qualities of triggers and the effects produced."[42] Finally we have psychedelic psychiatrist Claudio Naranjo, who reminds us that the psychedelic state is also a trance state, and that to enter it fully one must *relinquish every intention aside from that of mere experiencing*: "[Contemplation] is a state in which the habitual duality of subject and object is reduced or may disappear, so that the contemplator is absorbed in the object of his contemplation. In the 'hallucinogenic trance,' as we may also call this particular effect of the LSD-like psychedelics, the individual feels inclined to lie down and usually to close his eyes, relinquishing every intention aside from that of mere experiencing while the characteristic perceptual and spiritual effects . . . unfold."[43]

Music as "Jungle Gym" and "Carrier Wave"

As we speak of letting go, of allowing ourselves to surrender to the process, we recognize that music itself responds to that surrender by becoming a support, a container, or a structure guiding the experience. Because psychedelic states facilitate de-habituation and de-familiarization, one may be left feeling disoriented. In the psychedelic state, music itself becomes, one might say, a kind of placeholder for the inner psychic structure that has been temporarily deconstructed. Marlene Dobkin de Rios, who spent decades studying ayahuasca culture and ritual in the Amazon, provides a useful metaphor: the jungle gym found in some children's playgrounds, which, extending the metaphor, may serve as a "substitute psychic structure":

> Given the anxiety, fear, and somatic discomfort that many people experience when they have unexpected access to unconscious materials, the shaman guide creates a corpus of music that de Rios has called "the jungle gym in consciousness." The intrinsic structure of the music provides psychedelic users with a series of paths and banisters to help them negotiate their way during the psychedelic experience. Moreover, music, with its implicit structure, may provide a *substitute psychic structure* during potentially frightening periods of ego dissolution.[44]

J. Ross MacLean et al. offer a related structural image: "Not only does music have certain abreactive [emotion or trauma releasing] properties, but our patients appear to use it as 'sound posts' in their journey, just as the traveler uses sign posts."[45]

Though useful, these analogies, like any, are limited. Music is far less tangible and far more malleable than a metal system of hard verticals and horizontals. Rather than a rigid structure that forcibly shapes or directs the experience, music simply provides a safe space for the free play of imagination. When the usual conditioned (default) forms of consciousness are de-activated, a piece of music can serve as a safe container for the flow of consciousness, or a comfortable home base from within which one can dive into the depths of being or set out to explore the cosmos of consciousness.

Benny Shanon offers a further insight on the structural support provided by music. He explains that music's internal structure and directionality (it moves through and marks off time) can help relieve the fear or anxiety that may accompany the sense of chaos brought on by a feeling of timelessness:

> Music also exhibits internal structure and directionality, which carry over to the Ayahuasca experience rendering it less chaotic and more manageable. . . . With Ayahuasca time perception may be greatly modified. Often, a moment seems to last an

eternity, and if what one is seeing at that moment is frightening, the experience can be quite terrifying, in which case the music being played or sung can be most helpful. Subjectively, one may feel that the experience will never end, yet at the same time, listening to a familiar song may provide some temporal perspective and security.[46]

Jane Dunlop, in one of the earliest (1961) published accounts of LSD experience by a non-clinician, describes music as a stabilizing force amid the turbulence of powerful emotions: "As visions shifted continuously with breath-taking speed and thoughts pelted my brain, the music . . . was the stabilizing influence which maintained my sanity as wave after wave of soul-shattering emotions engulfed me."[47] A better-known, oft-cited reference to waves is offered by Stanislav Grof, an image that suggests, to this mind at least, an idealized image of surfing: "The continuous flow of music creates a *carrier wave* that helps the subject move through difficult experiences and impasses."[48] Sharks or no sharks plying the tempestuous emotional waters below, the psychedelic surfer is kept afloat and moving along on a perfect, glistening wave of psychedelically enhanced music.

Let us tie a bow on this subject with a vignette that speaks volumes: "What's that music you're playing in the background?" he asked. "Bach," I told him. "It's the only thing that's keeping me together."[49]

4

Timelessness, Hypersensitivity, and "Becoming" the Music

Timelessness

In an early article titled "Psychedelics and Religious Experience,"[1] Alan Watts describes psychedelic states as "virtually indistinguishable from genuine mystical experiences." He conditions his claim by relating that his very first experience with LSD under controlled conditions—at the Neuropsychiatric Clinic of the UCLA Medical School with 100 micrograms of Sandoz—"was not mystical," though "it was an intensely interesting aesthetic and intellectual experience which challenged my powers of analysis and careful description to the utmost." Though it didn't meet Watts's technical criteria for what constitutes the "mystical," it was still quite a ride, which he described several years later in his autobiography: "For me the journey was hilariously beautiful—as if I and all my perceptions had been transformed into a marvelous arabesque or multidimensional maze in which everything became transparent, translucent and reverberant with double and triple meanings. Every detail of perception became detailed and important . . . and time slowed down in such a way that people going about their business outside seemed demented in failing to see that the destination of life is this eternal moment."[2]

Some months following this first experience, he tried LSD twice more (no mention of dosage) at the invitation of two psychiatrists from the Langley-Porter Clinic in San Francisco "who thought I should reconsider my views" (i.e, aesthetic vs. mystical),[3] this time with different results: "I was amazed and somewhat embarrassed to find myself going through states of consciousness which corresponded precisely with every description of major mystical experience that I had ever read"—a significant statement coming from one of the great modern scholars and interpreters of comparative mysticism. He goes on to describe what he found to be "four dominant characteristics" of psychedelics, the first one being "a slowing down of time, a concentration in the present . . . One's normally compulsive concern for the future decreases, and one becomes aware of the enormous importance and interest of what is happening at the moment. . . . One therefore relaxes, almost luxuriously, into studying the colors in a glass of water, or in listening to the now highly articulate vibration of every note played on an oboe or sung by voice."[4]

Ah, timelessness: that delicious, rarified atmosphere of expansive calm, the world stilled, nothing demanding one's attention, freeing one to exist in a state of uninterrupted, simple Beingness. In his essay "The New Alchemy," Watts connects this felt sense of timelessness to that of purposelessness, the freedom from the compulsion to be, act, and do:

> Our selection of some sense-data as significant and others as insignificant is always with relation to particular purposes—survival, the quest for certain pleasures, finding one's way to some destination, or whatever it may be. But in every experiment with LSD one of the first effects I have noticed is a profound relaxation combined with an abandonment of purposes and goals, reminding me of the Taoist saying that "when purpose has been used to achieve purposelessness, the thing has been grasped." I have felt, in other words, endowed with all the time in the world, free to look about me as if I were living in eternity without a single problem to be solved.[5]

I've always been struck by those words, "endowed with all the time in the world . . . as if I were living in eternity without a single problem to be solved," because it so perfectly describes a profoundly sublime feeling unique to the mystic and to the fortunate psychonaut. Time stops, the relentless metronome of clock-time ceases, the grinding forward movement halts, the demands of circumstance evaporate. All that, plus the imperious egoic narrative dissolves into nothingness. One is left fully free to experience and explore the riches and subtle mysteries of the present moment: which has a way of opening up, or bottoming out, into Eternity. Contrary to common assumption, declares philosopher Ludwig Wittgenstein, Eternity need not be accessed through death and entrance into Everlasting Life but through a simple immersion in the present moment: "If we take eternity to mean not infinite temporal duration but timelessness, the eternal life belongs to those who live in the present."[6]

Once, while slowly disembarking from an LSD trip, I made an attempt to put into words that ineffable feeling of timelessness, knowing that it would soon dissipate:

> When the resistances are gone and you experience, perhaps for the first time, a state of serene timelessness, with nothing bearing down on you, nothing to accomplish, nothing to sustain or maintain or explain, nothing to defend or protect, nothing to get to, no task to complete—just you in a still, serene state of quietude, resting in an "empty" mind, expecting nothing, fearing nothing, open to everything. In that rarefied state, when something enters your field of awareness—an object, an image, a sound—let's say some music—that music energy and your consciousness are now the only existents in the universe. The resultant absolute immersion and intimacy is sublime beyond description. . . . Similar in principle to the way a photograph stops time in its tracks, snatches, in a flash, a minuscule moment out of the moving river of time, places it in a frame and puts it before our curious eyes and minds for patient, unhurried contemplation. The fleeting moment is no longer fleeing, but is now stilled, tamed, enshrined in the here and now and available for uninterrupted probing perception. Clears a wide space for our fullest attention, brings that ephemeral moment to the center of our awareness to be seen, reflected upon, and imprinted deeply within consciousness and memory.[7]

Among my favorite visual analogues to this state of timelessness and purposelessness are some of Maxfield Parrish's otherworldly, minimally peopled landscapes, where one might view, for instance, a pair of young women reclining gently on the earth beneath a protective tree, doing nothing but absorbing the acadian ambiance (*Hilltop*, 1926), or stretched out on a boulder overlooking an alpine waterfall with nothing to do but observe in a state of calm delight (*Waterfall*, 1940), or a single maiden wearing nothing but infinite curiosity perched on a rock in water gazing up into an infinite blue sky (*Dreaming*, 1928). Perhaps what we call "nostalgia for Paradise" is the soul's deeply implanted memory of these kinds of transcendent visionary states, experienced in whatever mysterious, forgotten realm, flashes of which we sometimes encounter in psychedelic states, and which, whatever their ontological status, provide a much-needed sense of untarnished, soul-filling beauty.

Watts compares this essentially mystical state of timelessness and purposelessness to music (as well as to dance) itself, "where the point of the action is each moment of its unfolding and not just the temporal end of the performance."[8] Music is, might we not say, an ontological cousin of the psychedelic state itself: an intangible, ineffable, nondefinable, flow of concentrated, heightened experience. Watts concludes with a hint of autobiographical candor: "Such a translation of everyday experience into something of the same nature as music has been the beginning and the prevailing undertone of all my experiments."[9]

Cannabis use being more widespread than psychedelics, it is fairly common knowledge that being stoned increases absorption in and enjoyment of music. In fact, "the most characteristic effect of marijuana intoxication is an auditory one," reports Charles Tart in his early study *On Being Stoned—A Psychological Study of Marijuana Intoxication.* With particular reference to the experience of time, Tart states: "Changes in time perception are striking. Characteristically, time seems to pass more slowly, and the user feels much more in the here-and-now, totally immersed in the present situation without thinking about its relation to the past or its possible future developments. . . . Time may seem to stop, i.e., it's not just that things take longer but certain experiences are simply timeless; they seem to occur 'outside' of time."[10]

Mirroring Tart's assertion, German researcher Jorg Fachner cites fellow scientist P. Hess's finding that the "clearest indications of hashish intoxication" were found in subjects while they listened to music.[11] Here again, the enhanced experience of music is declared to be *the clearest indication* of hashish intoxication, it's most notable effect. Focusing on changes in time perception, Fachner explains: "Drugs have the capacity to reframe perspectives on musical materials through an altered temporality . . . [creating a] set and setting that significantly influence the listener's focus of attention on the musical time-space . . . [whereby] the brain has various strategies available to it to zoom into particular parts of the music in order to process musical elements more distinctly and in a more focused manner, in a hypofrontal state of enhanced sensory perception."[12] Waxing inscrutably scientific, Fachner elaborates: "The topographic pattern of music listening . . . is intensified on the alpha band after consumption.

On the basis of increased parietal alpha, we may assume that consumption directs specific attention to acoustic perceptual processes. Consequently, cannabis seems to have the same effect as psychoacoustic enhancers, exciters or modulation units as utilized in studio technology that make sound appear more transparent, with clearer contours."[13]

Musical sensitivity as the most distinguishable characteristic of hashish/cannabis intoxication is not a recent discovery. Well over a century before these studies, French psychiatrist Jacques-Joseph Moreau, writing in 1845, stated: "the overstimulation caused by hashish throughout the entire nervous system is felt most particularly in the portion of this system concerned with perception of sounds. Hearing acquires a delicacy, an unbelievable sensitivity."[14] Though his reference here is to "sounds" and "hearing," in the same publication he devotes much attention to intensified musical experience under hashish.[15]

What's true for cannabis and hashish is predictably magnified under psychedelics, often exponentially. One tripper (on LSD) describes the sensation of time slowing and stretching out, permitting a kind of microscopic penetration into musical flow:

> As speech became increasingly difficult, I abandoned conversation altogether. Instead, I sat back down in the armchair and listened to the music. I tried closing my eyes. Instantly, the sound seemed to enclose me physically, and my sense of orientation with respect to the room vanished. The universe appeared to be occupied entirely by sound.
>
> What followed was rather unlike any musical experience I have ever known. In the first place, my speeding brain seemed to assimilate the notes at a considerably greater rate than the musicians were able to play them. Thus, *each note appeared to be separated from the next by a leisurely interval, so that I had ample time to consider the relationship of each note played to the entire composition, before the next note sounded* [emphasis added]. Secondly, my apparent ability to comprehend so many factors at once, enabled me to perceive the contribution of each musician to the entire musical production. The intentions of each musician became transparent: I knew "why" each one played the notes he did.[16]

Like a small insect exploring the inner structure of a flower, another tripper describes a similar experience of a laser-like miniaturization of musical perception made possible by an uncanny slowing of time: "I had the sense of actually being able to crawl between the notes and get into the spaces in the music. Also, as the bow moved across the violin, or even more so across the cello, I could hear cell by cell as that bow, slowly, and what sometimes seemed forever, moved across the string it was playing."[17] The French philosopher Gaston Bachelard (1884–1962), a philosopher of science with the soul of a poet, describes this sensation of timelessness as the basis of "reverie" or "cosmic reverie," and one capable of entering such a state as a "world dreamer" who experiences the world in a mythopoetic manner. His description of the timelessness and detachment that typify the act of reverie, a state of intuitive openness and receptivity, cannot but remind us of the psychedelic state:

> When a dreamer of reveries has swept aside all the "preoccupation" which were encumbering his everyday life, when he has detached himself from the worry which comes to him from the worry of others, when he is thus truly the author of his solitude, when he can finally contemplate a beautiful aspect of the universe without counting the minutes, that dreamer feels a being opening within him. Suddenly such a dreamer is a world dreamer. He opens himself to the world, and the world opens itself to him. One has never seen the world well if he has not dreamed what he was seeing. In a reverie of solitude which increases the solitude of the dreamer, two depths pair off, reverberate in echoes which go from the depths of being of the world to a depth of being of the dreamer. Time is suspended. Time no longer has any yesterday and no longer any tomorrow. Time is engulfed in the double depth of the dreamer and the world. . . .
>
> The communication between the dreamer and his world is very close in reverie; it has no "distance," not that distance which marks the perceived world, the world fragmented by perception.[18]

Musical Hypersensitivity

Beyond the psychedelically induced slowing of time (providing the listener "all the time in the world" to inhabit, explore, and relish music), there are various other ways in which psychedelics profoundly deepen the experience of music. We begin our exploration with the hypersensitization of hearing itself, in terms both of musical sound and musical "meaning."

Philosopher, science writer, and friend to Aldous Huxley, Gerald Heard, describes the uncanny aesthetic sensitivity bestowed by LSD:

> For many who have taken [LSD] under proper, controlled conditions, it has brought about an astonishing enlargement of sensitivity and perceptiveness . . . You see and hear this world, but as the artist and the musician sees and hears. . . . Music frequently becomes an absorbing delight even to the nonmusical—while to the musical it has on occasion become almost unbearably intense. "Under LSD I asked that my favorite recording of my favorite Beethoven quartet (Opus 135) be played," one musical [listener] reported; "but after a few minutes I had it turned off. Its emotions had become too searing—and besides, I had suddenly made the discovery that one of the instruments was playing ever so slightly off pitch."[19]

Michael Pollan describes his own more nuanced processing of musical tones and their emotional flavorings: "There is research to suggest that people hear music differently under the influence of these drugs. They process the timbre, or coloration, of music more acutely—a dimension of music that conveys emotion. When I listened to Bach's cello suite during my psilocybin journey, I was certain I heard more of it than I ever had, registering shadings and nuances and tones that I hadn't been able to hear before and haven't heard since."[20] Peter Michael Hamel, a German composer here writing as a musician, describes the experience of creating and playing music while on psychedelics:

> The musical LSD-trip was able to help many a previously mindless note-spinner to achieve a pitch of self-knowledge that was to influence his whole subsequent output. A prolonged note would be heard across a new and much greater range of overtones. The harmonic series would reveal itself to the sensitized ear like some secret message. A whole universe of the finest microintervals was perceived and translated into music. Suffused by an overpowering sense of joy, one could submerge oneself in one's music, experience a grace and an almost holy

awe. With other musicians one felt a marvelous oneness, while retaining nevertheless the feeling of one's own identity amid the whole. This experience, which one could almost call mystical, culminated in spontaneous, deep insights into the relationship of man to the world of sounds.[21]

One not uncommon effect (echoed earlier in Gerald Heard's description) is the ability of the hearer to acoustically isolate one instrument among even a large group of instruments. Malden Grange Bishop reports, "My hearing was very sharp. I could listen to any one instrument in an orchestra if I wanted, or hear any one singer in a choral group."[22] A more dramatic example of such close and selective hearing is found in the Fitz Hugh Ludlow drug classic *The Hashish Eater* (1857), as summarized here by Lester Grinspoon: "The next evening . . . he took approximately 25 grains [of hashish] and then went to the theater, where he experienced 'a most singular phenomenon.' He could distinguish the exact notes played by each of two different violinists, both playing the same part, and both in the middle of the full orchestra 'as distinctly as if the violinists had been playing at the distance of a hundred feet apart, and with no other instruments discoursing near them.'"[23]

For one pioneering psychonaut, R. H. Ward, LSD acted to deconstruct music, narrowing attention onto individual notes:

> In these circumstances it was not the music, but the notes, which so strongly engaged my attention and feelings. [I was] not much interested in the concerto's melodies, structure or style, but cared primarily for the individual sounds involved . . . The state of consciousness induced by the drug may be said to have taken the music as such to pieces, and to have [highlighted] each note for its own sake. Even in passages for many instruments, it seemed to me that I could separately hear the notes played by each instrument in a way which I should normally find impossible; so that the drug appeared to lend me the trained ear of a musician. . . . It was as if one had never heard music before.[24]

For the same writer, LSD could also create the opposite effect: that of organizing the "raw materials of music" into complex entities of "new and more wonderful meaning," as well as bestowing on the hearer a more sophisticated musical ear:

> There was one lyrical phrase in the slow movement which, each time it was repeated, increased in significance until I felt that I understood how the separate notes, or raw materials of music, when brought together to form a new and more complex entity, acquired a new and more wonderful meaning. . . . I felt that in this particular combination of sounds, the quality of which seemed in some way different from that of the rest of the music, a "deed" had been done which is in fact the deed of creative art, a deed which approaches as nearly as possible to the essential truth. It is probable that not everything which goes by the name of art would commend itself as such to the "higher criticism" of a state of consciousness higher than that in which critics ordinarily find themselves.[25]

Charles Bush describes an LSD experience where he finds himself in the midst of a "surround-sound Cinerama"[26]:

> As things got more intense, I lay back on the couch and closed my eyes. Imagine never having seen a movie of any kind and being transported instantly into the middle of the finest Cinerama—with full surround sound, full surround vision—and then they turn the speed of the film up to about four times normal. I was able to see every detail in the entire sphere that surrounded me in brilliant color. All of a sudden, I was in the theater of visions. That went on for what must have been at least forty-five minutes before I opened my eyes and went, "Wow."
>
> At some point, somebody put music on, and the inner display danced and changed in perfect coordination with the music, which was multidimensional. . . . I felt there was infinite time between every moment of the music to reflect on it and get its meaning. My auditory universe had developed a depth like seeing for ten miles, only I was hearing for ten miles—not *out* but deep *inside* the sound itself. . . . an auditory universe full of meaning and precision that I participated in fully.[27]

Benny Shanon explains how under ayahuasca, as with any psychedelic, the effects of music become "greatly amplified and accentuated" to the point of spiritual ecstasy:

> The brew significantly enhances people's aesthetic sensitivity and appreciation, and under intoxication people experience manifestations of beauty they deem to be truly fabulous. This is the case in all sensory modalities, and pertains both to perceptions of stimuli actually existing in the external world and to inner, subjective experiences. Thus, under intoxication music sounds immensely beautiful, and is often felt to be enchanting. It evokes strong emotions and deep sentiments, profound meanings are often discerned in it, and it is likely to be characterized as heavenly and/or divine.[28]

Shanon explains another psychedelic effect expressed in some trip reports and that he experienced himself: the compelling sense that one is being gifted with profound intuitive insights into the creative intentions and technical strategies of a composer:

> Overall, Ayahuasca induces an enhanced conferral of meaningfulness and the feeling of heightened understanding. This is especially marked with music. Listening to pieces of classical music that I had heard many times before, it seemed to me that I was hearing them precisely in the same manner that their composer did. I also felt that I had clear understanding of what the composer was doing in the music, what he wishes to convey, and how he had decided to do it. I understood the harmonies, the development of the melodic lines, their modulations and resolutions. Indeed, often I felt I could anticipate what the composer was going to do next, as did several of my informants who reported similar experiences.[29]

Such heightened intuition may provide insight not only into the creative intentions and strategies of a composer, but also into his or her innate "sincerity." A subject listening to music on hashish offers the following testimony, stating that for him the drug seems to strip away from music all that is phony or pretentious. Citing Baudelaire's declaration (in

Les Paradis Artificiels) that "Over the surface of man's ordinary life the power of hashish spreads a magic glaze, coloring it with solemnity, bringing to light the profoundest aspects of existence," he comments:

> This magic glaze can spread over any form of experience. For many, it exerts its greatest power in connection with music. Patterns entirely unsuspected emerge from the sound. The ear becomes fascinated with a minor theme, follows a single instrument to the exclusion of all the others. Music that seemed clever or even brilliant may, under the hashish influence, stand revealed as phoney and insincere. The merciless spirit of hashish strips from all art forms the overlay of egotism, illuminating with a pitiless radiance the underlying reality. For genuine artistic creation its praise is unqualified; for the contrived, the slick, the merely clever its contempt is biting: "How this fool tries to show off! What a jackdaw in peacock's feathers!"[30]

This heightened capacity to assess sincerity versus egotism in music is evidenced as well in this report from a composer who describes listening to various works:

> Mozart, Bizet Symphony, Mussorgsky Pictures, the suite from Strauss's Der Rosenkavalier and my own incident music. My reaction to these pieces began with the conventional response but gradually took on a new character. It was as though the remaining ecstasy that flowed through me had washed away my patience with the exterior posturing of music. I felt that I saw directly into its heart and was interested only in what the music was really saying, remaining totally indifferent to how it was dressed.[31]

One final example of such psychedelically enhanced discernment comes to us from clinician and noted music therapist Helen Bonny and co-author Walter Pahnke, who describe that "A frequent patient comment on a poor recording [i.e., a particular performance of a classical piece] is that 'the musician did not believe in what he was singing or playing,'" which, the authors point out, "is indicative of the hypersensitivity to the quality of stimuli that a patient exhibits in an altered state of consciousness."[32]

"Becoming" the Music

In his famous poem *Four Quartets*, T. S. Eliot wrote of "Music heard so deeply that it is not heard at all, but you are the music while the music lasts." Many on psychedelics speak of the felt sense of "becoming the music." This merging of personal consciousness with music implies that something has been removed, some filter standing between the perceiving self and those lovely, multidimensional sounds. What might that be? Well, the same things that ordinarily intercede between perceiver and perceived, experiencer and experience, in any circumstance: associated memories, half-conscious comparisons, half-baked ideas, fleeting distractions, and other vague cerebral irritations: all those furry little things scurrying around the dimly lit cerebral attic (or basement) looking for something to chew on. Even the fittest, finest among such inchoate cerebral irritants serve only to distract, to prevent and inoculate us against direct, "unmediated" experience of the "thing" itself, i.e., the music.

During an early psychedelic conference, a Huxley less familiar to us, Francis (Aldous's nephew), a botanist and anthropologist, offered these comments on overcoming the subject-object split that preempts direct experience:

> One of the most fascinating experiences to be gained under LSD is that during which the subject-object distinction is done away with. It is replaced, not by that state imputed to infants unable to distinguish things in the outside world from themselves, but by a recognition that nothing that exists and is experienced can be properly classified as "an object" since the very act of experiencing it makes it part of yourself and therefore of your subjectivity. Strangely enough, however, this recognition does not necessarily destroy the thing's individuality: it remains itself however much it also becomes a vehicle for the awareness of yourself.[33]

Rather than an abstract, idealized or vague metaphorical conceit, "becoming one" with music is an experiential fact in psychedelic states. Michael Pollan offers this eloquent, up-close look at his experience of "becoming" music while on magic mushrooms:

> Four hours and four grams of magic mushroom into the journey, this is where I lost whatever ability I still had to distinguish

subject from object, tell apart what remained of me and what was Bach's music. Instead of Emerson's transparent eyeball, egoless and one with all it beheld, I become a transparent ear, indistinguishable from the stream of sound that flooded my consciousness until there was nothing else in it, not even a dry tiny corner in which to plant an I and observe. Opened to the music, I became first the strings, could feel on my skin the exquisite friction of the horsehair rubbing over me, and then the breeze of sound flowing past as it crossed the lips of the instrument and went out to meet the world, beginning its lonely transit of the universe. Then I passed down into the resonant black well of space inside the cello, the vibrating envelope of air formed by the curves of its spruce roof and maple walls. The instrument's wooden interior formed a mouth capable of unparalleled eloquence—indeed, of articulating everything a human could conceive.[34]

Immersed in the stream of sound, there was, for Pollan "not even a dry tiny corner in which to plant an I," a separate observing self distinct from the inward flowing music. He could well have quoted the mystic Meister Eckhart: "What absorbs me, that I am, rather than mine own self."[35]

For another informant describing listening to music on LSD, you, the listener, do not *hear* the music, you *are* the music:

> I lay quietly and listened to the music I had brought with me. . . . Slowly the music seemed to absorb all my consciousness. *It is as though all previous hearing of music had been deafness* [emphasis added]. It seemed to me as though the music and I became one. You do not hear it—you are the music. It seems to play in you. I thought that perhaps this complete experiencing of it is the way a real musician perceives it all the time.[36]

A ministerial student participating in a psilocybin study in Germany reports that

> It is misleading even to use the words "I experienced," as during the peak of the experience there was no duality between myself and what I experienced. Rather, I *was* these feelings. . . . This was especially evident when, after having reached the mystic

peak, a recording of Bach's Fantasia and Fugue in G Minor was played. It seemed as though I was not my usual self listening to a recording, but that I was the music itself. Especially at one climax in the Fantasia, love became so overwhelming as to become unbearable or even painful. I shed tears at this moment, not of fear, but of uncontainable joy.[37]

Another subject describes his psychedelic absorption in music as "pure synesthesia" and as "the most profoundly consuming aesthetic experience" of his life:

This was more than music: the entire room was saturated with sounds that were also feelings—sweet, delicious, sensual—that seemed to be coming from somewhere deep down inside me. I became mingled with the music, gliding along with the chords. Everything I saw and felt was somehow inextricably interrelated. This was pure synesthesia, and I was part of the synthesis. I suddenly "knew" what it was to be simultaneously a guitar, the sounds, the ear that received them, and the organism that responded, in what was the most profoundly consuming aesthetic experience I have ever had.[38]

"Becoming the music" can sometimes take on a more explicitly physical quality, with the body itself becoming an active resonator, either physically or metaphorically. Stanislav Grof notes that "Frequently, music seems to resonate in different parts of the body and to trigger powerful emotions."[39] We find this phenomenon expressed by two different participants in pioneering LSD studies conducted by Oscar Janiger. Both express "becoming the music" in raw physical terms:

I have grown extremely sensitive. My flesh is charged with emotional responsiveness to the Mozart E-flat symphony. My skin seems microscopically thick and porous so as to admit the music more easily. The inner lines of counterpoint are suddenly so clear. The dissonances are so penetrating, and the bass-line is positively alive. It jumps and strides with a kind of cosmic purpose.[40]

My body was now a torrential river, streaming and flowing. At the same time it felt like some unknown stringed instrument being played by an unseen hand, which drew its bow across me to release a kind of music for which there are no words. Totally indescribable.[41]

Another trip report offers a different perspective. Rather than classical music, the music in this case is from India and Africa. While involving profoundly physical sensations, there is also a strong visionary component involving the experiencer as both mother giving birth and child being birthed:

> This vision was erased by the next record—Ravi Shankar, followed by about five other recordings of Indian music. I inhaled the tabla; the sitar entered through every hair in my body; the vibrating warmth of the tamboura filled my belly where I rested waiting to be born. . . . [After the final record] there was no tamboura to relax the child in my womb. The prominence of the drum awakened the child, and the contractions began to come more and more frequently. The final record was playing at the moment of birth—Olatunji and the Drums of Africa. Passionate; moving fiercely. From the African drums came warmth, and from the passion of the music, the strength for the final effort, for the delivery of myself out of the universe to the earth.[42]

5

Music, Emotion, and Aesthetic Ecstasy

The fact that most of us live lives of blunted, censored emotion was perceived clearly and stated eloquently by D.H. Lawrence when he wrote,

> Our education from the start has taught us a certain range of emotions, what to feel and what not to feel, and how to feel the feelings we allow ourselves to feel. . . . This feeling only what you allow yourselves to feel at last kills all capacity for feeling, and in the higher emotional ranges you feel nothing at all: This has come to pass in our present century. The higher emotions are strictly dead. They have to be faked.[1]

Though this may sound overstated, its essential truth is revealed when the egoic straightjacketing of emotion is lifted, or partially so, during a psychedelic journey. In these states one may discover depths and subtleties of emotion, of intense soulful awareness and responsiveness, that seem both natural—an authentic expression of one's inner being—and an extraordinary gift.

The experience of strong, often intense emotion is a characteristic by-product of the psychedelic state, especially in higher doses, and is often related to music. Walter Pahnke (and co-authors) explain that within the context of psychedelic psychotherapy: "the function of the music is to help the patient let go more easily, to enter more fully into his unfolding inner world of experience, and to facilitate the release of intense emotionality. . . . The major dimension of drug-altered reactivity with therapeutic relevance is the affective or emotional sphere; intense, labile, personally-meaningful emotionality is uniformly produced, with periodic episodes of overwhelming feeling."[2] Whether in a therapeutic or a less-structured setting, psychedelics provide deep access to human feeling and emotion, with music often acting to catalyze, channel, and give form and structure to emotion in its infinite varieties. As Benny Shanon explains, "Music makes us experience joy and sadness, hopelessness and the regaining of hope, the open-endedness of possibilities, the quest for freedom and the allure of personal aspiration, solemnity and frivolity, the acceptance of one's lot in life and the tragic dimension of existence."[3]

Among the various art forms, music is often credited with exercising the most powerful effects on the emotions. As Eduard Hanslick (1825–1904), the Austrian aesthetic theorist, music critic, and author of the foundational work *On the Musically Beautiful* (1854), wrote:

> Even if we have to grant all the arts, without exception, the power to produce effects upon the feelings, yet we do not deny that there is something specific, peculiar only to [music], in the way music exercises that power. Music works more rapidly and intensely on the mind than any other art. With a few chords, we can be transported into a state of mind that a poem would achieve only through lengthy exposition, or a painting only through a sustained effort to understand it . . . the effect of tones is not only more rapid but more immediate and intensive. The other arts persuade, but music invades us.[4]

On Strong Emotion in Psychedelic States

What might appear to an outside observer to be an artificially induced intensification or exaggeration of emotion will likely feel, to the experiencer herself, the most authentic expression of her deepest experiencing self, an outer manifestation of profound inner awareness, a spontaneous outpouring of the soul unearthed and uncensored. The neural reducing valve that is (in the Bergson/Huxley model) meant to protect us from the full force of Being ("Mind at large") has been temporarily disabled; the ego, that meddlesome overseer, is on hiatus; and we are left to swim within our own deepest psychic and spiritual reservoirs.

As the session progresses, especially if the experiencer has some familiarity with this state, one may find oneself feeling strangely "at home" in this intensified inner environment, sensing in it something fundamental, something primeval and utterly authentic. There may arise an ineffable sense of having rediscovered something precious beyond words, something that somehow had been lost for eons. One may find oneself overwhelmed by a sense of appreciation, gratitude, for what now appears a kind of super-sanity, a more evolved mode of being, a more sublime ontology—compared with which "normal" life may now seem, in comparison, one-dimensional, a dim, tepid reflection. One may then look out on the world of properly socialized humans as strangely robotic, blinkered, tuned-out, and our collective, conditioned state as tragically impoverished. Why, in "normal" life, does a masterful piece of art not bring tears of appreciation to our eyes? Why are we not seeing? Why does a fresh bloom or a multi-hued sunset or a shape-shifting cloud not give us chills and exultations? Why do we not notice? Why does our intrinsic humanity not fill us with vibrant empathy, with profound interpersonal sensitivity and humane responsiveness toward others? Why are these beautiful, natural, exalted emotions so inaccessible?

Some of that deadening of our innate sensitivity, of our very humanity, is, of course, an inevitable consequence of living in a world of pathologic overstimulation, which causes a defensive hardening of the senses and mind. Lawrence Kramer, prolific scholar and writer on music, reflecting on our relative inability to become absorbed in a piece of music, summarizes an early sociological assessment of our shared condition of *inattention*, an assessment striking for having been articulated well over a century ago:

> In a famous essay of 1903, "The Metropolis and Mental Life," the German sociologist Georg Simmel drew out the consequences of the widespread feeling that modern life in the cities of the West was fraught with too much perceptual stimulation, one result of which was a loss of both the power and the opportunity to concentrate one's attention. This was not a byproduct of modernity but its essence, the consequence of the drastic speeding up of work, transformation, and communication that would repeat itself a century later in digital form. Beset at "every crossing of the street" by the "tempo and multiplicity of economic, occupational, and social life," accosted by "the

rapid telescoping of changing images, pronounced differences within what is grasped at a single glance, and the unexpectedness of violent stimuli," the citizen of the modern metropolis develops a hard defensive shell, a "blasé" attitude that serves as a shield against distraction or paralysis. Attention is withheld, husbanded; just enough goes out to the world to avoid being injured by it. The "metropolitan person" is thus removed to "a sphere of mental activity which is the least sensitive and which is the furthest removed from the depths of the personality."[5]

How understandably radical, then, is the sudden prying loose of mental defenses, the prying open of our senses and deeper sensibilities, the dissolving of the constructed psycho-social cocoon, represented by taking a psychedelic. How more comprehensible it should be, then, why psychedelics may effect a powerful emotional release. I think it important that we be able to deal with the question of emotion in psychedelic states not as "objective" observers studying and measuring anomalous drug reactions, but rather as sensitive observers (psychedelically experienced or not) of the extraordinary properties of expanded states of consciousness—rooted, as they are, in our deepest selves.

Why Is Discussing Deep Emotion Awkward for Many Writers on Psychedelics?

Academic and other "respectable" authors of books and articles on psychedelics are generally cautious about appearing overly enthusiastic about their subject. Both out of a well-founded fear of being seen as advocating the use of illegal substances, as well as a concern not to appear naively enthusiastic (which is incompatible with scholarly or scientific detachment), the subject of emotion, and certainly of ecstatic states, is rarely explored openly or in depth (except, in a limited sense, in the psychotherapeutic literature, where the focus is often on practical approaches to dealing with trauma and abreaction). Ecstatic emotions in psychedelic states present a particular set of challenges for researchers, inasmuch as ecstasy is closely associated with mysticism and mystical states, a topic considered off-limits, or at least dangerously liminal, to mental health professionals. As Roseman et al. state the problem: "The so-called 'mystical' experience has been a classic problem area for mainstream psychology—if not science more generally. The term 'mystical' is particularly problematic, as it suggests associations with the supernatural that may be obstructive or even antithetical to scientific method and progress."[6] Mainstream psychologists and secular scholars, with rare exceptions, do not like to be seen as dabblers in, much less bold explorers of, the supernatural.

The avoidance of the subject of deep emotion occasioned by psychedelics is also due, in part, to a kind of felt awkwardness or even embarrassment about the kinds of profoundly vulnerable states that are commonly experienced under psychedelics, when ego defenses are down and psyche and soul exist in states of existential nakedness. Confronting such unusual states, which transcend and confound conventional psychological categories, along with the unabashed, heartfelt earnestness with which they are often voiced, writers on psychedelics who operate within professional institutions and have reputations to protect are forced to effect an analytical cool: anything to avoid appearing to have been evangelized or spiritually co-opted.

Based on her own extensive psychotherapeutic experience, psychologist Betty Grover Eisner believed that often it is the most successful, well-established people in society (including academics and mental-health professionals) whose egos are particularly strong and well-fortified and who thus may resist the "letting go" necessary to the psychedelic process. In a letter to a colleague, she wrote, "I learned something about the well defended, successful people: they are more difficult to open because their defensive system has been so beautifully rewarded and sanctioned by society. And their anxieties are deeply buried along with their unacceptable drives. I also have a hunch that individuals in the psychiatric field or allied ones are also more defended along these lines"[7]—their "metaselves" (see chapter 3) perpetually alert, on guard against vulnerability, emotionality, and the embarrassment of "not knowing." This suggests that one seeking psychedelic therapy from a mental-health professional may want to inquire beforehand whether or not that professional has had significant personal experience with psychedelic states. One who themselves is "overly defended" is less likely to be able to help support a client opening to inner experience.

Another major contributor to this avoidance of a frank acknowledgment of—much less a deep intellectual or philosophical engagement with—profound emotion in psychedelic states is the ideology of reductionistic materialism that defines and dominates much of the physiologically based "scientific" study of psychedelics. Now the dominant force in psychedelic research, this ideology posits consciousness (including emotion) as essentially a product of, and dependent on, brain activity. It is one thing to point out that states of consciousness are reflected in—that is, have physical corollaries within—the gray matter, and another to insist that human awareness is simply a by-product or epiphenomenon of neurological activity. This guiding conviction—which keeps subjective and qualitative phenomena like consciousness and emotion at arm's length and essentially devalues them—is stated, with undisguised bluntness, by Dr. Ben Sessa, a psychedelic researcher affiliated with Imperial College London: "As a scientist and a materialistic reductionist I would argue that the spiritual experience that humans have is a feature and a factor of a complex neural algorithm. If you make neural networks complex enough, at first they'll come up with consciousness and then a bit later they'll come up with spirituality. But actually these are organic processes produced by organs, brains, and thus consciousness and spirituality is a by-product of that complexity."[8]

The key term here is, of course, "materialist reductionism," a doctrine (or, more accurately, a dogma) that denudes human experience (intellectual, emotional, spiritual) of its essential meaning, its innate and ultimate ontological significance, reducing the immense complexity and subtlety of human experience to "neural algorithms." Such thinking is the antithesis of an enlightened humanism that places a high value on the content and significance of individual human experience, including the vast, nuanced, and fluid realm of the emotions. It is also the antithesis of the kinds of profound psychological insights and aesthetic experiences, not to mention spiritual wisdom, that typically flow from psychedelic states. No wonder, then, that psychedelic-assisted therapists whose thinking, knowingly or unknowingly, is colored by neurological reductionism are often out of their depth when faced with clients who are having profound experiences and emotions of a spiritual, religious, or existential nature.[9]

A good contrast to this reductionist approach to psychedelics can be found in the experiences and reflections of those who are more at home in studying consciousness as an essential and irreducible expression of human life: philosophers, humanistically and transpersonally oriented psychologists, and scholars of religion genuinely interested in the human quest for existential and spiritual meaning. An example of the latter is the brilliant religion scholar Huston Smith, whose initial exposure to psychedelics was described in chapter 1. Author Christopher Partridge describes the aftereffects of that exposure:

> Following this experience, for a number of years psychoactives became central to Smith's thought. "Reflectively, to have become overnight a visionary—one who not merely believes in the existence of a more momentous world than this one but who has actually visited it—was no small matter. How could what felt like an epochal change in my life have been crowded into a few hours and occasioned by a chemical?" While he was, as Huxley had been, fully aware of the findings of scientific research, which typically explained the psychedelic experience in physiological terms, he could not suppress the conviction that there was more to it than this.[10]

Smith became involved in the psychedelic project based at Harvard University and found himself a participant in a kind of underground psychedelic salon with other spiritually open intellectuals, the organizing principle of which was a "resistance to epiphenomenal, reductionistic explanations of our revelations, and our certainty . . . that it was impossible to close our accounts with reality without taking these revelations into consideration."[11]

Returning more directly to our discussion of emotion, it's worth noting that strong emotion tends to be avoided or overlooked by many who study and write on psychedelics, in part because we tend to associate emotion with potentially unpleasant or disruptive states: fear, anger, rage, frustration, resentment, sorrow, not to mention the fear of losing control, of coming "undone," of going over some metaphorical "edge." Our common social sensibilities, our ego strategies, prevent us from exposing or confessing our deepest vulnerabilities. The public persona must be maintained. Who, after all, wants to be observed and judged while in the throes of overpowering, destabilizing emotions?

This reticence applies also, somewhat ironically, to highly expressive *positive* emotions (joy, awe, exultation), especially when they're associated with psychedelic states. What self-respecting psychedelic scholar or therapist will not feel a twinge of embarrassment at the prospect of being viewed by their colleagues not as a detached, intellectualizing observer but as some wide-eyed, blissed-out, humanity-embracing, cosmos-loving "hippie"? After all, the traditional hippie stereotype is not one to be coveted, although, in truth, it amounts to little more than a debased version of someone reaping the benefits of a particularly fruitful psychedelic experience. That image, paradoxically or not, mimics the descriptions, articulated in almost every religious tradition, of God-intoxicated mystics and saints: those entranced by inner states, absorbed in the moment, taking no thought for the morrow, spontaneous, unpredictable, living in caves or trees, in love with all creatures, talking to the birds, offering prayers to "Brother Sun" and "Sister Moon." How embarrassing it would be to be discovered cavorting beyond the boundaries of normative human behavior, of being . . . unprofessional!

Relating this directly to music, the experience of music in psychedelic states does indeed generate a wide variety of powerful emotions. Philosopher Vladimir Jankelevitch addresses the fear of music's emotional component in his acerbic comments about music critics who talk incessantly about music while avoiding its living essence. He repeatedly refers to that essence as music's *Charm*: its ineffable, quasi-magical allure that invokes enchantment in those who can truly listen and hear.[12] He points out that music critics keep music's disarming charm at bay via intellectual distancing. This provides useful clues into our own self-alienating tendency to effectively deny or minimize our deepest emotions as they reveal themselves in psychedelic states, especially if those experiences happened many years ago and can now be disowned as "youthful indiscretions." He views the technical analysis offered by music critics as a kind of shield against the embarrassment of emotion, of feeling music deeply, of being "bewitched." Technical analysis, he writes, is an affectation that is

> simply a means of not sympathizing, not being touched by the Charm, of sundering the covenant made with innocence and naivete, on which all enchantment depends . . . Everyone knows the type, the cool cerebral people who affect interest in the way the piece is "put together" after the concert. Technical analysis is a means of refusing to abandon oneself spontaneously to grace, which is the request the musical Charm is making. *The phobia about consent, the fear of appearing bewitched, the coquetry of refusal, the resolve not to "submit," are the social and sociological forms assumed by alienation.*[13] [emphasis added]

It is this very capacity for sympathetic self-abandonment to music's ineffable charm that provides access into the psychedelic realm—a realm where, having arrived, one discovers that that "charm" is no mere aesthetic attraction but a virtual conduit into metaphysical and spiritual realms.

Widening the Meaning of Emotion

The term "emotion" feels constrained, in that it tends to register as a transient, distinct feeling, a circumscribed psychological reaction to some particular stimulus that fades after the stimulus disappears. Better, perhaps, to think of emotion in broader terms, as a general, fundamental constituent of consciousness, a capacity for sensitivity toward and empathic awareness of whatever may present itself within our conscious environment. We might think of emotion as a free-flowing continuum of deeply felt awareness, capable of assuming a virtual infinity of forms of greater or lesser complexity, fluidity, depth, or nuance. This is not a perfect definition, perhaps—admittedly it is rather loose and abstract—but at least it provides the aroma of an idea: something to help expand the notion of emotion beyond the image of a small box containing a collection of preprinted labels: happy, sad, angry, and so forth. It offers a way, perhaps, to more fully appreciate emotion in highly sensitized psychedelic states, during which an unending flow of visions, memories, and insights are each eliciting dynamic affective responses.

Music and Emotion: Perennial Views

Before moving on to first-person testimonies concerning music and emotion in psychedelic states, I'd like to place the subject within the broader context of how music has always catalyzed and expressed human emotion by invoking the thoughts and words of several writers who've given the subject serious reflection. Although only one of these is affiliated directly with the study of psychedelics, their views are most relevant to our subject: how psychedelics dramatically deepen and intensify the experience of music and how that intensification has a way of uncovering a remarkable depth, range, and subtlety of human emotion.

For many writers, music is the preeminent expression and transmitter of the mysteries and subtleties of human emotion. For Tolstoy, "Music is the shorthand of emotion. Emotions, which let themselves be described in words with such difficulty, are directly conveyed to man in music and in that is its power and significance.[14] For essayist and naturalist Diane Ackerman, "Music is a controlled outcry from the quarry of emotions all humans share."[15] An insight with uncanny relevance to music heard on psychedelics comes to us, again, from the author of *Music and the Ineffable*, who explains that music not only expresses emotions with which we are familiar, but also reveals those that have been hidden from conscious awareness, including spiritual emotions such as joy: "[Music] reveals to us our own profound joys, our unknown joys, the ones we never recognized, concealed as they were by care and hidden by petty emotions."[16] Schopenhauer offers a similarly important insight into the nature of the musically generated emotions experienced in psychedelic states, given their archetypal quality: "[Music] never expresses the phenomenon, but only the inner nature, the in-itself, of every phenomenon. . . . Therefore music does not express this or that particular and definite pleasure, this or that affliction, pain, sorrow, horror, gaiety, merriment, or peace of mind, but joy, pain, sorrow, horror, gaiety, merriment, peace of mind themselves . . . in the abstract, [in] their essential nature. . . . Nevertheless, we understand them perfectly in this extracted quintessence."[17] Although absorbed into consciousness in abstracted form—in their "extracted quintessence"—music-borne emotions, once internalized and personalized within an individual consciousness, may evoke a myriad of personal, autobiographical (or more universal or transpersonal) responses. Now, as I write these words, I realize how abstract this description is. This is yet another reminder that words are simply weak signals, pointing, ineptly, to matters that are irreducibly experiential. We can, at least, try to "translate" these abstractions into something more tangible, more familiar, by scanning our own memories and intuitions for experiences that may, at least partially, express and ground those abstractions.

I have one more "perennial" view on music and emotion to present to you, one that is particularly impassioned, rich with implications for psychedelia, and one that calls for a deeper inspection. Its source is Paul Elmer More (1864–1937), who taught Sanskrit at Harvard and Bryn Mawr, wrote books on Greek philosophy, and was a prolific literary critic and essayist. He wrote the following paean to the power of music to enter the deepest realms of our being, realms beyond conscious awareness:

> When we listen to the harmonies of instrumental music or the melody of the human voice, there arises a strange emotion within us which seems to magnify us out of ourselves into some

expanse of illimitable experiences, to lift us above the present cares of our petty life into some vast concern—so vast that the soul is lost between the wonderings of divine hope and divine fear. Great music is a psychical storm, agitating to fathomless depth the mystery of the past within us. Or we might say that it is a prodigious incantation. There are tones that call up all ghosts of youth and joy and tenderness;—there are tones that evoke all phantom pains of perished passion;—there are tones that revive all dead sensations of majesty and might and glory,—all expired exultations,—all forgotten magnanimities. Well may the influence of music seem inexplicable to the man who idly dreams that his life began less than a hundred years ago! He who has been initiated into the truth knows that to every ripple of melody, to every billow of harmony, there answers within him, out of the Sea of Death and Birth, some eddying immeasurable of ancient pleasure and pain.[18]

This wonderfully impassioned statement draws our attention to how, in psychedelic states, music may penetrate very deeply into inaccessible realms of consciousness, both subconscious and transpersonal—far beyond the limits of what William James called the "hot spot" of consciousness, our present, narrowly focused attention. William Barnard, a specialist in the comparative philosophy of mysticism, explains James's view:

James's psychology stresses that our consciousness always has a "hot-spot," a center of gravity, a focus of attention. Surrounding this central focus of our awareness, however, is a vaguely felt, but crucially significant, penumbra of tacit assumptions, memories, hopes, and prejudices that operate below the surface of our conscious awareness and strongly influence how we perceive and interact with the world around us. In addition, *encircling this fairly accessible preconscious background, there is another, deeper level of subconscious awareness, an awareness that appears to be active below the surface boundaries of our consciousness and which occasionally erupts into our lives with powerful and undeniable force.* [emphasis added][19]

It is that "deeper level of subconscious awareness" that often "erupts" into consciousness during a psychedelic experience, and often it is music that is its vehicle. Barnard cites another James scholar, Eugene Fontinell, who describes

James's comprehensive vision of reality as one of "fields within fields within fields," an image that will resonate with psychonauts. Barnard explains:

> This field model of reality sees individual selves not as self-contained monads with an unchanging, essential core, but rather, as swirling vortices of interpenetrating, interdependent fields whose boundaries are, according to Fontinell, "open, indefinite, and continually shifting such that other fields are continually leaking in and out." *The Varieties of Religious Experience* depicts a world in which these fields within fields not only take the form of our ongoing stream of consciousness, but are themselves surrounded by another whirling miasma of interpenetrating fields: the subliminal self, that bubbling cauldron of intuitions, passions, delusions, fantasies, paranormal cognitions, and mystical ecstasies that from time to time spills over into our consciousness . . .[20]

In other words, in psychedelic states, we may assume that music heard in the absence of the controlling, self-limiting, censoring ego penetrates to unknown depths of consciousness, which, in turn, interpenetrate and reverberate within expanding fields of awareness, including the transpersonal. Although what I've offered here is but a tentative, conceptual formulation of an ineffable process, it does provide a meaningful clue as to why music in entheogenic states becomes such an eloquent and revelatory language not only of emotion, but also of existential and spiritual being.

Music and Emotion in Psychedelic States: Firsthand Accounts

The matter of *how* music elicits emotion is a complicated one—the mechanics or dynamics of the process a subject for endless discussion and debate among neuroscientists, psychologists, musicologists, and those who practice various forms of music therapy. Since our focus is on the experiential dimension of psychedelics, our best informants are those with firsthand experience of the territory. For one LSD subject, "This was more than music: the entire room was saturated with sounds that were also feelings—sweet, delicious, sensual—that seemed to be coming from somewhere deep down inside me."[21] Another LSD subject reflects philosophically on music's ability to unearth and articulate emotions of all kinds that we keep hidden within us: "As I watched these visions, it occurred to me that the importance of music was, like art, its power to convey emotions we were too hurt, too timid, or too inarticulate to express directly: love, compassion, sweetness, tenderness, warmth, loneliness, sadness, despair, discouragement, and the gamut of pains and joys. It seemed to me that music was great only in so far as it could catch and interpret these universal feelings."[22] Another subject, also on LSD, seems to experience a perfect blending of the aesthetic, the emotional, and the spiritual:

> Listening to music, one understands Mozart for the first time—as each phrase unfolds, waves of contentment—so pure, so serene—pour their lambent light upon the languishing soul, drunken with sheer bliss! Every silvery sigh, every shudder of peace and fulfillment rises clear and transparent before the senses, like bubbling water in mother-of-pearl chambers! The pure, oily, gut-richness of string tones sound with poetic sensuousness that they never before possessed. Every pulse of an instrument is a perfect sigh, every nuance an expression of perfect emotion. How intricate and lovely the interweaving of naked sound—the pure presence of eternal harmony and experienced sensation![23]

For an example of explicitly religious emotions flowing from music experienced under a psychedelic, we have Dr. Huston Smith's personal account of his participation in the famous "Good Friday Experiment," the basis for Walter Pahnke's doctoral dissertation on psilocybin as a reliable catalyst for mystical experience:

> For me, the climax of the service came during a solo that was sung by a soprano whose voice (as it came to me through the prism of psilocybin) I can only describe as angelic. What she sang was no more than a simple hymn, but it entered my soul so deeply that its opening and closing verses have stayed with me ever since.
>
> *My times are in Thy hands, my God, I wish them there;*
> *My life, my friends, my soul, I leave entirely in Thy care....*
> *My times are in Thy hands, I'll always trust in Thee;*
> *And after death at Thy right hand I shall forever be.*

> In broad daylight those lines are not at all remarkable, but in the context of the experiment they said everything. The last three measures of each stanza ascended to a dominant seventh which the concluding tonic chord then resolved. This is as trite a way to end a melody as exists, but the context changed that totally. My mother was a music teacher, and she instilled in me an acute sensitivity to harmonic resonances. When that acquisition and my Christian nurturance converged on the Good Friday story under psilocybin, the gestalt transformed a routine musical progression into the most powerful cosmic homecoming I have ever experienced.[24]

Another example of deeply religious emotion flowing from music involves music not literally heard but imagined (a subject we explore in chapter 7). It involves noted Harvard theologian Harvey Cox as a participant in an all-night peyote ritual in the Sierra Madre mountains of Mexico under the guidance of a Huichol shaman sometime in the late 1970s. When one of the other participants noticed and pointed out the "morning star" (i.e., Venus or Sirius) "glistening like a crown jewel over the eastern horizon," Cox began hearing a favorite hymn, "Bright Morning Stars Are Rising," in his head, "sung by a fifty-thousand-voice choir . . . and it was all for me." This is how he describes and reflects on his resultant emotions:

> That night the morning star became for me the sign of a universe that throbbed with love—not just general beneficence, but personally focused love, pouring through real people. Watching the morning star I felt more intensely than I ever had before what I have nearly always believed, and had sensed on some previous occasions: that "God is love" is not just a pious hope but a factual statement about the character of the universe. The morning star and the song about it fused. The song was the star and the star was the song.
>   The feeling was too strong. At first I staggered out into the desert reaching toward the morning star. Then I fell, knelt, wept and cried, stood up, fell again. My knees shook and I trembled. Twice I tried to turn back toward the fire, away from the star. But each time its power turned me around and I was drawn toward it, only to stumble and fall again. I was

deliriously happy. I thought of my family and my students, neighbors and friends—all the people whose love for me is a vehicle of the vital energy of the cosmos. Finally, exhausted from crying and weak with joy, I crept back to my colleagues around the fire and lay still.[25]

A final example of the blending of music and emotion stands a bit apart from the others on three counts: first, it's age (it was written in 1845); second, it melds together first- and secondhand description; third, it involves hashish, which was often taken in "psychedelic" doses in the nineteenth century. This account was written by French psychiatrist Jacques-Joseph Moreau (1804–1884), who had first encountered hashish during his travels in North Africa. A brief biographical sketch explains that he "must also have tried it himself since in his travel reports he writes rather lyrically about 'pleasures impossible to interpret' which this 'marvelous substance' brings about and which 'would be impossible to describe to anybody who had not experienced it.' "[26] In fact Moreau insisted that to be a credible researcher into the psychological effects of hashish one must experiment on himself:

> I [became] acquainted with the effects of hashish through my own experience, and not merely from the reports of others. . . . At the outset I must make this point, the verity of which is unquestionable: Personal experience is the criterion of truth here. I challenge the right of anyone to discuss the effects of hashish if he is not speaking for himself and has not been in a position to evaluate them in light of sufficient repeated use."[27]

Here, Moreau describes the emotional effects of music on those using hashish:

> The sense of hearing, like all the other senses, becomes extremely keen under the influence of hashish. . . . This excessive development of the sense of hearing must be attributed, at least in part, to the powerful influence that music exerts on those who take hashish. Words fail to portray the variety of emotions that harmony can produce. The crudest music, the simple vibrations

of the strings of a harp or a guitar, rouse you to a point of delirium or plunge you into a sweet melancholy.

I have observed these effects in several people. I have witnessed their cries of joy, their songs, their tears and their laments, their deep depression or their frantic elation, depending on the harmonic mode in which the sound reached them. Several months ago *Experience* published an article in which Carriere [one of Moreau's medical-student assistants] described, with the great wit and accuracy of observation for which he is known, the state of excitement in which he saw several medical students to whom I had given hashish:

> A colleague, Dr. . . . , wishing to know for himself the effects of hashish, swallowed several grams of *dawamesc* [a form of hashish]. The dose was minimal, and some time elapsed before Dr. . . . felt anything extraordinary. Then a female voice was heard. It was a maid busy tidying up in the room next to the one we were in. This voice was not disagreeable, which is about all one could say for it. Nevertheless, our colleague paid close attention to it. Soon he approached the door of the room where the songs came from and glued his ear to the keyhole in order not to miss a single note. He remained there, spellbound, for nearly a half-hour and left only when his siren in dustup and wooden shoes could no longer be heard.

Moreau continues:

> I would try in vain to convey the extent to which music affects me in the same circumstances. Agreeable or disagreeable, happy or sad, the emotions that music creates are comparable only to those experienced in a dream. It is not enough to say that these emotions are more vivid than those of the waking state. Their character is transformed, as it were, and it is only upon reaching a hallucinatory state that they reach their full strength and can induce actual paroxysms of pleasure or pain. At that moment the immediate, direct action of harmony and the actual sensations on the ears are combined with the fiery and

varied emotions resulting from associations of ideas caused by the combination of sounds.[28]

Subtle Emotions

The profound emotions that music generates in psychedelic states are not limited to those that might be described as intense or of great existential import, but include also the most exquisitely subtle of emotions: gentle, sublimely nuanced variations of mood and sentiment. In the earlier discussion of "Musical Hypersensitivity" in chapter 4, the focus generally was on heightened perception of the subtleties of music itself, rather than on the emotions they produce within consciousness. Here I focus briefly on how, in psychedelic states, the emotions inspired by music may take extraordinarily subtle and nuanced forms beyond the reach of descriptive language. Aaron Copland, one of the most respected composers of the twentieth century, offers a critical insight in this regard:

> Refinement in musical taste begins with the ability to distinguish subtle nuances of feeling. Anyone can tell the difference between a sad piece and a joyous one. The talented listener recognizes not merely the joyous quality of the piece, but also the specific shade of joyousness—whether it be troubled joy, delicate joy, carefree joy, hysterical joy, and so forth. I add "and so forth" advisedly, for it covers an infinitude of shadings that cannot be named, as I have named these few, because of music's incommensurability with language.[29]

I have to say that encountering this comment by Copland struck a deep chord. Through years of preparing a series of psychedelically oriented playlists on Spotify, I've devoted a good bit of time to the classical genre. Aside from the principal featured classical playlist ("Classical Music for Psychedelic States"[30]), I've spent innumerable hours creating a number of subsidiary classical lists, the majority being focused on one particular emotional or attitudinal sentiment. It was in the course of repeated listenings to numerous individual musical works (to determine in which of these various playlists they belonged) that I found my capacity for deep and discerning listening to evolve over time. It was particularly while absorbing myself in the contents of any one particular list (e.g., "Compassion") that I found myself becoming increasingly sensitive to the kinds of emotional nuance that Copland addresses: the "infinitude of shadings" to be found in musical expression. This often included repeated listening to several different performances (i.e., various interpretations) of the same piece. This deeply immersive experience, extending over several years, has served as an extraordinary education in the art of "deep listening," and likewise in the subtleties of musical composition: the essential miracle of creating and artfully assembling sound vibrations into ineffably expressive wholes. It is often in the psychedelic state that those of us not born with advanced musical gifts can savor the deepest beauties and sublimities of music and be directly moved by the emotional wisdom they embody. In a journal I kept during the early phases of this extended curation process, one entry reads:

> Listening to a piece of music, a certain mood or emotional flavor may predominate, may draw you like a magnet into its living core, constituting a journey into the complex soul of a particular human feeling (encompassing emotion, sensation, and awareness). This singular, distinctive music-feeling may seem to possess infinite import, containing within it the very soul of existence.
>
> Or, while listening, the mood in a piece may evolve, may slip into a new variation, a different register, shift to a higher frequency, a subtler refinement, colored by a new light. And you find yourself simply flowing with that—without need for inner analysis or commentary, no need to document it as a facet of perception, something to recall or try to express. It just is, and it is everything.[31]

6

Music, Creator of Worlds

Synesthesia and Eidetic Visions

> There are layers upon layers upon layers of consciousness within—literally worlds upon worlds, countless dimensions of consciousness, that can be accessed via psychedelics—if we are willing to approach them with care and respect.
>
> —G. William Barnard

Even under "normal" circumstances, music, when allowed to fill one's awareness, has the power to create alternate worlds. Although this metaphor refers to the creation of a consuming atmospheric mood or feeling, in the psychedelic realm it becomes more like a literal reality because of the phenomenon of synesthesia, defined as a perceptual phenomenon in which stimulation of one sense generates a simultaneous sensation in another. As the *Psychology Today* website describes it, "[W]hen one sense is activated, another unrelated sense is activated at the same time. This may, for instance, take the form of hearing music and simultaneously sensing the sound as swirls or patterns of color."[1] A nod to psychedelia, perhaps?

The concept/phenomenon of synesthesia goes back a long way. Mike Jay gives a brief overview of its history:

> "Coloured hearing" had been described in classical Greece and studied by German psychologists since the early nineteenth century; but the scientific term "synaesthesia" was freshly

minted by the American psychologist Mary Whiton Calkins[2] in 1893. At the moment of [Havelock] Ellis's experiment,[3] the phenomenon was of intense interest to scientists, artists and occultists alike. . . . Thanks to Charles Baudelaire's famous account,[4] it was already recognized that hashish could prompt episodes of synaesthesia, and that these were associated with ecstatic states and creative inspiration.[5] Arthur Symons echoed Baudelaire with his description of the drug as "a magician who turns sounds into colors and colors into sounds" [in *The Symbolist Movement in Literature*, 1899].

Synaesthesia was taken as evidence, both scientific and artistic, that hashish—and now peyote—had the power to create sensory experiences that were unattainable in normal life to all but the exceptional few. As to its cause, psychologists offered competing theories. . . . Occultists and spiritualists saw synesthesia as evidence . . . of a higher form of consciousness, perhaps even the arrival of a new stage in human evolution.[6]

Baudelaire was especially influential in establishing the aesthetic category of synesthesia (decades before the term came into use). He "had already evoked this sensation in his poetry, notably in 'Correspondences' (1857), in which perfumes are 'sweet like oboes, green like prairies,'"[7] and in Les *Paradis Artificiels* (Artificial Paradises), published in 1860, he described "Sounds . . . clothed in colours and colours in music."[8] "Over the next decades," Jay writes, "synesthesia became a signifier of spiritual and artistic peak experience."[9] Madame Helena Blavatsky, the Russian-American mystic who cofounded the Theosophical Society in 1875, cited Théophile Gautier's essay "Hashish," where he describes his own experience with synesthesia: "My hearing acquired marvellous capacities: I heard the music of the flowers; sounds—green, red and blue—poured into my ears in clearly perceptible waves of smell and colour. A tumbler upset, the creaking of an armchair, a word whispered in the lowest tones vibrated and resounded within me like so many claps of thunder. At the gentlest contact with objects—furniture or human body—I heard prolonged sounds, sighs like the melodious vibrations of an Aeolian harp."[10]

A common but not necessarily universal feature of psychedelic experience,[11] synesthesia is experienced when music, especially with eyes closed, generates elaborate visual phenomena, generally of great complexity, beauty, and felt profundity. Images might flow from the music with such seamless instantaneity and harmonious fit between sound and image that it may seem as if the images had been encoded into the music as part of its sonic DNA. These elaborate, often breathtaking images may assume the form of rich, complex abstract designs (e.g., geometric, kaleidoscopic, mandalic, etc.) or exotic architecture, otherworldly landscapes, alien worlds, or any other creation of a liberated imagination. As I described in the introduction, music seeds visualizations, visions, whole worlds of eidetic (virtual) reality, creating vast spaces for the free flow of consciousness. Benny Shanon describes this phenomenon: "[Psychedelics amplify] an affect intrinsic to music . . . its capacity to generate an otherworldly mode of existence. Even in the ordinary state of consciousness, listening to music can transport people to a different temporal matrix, defined not by the clock but rather by the intrinsic dynamics of the composition. With Ayahuasca this effect is greatly magnified and one may indeed feel absorbed and swept into what is experienced as another frame of being, or another reality altogether."[12] Nick Bromell writes of the "stunning synergy" between music and psychedelics in the creation of visionary worlds: "Together, psychedelics and music achieve a stunning synergy because music, too, is felt as something very near to us and at the same time as a world that is quite distinct from the world mapped by vision and touch. . . . Music creates an ontological framework, or world, independent of the everyday yet present beside it, and requiring only the slightest stimulus (a voice raised in song, the vibration of a guitar string) to call it into being."[13]

The idea of music creating worlds, expanding into cosmic and visionary realms, is both ancient and modern. As music historian Mark Evan Bonds notes, "from the Pythagorean perspective, to experience music as sound was to perceive through the senses that which lay beyond the realm of the senses: the very structure of the cosmos itself."[14] (This matter of music creating, invoking, or opening portals to other worlds was initially introduced in chapter 2.)

In her book *Deep Listeners: Music, Emotion and Trancing*, Judith Becker intriguingly explains that when music is heard in trance states, *imagination becomes experience*, a phenomenon that releases one from "quotidian time and space": "Music provides a link between alternate selves and alternate places and alternate times that become real places and real times in trance experiences. By enveloping the trancer in a soundscape that suggests, invokes, or represents other times and distant spaces, the transition out of quotidian time and space comes easier. Imagination becomes experience. One is moved from the mundane to the supra-normal:

another realm, another time, with other kinds of knowing."[15] Scholar of religion Lawrence Sullivan supports this idea, explaining that music, being the most potent expression of human imagination, can stimulate the imaginal realm into "all realities":

> Humans, who are the musical beings par excellence . . . participate in material reality through their bodily life but also in immaterial reality through the life of the imagination. Human fantasy allows the human spirit to conjure within itself images that resemble any and all forms of reality—material, spiritual, or even divine. . . . Music is the most malleable and most profound expression of this human imaginal power to reflect all realities in the [musical] phantasms it generates.[16]

Experiencing Synesthesia

Benny Shanon explains the basic principle, dynamics, and categories of auditory to visual synesthesia experienced on psychedelics, with ayahuasca as his usual point of reference:

> Ayahuasca is especially famous for the visions it induces. . . . These are of various structural kinds. In progressive order of increasing richness, complexity, and strength, they may consist of geometrical patterns without any semantics, of simple figurative items that do have semantics, and of entire scenes. In the latter case, various forms of interaction with what is seen in the visions may be experienced; when most powerful, the visions involve full immersion and turn into veritable virtual realities. Paradigmatically, music has great influence on the contents of the visions, their dynamics, and their progression.[17]

Let us now look at some first-person accounts of audible-to-visual synesthesia under psychedelics. Partially adapting Shanon's schema, I divide these into two loose categories: "simple" (mostly visual, involving patterns, figures, and designs, with or without implied meaning or symbolism); and "complex" (more highly elaborated visions within fully immersive, interactive virtual realities). Both can be *eidetic* (involving extremely vivid visual content), but by "complex" I mean those visionary experiences that possess a greater and richer profusion of content, often unfolding in a fully immersive narrative or "cinematic" environment.

British poet/mystic William Blake (1757-1827) offers what may serve as an apt, still useful definition of "eidetic vision": "A Spirit and a Vision are not, as the modern philosophy supposes, a cloudy vapor or a nothing: they are organized and minutely articulated beyond all that the mortal and perishing nature can produce. He who does not imagine in stronger and better lineaments, and in stronger and better light, than his perishing eye can see, does not imagine at all."[18] In more modern language, R. Gordon Wasson, describing a magic mushroom trip, wrote, "The visions were not blurred or uncertain. They seemed more real to me than anything I had ever seen with my own eyes."[19] As if to make absolutely clear this overpowering sense of reality—the undeniable immediacy, clarity, and substantiality of these visions—Wasson writes elsewhere,

> No patina of age hung on them. They were all fresh from God's workshop, pristine in their finish. . . . They seemed the very archetypes of beautiful form and color. We felt ourselves in the presence of the Ideas that Plato had talked about. In saying this let not the reader think that we are indulging in rhetoric, straining to command his attention by an extravagant figure of speech. For the world our visions were and must remain "hallucinations." But for us they were not false or shadowy suggestions of real things, figments of an unhinged imagination. What we were seeing was, we knew, the only reality, of which the counterparts of every day are mere imperfect adumbrations.[20]

Alan Watts makes the same point in his own way, explaining that "the classic psychedelics induce a sensation of intense though relaxed awakeness in which all details become vividly clear and astonishingly interesting. . . . It should be noted that visual images of these experiences presented in the popular press and in such films as *Easy Rider* are completely misleading, for they're not vague or bizarre but as clear and articulate as, say, Persian miniatures or the stained glass of Chartres or the photographs of Eliot Porter."[21]

Although the term "simple" synesthesia does little justice to what may involve breathtaking visions, it does provide a provisionally useful distinction. One LSD subject reports, "I could not for a time distinguish between sight and sound. . . . Mozart's melodic line was filling the room . . . woodwind harmonies released ethereal glowing purples and pinks in shafts of radiant light which streamed out from a picture in precise synchronization with the music.[22] Alan Watts, also on LSD, writes, "Listening to music with closed eyes, I beheld the most fascinating patterns of dancing jewelry, mosaic, tracery, and abstract images."[23] A more dramatic example, stretching the designation "simple" synesthesia to its limits, comes to us from author Mark Seelig describing an ayahuasca experience: "Music becomes 'visible' during the ceremonies in a way that is hard to put into words—rainbow colors shape-shifting into garlands, ornamented with billions of glittering crystals and jewels, twist and turn around their own axis and explode into kaleidoscopic supernovae that dance with every note of the track."[24] A final account of "simple" synesthesia, again pushing the limits of that term, comes from 1960s musical icon Donovan, who records the following trip sequence in his autobiography *The Hurdy Gurdy Man*:

> Suddenly, a brilliant beam of light flashed into the room. . . . Colours began to vibrate intensely. A Ravi Shankar record, newly arrived in London, was on the turntable and I closed my eyes. The vibrant colours were inside me also, in circular, pulsing patterns, flowers of light and energy. The inner mandalas vibrated and changed through incandescent hues of living light. . . . I stared at the carpet and became transfixed with the interlaced patterns moving to the slower raga which Ravi now played. . . . Exquisite sounds from another world and glowing patterns led me into a realization of great meaning. I became Awareness. Descriptions of the Divine Vision which I had read of in Buddhist books were now my own.[25]

Examples of what I've termed "complex" synesthesia under psychedelics are quite extraordinary, and arguably add an important new chapter to the literary history of mysticism. I encountered a fair number of these transcendent narratives in my research and have chosen to highlight four representative cases. As their authors took pains to describe their experiences as fully as possible, I present them as they did, without undue interruption or commentary.

The first comes from renowned British poet, historical novelist, and critic Robert Graves. It is an excerpt from *The Poet's Paradise*, a version of an address given in the early 1960s to the Oxford University

Humanist Society while Graves was a visiting professor of poetry there. In this excerpt, he describes taking magic mushrooms in the company of R. Gordon Wasson. It was the legendary *curandera* and wise woman María Sabina who introduced Wasson to the magic mushroom experience in Oaxaca, Mexico, in the mid-1950s, and it is a recording of her voice (presumably singing icaros—spontaneous, divinely inspired songs) that Wasson played during this session:

> Gordon Wasson had switched on the tape-recorder [with] the *curandera*'s voice . . . Every now and then she would change her mood and song; could mourn, triumph, or laugh. I fell wholly under her spell, and presently enjoyed the curious experience of seeing sound. The song-notes became intricate links of a round golden chain that coiled and looped in serpentine fashion among jade-green bushes; the only serpent I met in Eden . . . Each song was followed by a pause, and always I waited in a lover's agony for her to begin again, tears pricking at my eyelids. Once the *curandera* seemed to sing off-key. Perhaps this was quarter-tone music; at any rate, my ear was not offended: I knew what she meant when I saw one edge of the golden chain band now formed by the sound spread out into a spectrum; and laughed for pleasure. Towards the end came a quick, breathless, cheerful song of creation and growth. The notes fell to earth but rose once more in green shoots which soared swiftly up, putting on branches, leaves, flowers—until it dominated the sky like the beanstalk in the fairytale.
>
> My spirit followed after into the clear blue air, gazing down on cornfields, fields of poppies, and the spires of a heavenly city, and Thomas Traherne's orient and immortal wheat, "which never should be reaped nor ever was sown."
>
> At last the music ended. The visions were fading now. My corporeal self sighed, stretched luxuriously, and looked around. Most of the company had left the room. Only one friend remained. I asked him: "So the journey seems to be over?"
>
> "Ah, but close your eyes, and you can get back at once," he said.
>
> "How do you feel?"
>
> "My mind has never been so clear! Did you hear such

music in all your life?"[26]

This next episode of "complex" synesthesia was recorded by a female patient of pioneering psychedelic psychotherapist Dr. Sidney Cohen. For this woman on LSD, music became a magical force lifting her into a soaring, aerial flight above a breathtaking panorama of pristine nature, with the music (she mentions Mozart and Beethoven) keeping her aloft:

> The music seemed to take over the direction of the experience. I began to feel disembodied, and a marvelous weightlessness commenced. My consciousness seemed to rise into a wonderful limitless space, infinite and curving as the sky, with the earth and sea below. . . . The colours of the sky and sea and mountains were marvelously beautiful in a sort of shining air. There was only nature, no buildings anywhere. Only the land, the ocean and the limitless vaulted sky. It was absorbing and beautiful, beyond speech. I wanted not to speak, only to experience it silently. The music seemed to speak beyond any eloquence. Nothing in words could conceivably add to it. . . .
>
> Throughout everything the music seemed an intrinsic part of the experience. I couldn't then or now imagine what it would have been like without it. . . . The prevailing feeling was the marvelous soaring in the universe, the immense light, and a being borne aloft by the music.[27]

This next example of complex synesthesia comes from renowned science journalist and best-selling author Michael Pollan (quoted earlier), author of *How to Change Your Mind*, a highly informative and widely influential survey of contemporary psychedelic research and therapeutics. Here he describes an LSD experience with music "summoning into existence a sequence of psychic landscapes":

> [I]n this dreamy state, so wide open to suggestion, I was happy to let the terrain, and the music, dictate my path. And for the next several hours the music did just that, summoning into existence a sequence of psychic landscapes, some of them populated by the people closest to me, others explored on my own. A lot of the music was New Age drivel—the sort of stuff you might hear while getting a massage in a high-end

spa—yet never had it sounded so evocative, so beautiful! Music had become something much greater and more profound than mere sound. Freely trespassing the borders of the other senses, it was palpable enough to touch, forming three-dimensional spaces I could move through.

The Amazonian-tribal song put me on a trail that ascended steeply through redwoods, following a ravine notched into a hillside by the silvery blade of a powerful stream. I know this place: it was the trail that rises from Stinson Beach to Mount Tamalpais. But as soon as I secured that recognition, it morphed into something else entirely. Now the music formed a vertical architecture of wooden timbers, horizontals and verticals and diagonals that were being magically craned into place, forming levels that rose one on top of the other, even higher into the sky like a multistoried tree house under construction, yet a structure as open to the air and its influences as a wind chime.

So it went, song by song, for hours. Something aboriginal, with the deep spooky tones of a didgeridoo, put me underground, moving somehow through the brownish-black rootscape of a forest. I tensed momentarily: Was this about to get terrifying? Have I died and been interred? If so, I was fine with it. I got absorbed watching a white tracery of mycelium threading among the roots and linking the trees in a network intricate beyond comprehension. I knew all about this mycelial network, how it forms a kind of arboreal Internet allowing the trees in a forest to exchange information, but now what had been merely an intellectual conceit was a vivid, felt reality of which I had become a part.[28]

This final example of a complex visionary state was, like the others, evoked by music, but also features music as its ultimate narrative focus. The author of this testimony is a female "twenty-four-year-old university instructor [on] 225 micrograms of LSD" whose recorded vision possesses the coherence and prophetic solemnity of a religious allegory:

A Bach toccata then was put on the phonograph and the music of the spheres left their archetypal abode and took up residence in the walk-up on ___ Street.

It was at this time that I closed my eyes and experienced

a vision of the future that unfolded in vivid colors before my closed eyes and was accompanied by voices that were audible, however, only inside my head. I found myself and the rest of mankind standing together on the foothills of the earth, being addressed by two splendid and luminous figures many hundreds of miles high. They could be seen plainly in spite of their height and they told us that they were the elders of this particular part of the cosmos and had lost their patience with the human creatures of this earth. The recalcitrance of greedy, warring, barbarous mankind had over-exceeded itself and now that nuclear power had been discovered the outrageous breed evolved on our planet might yet attempt to subvert the whole cosmos. And so it had been decided in the Council of Elders that unless mankind could find something in its creations with which to justify itself, it would have to be destroyed.

Having heard this message, we earthlings scattered and searched our libraries, museums, histories and parliaments for some achievement that might be seen as a justification for our being. We brought forth our greatest art objects, our Leonardos, Michelangelos, Praxiteles—But the elders only shook their heads and said solemnly: "It is not sufficient." We brought forth our great masterpieces of literature, the works of Shakespeare, Milton, Goethe, Dante. But these also were deemed insufficient. We searched in our religious literature and offered the figures of the religious geniuses—Jesus, Buddha, Moses, St. Francis, but the elders only laughed and said: "Not sufficient."

It was then, when destruction seemed imminent and all had given themselves up to their fate, that I came forward and offered to the elders the music of Johann Sebastian Bach. They listened to the entire corpus and great silver tears of incredible brilliance shimmered and trickled down the length of their luminous bodies, after which they were silent. On and on this silence extended, until they broke it to say only: "It is sufficient. You of the Earth are justified." And then they went away.

For a period of time I had neither capacity nor wish to measure, I pondered this vision. Then, when the music had ended, I lay on my back and looked up at the ceiling where a kaleidoscope of images from ancient civilizations flickered rapidly before my eyes.[29]

In closing this chapter, I should point out that not everyone experiences music-to-visual synesthesia while on psychedelics. I had simply assumed it was a universal feature of the experience because it was such a prominent feature of my own, and I'd begun to encounter quite a bit of confirmation in the literature. However, once, during the early days of this project, I happened to be attending a small psychedelic gathering in the Bay Area and was chatting with a respected elder of the psychedelic community. While describing my incipient music project in hopes of receiving some sage advice or inspiration, I raised the topic of musically induced synesthesia. He informed me, matter of factly, that this was something he himself did not experience in his journeys. While he relished listening to music on psychedelics, synesthesia was not part of the equation; no elaborate inner cinematography rose from whatever music was entering his ears. I recall being surprised, my facile assumption about the universality of synesthesia under psychedelics shattered. I somehow also felt a bit sad for his missing out on what to me was a cherished aspect of the experience, and perhaps slightly embarrassed for having raised the topic. It didn't seem to bother him.

We do know, however, that Aldous Huxley described himself as a "poor visualizer" (with and without the presence of music) under psychedelics (this, apart from his extremely poor eyesight). In a letter to Humphry Osmond, he wrote:

> We had our LSD experiment last week, with Al, Gerald and myself taking 75 micrograms. . . . I had no visions with my eyes shut—even less than I had on the first occasion with mescalin, when the moving geometries were highly organized and, at moments, very beautiful and significant (though at others, very trivial). This time even the patterns were poorly organized. . . . Evidently, if you are not a congenital or habitual visualizer, you do not get internal visions under mescaline or LSD—only external transfiguration.[30]

In his response, Osmond reminds Huxley that 75 micrograms of LSD "is a minimal dose." However, even on a comparatively much higher dose (500 mg) of what Huxley refers to as "a particularly pure brand of mescaline," the visual effects increased, but only to a limited degree: "The effects were powerful. A good deal of vision with your eyes closed—though never consistent or long-drawn, just moving geometries modulating or on the verge of modulating into architectures."[31] Of course, what Huxley may have lacked in synesthetic visualization was dramatically compensated by an exquisite sensitivity to music itself, as we've already heard.

I learned from my own encounter with a "non-visualizer" that one should be cautious in assuming too much about what others experience on psychedelics. I have no idea whether this individual's lack of a synesthetic response to music is uncommon and, if so, how uncommon. I happen to be a strongly visual person (I was a visual artist in photography for many years), so perhaps my own experiences are less typical than I had imagined. I've not come across any relevant statistics, but based on having accumulated numerous accounts of the phenomenon, I have to assume that it is reasonably common.

However, if not so for you, there are ample alternative sources of visual stimulation while on a psychedelic. I would especially recommend the beauties of nature and the infinite varieties of fine art. The natural world offers limitless wonders, if you can make your way to a safe and secluded spot. If that's not possible, you can utterly lose yourself in images of nature in books containing good-quality reproductions of photographs, paintings, watercolors, or other media. My second recommended source for visual stimulation is visual art in general, in whatever form. I always have a pile of favorite art books on hand for special occasions. As in a child's fantasy or a magical tale, simply turn the pages and the images will come alive, expand beyond the page, become animate like lucid dreams, portals to other worlds.

7

Music from "Nowhere"

Hallucinating Music

> The sense of limitation—of the confinement of our senses within the bounds of our own flesh and blood—instantly fell away. . . . harmonies, such as Beethoven may have heard in dreams, but never wrote, floated around me.
>
> —Bayard Taylor[1]

When I was about fifteen and still a psychedelic neophyte, I returned home late one Saturday night after a psychedelic day with friends, still slightly under the influence. I tiptoed upstairs to my bedroom, got undressed, slid into bed, closed my eyes, and watched the kinds of late-trip, low-grade cartoonish residuals that linger and gradually dissipate. At one point, out of nowhere came the sound of orchestral music, as if Mozart or Tchaikovsky (I wouldn't have known the difference) were playing on a turntable by the bed. The music was not faint or vague, neither sporadic or disjointed, but as smooth, consistent, and refined as one might expect from a professional recording of a major symphony orchestra. Coming late in the trip, the music didn't generate the kind of intense aesthetic excitement it might have provoked earlier, during peak hours, so it didn't register as a highly significant experience, the kind that might have sparked a lively new interest in classical music. But the realization that this music was coming from within (where? how?), that it had no source outside my own inner being, was a striking novelty.

I'd never given the incident much thought until I learned many years later (while researching this book) that my experience was not unique. Psychedelic pioneers Helen Bonny and Walter Pahnke commented on this phenomenon of hallucinated music: "During Phase 5 (4.5 to 7 hours), experiences are sometimes reported of hearing spontaneous internally produced music of great beauty. The incidence of spontaneously produced music can frequently be enhanced by the introduction of periods of silence or in response to minimal auditory stimulus."[2] Jane Dunlop reflected on her experience of the same phenomenon: "My thoughts turned to the almost unbelievable fact that beautiful original music was somehow stored deep inside me. . . . I felt convinced . . . that deep inside every person must be a fount of music which men like Brahms, Beethoven, Mozart, and Schubert had been able to reach. Only later did I learn that other persons given LSD had reported hearing exquisite music not played by human hands."[3]

In this chapter we encounter elaborate descriptions of hearing music in psychedelic states in the absence of any external source of music. It's notable that most of these episodes involve more than just listening to internally broadcast music. They often involve (as in the previous chapter's discussion of synesthesia) full-fledged visionary experiences wherein music is not only heard, but where music and music making become subjects in and of themselves, often central to the visionary narrative. But before diving in, it's worth exploring the fact that musical hallucination is not unique to psychedelic states. One finds a certain esoteric history of the phenomenon in at least three other areas—neuropathology, mystical religion, and the paranormal—each of which I review briefly.

Neuropathology

There is an entire chapter on "Musical Hallucinations" in Oliver Sacks's book *Musicophilia: Tales of Music and the Brain*. There he explains: "Brain imaging [has] recently shown that the 'hearing' of musical hallucinations was associated with [unusual] activity in several parts of the brain: the temporal lobes, the frontal lobes, the basal ganglia, and the cerebellum—all parts of the brain normally activated in the perception of 'real' music."[4] This means that those who, because of some irregularity in brain function, may "hear" music in the absence of external causes are not, strictly speaking, "imagining" it, in the sense of conjuring it out of a void. At least in some cases (as Sacks assures a concerned patient), musical hallucinations are "not imaginary, not psychotic, but real and physiological"—though the symptoms are generally distressing and can only be partially blunted with certain medications. Relatedly, even under "normal" circumstances when we "play" a piece of music in our heads, the brain's music centers are activated: "Increasingly sophisticated brain-imaging techniques have shown that imagining music can indeed activate the auditory cortex almost as strongly as listening to it,"[5] indicating the subjectively highly realistic nature of inward "hearing."

Some classical composers are known to have been subject to this phenomenon. Sacks gives the example of Robert Schumann: "Robert Jourdain, in *Music, the Brain, and Ecstasy*, cites Clara Schumann's diaries describing how her husband heard 'music that is so glorious, and with instruments sounding more wonderful than one ever hears on earth.' One of his friends reported that Schumann 'unburdened himself about a strange phenomenon . . . the inner hearing of wondrously beautiful pieces of music, fully formed and complete! The sound is like distant brasses, underscored by the most magnificent harmonies.'"[6] Sacks explains, however, that "Schumann probably had a manic-depressive or schizo-affective disorder, as well as, towards the end of his life, neurosyphilis," which, in the end, caused his musical hallucinations to take a very dark and tormenting turn.[7] Another possible example is Tchaikovsky: "As a child, Tchaikovsky was supposedly found weeping in bed, wailing, 'This music! It is here in my head. Save me from it.'"[8]

Religious Mysticism

Individuals who experience auditory musical hallucinations turn up in a variety of religious and mystical traditions. A handful of Christian saints and mystics, along with a few examples from the Hindu tradition, will suffice to illustrate the point.

While reading the 1845 book *Hashish and Mental Illness* by Dr. Jacques-Joseph Moreau, I came across a one-line reference to a "Saint Cedily," who, Moreau informs us, "performed on the harpsichord the sublime harmony that a troop of celestial spirits created in the heavens."[9] A search for "Saint Cedily" yielded, more properly, "St. Cecily," another name for St. Cecilia, third-century Roman virgin martyr, venerated throughout the Christian world as the patron saint of music (as well as of musicians, composers, instrument makers, and poets—quite a portfolio). According

114 | Tuning In

to the website "Catholic Online," "St. Cecilia is regarded as the patroness of music because she heard heavenly music in her heart when she was married."[10] In art she's often represented playing the pipe organ (or other keyboard instrument), as well as violin, lute, and harp. She is honored in French composer Charles Gounod's well-known "St. Cecilia's Mass" (1855).

Another Christian mystic, the German Dominican friar Henry Suso (1295–1366), reportedly experienced his own musical hallucinations:

> Now, on the night before the feast of All Angels, it seemed to him in a vision that he heard angelic strains and sweet heavenly melody; and this filled him with such gladness that he forgot all his sufferings. Then one of the angels said to him: "Behold, with what joy thou dost hear us sing the song of eternity. . . ."
>
> The heavenly spirits began with loud voice to intone the beautiful responsory. . . . They had scarcely sung a little, when his soul became so full of the heavenly strain, that his frail body could bear no more, and opening his eyes, his heart overflowed, and the burning tears streamed down his cheeks.[11]

Our next musical hallucinator is Protestant mystic Jacob Boehme (1575–1624). In his classic study *Cosmic Consciousness*, Richard Maurice Bucke describes that hours before his death, Boehme "called his son Tobias to his bedside and asked him whether he did not hear beautiful music, and then he requested him to open the door of the room so that the celestial song could be better heard."[12]

Jumping ahead several centuries, we encounter the short-lived French Carmelite nun St. Thérèse of Lisieux (1873–1897). As recorded in Francis Younghusband's *Modern Mystics*, just before her death the saint stated, "Mother, some notes from a distant concert have just reached my ears, and the thought came to me that soon I shall be listening to the music of Paradise."[13]

Moving on to traditional Hinduism, in his book *Yoga: Immortality and Freedom*, noted Indologist and religion scholar Mircea Eliade cites the *Nadabindu Upaniṣad*, which describes "auditory phenomena that accompany certain yogic exercises":

> At first, the sounds perceived are violent (like those of the ocean, thunder, waterfalls), then they acquire a musical

structure (of *mardala*, of bell and horn), and finally the hearing becomes extremely refined (sounds of the *vina*, the flute, the bee). . . . Finally, the yogin will experience union with the *parabrahman*, which has no sound. . . . This Upanisad . . . was certainly composed in a yogic circle that specialized in "mystical auditions,"—that is, in obtaining "ecstasy" through concentration on [inner] sounds. But we must not forget that such concentration is acquired only by the application of a yogic technique (*asana, pranayama*, etc.) and that its final objective is *to transform the whole cosmos into a vast sonorous theophany* [emphasis added].[14]

My final example of this phenomenon is one with which I had a close personal connection as both witness and participant. On a sunny spring day in Boston in 1990, I was walking along Boyleston Street adjacent to the Boston Gardens with a special friend who was visiting from Europe. Mira was a twenty-nine-year old Belgian devotee of Krishna and a born mystic, some of whose story I recount in my book *India in a Mind's Eye*. I'd met her a few years earlier in India at one of the ashrams of the Krishna Consciousness movement. My trusty saint/mystic antennae had led me to her, and I'd become a close confidant to this spiritually gifted soul who, like other mystics throughout history, lived precariously within a conventional religious institution—the kind whose members have ambivalent (and often resentful) feelings toward those in their midst who authentically vivify those sacred teachings that remain distant abstractions to most members.

As we walked along, at one point Mira's pace slowed and she began to falter. I tried to steady her with my one free arm as she slowly crumpled to the pavement, fainting dead away. She'd previously told me of her history of fainting and falling into trances, but this was my first encounter. I gently picked her up and carried her into the park, placing her sitting on the ground leaning against a tree. Various concerned strangers, including two young policewomen, approached and inquired if my friend needed help. I reassured them she'd be fine soon. Mira had told me about unnecessary, counterproductive, and even traumatic hospital interventions following past fainting episodes, so I was determined not to let that happen this time.

As we sat together I held Mira's hand and gently rubbed her shoulder. After several long minutes her eyes began to flutter open, although she seemed to linger in trance. Leaning against my shoulder, eyes streaming tears, in a weak voice she asked, "Did you hear that beautiful music?" When I replied apologetically that I hadn't, she seemed incredulous. "You didn't just hear that celestial (she might have used the word "heavenly") music?" Mira seemed genuinely surprised and a little disappointed. It had been that real to her. I asked if she might be able to describe to me what she'd just experienced. Aside from the indescribable music, she remembered being in what sounded like some paradisiacal, heavenly environment: a beautiful lake surrounded by trees and flowers. My heart melted, and I wished I could have participated in her vision and been privy to such an unworldly scene.

After a while (I'd lost any sense of time), Mira, now revived and ready to continue our walk, asked if we might go and get some ice cream, as we'd planned earlier as part of our outing. Not confident she was quite back to normal, I suggested we instead return to the ashram on Commonwealth Avenue, which we did.

During the following days, now staying with me at my apartment in nearby Somerville, Mira experienced a few more similar episodes, but they occurred during "conscious" trance states and while safely indoors. The attendant memories of these events are indelible. Mira passed away about a decade later from cancer, aged forty. I miss her and think of her often. When I do, I inevitably feel gently transported. Fortunately I'd made recordings of some of our conversations, and the sound of her dulcet, lilting voice, colored by a strong Flemish accent, still sends chills down my spine.

Paranormal/Spiritism

The annals of research into what is commonly referred to as "the paranormal" is rich with accounts of out-of-body and near-death experiences, which sometimes include disembodied music. D. Scott Rogo is the author of two books originally bearing the main title NAD. Nad (*nada*) is the Sanskrit term for "sound." It is commonly used in the compound *nada-brahman*, meaning spiritual, sacred, or transcendent sound or, in Rogo's words, "transcendental, astral, psychic, or paranormal music—music heard from no apparent source."[15] This pair of books presents myriad historical incidences of musical hallucination, drawn from paranormal and spiritualistic literature going well back into the nineteenth century. In another work he offers some metaphysical context for the phenomenon, in that instance using the Pythagorean term "music of the spheres":

> Perhaps the "music of the spheres" is some sort of property of the higher spheres—spiritual realms existing within the Universe that interweave with the physical world in which we live. Perhaps this is the realm we enter when we die. When a person comes close to death, perhaps a rift opens between our terrestrial dimension and the Great Beyond, so that the patient can momentarily experience its pleasures and music. . . . People enjoying out-of-body experiences might perceive the music, since a similar rift in the fabric of reality could easily take place during these mysterious excursions.[16]

In one of the Nada books Rogo describes an instance of music hallucination occurring during an NDE (near-death experience). During the spring of 1880, a boy of fifteen had been sick for ten days with pneumonia when the doctor told the family he thought the boy had little time left. The boy's brother relates:

> My brother had been unconscious for two or three days, so on that night that the doctor was expecting him to die, one of our neighbors and myself kept watch by his bedside. He had not spoken or showed any sign of life for more than 24 hours—and at midnight he roused up and opened his eyes and asked us to *listen to that sweet music*—he repeated it several times, saying *it was the prettiest music he ever heard and asked us if we did not hear it*. . . . After he had spoken several times about hearing the sweet music, he went to sleep and when he awoke he was much better and continued to improve until he got well—he is living today.[17]

Rogo also describes an instance of "music in the afterlife" as related via a mediumistic communication—that is, someone who has "passed over" speaking to the living through a professional medium. Rogo sets the scene: "Just about every book on the afterlife has some descriptive matter concerning the music of that world. Consistent with what is reported by percipients of psychic music, 'communicators' usually describe music as either choral or orchestral, and usually as inconceivably more beautiful than anything ever heard on earth."[18] He quotes from the book *Light in our Darkness*,[19] where a denizen of the Beyond describes, through a medium, how one arriving in that higher realm experiences the music there:

> Presently, when their eyes are no longer dazzled by the exquisite scene, sounds of music seem to echo from the sky and to float in the colored atmosphere. You have music on earth, but perfect harmony is impossible in your present vibration. Your ears are not fine enough to realize this, but here the vibrations are made so delicate that a fractional difference of tone would strike one as discord. Imagine therefore an orchestra in which every instrument was perfect in tone and time. Even you would not realize what music might be.[20]

To conclude this introductory section: as in other matters, it is apparent that "psychedelic" experiences are not necessarily sui generis but are more intensified versions of generic human experiences—even if, as in the above cases, uncommon ones.

Hallucinating Music in Psychedelic States

In cases of psychedelically induced "hallucinated" music—music heard in the complete absence of any source of music in the immediate physical environment—music, often of a celestial or divine nature, is experienced as a living reality, whether perceived as "internal," "external," or as all-pervasive. Such music is typically accompanied by visions (as in "normal" synesthesia), often involving scenes of music making or musical revelry.

This first example, from 1912, actually involves not a traditional psychedelic but hashish. As mentioned in earlier chapters, classic nineteenth- and early twentieth-century reports of hashish intoxication usually involve very substantial doses worthy of the description "psychedelic." As author Mike Jay explains in *Emperors of Dreams: Drugs in the Nineteenth Century*: "The high-flown descriptions of hashish intoxication by writers like Charles Baudelaire and Fitz Hugh Ludlow can seem hilariously overblown to contemporary readers, but we must remember that the few hashish-eaters of the nineteenth century were eating mind-blowing doses of three or four grammes, at which level cannabis is no gentle mood elevator but an intensely powerful hallucinogen."[21] Elsewhere, he elaborates: "These oral preparations had long been consumed in doses that produced powerful and unpredictable effects. Often their subjects would remain prostrated for several hours, unable to move or speak, immersed in visions and fantasies that succeeded each other too rapidly and chaotically to describe. . . . In their spectrum, intensity and duration, these effects were comparable to what we now call psychedelic drugs."[22]

In Victor Robinson's 1912 work, *An Essay on Hasheesh*, he describes how internally perceived music sends him on a miraculous, cosmic journey:

> I hear music. There is something strange about this music. I have not heard such music before. The anthem is far away, but in its very faintness there is a lure. In the soft surge and swell of the minor notes there breathes a harmony that ravishes the sense of sound. A resonant organ, with a stop of sapphire and a diapason of opal, diffuses endless octaves from star to star. All the moon-beams form strings to vibrate the perfect pitch, and this entrancing unison is poured into my enchanted ears. Under such a spell, who can remain in a bed? The magic of that melody bewitches my soul. I begin to rise horizontally from my couch. No walls impede my progress, and I float into the outside air. Sweeter and sweeter grows the music, it bears me higher and higher, and I float in tune with the infinite—under the turquoise heavens where globules of mercury are glittering.[23]

Henry Luce, the American magazine magnate who founded *Time*, *Life*, *Fortune*, and *Sports Illustrated*, had an early interest in psychedelics. Along with his wife, Clare, he had his own musical hallucination under the influence of LSD: "Well before the hallucinogenic drug LSD hit the headlines, Luce was interested. One Luce houseguest was Dr. Sidney Cohen of Los Angeles, who had been studying the effect of LSD on actors and other creative people. The Luces took a "trip" under Cohen's guidance. Clare reported an enhanced appreciation of colors in her paintings, while the tone-deaf Luce heard music so bewitching that he walked out into the cactus garden and conducted a phantom orchestra."[24]

In *The Diary of Anaïs Nin, 1947–1955*, the celebrated writer provides one of our most eloquent descriptions of internally generated music. Drawn from a 1955 LSD trip under the auspices of Dr. Oscar Janiger, it is of special interest because—unlike the usual pattern of synesthesia highlighted in chapter 6, that of audible to visual—in Nin's description various visions seem to generate their own musical accompaniment:

> [T]here was a door leading to the garden. Gil opened it. The dazzle of the sun was blinding, every speck of gold multiplied and magnified. Trees, clouds, lawns heaved and undulated too, the clouds flying at tremendous speed. I ceased looking at the garden because on the plain door now appeared the most delicate Persian designs, flowers, mandalas, patterns in perfect symmetry. As I designed them they produced their matching music. When I drew a long orange line, it emitted its own orange tone. . . . the colors in the designs gave me pleasure, as well as the music. The singing of mockingbirds was multiplied, and became a whole forest of singing birds. My senses were multiplied as if I had a hundred eyes, a hundred ears, a hundred fingertips. The murals which appeared were perfect, they were Oriental, fragile, and complete, but then they became actual Oriental cities, with pagodas, temples, rich Chinese gold and red altars, and Balinese music. The music vibrated through my body as if I were one of the instruments and I felt myself becoming a full percussion orchestra, becoming green, blue, orange. The waves of the sounds ran through my hair like a caress. The music ran down my back and came out of my fingertips.
> . . . I returned to my starting point. I was standing in front of an ugly door, but as I looked closer it was not plain or green but it was a Buddhist temple, a Hindu column, a Moroccan ceiling, gold spires being formed and re-formed . . . Each form, each line emitted its equivalent in music in perfect accord with the design. An undulating line emitted a sustaining undulating melody, a circle had corresponding musical notations, diaphanous colors, diaphanous sounds, a pyramid created a pyramid of ascending notes, and vanishing ones left only an echo. These designs were preparatory sketches for entire Oriental cities. I saw the temples of Java, Kashmir, Nepal, Ceylon, Burma, Cambodia, in all the colors of precious stones illumined from within. Then the outer forms of the temples dissolved to reveal the inner chapels and shrines. The reds and golds inside the temples created an intricate musical orchestration like Balinese

music. . . . The temples grew taller, the music wilder, it became a tidal wave of sounds with gongs and bells predominating. Gold spires emitted a long flute chant. Every line and color was constantly breathing and mutating.[25]

A poignant account of sacred music flowing from within is given by Harvard theologian Harvey Cox, describing his participation in a native-lead peyote ceremony in the Sierra Madre mountains of Mexico.[26]

Since we had no watches, I had no idea what time it was when one of the patients first noticed the morning star and pointed it out to us, glistening like a crown jewel over the eastern horizon. The other patients saw it and agreed it was beautiful, and then went back to whatever they were doing before. But I could not go back. In the church I belong to there is a group of young adults who like to sing selections from a nineteenth-century collection called *The Sacred Harp*, the oldest hymnbook still in use in America. They perform these old hymns with the same precision that other people devote to motets. One of the songs in this collection is a simple, stirring one entitled "Bright Morning Stars Are Rising." When I saw the morning star in the desert sky over San Luis Potosi State, I heard that hymn sung by a fifty-thousand-voice choir, or so it seemed. And it was all for me. . . . The morning star and the song about it fused. The song was the star and the star was the song. . . . No theory that what happened to me was "artificially induced" or psychotic or hallucinatory can erase its mark. "The bright morning stars are rising," as the old hymn puts it, "in my soul."[27]

The remaining examples of hallucinated music derive from two particular sources: the writings of anthropologist Benny Shanon describing experiences under ayahuasca, and those of Jane Dunlop on her experiences with LSD. We begin with Shanon, who explains that "A full-fledged hallucination is one that is not evoked by any stimulus in the real world." Stating that both the anthropological literature and his own informants have described incidents of hallucinating "angelic music performed in the heavens" (characterized as "the most beautiful music they have ever heard"), he relates his own similar experiences in the company of Indigenous practitioners in southern Colombia while on "a large dose of Ayahuasca." In one case, a particular vision inspires him to sing:

> The words that spontaneously came out of my mouth were (in Spanish) *Gloria a Dios* (in English, Glory to God); the melody was being composed as it was being sung. As I was singing, I found myself to be surrounded by an immense choir of angels—I was taking the leading role and they accompanying me. The music was exceedingly beautiful. Every now and then the choir was joined by guest groups that came in, performed, and then left. One such group that especially impressed me was one of Black, very sensuous players. The music they played was very different from that sung by the angels, but it all fitted very well and the ultimate meaning and purpose of it all was one and the same—*Hallelujah*, that is, the singing of God's praises.[28]

Shanon explains that sometimes "music itself can be the theme of one's visions," and describes that on some occasions "my visions were associated with new comprehensions of specific musical compositions and with insights regarding the phenomenon of music, the relationship between music and the human psyche, and the process of musical creation." Here he describes, like a beautiful dream, one such music-themed vision:

> High above, in a superior realm, immersed in nebulous transparency, subtle energy was vibrating. It was fresh, delicate, pristine. Carried along the waves the energy was creating and in perfect tune to its movement and rhythm, a fair maiden (now as I am writing this, I think of the woman in Botticelli's *Primavera*) was circling round and round. She was clad in very fine chiffon and her smooth, gentle movements flowed with delightful calm. She was floating in thin air, her feet bare, and her arms spread in an open, yet not too wide, inviting embrace. It all exhibited perfect serenity, deep self-assurance, and gay benevolence. The fine waves of energy washed over the woman, and like pearls of sparkling dew they scintillated with mellow pastels of celestial light blue and faint pink and the whitish green of buds that are just about to bloom. Through her dance the energy magnified and relayed ahead further and further. Like rain, it showered down and watered all creation. As they

passed, the undulations gained ever more substance and, lo and behold, turned into music. It was music so sublime that no mortal could hear. By now, I realized, they had well-defined shape and form, so that they were so less abstract than the primordial energy from which they had originated. Yet, surely, they were still more abstract than pictures, more abstract than any sign or expression, more abstract than any word would be. This is, I comprehended, why music can exercise this unique, enchanting [*encantamento* (enchantment), *canto* (song), *cantare* (sing), I associated in Portuguese] power that it has on the human psyche. Down there on Earth, I knew, there were men and women and children who, unbeknownst to themselves, were drawing their hearts, like the heads of flowers toward the sun, so that they could be nourished and lovingly nurtured by the music of the spheres.[29]

Shanon introduces a particular type of musical hallucination that he terms "hearing-as," where one sound is subjectively transformed into another, the original sound and its transformation being either musical or non-musical. In one case a far-off motorcycle "sounded as if a great, ill-comprehended, cataclysmic event was approaching." In another, which he describes as "the auditory episode that puzzled me most," clarinet music played by a native (Brazilian) participant in an ayahuasca session entered Shanon's awareness as perfectly executed "traditional Jewish Hassidic melodies."[30]

Our next prodigious experiencer of music hallucinations under psychedelics was the prominent American nutritionist and author Adelle Davis (1904–1974), writing under the pseudonym Jane Dunlop. Ms. Dunlop produced one of the first published books on LSD (in 1961), a chronicle of a series of LSD trips taken under the auspices of psychiatrist Oscar Janiger and clinical psychologist Robert S. Davidson. Her book, *Exploring Inner Space: Personal Experiences under LSD-25*, consists of narratives extraordinary for their sheer volume of descriptive detail. She articulates, with literary flair, densely visionary, deeply mystical inner journeys. Of that work, Myron Stolaroff wrote several decades later, "More beautifully written and profound descriptions of remarkable LSD experiences probably don't exist."[31]

Dunlop's psychedelic narratives are notable for repeated instances of music arising independently within the context of fantastic visionary tableaus. As she describes it, "With each vision I heard exquisite music. Familiar symphonies, songs, and hymns, far surpassing their actual beauty, were intermingled with magnificent music which my brain composed with amazing spontaneity." Out of numerous possibilities, I reproduce here five passages from her book, chosen for their explicit attention to the role of music and music-related visions. I've provided each with a brief title, either my own or one drawn from the author's lyrical text:

"Only a snowflake could have ears sensitive enough to hear this captivating delicacy of sound"

Then, with no sensation of cold, I watched huge snowflakes falling, their movements like those of a gently waving curtain. Next I became a snowflake and at the same time viewed, as if under a microscope, my intricate symmetrical beauty set with glittering diamonds. As this snowflake I felt the intense aliveness, joyousness, boundless energy, and . . . many other glad emotions . . . With other snowflakes of various exquisitely delicate designs, each flake sparkling with ever-changing iridescence, I danced in golden sunlight to the alluring rhythm of a symphony of the snows. This music, slightly suggestive of Tchaikovsky's Waltz of the Flowers [from The Nutcracker], if played softly, seemed so lovely I felt it could not be surpassed in beauty. "Only a snowflake could have ears sensitive enough to hear this captivating delicacy of sound," I thought, awed by the wealth of both visual and auditory delights.[32]

In the realm of music fairies

Soon I was back under the drug. This time I became part of a golden autumn afternoon, the sky so clear that I was lifted into it, seemingly by beauty itself. Balmy Indian-summer breezes blew me far above trees in gaudy dress. All about me were fairies of milkweed seeds, their fragile silken wings delicately lit from within. The fairies, their slender arms and legs moving with infinite grace, seemed to toe-dance on miniature feet covered with pointed slippers glistening with jewels. I had been so fascinated by watching them that I had not at first realized that I too was a fairy. The discovery of my tiny body, my lovely opalescent wings, and my graceful movements caused an excess of joy to penetrate every cell of my actual self. With a combination of dancing, flying, and floating, each movement ecstasy translated into rhythm, we went ceaselessly upward to dainty pastel clouds which we used as seats. Then in our hands there materialized tiny golden flutes, lyres, harps, and mandolin-like instruments inlaid with precious stones. Together we made music such as, I suspect, even angels have never heard. The total beauty was so profound that it changed into pain, and I sobbed, bursting with happiness and yet feeling I could stand no more.[33]

"As both music and light, I danced joyously"

As soon as I was comfortable on the couch once more, I became in quick succession a golden harp and then a violin, each instrument being played by unseen hands; many woodwinds blown by unknown lips; and a great ray of sunlight which broke into the colors of the spectrum. The gay, happy music of the instruments became shifting, brilliant lights and colors, and the spectrum became music of great purity and delight. As both music and light, I danced joyously to rhythms identical to those of the forms of life I had already experienced.[34]

A cascade of musical visions

I became the spirit of music, another aspect of God and my soul, which filled me anew with reverence and all-encompassing love. I danced weightlessly in midair while before me appeared a hundred or more visions: symphony orchestras playing in bowls and concert halls; nude African natives beating strange-shaped drums in small clearings in dense jungles; congregations singing hymns in churches large and small; warm-hearted Hawaiians leisurely strumming ukuleles; devout monks chanting in the predawn darkness of chilled chapels; West Indian Negroes shaking gourds and joyously clanging tops of carefully reshaped oil drums; a great choir praising God with the Hallelujah Chorus; family groups gathered around living-room pianos; muffled and mittened children caroling Christmas joys;

cowpunchers, boy- and girl-scout troops, and camping parties of many varieties encircling bonfires; and lastly an orchestra of crickets amid wildernesses of stems of grasses, grains, and weeds, singing through lazy afternoons, balmy twilights, and star-filled nights. With each vision I heard exquisite music. Familiar symphonies, songs, and hymns, far surpassing their actual beauty, were intermingled with magnificent music which my brain composed with amazing spontaneity.[35]

In the mystic hall of music

There came a feeling of floating in rapidly moving water as the drug again took possession of me. This time I swirled into a cavern of phosphorescent stones which glowed with warm yet striking brilliance. Many smaller chambers opened from the main one, partly concealed by the many narrow columns of fused stalactites and stalagmites, each phosphorescent like the whole. The pool by which I had entered twisted and eddied, splashed into a broad waterfall which spread into a thin sheet over bright stones, and bubbled and foamed as it landed, creating a symphony of its own and causing luminous colors to flicker, deepening and brightening to the rhythm of its making. The exquisitely lighted walls were glassy smooth from being caressed by the musical flowing of waters which had formed them; and I knew this cavern symbolized the hall of music which was a part both of God and of the soul of every person.[36]

These extraordinary narratives concerning interior worlds of vision and music are only one element in a work that traverses a multiplicity of inner landscapes and powerful emotions, both heavenly and hellish, many being of a deeply spiritual and religious nature. The author concludes her book with a chapter she calls "Aftermaths and Rewards," in which she describes with clarity of detail, but with lingering poetic flavor, how her LSD experiences changed her life. Its importance lies in its deeply honest, probing insight into her own personality and the transformations it underwent after her several LSD sessions:

Within a week after my first sojourn into other worlds I noticed that I seemed to have two personalities: a pre-LSD personality in which my own feelings stayed dominant and to which I reverted under stress; and a post-LSD personality characterized by serenity, tolerance, optimism, and a forgetfulness of self. When the latter personality was uppermost, I could at times sense the feelings of others with an amazingly accurate intuition. The two personalities became more evident with each experience, but after a period of months they apparently became amalgamated and were no longer separately recognizable.[37]

Dunlap describes at length what we now call post-trip "integration." In this process she was guided not, however, by a credentialed or self-designated integration counselor or therapist (currently a professional growth industry), but by simply living her life with deep introspection, self-awareness, and a continuing quest for spiritual meaning in life—a quest often suggestive of a movement toward a kind of cosmic consciousness.

8

Music in Psychedelic Psychotherapy

Early Research in Psychedelics

The scientific study of psychedelics and their use in psychotherapy has its origins in the nineteenth century and has a long and complex history.[1] We might say, however, that the first wave of research in recent memory lasted roughly from the early 1950s through the mid- to late 1960s, at which time the US government called a halt to nearly all such research. This early wave of scientific and psychoanalytic interest in psychedelics involved scientists, psychiatrists and psychologists attached to various medical and academic institutions and holding widely divergent views concerning the essential characteristics of these substances and their usefulness as psychotherapeutic aids. These early researchers engaged in a wide variety of therapeutic practices and experimentation, with their motives ranging from a sincere desire to alleviate human suffering to experimentation involving reckless dosing of adults, children, and animals to satisfy personal curiosity and keep publications going out and grants coming in.[2]

In going through some of the early published volumes of scientific and psychotherapeutic studies, one is struck by several things. Early researchers, for example, expressed amazement about the psychotherapeutic successes being reported with patients. Many shared the sense that a super-drug had been discovered that worked virtual magic with alcoholics, schizophrenics, depressives, and other patient populations. Another response was the surprised and enthusiastic reactions of psychiatrists themselves who had self-administered a psychedelic (usually LSD) and had had, shall we say, their minds blown. There was also admitted confusion about the nature of the substances themselves: how and why they worked (neurologically or psychologically) and what kinds of language might be used to describe their effects. Finally, one discovers the undeniable cruelty, on the part of some researchers, with which these drugs were experimentally administered to animals and their seemingly reckless use with children as young as five.

One early volume that reports some of these findings is *The Use of LSD in Psychotherapy*. Edited by Dr. Harold A. Abramson and published in 1960, it was based on a conference held the previous year in Princeton, New Jersey. During an open discussion initiating the conference, Dr. Mortimer A. Hartman of the Psychiatric Institute of Beverly Hills reports:

> About a year and a half ago, Dr. Wesley told me that Dr. Cohen and Dr. Eisner had achieved some spectacular results with a hallucinating agent called LSD, and I joined Dr. Wesley in some research on it. When I took the drug myself, I found that I was suffering from the delusion that I had been psychoanalyzed. I had spent seven and a half years on the couch and over $20,000, and so I thought I had been psychoanalyzed. But a few sessions with LSD convinced me otherwise.[3]

Dr. Sidney Cohen (cited above) of the Neuropsychiatric Hospital, Veterans Administration Center in Los Angeles, briefly mentions his own first experience with LSD and admits the futility of understanding the psychedelic phenomenon using the standard tools of psychiatry:

> My first subject was myself, and I was taken by surprise. This was no confused, disoriented delirium, but something quite different. Just what it was, I could not say. But since then, our efforts toward understanding and defining this remarkable experience have been futile. Though we have been using the available measuring instruments, the check lists, the performance tests, the psychological batteries, and so forth, the core of the LSD situation remains in the dark, quite untouched by our activities.[4]

That's an extraordinary admission coming from a contemporary leading "expert" in the field. Clearly, then, these early researchers were working more or less in the dark, faced with a new and quite mysterious phenomenon that resisted their standard armamentarium of empiric tools.

Towards the end of the same volume, after endless discussions—a babel of theories, speculations, agreements, disagreements, gentle put-downs, and retorts—the doctor representing the institutional body sponsoring the conference, Frank Fremont-Smith of the Josiah Macy Jr. Foundation, interjects this frankly pessimistic assessment:

> The striking feature of the Conference so far is that we have not communicated. The verbal image that was good for one of us was not good for eight-tenths of the others. This has happened again and again in this Conference, and is perhaps one of the most worth-while things which has happened to us, if we see that we really aren't yet able to communicate really adequately with each other about the problems under discussion. We really aren't successful in communicating, we mesh only occasionally. Every once in a while, two people agree, and there is a flash of communication between them.[5]

One can appreciate the unexpected honesty in that statement. Seconding and broadening this view to encompass the psychiatric profession as a whole, we have psychedelic pioneer Dr. Humphrey Osmond (coiner of the term "psychedelic"), not a participant in this particular conference but in many others, stating (with a co-author) the following:

> Any intelligent and critical person allowed to overhear conferences in most psychiatric centers, in this or other countries today, would be profoundly puzzled, not merely by the differences of opinion but by the lack of common ground among the discussants. Conversations can be heard which strongly resemble the Mad Hatter's tea party, and even when clearcut differences of opinion occur which might result in rational confrontation and serious debate, the contestants are likely, after a few rhetorical statements, to ride off in all directions.[6]

Animal Experimentation

Besides remarkable results with patients, mind-blown psychiatrists, and various well-funded babels and Mad Hatter affairs, early researchers experimented with the effects of psychedelics on animals. At the same conference mentioned earlier, researcher Dr. Sidney Malitz of the Department of Experimental Psychiatry, New York State Psychiatric Institute, presented a film made by his co-researcher, Dr. Leon Roizin, chief of Neuropathology at the same institution. The lights go off, the film switches on, and the attendees are treated to the spectacle of two monkeys sharing a cage who had been receiving daily subcutaneous injections of LSD over a period of time. They were first given a low dose, working up to admittedly "enormous" doses: based on the monkeys' differential relative weight, the doses were equivalent in human terms to 9,800 and 16,800 micrograms. "Enormous" is a timid description. Narrating, Malitz explains:

> These animals seem to reach out for things that aren't there. They hurt themselves by banging into the side of the cage, which they ordinarily do not do. Their proprioception seems impaired. They jump as if the cage were too small or too big, and they misjudge the distance of the cage walls. They don't know what is going on; they hurt themselves and fall to the bottom of the cage as if their perception were distorted. . . . They are quite sluggish and do not jump about the cage as they did before. . . . Of course, the ordinary macaque will bite someone putting his hand in the cage. They are quite vicious animals.[7]

Vicious indeed. Malitz continues, "By the way, these animals are still alive. This experiment has been repeated many times. They will be sacrificed sometime in the near future and their brains will be examined." One has to wonder what of possible value these respected men of science found in the dissected brains of these tormented, sacrificial creatures. Responding to this film, Dr. Sidney Cohen properly points out that "these dosages are so far out of line with human LSD levels that they may have no application whatsoever" and that the whole enterprise "seems a bit dubious."[8] Someone else changes the subject.

Dosing Children

At the same conference, psychologist Betty Eisner asks Dr. T. T. Peck Jr. of the Psychiatric and Public Health Departments, San Jacinto Memorial Hospital in Baytown, Texas, if he's given LSD to children. Yes, indeed he has: "Age 5, 7, 9, 11, and 14." He describes the case of a "completely rebellious" five-year-old:

> The 5-year-old girl was a real behavior problem, completely rebellious about everything. Knowing her background I wouldn't blame her. We gave her about 40 [micrograms] over a 1 1/5-hour period, and she became completely uninhibited. It was a typical schizophrenic reaction. Afterward, she was very happy. The only untoward reaction was a very slight tremor and an over-elation, to some extent. But, for 2 weeks, she was just a perfect child. Of course, she went back into the same environment and continued much the same pattern. But then we showed the parents where they were really planting the seeds of her difficulties in her. By changing the environment, we solved the problem.[9]

We must, I suppose, take him at his word that he "solved the problem." Another psychiatrist, Robert C. Murphy Jr. of Waverly, Pennsylvania, offers that he, too, had great success with a child, an eight-year-old girl. She was a bed-wetter with "deep sexual conflicts" who was administered doses up to 300 micrograms—"regularly, once a week":

> She had a long-standing extremely chronic, and extremely resistive character disorder. She was an enuretic child [wet her bed] with deep sexual conflicts, whom I had had in unsuccessful psychotherapy for a year before she started LSD. I was getting absolutely nowhere with her. In treatment, she worked up to 300 [micrograms] and took them regularly, once a week. . . . There was a very thoroughgoing change in the child. . . . Her [bed wetting] which had been with her every day for several years, stopped after the second session, *a very violent one, in which she became disoriented and called continually for her mother* [emphasis added]. But then she went on to a great deal of characterological change [on which the doctor elaborates]. . . . Like the adults who have done well in treatment, she participated in every decision to increase her dosage, and it was she who decided when she was through.[10]

One is left to ponder what unspoken trauma lay behind this case, as well as try to imagine the girl's nightmarish ordeal during therapy. The odd claim that an eight-year-old patient was consulted on critical decisions regarding dosage (topping out at 300 micrograms, a very considerable dose, administered weekly!) and on when to terminate treatment is particularly baffling. The self-serving, even boastful claims of success made by these psychiatrists raises its own questions, to say the least.

Some Dissenters to the Psychiatric/Psychological Model

Despite these disturbing examples of early abuses (how common I do not know), a wide variety of psychedelic therapists have reported, through several decades, the positive benefits of using psychedelics, along with music, in their therapeutic practices. Before delving into that subject, however, it will be helpful to place it in the broader context of discussion and debate concerning the dominant role that psychiatry and psychology have always assumed in the study of psychedelics. We'll do that by hearing from a few authors who, while acknowledging the value of psychotherapeutic applications, have questioned the historical dominance, even hegemony, of psychology and medical psychiatry over the field—viewing it either as harmfully reductionistic or simply as a limited approach. Dr. Erika Dyck, who has written much on the history of psychedelic psychotherapy, describes the divisions that arose as early researchers tried to define the scope and purpose of their work, divisions that often "emerged along scientific versus spiritual lines":

> Efforts to consolidate a psychedelic program . . . exposed significant differences in how various people prioritized the research objectives. . . . Members of the wider psychedelic community expressed conflicting views on the importance of these drugs for developing deeper philosophical, religious, scientific, or medical insights. As the experiments continued, divisions emerged along scientific versus spiritual lines. [Pioneer Al] Hubbard summarized his feelings regarding this split: "My regard for science, as an end within itself, is diminishing as time goes on . . . when the thing I want with all of my being, is something that lives far outside and out of reach of empirical manipulation." Hubbard was not alone in feeling that the psychedelic experience defied scientific explanations and that, in fact, the scientific vocabulary was insufficient for describing the kinds of insights that one might achieve.[11]

The author of *Psychedelia—An Ancient Culture, A Modern Way of Life* offers this insightful critique on the reductionistic impulses of psychology, as well as of its inability to fully encompass an experience that manifests phenomena that exceed the intellectual and philosophical limits of the discipline:

> Much of what has been written and said about the psychedelic experience over the past century has been surprisingly narrow in scope. Enthusiasts have been so bowled over by their early journeys into Innerspace that they've rushed to apply the first paradigm that seemed to fit. Not infrequently, this paradigm has been psychotherapeutic. The use of LSD and mescaline as useful adjuncts to analysis notwithstanding, an important reason for this is simply that so many of the early experimenters were psychologists by profession. In the otherworldly swirl of symbols and emotion and memory, they reached for a framework that seemed to offer stability; i.e.: their branch training. But Psychedelia blows past the boundaries of psychology into domains never accounted for in the field. The psycho-dynamic frame is much too small; it may even seem ridiculous. . . .
>
> The direct experience of the otherworldly that the major psychedelics produce is a singular event, which cannot be explained or incorporated by anything else. It should not be metaphorized in any serious context, but should be approached with a clean mental slate, as objectively and as respectfully as an artifact from another planet.[12]

The authors of *The Varieties of Psychedelic Experience* argue for a substantially wider use of psychedelics beyond medicine, psychiatry, and psychotherapy:

> Even the [psychologically based] materials already presented should suggest that the psychedelic drugs have legitimate uses beyond the strictly medical, or still more limited experimental psychiatric and psychotherapeutic, ones to which some persons would restrict them. Support for a wider use has come from prominent individuals in a variety of fields who believe that psychedelic research will be of great value in such diverse areas as philosophy, parapsychology and the creative arts, and in the study of literature, mythology, anthropology, comparative religion, and still other fields. . . . Even so, the effort to close off non-medical research has been very largely successful.[13]

Another dissent against the excessive psychologizing of the psychedelic experience is offered by Alan Watts. He describes his own manner of tripping, which appears to have been based on a kind of heightened form of introspection—psychedelically catalyzed thought experiments, if you will. As he described it, he would choose a theme for contemplation "and then allow my heightened perception to elucidate the theme in terms of certain works of art or music" (as well as natural objects, religious and mythological archetypes, etc.). "From these reflections there arise intuitive insights of astonishing clarity," which he would write down and ponder over during the following days and weeks. He concludes: "The drugs appear to give an enormous impetus to the creative intuition, and thus to be of more value for constructive invention and research than for psychotherapy in the ordinary sense of "adjusting" the disturbed personality. Their best sphere of use is not the mental hospital but the studio and the laboratory, or the institute of advanced studies."[14]

As a final example, speaking at a psychedelic-themed conference in 1994, Ram Dass (Dr. Richard Alpert), while acknowledging their therapeutic value, emphasized psychedelics' more fundamental power to deconstruct cultural conditioning and revive a kind of existential innocence: "It's obvious that psychedelics, properly used, have a behavior-change psychotherapeutic value. But from my point of view, that is all underusing the vehicle. The potential of the vehicle is sacramentally to take you out of the cultural constructs [of] which you are part of a conspiracy in maintaining and giving you a chance to experience once again your innocence."[15]

Enlightened Views among Some Psychedelic Pioneers

Long before the first hippie sprouted from a garden bearing a flower and a beatific grin, psychologists and others were, as we've been seeing, trying to figure out what to do with LSD. Ample evidence of that interest is recorded in the voluminous proceedings of a 1965 conference published in 1967 titled *The Use of LSD in Psychotherapy and Alcoholism*.[16] More than a few of its contributors, both scientists and non-scientists, were humanistically oriented intellectuals, serious thinkers who seemed genuinely impressed by the strange powers of this new drug to reveal the inner workings of consciousness. Some were even hopeful that it might not only ease human suffering but also provide important philosophical and even metaphysical insights. In his contribution to the volume, Abram Hoffer, MD, quotes from an earlier published article by fellow conference attendee Dr. Humphrey Osmond where he wrote:

> Whether we employ [the psychedelics] for good or ill, whether we use them with skill and deftness or with blundering ineptitude, depends not a little on the courage, intelligence and humanity of many of us working in the field today. I believe that the psychedelics provide a chance, perhaps only a slender one, for *Homo faber*, the cunning, ruthless, foolhardy, pleasure-greedy toolmaker, to emerge into that other creature, whose presence we have so rashly presumed, *Homo sapiens*, the wise, the understanding, the compassionate . . . Surely we must seize the chance.[17]

Betty Grover Eisner, PhD, in her contribution "The Importance of the Non-Verbal," speaks of increased access to "a new dimension in consciousness":

> We are in the pre-dawn of knowledge about the human mind and the universe. Because communication of knowledge occurs through the verbal, we must not make the mistake of assuming that it occurs because of the verbal. Nor are perception, knowledge—and wisdom—limited to the vehicle of the six senses. It appears that we are on the verge of a new dimension in consciousness—probably several dimensions. It is possible that psychopharmacology used in conjunction with therapy is one of the media by which the parameters of these new dimensions may be surveyed.[18]

In "Dimensions in Psychotherapy," G. W. Arendsen Hein, MD, invokes the prominent existential/humanistic psychotherapist Dr. Victor Frankl (author of *Man's Search for Meaning*, *The Will to Meaning*, etc.), who here questions the capacity of rationality to satisfy the human hunger for the spiritual: "Is man of the 20th century now beginning to discover, that in spite of his rationalistic and technical achievements, these sources prove to be inadequate to meet his deeper spiritual needs; that he only finds peace and harmony when he transcends the ego-boundaries and becomes aware that the most elementary source of power, love, etc., is not in himself but in his oneness with God's universe?"[19] Hein comments on the relevance of LSD to these concerns, offering in effect a brief but compelling manifesto for a spiritually informed approach to psychedelic psychotherapy. He begins, provocatively, by asking, "Have not most of us been living in a state of complete unawareness of our roots in the transcendental, until we saw this clearly under the influence of LSD? We might call this underdeveloped area our cosmic or universal unconscious." He continues:

> There is the fourth dimension of human existence, a divine reality beyond time and space, beyond life and death, beyond thou and I, beyond all the antagonisms that puzzle the human mind, where man discovers the origin of his true self, his essential being. There he finds joy, faith, love, strength—whatever he needs, independent of the worldly position of his ego. When the claims of the ego are given up, man becomes enlightened and open to his participation in greater life. This kind of experience also provides the patient with a totally different outlook and attitude toward himself and life in general. . . . The true self of the human being is not really affected by the neurotic distortions in the super-structure, although the true self may be imprisoned and its creativity tied up.
>
> A further consequence of this concept of man is that we psychotherapists, not knowing the deeper core of man's personality or his ultimate destiny, cannot pretend to help him basically in this sense. Nevertheless we assist him to function better in his role and discover the true self which becomes visible when the neurotic disguise is removed. Our medical task is then to prepare him to the extent that he becomes aware of the deeper longings of his true self and that a serious wish may emerge to remove the obstacles for a breakthrough towards greater life.[20]

It is this more than occasional openness to deep philosophical, moral, and existential questions that surprised me as I went through this very interesting collection of papers. We should note, however, that these conference participants were not the first scientists to take seriously the potential human benefits of psychoactive drugs. In his book *Emperors of Dreams: Drugs in the Nineteenth Century*, author Mike Jay characterizes the attitudes and motivations of that century's scientific explorers of artificially induced exceptional states:

> From Humphry Davy's first nitrous oxide revelation to Havelock Ellis' New Artificial Paradise a century later, the majority of the nineteenth century's recorded drug experimenters felt they were engaged in a project with its roots essentially in the Enlightenment: a scientific mapping of the unexplored realms of the mind whose future outcome would be a more highly evolved understanding of what it means to be human, a broadening of control over our moods, our abilities and ultimately our mental health.

Jay continues: "Most of them would have been astonished to discover that the twentieth century would be characterized by an intense, often fanatical effort to banish these new dimensions of mind from the civilized consensus, and to insist that the use of drugs belongs not to humanity's future but to its primitive and atavistic past."[21] While many mental-health professionals have lent their professional credibility to these kinds of reactionary views and policies, many others, as we've been seeing, have allowed their humane instincts and genuine scientific inquisitiveness to guide their actions. We'll hear from more of those now, with particular regard to their use of and attitudes about music in their psychedelic-assisted psychotherapeutic practices.

Music in Psychedelic Therapy

We begin with a bit of historical background offered by psychedelic pioneer William A. Richards. He cites his mentor, German psychiatrist Hanscarl Leuner, as the first to combine music and psychedelics:

> Hanscarl Leuner, who developed a psychotherapeutic technique known as Guided Affective Imagery, or GAI . . . may be credited as being the first to combine imagery with music and then to combine both with the use of entheogens. His techniques, combined with the experiences of others who employed music in the early days of psychedelic research in Canada, the United States, and Europe, were further refined and systematized by

> Helen Lindquist Bonny, a music therapist at the Maryland
> Psychiatric Research Center.[22]

Having "experimented with the use of music in more than six hundred drug sessions during a period of several years" at MPRC, Helen Bonny and co-author Walter Pahnke describe how music had proven to be "a very effective stimulus and complement to drug action": "Music complements the therapeutic objectives in five interrelated ways: 1) by helping the patient relinquish usual controls and enter more fully into her inner world of experience; 2) by facilitating the release of intense emotionality; 3) by contributing toward a peak experience; 4) by providing continuity in [the midst of] an experience of timelessness; 5) by directing and structuring the experience."[23] The authors explain how LSD "greatly amplifies" music's innate ability to uncover unconscious materials and release emotion:

> [Music] opens the doors to the unfolding contents of the unconscious. . . . A theory called "depth provocation" explains that "music, because of its abstract nature detours the ego and intellectual controls and, contacting the lower centers directly, stirs up latent conflicts and emotions which may be expressed and re-enacted through music." . . . This ability of music to release emotion is greatly amplified by the use of a psychedelic drug, which allows the listener to project his personal experiences and visual fantasies into the unfolding experience. The evoked material may become so meaningful that the patient may exclaim, "I have heard the music before but never has it spoken so directly to me, and to my needs."[24]

Stanislav Grof, also active at MPRC for many years, affirms Bonny and Pahnke's views: "We used music systematically . . . and have learned much about its extraordinary potential for psychotherapy. . . . It mobilizes emotions associated with repressed memories, brings them to the surface, and facilitates their expression. It helps to open the door into the unconscious, intensifies and deepens the therapeutic process, and provides a meaningful context for the experience."[25] Elaborating on "context," Grof introduces his oft-cited analogy of music serving as a "carrier-wave" during a psychedelic session: "[This] continuous flow of music creates a carrier wave that helps the subject move through difficult experiences and impasses, overcome psychological defenses, surrender, and let go."[26] Music thus "provides a meaningful structure for the experience . . . a sense of continuity and connection in the course of various unusual states of consciousness."[27]

Clinical psychologist Betty Grover Eisner discusses how in psychedelic therapy, music "potentiates" the drug, helps move the patient away from the verbal toward emotional and symbolic levels of consciousness, and helps the patient work through difficult areas:

> From our very first experiences with LSD, it became apparent that subjects or patients were able to go more deeply into the drug and to experience insights more integratively when there was no pressure on them to translate the experiences immediately into words. . . .
>
> Music is an indispensable aid in deepening the drug effect—taking the experience out of the intellectual and into the feeling area. . . . Music is used routinely in all our drug sessions to potentiate the drug and move the patient easily and pleasantly away from the verbal toward emotional and symbolic levels of consciousness. . . . Music will undoubtedly come into its own as one of the important aids in psychotherapy as we move from intuitive hunches, gleaned from empirical observation, toward more precision of usage.[28]

Aside from using music during one-on-one psychotherapeutic sessions, other pioneering psychedelic therapists—some working "underground"—have used music in guiding both individual and group sessions, whether with patients or with people simply seeking personal growth. Pioneer therapist Myron J. Stolaroff describes his use of music in these kinds of settings:

> The first several hours are spent encouraging the subject to search deeply within her/himself. This is facilitated by having the subject lie down and put on a good pair of stereo headphones, then covering his/her face with a velvet cloth. The first few hours are spent listening to music, which greatly encourages the unfolding and focusing of the experience. The beauty and wonder of music as experienced under the sacrament eases any encounter with unpleasant material and is often in itself a source of extreme enjoyment and even amazement.[29]

Here, Stolaroff interviews fellow pioneer "Jacob" (Dr. Leo Zeff), who, in his characteristically informal, colloquial manner, describes his own arrangements for music listening in group sessions:

> JACOB: We all gather in the living room [and have] our dropping ceremony. . . . After everybody's dropped, they wander around, they're quiet. We ask them to still be quiet, until they feel themselves starting to turn on. . . . When they start to turn on, they go to their pads, lie down, put the eyeshades on and the earphones on and there's music playing already. They just lay there until they turn on.
>
> MYRON: All the time they're really in it, they're laying there listening to music?
>
> JACOB: Right. . . . [At the end of the day] the music continues so they can listen to it if they want to, until they're ready to go to bed.[30]

Elsewhere in the interview he elaborates:

> JACOB: I mention to them, "Look, sometimes you get real turned on by a piece of music and it's a great experience and it ends and you're kind of disappointed. All you have to do is say, 'Play it again,' and I'll play it again for you. You go right back out again." I tell them that *music is the vehicle that takes you to all the different places you go on your trip* [emphasis added] . . .
>
> MYRON: Isn't silence the vehicle sometimes?
>
> JACOB: Oh yeah. I say, "If you ever want to be quiet, have silence, let me know." Most of the time they want the music. Sometimes I'll just not play anything for a while but in just a little bit they'll say, "The music's off." You've never heard music in your life . . . until you've heard it on the trip. Which is true, everybody knows who's had that. I tell them, "Anytime I'm playing a piece of music that's not consonant with where you are, that's bothering you or you don't like it, just say, 'Change the music,' and I will." Once in a while that

happens. Most of the time with the kind of music I have they dig it all the way through.[31]

Underscoring "Jacob"'s recommendation about wearing eyeshades while absorbed in music, Jim Fadiman advises:

> Listening to music with closed eyes increases its value and its potential impact. An eyeshade, an eye pillow, or a folded washcloth or scarf makes it easier for the music to be experienced internally. There are valuable facets of consciousness to enter with the eyes open or closed, but many guides recommend that a voyager spend most of the time, especially during the period of intensely heightened awareness, with closed eyes. As one guide said, "It's amazing how much one can 'see' with eyes closed."[32]

Stan Grof likewise emphasizes the importance, particularly in high-dose sessions, of keeping the experience within the internal realm by keeping the eyes closed: "In the higher dosage range [250–500 mcg], it is important to keep the session internalized; this makes it possible to see and understand what is emerging from the unconscious and what we are dealing with. Leaving the eyes open and interacting with the environment in high-dose LSD sessions is dangerous and unproductive. It confuses and mixes the inner and outer and makes self-exploration impossible."[33]

General Guidelines in the Choice of Music

Helen Bonny and Walter Pahnke emphasize that the therapist should be sensitive in choosing music that is responsive to the evolving interior state of the experiencer:

> The extreme vulnerability of this state requires a sensitive and responsible use of the medium. The therapist chooses the recordings which will be played at various phases of the drug action because he has, through repeated experience, found that some selections are much more effective than others. His choice is further determined by the reaction of the patient to the evolving session material. At critical times during a session

the therapist may variously use the music to communicate a reassurance, to deepen an experience, or to lead the patient into an area of therapeutic confrontation.[34]

Stanislav Grof concurs: "Each therapeutic team develops, after a certain time, a list of its favorite pieces for various phases of LSD sessions and for certain specific situations. The basic rule is to respond sensitively to the phase, intensity and content of the experience, rather than to try to impose a specific pattern on it. Preference should be given to music of high artistic quality, but little concrete content."[35] Expanding on the importance of choosing music of "high artistic quality," Bonny points out how extraordinarily, sensitively attuned to music the psychedelic client may be, suggesting that the guide, or whoever may choose the music, should ideally possess some degree of musical sophistication:

> Good recorded or live music should be chosen, with an effort to present the best available performance of the selected composition. Attention should be given to the musical interpretation of the artist and to his sincerity of thought. A frequent patient comment on a poor recording is that "the musician did not believe in what he was singing or playing," which is indicative of the hypersensitivity to the quality of stimuli that a patient exhibits in an altered state of consciousness.[36]

Complicating the matter of music choice, Grof makes a critically important point concerning the very subjective nature of music reception during a trip (a subject which I explore in more detail in chapter 9), indicating the challenge involved in predicting the effect that any particular piece of music may have on a listener:

> If the subject is in an extremely difficult emotional place, any music, no matter how inspired and ethereal, will be distorted and may sound like a dirge. Conversely, during a deep positive experience just about any music will be enthusiastically accepted by the subject, who will find it fitting and interesting from some point of view. Only in the medium range somewhere between these two extremes can music effectively shape the experience. Even then, although a certain general atmosphere or emotional tone will be suggested from the outside, the subject

will elaborate it very specifically. The resultant sequences will still be manifestations of the individual's own unconscious, reflect the content of his or her memory banks, and represent a meaningful self-revealing gestalt.[37]

Numerous differing suggestions concerning choices and uses of music in psychedelic therapy are offered in the literature, which should discourage any kind of rigid, programmatic, or dogmatic approach. Personally, my favorite *general* recommendation comes from Walter Pahnke, who favored "smooth, peaceful, and majestic music."[38]

Psychiatrist Claudio Naranjo places special emphasis on relying on personal intuition and spontaneity when choosing music, in this case for group sessions:

> What to say of the opportuneness with which these musical works are offered to the group? Or of the sequence in which they are presented? I would say that in this I have known how to practice a certain art that I never attempted to put into words. . . . On occasions my musical preference of the moment has been induced by the experience of a particular person or, sometimes, by a wish of his or hers, or by a simple wish to say "hello" to him or her, but in general I allow myself to be guided by what I intuit as appropriate to the "group atmosphere," and many times people in the group have told me that the music reached them in the most opportune way for their inner process that could be imagined, as if programmed from an omniscient mind.
>
> I confess myself innocent of such omniscience, but open to the idea that spontaneity can be very wise. . . . It seems to be that a person that teaches from a certain level of inspiration is secretly in touch with what happens without realizing it.[39]

Music for Different Phases of the Psychedelic Session

As in many matters concerning choice and scheduling of music, whether in a therapeutic context or otherwise, different (and conflicting) opinions and approaches have always existed when it comes to (1) differentiating or mapping the progressive phases or stages of a psychedelic session, and (2) assigning different kinds of music to suit each phase (usually determined by the degree of emotional intensity assumed to be characteristic of that phase). I am among those who are wary of rigid rules and programmatic approaches to these matters, for the simple reason that music is a highly subjective experiential phenomenon, especially in psychoactive states. However, to provide the reader at least some historical sense of how this issue has been approached by leading figures in psychedelic psychotherapy, I offer the following brief overview. I've removed references to individual pieces of music, sticking to generalities. (Some specific recommendations in music by these and other individuals can be found in chapter 10, "Is Classical Music Still Relevant?")

The general principle concerning matching trip phases with appropriate music is stated succinctly by Stanislav Grof: "In general, the music chosen reflects the usual experiential trajectory of the psychedelic sessions."[40] Betty Eisner notes: "Al [Hubbard] had found music to be effective in enhancing the action of the drug, which we corroborated personally and with our first subjects. In fact, we found that the type of music and the period when it was played in a session could have a profound effect."[41] One might characterize the variety of trip-mapping models as generally including five stages: (1) early, (2) "building toward peak," (3) peak, (4) descent, and (5) resolution.

For the "early" phase, Grof suggests "quiet, flowing and calming music."[42] Betty Eisner encouraged " 'light' classical music." For Myron Stolaroff, "the initial musical selections are quiet, lyrical compositions that encourage relaxation and sentimentality and convey a sense of mystery."[43] Helen Bonny and Walter Pahnke suggest "for a smooth entry into the experience, music of a quiet but positive and reassuring mood," and add that "when unmistakable drug effects are noted . . . [the patient] is directed to lie down on the couch and given the eyeshades and earphones that will enable him to go more deeply into the powerful stimuli of drug and music."[44]

For the phase sometimes referred to as "building towards peak," Grof recommends "music which has an opening-up and building-up quality."[45] For Betty Eisner, who termed this phase "the deepening and integrative period of the drug action," concertos were ideal since they "[seem] to express and enhance the relationship of the individual to the environment as expressed by the interaction of the soloist with the orchestra."[46] Bonny and Pahnke, who devote more attention to this periodization theme than do anyone else I've come across, suggest:

During this period when the drug effects are increasing and strongly building toward peak intensity, the overwhelming nature of the experience . . . can lead to resistance, fear and an eagerness to escape the deepening effects of the drug . . . but careful selection of music can be a great help in going through to deeper levels of positive emotion. The choice of music as amplifier and stabilizer is crucial. Instrumental and vocal music are often used alternately. Instrumental music can provide underlying support and structure as the patient works through his evolving conflicts and problems. Vocal music often emphasizes human relationships and tends to encourage feelings of closeness and humanness, and, if positively oriented, can establish a mood of reassurance and comfort.[47]

Moving on to the "peak" period of a trip, Stan Grof writes that this stage gives the patient "an opportunity for a major emotional or spiritual breakthrough, depending on the level on which the session is experienced. It seems appropriate at this point to introduce powerful, overwhelming music with a transcendental quality."[48] Stolaroff similarly suggests that "more dramatic music can be introduced."[49] Bonny and Pahnke similarly state that

In the repertoire designated as peak music are certain selections which have been shown by experience to evoke powerful emotions and to aid greatly in facilitating the occurrence of peak experiences if played at the proper time. *If these selections are played at an improper time, the potential effect can be wasted and a negative musical imprint for that particular selection may result* [emphasis added]. The therapist must first determine the psychological state of the patient and then choose a selection that implements the treatment aim.[50]

During the extended period of descent following peak stage, Stan Grof recommends "quiet, relaxing, and flowing music with a timeless quality."[51] Referring to "the latter part of the re-entry phase," Bonny and Pahnke write, "Musical selections of a lighter type are played. The increased awareness of the aesthetic beauty of sound, amplified by the drug, is still in effect. Familiar music now may be greatly enhanced and especially meaningful to the patient."[52] Stolaroff writes, more universally,

"Toward the end of the inward exploring period, and especially if the subject approaches transcendental levels, spiritual music is compelling."[53]

Concerning what I've almost arbitrarily termed the "resolution" of the psychedelic session, Stan Grof writes, "The late hours of the session, when no more therapeutic work has to be done . . . is a period of relaxation and the subject is given the opportunity to determine the nature of the entertainment."[54] William Richards concurs: "It may be noted that, as consciousness is returning to ordinary awareness after intense experiences of a mystical, visionary, or psychodynamic nature, most any style of music can be explored with delight. At this time, one's personal favorite selections may be enjoyed with fresh appreciation."[55] Bonny and Pahnke offer a different approach: "In the post-drug therapeutic hours, the playing of session music which was especially meaningful to the patient can elicit a repetition of affect and may provide an opportunity for a more thorough assay of both problem areas and positive experiences."[56] Humphrey Osmond is an outlier in this area, suggesting: "In the early part of the morning, stirring, exciting music was played; in the mid-morning, mystical, contemplative music; in the afternoon, selections were dramatic and integrative."[57] Though there is some overlap, it is clear that opinions vary involving timeframes and music choices.

Types of Music or Situations to Avoid

Music Containing Intelligible Lyrics

Whether coming from a lone voice or a large choir, lyrics carry "concrete content": specific thoughts, ideas, or sentiments that may interrupt the free flow of nonconceptual awareness, drawing one's attention back into the cerebral realm of words and concepts. The exception, of course, is words sung in an unfamiliar language, wherein the human voice remains a harmless abstraction or, better, becomes an additional layer of expressive sound. This advice is common in the psychedelic literature. Rick Strassman writes, "Music with understandable lyrics can sometimes be distracting or can constrain the experience. Instrumental music or world music with lyrics that are unintelligible may allow for more fluidity in reaction to it.[58] Bonny and Pahnke make the same point with regard to periods of emotional intensity: "The use of English words with music may not be advisable during periods of intensity and emotional turbulence, as it invites the activity of the rational mind and intellectualization at the expense of unfolding intuitive experience. . . . As the human voice itself can be very effective in periods of turbulence, music sung in an unfamiliar language is a useful substitute."[59]

Music with Overly Specific Associations

This is to be taken in a rather limited, conditional sense. Any and all music may invoke mental associations based on memory, unconscious material, or the play of imagination. And obviously a piece of music might carry particular associations for one person but not another. Grof presents two examples: (1) widely known pieces of music that produce a clichéd response and (2) music that may carry, for any particular person, strongly negative associations:

> It is preferable to avoid pieces with which clients have specific intellectual associations. Thus, the beginning of Beethoven's Fifth Symphony in C minor is usually associated with the imminence of a fateful event (Symphony of Destiny); the use of the wedding marches from Wagner's *Lohengrin* or Mendelssohn's *A Midsummer Night's Dream* suggest a nuptial atmosphere; and Bizet's *Carmen* would evoke through a similar mechanism the theme of a bull-fight. In Czech subjects, Liszt's *Les Preludes* tends to bring memories of the war, because it was used by Nazi propagandists as an introduction to the daily news broadcasted on street loudspeakers.[60]

Another therapist reported that "if one female client of mine heard solemn religious music, she had a memory of being sexually assaulted by a man of the cloth, triggering a massive outburst of rage."[61]

Music That Is "Jarring, Dissonant, and Anxiety-provoking"

Bonny and Pahnke note that "extremely discordant music . . . can unduly frighten the patient and throw him into a state of confusion or panic."[62] This should be fairly obvious, but I've come across quite a few examples of classical pieces that are recommended for the so-called "building up" or "peak" periods of a trip—music described, for example, as "powerful and emotionally highly evocative"—that, while not being overtly "discordant" or "dissonant," may still be overpowering for some listeners. Even under "normal" circumstances, loud or emotionally intense music may be experienced by sensitive listeners as aggressive, hyper-masculine, or dominating, the effect of which may be to frighten, intimidate, or overwhelm. Such forceful music may sometimes be appropriate in non-psychedelic holistic therapies such as Holotropic Breathwork, but may be destabilizing, even frightening, for one in a highly vulnerable psychedelic state.

The "Veto Rule" in Group Settings

Rick Strassman writes: "Music can evoke profound effects in a highly psychedelicized individual. It usually is easier to arrange music beforehand, either by the solo tripper or, in the case of a group session, in consultation with the sitter if there is one. In a group setting, it is advisable to consider a "veto" rule regarding music: If anyone finds the music intolerable, it must be discontinued."[63] Similarly, in the interview quoted earlier, pioneer therapist Leo Zeff hypothetically addresses those under his care: "Anytime I'm playing a piece of music that's not consonant with where you are, that's bothering you or you don't like it, just say, 'Change the music,' and I will."[64] William Richards suggests a "footnote" to this "rule" where, in certain therapeutic settings, a client may instinctively object to a piece of music that is in fact helping to uncover sensitive memories or emotions that are central to the psychotherapeutic effort.[65]

"Please Don't Stop the Music!"

Experienced psychedelic therapists and others have warned of the sometimes extreme discomfort experienced by clients (or themselves) when there are gaps in the flow of music. Stan Grof writes: "Another function of music is to provide a sense of continuity and connection in the course of various unusual states of consciousness. It is quite common that clients have difficulties with the periods when the music stops and the records or tapes are being changed; they complain that they feel suspended in midair, and sense a painful gap in the experience."[66] Bonny and Pahnke agree:

> Experience at MPRC has indicated the advisability of almost continual use of music during the session hours. Silences, although very brief in conscious time, may be experienced under the drug as unbearably long. The subject usually becomes

so accustomed to the music as a continuation and guide that the pauses between recorded selections can provide uneasiness, and seem interminable. Thus, it is very important to avoid unnecessary lapses into silence. Patient comment: "When the music stopped, the flow of imagery stopped and I felt suspended in a spaceless void. A renewal of the music was a reassurance that the experience was continuing."[67]

Guidance That Is Overly Rigid and Programmatic

Psychedelic psychotherapist Andrew Feldmár warns that "during these heady days of psychedelic renaissance . . . more and more training programs are springing up . . . Protocols are being manufactured, as if the interactions could be standardized and controlled. Experts are created, selection criteria are invented," and, he adds, "optimal musical backgrounds [he calls it "programmed music"] are offered, as if these were scientific matters.[68]

As I've pointed out more than once, there are few reliable generalizations one can make concerning how music in general, or any particular piece of music, will be received and processed within a particular consciousness, especially during a psychedelic state. As science, by nature, seeks to establish repeatable formulas and predictable results, the "science" in "psychedelic science" may act negatively to undermine therapeutic intuition: the spontaneous, in-the-moment, interactive dynamic between therapist and client. Whether literal, a paraphrase, or apocryphal, how appropriate is this pearl of wisdom attributed to Carl Jung: "Know all the theories, master all the techniques, but as you touch a human soul be just another human soul."

9

It's Subjective

Choosing Music

Any discussion about what music is appropriate for psychedelic use—which playlists to use, whose advice to follow, and, most certainly, which playlists are "scientifically" based (one online article promotes "5 scientifically approved playlists for psychedelic therapy")—has to be informed by the fundamental fact that the hearing/reception of music is a highly subjective, personal matter, particularly in psychedelic states. What I hear and internalize from a piece of music—how it "sounds," how it affects my consciousness, how it makes me feel, what "meanings" I might derive from it—is different from what you hear, how you are affected, and what meanings capture your imagination. One can no more create a standard playlist or system of playlists, or devise a standardized musical technology for psychedelic use, than one can standardize human consciousness itself. This should be self-evident, a matter of common sense, but the human obsession with standardization, predictability, scientific precision, and behavior control—the impulse to reduce human beings to stimulus-response machines—seems to be an inescapable derangement of our species, rooted in a pathological fear of freedom and spontaneity.

While briefly discussing the use of music in psychedelic therapy, British neuropsychologist Andy Mitchell, in his book *Ten Trips*, mentions a company created by a current psychedelic researcher whose "product mission," Mitchell explains, "is to deliver the world's first personalized playlists to facilitate 'experience as medicine.'" He quotes the company's founder: "We provide a new category of therapeutic tools, integrating psychedelic science, machine learning [i.e., artificial intelligence], music theory, psychotherapies and experience design." The business, in Mitchell's words, "is predicated on the ability of technology to 'instrumentalise' music, to give it a function that can be objectively measured and controlled." Mitchell is doubtful: "It's hard, perhaps impossible, to measure music in any useful way because it would rely on finding an objective way to measure the richness of experience itself: it would mean quantifying a quality." Interviewing the prominent American computer scientist, virtual reality pioneer, and composer Jaron Lanier, Mitchell describes Lanier's reaction to such attempts to standardize the use of music in psychedelic settings:

> His face screwed up as though he'd bitten a lemon. "The idea of music as some catalogue of triggers is just horrible. Music is more alive, more mysterious, more precious than that." It is also philosophically problematic: for Lanier, music is the only known thing in the universe that is its own context. "It's so unusual—unique in that it's pure form without content and somehow it still works. It's hard not to sound a little mystical around it . . . but music appears to support something very fundamental, bound up with the nature of consciousness itself."[1]

Scattered through various science and psychiatry journals, one finds, these days, growing numbers of articles by neuroscientists and psychiatrists (often in team or even herd formations) trying to unlock the secret science of music's efficacy in psychedelic psychotherapy, mostly with reference to brain anatomy and function. Some seek to determine, once and for all, which music is most appropriate for the job at hand—essentially reducing music to a cabinet of pharmaceutical agents or the "catalogue of triggers" mentioned above. Viewing human expressions of human experiences as merely "anecdotal," they set about quantifying qualities, objectifying the subjective, and reducing experiences to repeatable, predictable patterns and principles. Despite the apparent experimental rigor and the impressive statistical tables, one rarely feels one has learned anything of substance or relevance from these studies.

The conclusion, as always, is that human cognition of and aesthetic experience of music—subjective experience of any kind for that matter—resists meaningful reductive quantification. On the most fundamental level, we are all conditioned differently by life experiences (along with genetic and other predisposing factors), which creates a particular set of perceptual, cognitive, and emotional filters through which we perceive, process, and "make sense of" the external world. As Humphrey Osmond explains: "Our day to day experience of the world, each individual *umwelt*, can be surprisingly dissimilar. . . . Life, like art, is in William Blake's words, 'a matter of minute particulars.' We must accept, however difficult it may be to do so, that the 'minute particulars' experienced by one person may be very different from those experienced by other people."[2] Judith Becker adds, "It takes some adjustment to be able to accept the anti-intuitive idea that the tree that I look at, the tree that I 'see,' is not a straightforward mental representation of that tree out there. . . . The outside world is not represented [i.e., directly mirrored] in the brain but is interpreted and given meaning by the brain."[3] As Albert Hofmann explains, "reality is not a clearly defined condition, but the result of continuous processes, consisting of a continuous input of material and energetic signals from the outer world and its continuous decoding and transformation into psychic experiences and perceptions in the inner world. Reality is a dynamic process; it is constantly created new in every moment. Actual reality is consequently only in the here and now, in the moment."[4] This view is closely mirrored by neuroscientist Walter Freeman, whom Judith Becker quotes: "A stimulus excites the sensory receptors, so that they send a message to the brain. That input triggers a reaction in the brain, by which the brain constructs a pattern of neural activity. The sensory activity that triggered the construction is then washed away, leaving only the construct. That pattern does not 'represent' the stimulus. It constitutes the meaning of the stimulus for the person receiving it."[5] This meaning, Freeman states elsewhere, is "always and ever fluid."[6]

And so it is with music, which, far from existing as an objective external quantity, Becker notes, "invokes thoughts, memories, and feelings that are in no way intrinsic to the music signal itself."[7] Oliver Sacks, quoted earlier, reflects this theme when he writes: "Perception is never purely in the present—it has to draw on experience of the past. . . . We all have detailed memories of how things have previously looked and sounded, and these memories are recalled and admixed with every new perception, [whereby] every act of perception is to some degree an act of creation."[8] Anthony Storr, author of *Music and the Mind*, compares music's effect on a listener to the famous Rorschach inkblot test: "To some extent, a listener's response to a particular piece of music is governed by his subjective state of mind at the time; and some part of his experience is likely to be derived from the projection of his own emotions rather than being solely a direct consequence of the music."⁹ This is certainly true in the psychedelic state, where with increased emotional sensitivity to music "the listener . . . project[s] his personal experience and visual fantasies into the unfolding experience,"¹⁰ creating a totally unique experience of that music.

This inherent and universal (although not necessarily obvious) subjectivity of human perception and awareness must be taken into account when choosing music for psychedelic sessions, as Stanislav Grof pointed out in the previous chapter when describing the fluidity and unpredictability of music's effects during psychedelic states. Vladimir Jankelevitch, author of *Music and the Ineffable*, describes music, counterintuitively it would seem, as "inexpressive," but what he means by this is that music lacks a literal meaning as such, apart from how it is experienced, or imagined, within individual consciousness:

> The equivocal . . . is music's normal regime since it is a "language" that bears meaning only indirectly and suggests without signifying. . . . Music creates a unique state of mind, a state of mind that is ambivalent and always indefinable. Music is, then, inexpressive not because [it] expresses nothing but because it does not express this or that privileged landscape, this or that setting to the exclusion of all others; music is inexpressive in that it implies innumerable possibilities of interpretation, because it allows us to choose between them. As an ineffably general language . . . music is docile, lending itself to countless associations. Roussel attached the name "Evocations" to three orchestral "images" inspired by India: but music, with its double meanings, its readiness to oblige the most diverse interpretations, will evoke just as easily anything it pleases us to imagine. Sometimes music guides us, murmuring something, suggesting some unknown locale. . . . and yet, the name says to us, to our soul: choose your chimera, imagine what you will, anything is possible.¹¹

There are ample cases in the psychedelic literature showing that the subjectivity of music reception extends so far that a person who hears the same or a similar piece of music more than once (either within a single trip or in subsequent trips) may have radically different reactions. After rhapsodizing about a Bach piece during one psychedelic session, the same man, a half-year later, with a similar setting and dosing, turned to Bach to lift his spirits during an anxious phase. As he describes it, "I felt tightness in the solar plexus. I felt nervously restless and paced up and down the room. I felt no release from my ego, only more in its grip. I went to my room and tried to meditate but could not. I tried having a Bach record played. The music meant nothing to me but disconnected sounds."[12]

It should be no surprise, then, that there will be differences of opinion about what types and which pieces of music are most appropriate for psychedelic use. For one thing, people with highly developed tastes in music are often highly opinionated. Andrés Segovia, the famous guitar virtuoso, once described the piano as "a monster that screams when you touch its teeth" (one or two psychedelic therapists I've come across avoid using piano music because they find it too "percussive"). Sir Thomas Beecham, the legendary British conductor, described the sound of the harpsichord as "two skeletons copulating on a corrugated tin roof" (sounds like a good hypothetical example of synesthesia). So, while Aldous Huxley and James Fadiman both recommend Gregorian chants, Betty Grover Eisner thought otherwise. In a letter to a friend she warns, "Gregorian Chants are not good LSD music; they have invariably projected the subject into strong feelings of guilt, just as they did you that day: that was the Chants you got the reaction to—not the hospital—because I have had it happen several times until I realized what it was."[13]

Hanscarl Leuner, the professor of psychiatry mentioned earlier who developed psychedelic therapy in Germany, advised: "To start with, particularly soothing music is recommended, while later on the music rises to a peak of ecstasy—as in the Requiems of Mozart and Verdi."[14] However, Aldous Huxley strongly disagrees: "I feel sure . . . that it would be most unwise to subject a patient to sentimental religious music or even good religious music, if it were tragic (e.g., the Mozart or Verdi Requiems)."[15] The same two works of art, both famous requiems: in one set of ears it is ecstatic; in the other, sentimental or tragic. These examples demand an acknowledgment of the variability of musical taste (while also taking into consideration variations in set and setting) and should inspire us to become more attuned to and aware of our own intuitive responses to music.

It should be amply clear that, just as psychedelics themselves are not conventional pharmaceuticals with quantifiable, standardized effects, music itself is an intangible, perceptually fluid phenomenon, its reception and effects shaped by subjective consciousness—a factor multiplied manifold in psychedelic states, which themselves are characteristically protean and unpredictable.

In light of all this, one might legitimately ask why I have devoted years of effort to compiling multiple psychedelically purposed playlists on Spotify, "auditioning" thousands of pieces of music in multiple genres to include or exclude. The best response I can offer is that while being aware that we all hear music differently, at a basic level one can reasonably assess the *likely* effect of different qualities of sound and music on highly sensitized ears. Gentle, flowing, subtly suggestive music is, to state the obvious, likely to be more psychedelic friendly than, say, harsh, aggressive, or dissonant music. Music that is highly "declarative" will tend to feel manipulative, demanding a particular emotional response. Some music is very "busy," with torrents of notes flying in all directions, complicated by constant changes in theme and mood, leaving little room for individual consciousness to explore and play within the sound field. Further, some of the authors quoted in these pages have wisely indicated that there is a definite link between the quality of consciousness possessed by musical creators and their musical creations (how could it be otherwise?), implying that a good deal of the music to be found in any genre may be the expression, obvious or not, of forms of consciousness we may wish to avoid while in an exquisitely sensitive and vulnerable state. At a fundamental level, music communicates something of the inner experience, the inner being, of the composer, and a careful, open, intuitive listener is able to pick up on those expressive subtleties.

Some of these examples of the subjective qualities of music (e.g., harsh vs. gentle, manipulative vs. suggestive, busy vs. spacious) reflect fairly literal or exterior criteria that have helped guide me during this ongoing curatorial process. Beyond those external criteria, however, I have relied to a very large extent on personal intuition—an intuition, however, that over many years has been shaped, if I may claim as much, by a kind of "psychedelic" sensibility—a personal aesthetic inspired by intangible qualities such as beauty, mystery, wonder, awe, and the sublime—a sensibility shaped, in philosopher Schleiermacher's words, by "a sense and taste for the infinite."[16] My choices have been aided, at times, by the de-habituating, de-familiarizing effects of cannabis. A few tokes were generally all that was required to move the cerebral toggle switch from left to right brain, allowing for what Allen Ginsberg earlier described as a "more direct, slower, absorbing, occasionally microscopically minute engagement with sensing phenomena."[17]

I certainly have no expectation, and harbor no illusions, that every listener will respond positively to all of my music choices—but I suspect, or hope, that many will. In the end, I can only suggest, not prescribe. The musical choices I've provided are numerous and are offered as friendly, carefully considered suggestions. There are many genres to choose from and multiple choices within each. Explore to your heart's content, create your own personal playlist(s) out of these reservoirs of music I've assembled, and experiment freely. You will undoubtedly discover your own treasures.

If there is a conclusion here, it is this: one must remain flexible, intuitive, sensitive, and defiantly anti-dogmatic in the matter of selecting music for psychedelic use. Suggestions are, of course, always welcome and can be invaluable. But best be wary of any system or practice (especially those proclaiming "scientific" authority or promoting a commercial product) that claims to have discovered—by whatever means—which music is best for your own psychedelic consumption. In an age of growing psychedelic institutionalization, commodification, and careerism, we need to learn how to open our own ears, hearts, and souls to the extraordinary shape-shifting wonders of music, and to the multifarious ways it can deepen, nourish, and guide our psychedelic journeys.

10

Is Classical Music Still Relevant?

I am convinced that the great composers of the West have been teachers of humanity whose spiritual influence is ignored; and whether this statement is true or not for the majority of people today, I believe it is still true for those who listen to great classical music in their psychedelic journeys.[1]

—Claudio Naranjo

I longed further to pursue investigation of the properties of LSD in a musical atmosphere, in lovely surroundings and with stimulating company. . . . The concerto for flute and harp by Mozart was perceived in all its celestial glory, as heavenly music.[2]

—Albert Hofmann

Perhaps you've noticed that most of the musical works that have been cited in these chapters, generally from trip reports from psychotherapeutic sessions, come from the classical genre. Although classical music does not and ought not hold a monopoly in psychedelic practice, there are reasons for its apparent pervasiveness in these accounts. First, the modern age of psychedelic research and therapy began in the 1950s. Based on a widespread and continuing consensus that music with lyrics was to be avoided—because words evoke thoughts that may distract from the inner flow of experience—instrumental music (or choral music with foreign or unintelligible lyrics) was considered ideal by most practitioners. Further, since the other now most common musical genre used in psychedelic settings—various forms of electronica and ambient music—had not yet made its appearance, there were few obvious alternatives to classical music. The only alternatives mentioned in these earlier accounts include a very limited range of non-Western recordings (most commonly sitar music by virtuoso Ravi Shankar, whose recordings were available since the 1950s), along with very occasional references to jazz. Because classical takes many forms, encompassing a wide range of styles and moods and offering innumerable choices, it more than served the purposes of researchers and psychotherapists. As these early clinicians found classical to be suitable, even ideal, for psychedelic therapy, there was little to compel them to explore other musical modalities or to dislodge them from a kind of musical orthodoxy.

Another reason for the scarcity of non-classical musical references is that, as I discovered, the richest vein of published trip reports happens to be concentrated in the body of scholarly writings that appeared in response to the explosion of LSD use during the countercultural 1960s. The academic/intellectual interest back then (prior to the scientific rebranding of psychedelic studies) focused largely on the experiential dimension of psychedelics: what people actually were *experiencing*, that is, the psychological, aesthetic, and even spiritual dimensions of psychedelia. This "early approach" to the study of psychedelics "was the correct one," as Terence McKenna has insisted: "Intelligent, thoughtful people should take psychedelics and . . . share their experiences. It's too early for a science. What we need now are the diaries of explorers. We need many diaries of many explorers so we can begin to get a feeling for the territory."[3] Many of the richest, most subjectively expressive firsthand accounts of musical experience on psychedelics are therefore found in the literature (mainly trip reports) of that period, an era in psychedelic research strongly dominated by the classical genre.[4]

There is admittedly a tendency by many to dismiss classical music as (choose your adjective) antiquated, elitist, self-important, grandiloquent, impenetrable, unapproachable, and so on. No doubt some of those descriptors do apply to many individual pieces of classical music. I am certainly not an uncritical cheerleader for the genre, nor do I claim special expertise. But at the very least we should understand that there is no monolithic entity called "classical music." The term is used, commonly, to refer to a full millennium of music-making in the West involving a plethora of differing styles and movements and an endless variety of sonic experiences.

In the course of curating one major and several subsidiary classical playlists, I have spent literally thousands of hours exploring the genre's offerings. Now and then, while "auditioning" classical works for inclusion in a particular playlist, I have encountered a piece that touches me in some profound manner, music that seems to possess some undefinable charm, charisma, mystery, or magic—music that seems to possess something of the "psychedelic," as I intuit it. Admittedly, such found treasures are relatively few and far between: one in a hundred, or hundreds. Whatever your experience might be, whatever impressions or attitudes toward classical music you may maintain, I promise that if you sample some of the items in my classical playlists in the right frame of mind, you will find pieces that will charm, seduce, and fill you with wonder. Best to drop the preconceptions and expectations and simply dive in with an open mind and open ears.

Because this chapter is written in part to help clear away whatever prejudicial judgments (whether or not based in personal experience) that might keep one from embracing classical music as psychedelic worthy, I'd like to quote an ancient (1969) plea by the authors of *A Child's Garden of Grass* to their countercultural brothers and sisters, to whom they propose this challenge:

> If you hate classical music, get stoned and listen. Listening to music while stoned is a whole new world. . . . And grass will change your musical habits, generally for the better, stoned or not stoned. If you hate classical music, get stoned and listen, even to something very sophisticated. The sounds will take on new meanings and you will hear structures, instrumentation and passions which you never had the capacity to hear before. And often you'll get an insight into what the composer was trying to do, even though you've had no experience with classical music before.
>
> We're convinced that the Hi-Fi and stereo boom [remember, this is 1969] is to a great extent due to the fact that so many people are now getting stoned, because music, when stoned, becomes another world: intricate, three dimensional, visual, and completely understandable both intellectually and emotionally.[5]

It goes without saying that what's true for cannabis certainly applies, much more so, to psychedelics. Even without psychedelics, shedding timeworn stereotypes about classical can open up new worlds of experience. Lawrence Kramer, author of *Why Classical Music Still Matters*, writes:

> Despite the frigid connotations of its label, classical music . . . is the very opposite of frozen in its presumed grandeur. Lend it an ear, and it will effortlessly shuck off the dead-marble aspect of its own status and come to as much life as you can handle. It will invite you to hear meanings it can have only if you do hear them, yet it will give you access to meanings you had no inkling of before you heard the music. It has nothing to do with the classic in the sense of a timeless monument that dictates a self-evident meaning and demands obeisance for it. It opens itself like a willing hand or smile, making itself available to you for self-discovery, reflection, and, yes, critique. And at times . . . it will go further. It will offer you moments of revelation.[6]

Several psychedelic pioneers, mental health professionals who administered psychedelics to thousands of research subjects (both above- and below-ground), have documented the surprised reception to classical music on the part of many who were not accustomed to it. Myron Stolaroff reports, "In the research days of our Foundation [International Foundation for Advanced Study, Menlo Park, California], almost all who began the experience with a dislike of classical music ended up preferring it."[7] He elaborates:

> I don't think anybody could go through the program without leaving with a far greater appreciation of music, because listening to music is a remarkable experience under psychedelics. We always asked, "Well, would it be okay if we feed in a little classical music here and there?" And they'd respond, "Well, okay." They left loving classical music—much preferring it to popular music! I think that was true with almost 100 percent of them, although we didn't keep statistics on it.[8]

Stan Grof found a similar receptivity and transformation of musical tastes among alcoholics and narcotic addicts with whom he worked: "A number of our patients, who were alcoholics and heroin addicts with poor educational background, developed such deep interest in classical music as a result of their own LSD session that they decided to use their meager financial resources for buying a stereo set and starting a record collection of their own."[9] A similar finding from William Richards: "We discovered in early research in the 1960s, notably with some alcoholics who had never appreciated classical music, that Brahms symphonies and similar works resonated deeply within them and proved highly effective in providing nonverbal structure and support. Many of those people not only discovered an appreciation of classical music within themselves, but went out and purchased records, tapes, or [later] compact disks to facilitate the continuing integration of their experiences and for future enjoyment."[10] Based on these (and many similar) reports, Deutsche Gramophone, Sony Classical, Warner Classics, Decca, Hyperion, Naxos, and other labels that specialize in classical music should be lining up to donate large sums to psychedelic enterprises. You could add to that list major music conservatories like Julliard, The Royal Academy of Music, the New England Conservatory, and dozens more. It is not difficult to imagine psychedelics instigating a boon in the popularity of classical music—if psychonauts would simply lend an ear.

Moving now into the twenty-first century, we have a rock-loving British psychonaut, Christopher Gray, comparing himself to a "lovesick teenager" as he found himself falling in love with Renaissance music, aided both by psychedelics and cannabis:

> During the trip when I caught my first glimpse of the sacred, I had been listening to a CD of Hildegard of Bingen. The music must have touched me more deeply than I realized, because when I returned the CD to the library I borrowed two further discs of late medieval/early Renaissance music. I took them home and listened, though more dutifully than anything else, for they lacked the pristine clarity of St. Hildegard; and, if anything, sounded predictably churchy.
>
> However, one evening I'd had a smoke before I started to cook supper, and I put one of the discs, Ockeghem's fifteenth-century Requiem, on the stereo as background music. I was doing something at the stove when all of a sudden I heard it. It was as though my ears had been unblocked. . . . At first I was just amazed by the intricacy and richness of the counterpoint, the aesthetics of the voices dancing in and out of one another; then as I continued to listen, I became increasingly fascinated by the nature of the emotion the music was expressing. I couldn't find any adjective to describe it . . . but whatever it was, the lugubrious ecclesiastical quality had vanished. . . .

> For years, apart from some minimalism, I had hardly ever listened to Western classical music, but now I began to borrow more and more CDs of early Renaissance music from the library. At first most of them were like the Ockeghem, and I simply couldn't hear them; then suddenly, as though my ears had popped, I would be listening wonderstruck. A smoke usually did the trick. But I still couldn't pin down the nature of the emotion inspiring this music. Faith? Celebration? Rapture? Whatever it was, the complexity and need for split-second timing produced an exhilarating sense of purity, speed, and elation—qualities I'd certainly never associated with the church. Sometimes as I listened my body seemed to be melting or dissolving; and there was a marked sensation of soaring . . . of ascension, virtually of flight. . . .
>
> I hadn't been so involved with music since the early days of rock and roll. Indeed, I wasn't far short of a lovesick teenager . . . as I play[ed] and replay[ed] Lassus's *Infelix Ego*. With its dark ecstatic surges, surely the motet is one of the most haunting pieces of all Renaissance music. . . .[11]

Now, just because this particular author likes Lassus's *Infelix Ego* (which I first read, mildly stoned, as "inflexible ego") doesn't mean you will. No one piece of music is categorically psychedelic-friendly or otherwise. Personal taste (however shaped, expanded, or modified during psychoactive states), along with other variables, accounts for much. You will discover your own musical gems, your own harmonic ecstasies, your own musical crushes.

Earlier I was speaking of common attitudes about classical music that preempt unbiased listening. In his book *A Sound Mind: How I Fell in Love with Classical Music*, noted British rock critic Paul Morely set himself the task of starting from near scratch to understand what classical is all about, which amounted to a project of self de-conditioning. He describes his journey of discovery:

> I wanted to find ways to demystify a vast, complex world that seemed locked away behind a socio-politically constructed stuffy public image, as if it is a music that belongs only to a contrived elite obsessed with ossified geniuses and their timeless masterpieces. . . .
>
> I began to see a territory of classical music, the way one things leads to another, the way music moves forward by

becoming liberated from the historic implications loaded into it, in much the same way I have come to view the ebb and flow of pop music. Doing this allowed me *to smash through the barriers erected around the music and get to it simply as it is* [emphasis added], once all associations of time, history, fashion, prejudice and interpretation are stripped away—seeing [classical music] not as something that should only be appreciated in a very particular and formalized context, requiring sophisticated technical understanding and the correct clothing, but as *liberated sound existing in a pure metaphysical space reflecting timeless thinking and emotion* [my emphasis] . . . I began to view and understand music written even by the revered and mummified old masters as simply sounds being moved around through space and time in order to communicate feelings that spoken language or other artistic endeavors cannot come close to conveying. . . .

Kubrick and *2001: A Space Odyssey* has already made it clear that spaceships and classical music seamlessly fit together as if somehow they are related to each other, as ways of traveling through space and time, and deep into the mind, extending the idea, the very being, of humanity into new places of otherness. Great classical music is a kind of spaceship built to explore the vast unknown.[12]

Musicologist and author Robert Jourdain makes a brief but fascinating case for viewing classical music as inherently psychedelic. One may quarrel with his suggested associations between individual genres and particular drugs, but his point about the relation of classical music and psychedelics is intriguingly on the mark:

Before all else, people use music for mood enhancement. Psychologists have long known that different personality types are attracted to different kinds of drugs, legal and illegal. There's a parallel here. We "take" a certain kind of music to steer our central nervous systems toward a particular condition: hard rock as the frenzied rush of cocaine; easy-listening genres as a martini; cheery supermarket Muzak as a pick-me-up cup of coffee; cool jazz as a laid-back marijuana high; *the far-flung landscapes of classical music as the fantasy realm of psychedelics* [emphasis added].[13]

As Jourdain suggests, you could rightly think of many classical pieces as resembling landscapes. Unlike, say, most ambient music (which I also love), classical has definite shape and form, hills and valleys, winding roads, hidden grottoes, and fantastic beasts roaming about. There is a richness, variety, and unpredictability in many works that hold one's interest and fascination. Rather than just a tone, mood, or feeling, many classical pieces become, in psychedelic states, sacred journeys, heroic adventures, lush dreams, or magical mystery tours. See, or rather hear, for yourself!

I referred earlier (in chapters 5 and 7) to theologian Harvey Cox's peyote experience in the Mexican desert. Here I return to a different phase of that event that offers food for thought concerning our cultural and even spiritual bonds with the great Western composers. Told by the Huichol guide that "The gods and ancestors of the Huicholes are not your gods and ancestors," the group plays the music of Bach, Beethoven, and Mozart on a portable record player, whereby, in Cox's words, "the spirits of our gods and ancestors . . . would sing to us all that night":

> When I woke an hour later, the people in our group were gathering all the peyote we had cut into one batch to show our hosts. The Huicholes examined it closely and appeared to be blessing it. . . . One of them spoke.
>
> We had come to the desert in search of the little deer, he told us. We had been purified, had sought out the magical fawn and were now ready. This little deer, he continued, had for a very long time helped his people to talk with their gods and their ancestors. . . . They were grateful to the little deer, he said, for what it always did for them. Without it they could hardly live. But, he said suddenly furrowing his brown brow, "the gods and ancestors of the Huicholes are not your gods and ancestors." Now, he told us, we were on our own. The Huicholes could do nothing more for us. We should move our camp to a hill some two hundred yards away, and there, during the coming night and day, we should try, with the little deer's help, to talk with our own gods and our own forebears. He stopped, looked at each of us, and then turned and walked back with his companions to the fire that flickered only fifty yards away.
>
> The new camp we created looked more like a temple than had our first one, which had resembled a bivouac of inept

boy scouts. On the high ridge we dug a huge rectangular fire pit and arranged the bedding around it symmetrically. Some people dragged in piles of firewood while Roquet and his staff set up the portable hi-fi equipment through which the spirits of our gods and ancestors—Bach's B Minor Mass, Beethoven's Ninth Symphony, Mozart's Requiem, Gregorian chants and a record called "The Flutes of Israel"—would sing to us all that night. . . .

Seven patients, two staff members and I stayed up all that night around the fire, sang, laughed, cried and stared at the cosmic arch above us. . . .

As the choral movement of the Ninth Symphony came onto our portable hi-fi, Caterina, one of the young woman patients, looked at the sky, now resplendent with a million stars, and told us she was about to give birth to the whole universe. At the time nothing seemed more sensible to me. She lay back, drew up her knees, and with the rest of us attending, grunted and moaned in travail until she had birthed all the spiral nebulae and the milky way. After the astral birth, exhausted and satisfied by her labor, Caterina told us she would now die happy. But she didn't. After a half-hour death on her bedroll she was up dancing to a Mozart Kyrie.[14]

What I find striking and quite poignant here is the Huichol guide's words to the Western participants: "The gods and ancestors of the Huicholes are not your gods and ancestors." Westerners participating in ayahuasca, peyote, and other ceremonies with native or Indigenous guides sometimes feel ambivalent about their relationship with their hosts—personally, culturally, or spiritually—unclear about what is expected of them in terms of embracing a cultural or metaphysical milieu so far removed from their own. They question whether they are meant to commune with or submit to mysterious, otherworldly spirits or divinities.[15] The Huichol elder encourages this particular group of Westerners to try, with the help of peyote, "to talk with our own gods and our own forebears," as Cox puts it. We likely may not exalt Bach, Beethoven, and Mozart as divinities, but in some undefinable sense they are like tribal spirits, conveying through their music aspects of the accumulated experience, wisdom, and archetypal emotions of the civilizational heritage of the West, which is far from monolithic. A pinch of psychedelic may open a doorway into the psychological and spiritual offerings of these closer-to-home creators of musical worlds. As you'll recall from chapter 2, the philosopher Schopenhauer equated the musical composer (and artists in general) with the notion of "genius": one who acts as the natural conduit through which wisdom reveals itself—not necessarily as an enlightened soul but as a channel, even a naive channel, of higher truths. As Schopenhaeur put it, "The composer . . . articulates the most profound wisdom in a language that his reason does not comprehend; as the somnambulist under the influence of Mesmerism gives insights into things of which, waking, she has no concept." Sometimes that act of channeling is a conscious one, the composer inviting divine guidance. To offer only one of numerous possible examples from the realm of classical music, Johann Brahms described his own process of receiving inspiration:

> To realize that we are one with the Creator, as Beethoven did, is a wonderful and awe-inspiring experience. Very few human beings ever come into that realization and that is why there are so few great composers or creative geniuses in any line of human endeavor. I always contemplate all this before commencing to compose. This is the first step. When I feel the urge I begin by appealing directly to my Maker and I first ask Him the three most important questions pertaining to our life here in this world—whence, wherefore, whither [*woher, warum, wohin*]?
>
> I immediately feel vibrations that thrill my whole being. These are the Spirit illuminating the soul-power within, and in this exalted state, I see clearly what is obscure in my ordinary moods; then I feel capable of drawing inspiration from above, as Beethoven did. . . . Those vibrations assume the forms of distinct mental images, after I have formulated my desire and resolve in regard to what I want—namely, to be inspired so that I can compose something that will uplift and benefit humanity—something of permanent value.
>
> Straightaway the ideas flow in upon me, directly from God, and not only do I see distinct themes in my mind's eye, but they are clothed in the right forms, harmonies, and orchestration. Measure by measure the finished product is revealed to me when I am in those rare, inspired moods.[16]

Who is to say, then, that when deeply absorbed in the music of Brahms and other composers acknowledged as great, we are not, in some sense, communing with "our own gods and forebears"?

Which Classical Works Are Most Appropriate for Psychedelic Settings?

Before sharing with you the specific recommendations in classical music offered by various respected authors in the psychedelic field, I should mention the particular relevance of what is often referred to as "program music" along with "musical impressionism." While psychedelic-friendly music can be found in various quarters of the classical cosmos, these two fluid sub-genres deserve special attention due to their inherently "pictorial" quality: their creators' intention to "describe" visual scenes and narratives (a quality conducive to aural-to-visual synesthesia). Patrick Lundborg gives a concise, well-articulated description of these two subgenres, with specific application to psychedelic states:

> Program music accords to basic psychedelic principles, not just in that it stimulates the listener's visual imagination, but also with the full attention it gives to the listening experience, rather than to the composer's private agony, or meta-theoretical broodings. The most famous example of program music is probably Beethoven's *Pastoral Symphony*, and unsurprisingly this is also the Beethoven work which is most effective to score a psychedelic experience. . . .
>
> The French impressionists who succeeded [the] romantic era [Beethoven, etc.] would make vital contributions to the field of visually loaded music. Impressionism began as a movement within pictorial art, but soon emerged as a new style within contemporary music. An impressionist work of major importance as proto-Psychedelia is Debussy's *La Mer* first performed in 1905. While the impressionists ostensibly worked in opposition to the program music the romantic composers popularized, there is a clear affinity between Debussy's strongly evocative musical images of the roaring sea, and the visual music of . . . the *Pastoral Symphony*.

> The difference is that Debussy, in line with his aesthetics, offers not a narrative structure but the grandeur of the moment, or a set of discontinuous moments, in the life of the tumultuous ocean. There is no protagonist, but a sequence of purely musical images of currents and crashing waves, and via this design the listener becomes the protagonist; stepping into the world of the music, rather than passively receiving it. . . . With *La Mer* comes the idea of the abstract soundtrack, retaining the illustrative quality of program music, while dispensing with the need for a narrative framework. Impressionist music, as encountered in such a work, encapsulates the philosophical crux of psychedelic phenomenology . . . the all-important moment of pure perception.[17]

Examples of this type of music involving image and sensation is often reflected in the titles given by their composers: *The Enchanted Lake* (Anatoly Lyadov), *Poems of the Sea* (Ernest Bloch), *The Lark Ascending* (Ralph Vaughn Williams), *Hearing the First Cuckoo in Spring* (Frederick Delius), *The Lake at Evening* (Charles Griffes), *Stillness in Snow* (Takashi Yoshimatu). Here we have, in Lundborg's words, "the philosophical crux of psychedelic phenomenology . . . the all-important moment of pure perception." More than perception, *immersion*: a sense of being embraced by the spirits of the forest, mesmerized by the ocean's vast depths and moving surfaces, experientially participating in the endless flux of shape-shifting clouds, the flight of birds, the dream-like mystery of liminal twilight. More even than immersion, *revelation*: nature's deepest mysteries, the spirits that inhabit it, its healing energies, its ineffable embeddedness in the wider cosmos. This describes only one variety of classical music; there are many others.

Relatedly, we have a rich account of a spontaneous experiment by Havelock Ellis in his classic work *Mescal: A New Artificial Paradise*. As he explains it, "The chief object of the tests was to ascertain how far a desire on the composer's part to suggest definite imagery would affect my visions" while under mescaline. Here is his report:

> I . . . lay for some hours on a couch with my head more or less in contact with the piano, and with closed eyes directed towards a subdued light, while a friend played, making various tests, of his own devising, which were not explained to me

until afterwards. I was to watch the visions in a purely passive manner, without seeking to direct them, nor was I to think about the music, which, so far as possible, was unknown to me. The music stimulated the visions and added greatly to my enjoyment of them. It seemed to harmonise with them, and, as it were, support and bear them up. . . . The chief object of the tests was to ascertain how far a desire on the composer's part to suggest definite imagery would affect my visions. In about half the cases there was no resemblance, in the other half there was a distinct resemblance which was sometimes very remarkable. This was especially the case with Schumann's music, for example with his Waldscenen and Kinderscenen; thus "The Prophet Bird" called up vividly a sense of atmosphere and of brilliant feathery bird-like forms passing to and fro; "A Flower Piece" provoked constant and persistent images of vegetation; while "Scheherazade" produced an effect of floating white raiment, covered by glittering spangles and jewels. In every case my description was, of course, given before I knew the name of the piece. I do not pretend that this single series of experiments proves much, but it would certainly be worth while to follow up this indication and to ascertain if any light is hereby thrown on the power of a composer to suggest definite imagery, or the power of a listener to perceive it.[18]

A quite different type of classical music, less devoted to the "pictorial," is that of the baroque period (1600–1750), which has both positive and negative attributes for psychonauts, as suggested by Jourdain:

Not all music is expressive. For instance, a good deal of Baroque music moves along like a precision timepiece, having been written for eighteenth-century minds enamored of order and self-possession. Such music evinces a certain liveliness, but not the emotional drama that so dominates music written a century later. Yet we're still drawn to this "intellectual" music despite its lack of overt emotionality. The attraction of such music seems to reside in the elegance of its patterns. We admire it as pure structure.[19]

Some may feel that this description does limited justice to the varieties and nuances of Baroque. We are, after all, speaking of great works by composers such as Bach, Handel, and Vivaldi (some of whose works you'll find in my playlist recommendations). However it is generally true that music of the Baroque era is less overtly emotionally expressive, which may seem to suggest a lack of introspective or spiritual depth. Yet "the elegance of its patterns" may indeed satisfy a certain psychological need for predictable structure and order, if not also an aesthetic appreciation for the inspired geometries of musical form. If nothing else, the sheer "liveliness" of many Baroque pieces may dispel a dark mood with its optimistic, upward currents.

Though I've brought special attention to these particular types or genres of classical music—visually suggestive "program" music, musical impressionism, and, to a lesser degree, the Baroque—there is so much more within the classical genre to nourish and inspire psychedelic journeys. These include all those individual works that in a multitude of ways explore, with both depth and subtlety, the many dimensions of human feeling, sensation, and emotion.

Reflections and Recommendations (Mostly in Classical Music) by Psychedelic Authors

Several writers have mentioned their own particular favorites among the classical canon for use with psychedelics. We might, however, preface these recommendations with a sound piece of advice from Stanislav Grof concerning how to best listen to these works:

> It is particularly important to suspend any intellectual activity in relation to the music that is being played, such as trying to guess who its composer might be or from which culture it comes, exploring its resemblance to another piece that one knows, judging the performance of the orchestra, attempting to identify the key, or criticizing the technical quality of the recording or the music equipment in the room. The music has to be allowed to act on the psyche and the body in a completely spontaneous and elemental fashion. Used in this way it becomes a powerful means for inducing the supporting unusual states of consciousness.[20]

Starting our survey with Stan Grof, he offers a general recommendation of "less well-known symphonies, concertos, or overtures of famous masters," listing a number of composers without mentioning individual works. Focusing on the peak hours of a trip, he suggests "overwhelming music with a transcendental quality: oratoria, requiems, and masses, combining a full orchestra with a multitude of human voices." He mentions the "sacred music of Wolfgang Amadeus Mozart, Johann Sebastian Bach, George Frideric Handel, Hector Berlioz, Giuseppe Verdi, Charles Gounod, or Francis Poulenc." He also cites composer Alan Hovhaness, a gifted but often overlooked composer who was my own first cherished discovery as I began to explore the genre many years ago. Grof writes, "The music of American composer of Armenian-Scottish extraction, Alan Hovhaness, can be unusually powerful and effective in this context. It is extremely evocative and transcendental, yet not sufficiently well-known to produce standard associations."[21]

In another of his books, while discussing the use of music in Holotropic Breathwork, Grof becomes more specific in his recommendations, though it is not clear whether these pieces are meant specifically for use in Breathwork or more generally in psychedelic therapy. Works he mentions include Alan Hovhaness's *All Men Are Brothers*, *And God Created the Great Whales*, and *The Mysterious Mountain*, as well as Alexander Scriabin's *Poem of Ecstasy*, Pachelbel's Canon in D, and Samuel Barber's *Adagio for Strings*. It is notable that while discussing Holotropic Breathwork, Grof lists many works outside the classical genre.[22]

William Richards, himself an experienced musician, writes from a wealth of personal knowledge and experience: "After several decades of experimenting with the choice of many different styles of music to provide nonverbal support during the action of psychedelic substances, trying to differentiate between the 'very good' and the 'excellent,' I have personally concluded that there are works by Bach, Brahms, Mozart, and other composers usually considered 'Western classical' that definitely qualify as 'supremely psychedelic.'"[23] Richards offers specific recommendations drawing from the works of these composers. For Bach he cites both Kyrie's from the Mass in B Minor as well as the Fantasia and Fugue in G Minor; Brahms's majestic *German Requiem* (sections I, II and IV); Mozart's Clarinet Concerto (the *Adagio*) and his *Laudate Dominum*. Further works of psychedelic promise he cites in his book include Beethoven's Ninth Symphony, Handel's *Messiah*, and Samuel Barber's *Adagio for Strings* (citing its "transcendental yearnings and ethereal climax"). He describes these works as "pieces which are intuitively recognized as profoundly spiritual by many listeners."[24] A final recommendation is Chopin's Nocturnes ("with their many subtle nuances of emotional expression").[25]

Psychotherapist Claudio Naranjo comments at length on the value of several composers and individual works for psychedelic use. He has a particular fondness for the "sacred music of all cultures" including classical music that possesses "sacred content." Some of his favorites include Handel (whose *Water Music*, he says, accompanied his "entrance into the beyond"), Bach, Beethoven (Ninth Symphony), Mozart ("whose works so much communicate both the element of tenderness and the spirit of play"), and Schubert. He also offers high praise for Brahms, citing several works possessing "very particular therapeutic power" due to their "empathic, maternal, almost oceanic" qualities. With what seems a highly attuned musical ear, Naranjo's understanding of music should be of particular interest to psychonauts everywhere:

> When it comes to advising a repertoire for others, it seems to me that to induce spiritual states, nothing is more appropriate than sacred music of all cultures, but also classical music from diverse cultures can have a sacred content. Thus, when I attended Leo Zeff's group, I was deeply moved on several occasions by the music of Ravi Shankar that was popular in those days, and I think it ought to be part of a psychedelic guide's music collection.
>
> Coming back to Western music . . . it is of interest to pay great attention to Bach, the great genius of sacred Baroque music whose work constituted something like the foundation of later European music, until the beginning of modern times. When I was working with groups in Chile, I particularly used the Music[al] Offering and the Passion According to Saint Matthew. . . .
>
> If one had to choose one of Beethoven's works above all others, none would be more appropriate than the Ninth Symphony, whose first movement sounds like the voice of the Transcendent Father, the second movement like the voice of the Son in all of us, and the third—a lake of compassion—like the Mother, whereas the fourth choral movement represents an expression of humanity in harmony.

Perhaps there is no Romantic work that I have included more often in my sessions than Schubert's final string quintet, which, reflecting the composer's encounter with his very premature death, speaks to all of us mortals when, with the aid of psychedelics, we are able to open our ears to the experiential world underlying the musical world of sound and in this way receive nonverbal teachings from the composers.

Over the years, I have spoken at length about Brahms's very particular therapeutic power, who it seems attained a more balanced spiritual maturity than Beethoven, the titanic fighter in whom heroism prevailed both over tenderness and the spirit of play. Likewise of Mozart, whose works so much communicate both the element of tenderness and the spirit of play and the disposition to the pleasure of childhood. However, if we wish to find, in one single person, the full spectrum of the forms of love, it seems to me that Brahms sings with a fuller palette than the others, for the strong presence in his music of the empathic and maternal, almost oceanic component. I have made frequent use of Brahms's first two quartets, and also of the first sextet, as well as of Symphony no. 1. Parts of my repertoire have also been the quartets of Debussy and of Ravel, and Ravel's Piano Concerto in G major and his Bolero, as well Stravinsky's "The Rite of Spring" and "The Firebird."[26]

In their seminal article "The Use of Music in Psychedelic (LSD) Psychotherapy," Helen Bonny and Walter Pahnke cite numerous classical (and some non-classical) works. Here is but a small representative sample: Fauré's Requiem, Bach's *St. Matthew Passion*, Gounod's *St. Cecilia Mass*, Brahms's *German Requiem*, Smetana's *Moldau*, and Elgar's *Enigma Variations*. Aside from these recommendations of individual works, Bonny and Pahnke offer a unique observation which I've not seen repeated elsewhere, but which strikes me as significant, especially for psychedelic psychotherapy. They recommend the use of recordings of women's voices, presumably either singly or in choral settings: "Regression to early experiences of the mother-child relationship and subsequent reliving or reintegration of warmth and feeling at an infantile level may be facilitated and intensified by the female voice."[27] In a separate article, Walter Pahnke offers this general recommendation: "Music which intuitively appeals to the individual can be helpful; in general, smooth, peaceful, and majestic music is best."[28]

Betty Grover Eisner's choices in classical are well summarized by author Ido Hartogsohn: "[She] preferred Beethoven concertos, some Mozart, Bach's Arioso, recordings by Mexican mushroom healer Maria Sabina, the Pablo Casals recording of Bruch's Opus No. 47 (*Kol Nidrei*), and Chopin's Piano concerto No 1, which she especially favored. Eisner considered concertos particularly well suited for the therapeutic psychedelic experience because of the way that the soloist-orchestra dynamic mirrored the relationship between the individual and the environment."[29] Eisner herself writes, "Piano concertos were particularly good, especially Chopin's First and Second, and Beethoven's Fourth and Fifth."[30] In the context of a ketamine session, she mentions, without naming it, "a Mozart Concerto,"[31] and elsewhere, "Hindu ragas."[32]

James Fadiman reports that "Classical music tends to feel appropriate to most people, even if they have not chosen it." He personally recommends, "Hovhaness's Mysterious Mountain, Fauré's Requiem, Gregorian chants, solo piano, [and] piano with one or two other instruments." Departing from classical, he also recommends "unaccompanied flute, ragas, and indigenous drum recordings."[33]

Myron Stolaroff recommends for the initial part of the session "quiet, lyrical compositions . . . such as Respighi's Fountains of Rome or Ibert's Ports of Call." He continues, "As the subject goes deeper into the experience, more dramatic music can be introduced. Toward the end of the inward exploring period, and especially if the subject approaches transcendental levels, spiritual music is compelling."[34]

Though not a recommendation per se, we do learn from the book *Huxley in Hollywood* that during his maiden voyage on psilocybin (while in Cambridge in 1960 lecturing at MIT), Huxley listened to a mix of classical and non-Western music: "Leary brought the magic pills over to Huxley's apartment; they spent three hours listening to Bach, Mozart, African drums, and Ravi Shankar, Aldous cross-legged in lotus position, meditating behind closed eyes."[35]

In Praise of Quietude and Subtlety

Earlier in this chapter I mentioned in passing that I am sometimes surprised by certain of the classical musical choices made by well-meaning psychedelic guides who seem to think that the more intense hours of a psychedelic journey need to be artificially magnified using music described by them as emotionally intense, even "overwhelming"—as if a person in their most sensitive, open, and vulnerable state requires a form of musical shock treatment to reach a peak metaphysical climax. This seems to me counterintuitive. It is in those most sensitive, acutely responsive states of being during the height of a trip that the smallest, lightest, most effervescent thing can exert a tectonic or tsunamic force within consciousness. I appreciate Robert Jourdain's comment that "The voice of the muse is soft and delicate, audible only to a mind relaxed and free to drift. Its song is faint in our age of anxiety and distraction."[36] Vladimir Jankelevitch, author of *Music and the Ineffable*, provides a graphic image, suitable for psychonauts, illustrating the attitude with which one ought to receive the gift of music: "Imagine the look on the face of a man who had captured a barely perceptible message from some distant sphere: heart pounding, he would hold his breath, that all his senses might drink in the cryptogram, the unknown sign, the sign that has come to him across infinite space."[37] Grinspoon and Bakalar sagely point out, "The emotional atmosphere of a psychedelic session is spectacularly unstable. A minor change in the environment—a noise, the appearance of a new person on the scene, the sun passing behind a cloud—often creates an entirely new mood."[38]

On this point, how apropos is this simple story told by musician Bobby McFerrin concerning Yo-Yo Ma's visit to Africa. As author Elena Mannes explains, "The cellist visited a shaman and was so struck by his music that he asked the shaman to sing a particular song again so that Yo-Yo Ma could write it down in musical notation." McFerrin relates: "The shaman [is] singing and Yo-Yo says, 'Stop, wait, I need to write this down.' So he writes it down, and he says, 'Play it again. I want to make sure that I got it right.' And the shaman sings and Yo-Yo is saying, 'But that's not the piece you sang before.' And the shaman laughed and he said, 'Well, the first time I sang it, there was a herd of antelope in the distance. And a cloud was passing over the sun.'"[39] Such are the extreme subtleties of psychedelic perception, particularly during a high-dose trip. If even a cloud passing over the sun can "change everything," then a sudden storm of "overwhelming" music may cause devastation.

As I explained in the previous chapter, in curating playlists of both classical and non-classical music, I have excluded music that might provoke strongly negative emotions. Might one encounter, here and there, an occasional bit of drama or creative tension? Yes, one might, particularly in the playlist "Fantastic Journeys, Mystical Trips," inasmuch as any journey may entail obstacles and surprises, exultations and disappointments, crescendos and diminuendos. But in general I've excluded musical compositions that to most ears might seem angry, aggressive, bombastic, triumphalistic, chaotic, or dissonant, or in some manner emotionally manipulative. That restriction may indeed eliminate many "modern" and "contemporary" classical pieces, but certainly far from all (my playlists include numerous twentieth- and twenty-first-century pieces). Obviously what constitutes aggressive, insistent, or strongly declarative music is somewhat subjective, but I needed to trust my own intuition and exclude music that I thought might likely be problematic for those under the effect of a psychedelic. A tripping mind can, of course, turn hell into heaven and vice versa, but I thought it reasonable to exclude musical selections that, for most people, might communicate or invoke negative feelings.

Lest anyone wonder whether filtering out "darker" musical materials might leave one with a tepid sea of nondescript blandness, I assure you that is emphatically not the case. The classical music you'll find in my playlists embodies and communicates a vast range of human emotion and sentiment, a complex tapestry of human consciousness and feeling communicated though a broad range of styles, colors, tones and textures. I've traveled widely and inquisitively through the vast domain of classical music, and, like Darwin collecting rare and intriguing specimens from a totally unfamiliar world, I've searched out and collected the beautiful, the profound, the appealingly strange, and the sublime. Through these sojourns, my own knowledge and feeling for classical music have expanded beyond anything I might have imagined or hoped for.

Classical Playlists on Spotify for Psychedelic Delectation

1. "Classical Music for Psychedelic States" (principal playlist)

Classical music, intuitively and lovingly curated. Confounding stereotypes, it provides exquisite environments for the free play of imagination and emotion, windows on the subconscious, mirrors reflecting infinite shades of human feeling, and intimations of the sublime and divine.

https://open.spotify.com/playlist/1cIlMlQu7LaCMeGMc6UvCo?si=01422e86edf042ac

2. "Neo-classical for Psychonauts"

Contemporary composers engaging with electronica, minimalism, ambience, cinematic styles, and other experimental forms. May serve as "classical-lite" for some, yet here you'll find no lack of beauty, mystery, aesthetic depth, or visionary inspiration.

https://open.spotify.com/playlist/16yPohEXBCdDbxxXIe7Plg?si=-58893c27a67b4fb5

3. "Positive Mood"

Classical music can seem, from afar, serious, dry, or dour. But it also can be lighthearted, joyful, whimsical, exuberant, playful, festive, even comic, often without sacrificing musical sophistication, emotional subtlety, or aesthetic charm. It can lighten moods and inspire silly dancing.

https://open.spotify.com/playlist/1J13DYyqYRmSkHaMLJHhpJ?si=f-00c6c9c05b24546

4. "Innocence, Wonder, Awe"

Music that embodies and conveys emotions of innocence and awe: a fearless, trusting openness and in-the-moment curiosity about everything, unhindered by words and concepts. A Wordsworthian child wandering in a beautiful meadow witnessing cosmic miracles through pure, ecstatic eyes.

https://open.spotify.com/playlist/4y0F45iJm7TDsfm6QFehIA?si=33c-809073dc2449c

5. "Peace, Serenity"

Pastoral, lyrical music expressing peaceful, serene states of being: free from fear, worry, or existential angst. But can music free of emotional tension be interesting, engaging, transformative? Yes, these sound worlds encompass infinite shades and nuances of human experience, feeling, and knowing.

https://open.spotify.com/playlist/2v1W31awEzwzJ0nYhWjiwV?si=-d2a58480695e4972

6. "Compassion, Love, Benevolence, Tenderness"

Our deepest, most evolved humanity: compassion, empathy, love; these most poignant emotions are described in eloquent, sublimely subtle musical language. When heard in intensified or expanded states, this becomes Bodhisattva music.

https://open.spotify.com/playlist/4Il4xv1gv5YpyX22jGGrK5?si=f-c889d9dba7742ce

7. "Introspection, Reflection, Nostalgia"

Thinking, wondering, remembering, imagining. Wistful reveries on other times and places. Or feeling the poignant poetry of nature: swaying

branches, sailing clouds, birds in flight. Or observing the inner landscape with a calm and curious mind, lucid and unhurried.
https://open.spotify.com/playlist/0KxMprwUljEp02lCbPlORP?si=a509f4656d9a4477

8. "Fantastic Journeys, Mystical Trips"
Classical pieces with changing scenes, evolving moods, descriptive twists and turns—suggesting an unfolding of events: a fantastic dream, an epic journey, a sacred quest, or some other archetypal human drama. (Note: some pieces include passages of emotional drama and intensity; choose wisely.)
https://open.spotify.com/playlist/04AccwpzngXB5vtERQuVd2?si=8c61560d5d58448a

9. "Christian Mystical Music"
Music (often trancy and trippy) from Roman Catholic, Orthodox/Byzantine, and Protestant sources, from many lands and centuries. Whatever one's spiritual orientation, beautiful and profound music is what it is: artful expressions of deeper, subtler, and transcendent realms of human experience.
https://open.spotify.com/playlist/3hsBAxnKN0Lct3UzqzgXJY?si=d-27de35112c34e1f

10. "Hoping, Longing, Yearning"
Music that sings, in various idioms, of emotional and spiritual longing in the human heart.
https://open.spotify.com/playlist/6FuiQo5180atND8myebOBw?si=ae2fd7e60d21434d

11. "Sweet Sorrow"
Perhaps personal, circumstantial sadness: a tragedy, a grieving heart. But perhaps also an awareness of the melancholy of transience, a felt sense of the human condition, of the soul's difficult sojourn in an unfamiliar, cruel, and tragic world. A longing for return to one's eternal spiritual home.
https://open.spotify.com/playlist/3JKlmPLEbz6lU4rG3TEknz?si=-f151a6b29bf74fff

12. "Women Composers"
Classical, post-classical, film music, etc.

https://open.spotify.com/playlist/5hXyg58zOMwHkgALfQGp8r?si=6289db0e0ac04e92

11

Ambient Music for Psychedelic States

If I had no choice but to designate two genres of music as being most appropriate for psychedelic use, they would almost certainly be classical and ambient. Both have substantial and unique value for psychedelics. I have already discussed classical music at some length in chapter 10, in part to make a reasonable attempt to convince those who dismiss classical for whatever reason to approach it with a fresh, de-habituated mind. If there are still holdouts, psychonauts unable or unwilling to experiment with classical, they still have for their psychedelic delectation the beauties and deep pleasures of refined ambient music.

I offer the same to lovers of classical music who may wrongly suppose that ambient is just another name for "New Age" music, and therefore assume it to be lightweight, insipid easy-listening or "woo-woo" music. First of all, ambient music isn't the same as New Age, at least in my own thinking. Even if we lack clear, concise definitions that might neatly separate the two, in most cases I find little problem distinguishing between them. At the risk of courting controversy, I will simply say that, to my ears, New Age(y) music tends to have a more conventional, "safe," formulaic, generally more commercial sound. New Age music seems mainly meant to soothe and relax, to take the edge off life, to offer one feelings of safety and satiety. There are, of course, brilliant exceptions. But where New Age music seems to say "Be happy" or "Calm Thyself" or "Don't worry about a thing" or "Isn't life sweet?" or "Aren't we feeling spiritual today?," the more evolved ambient instead seems to say, "Prepare for a Cosmic journey," or "Behold the ineffable wonders," or "Turn off your mind and float into this multidimensional time warp." In the course of literally thousands of hours of deep listening to ambient music, along with varieties of music that may claim that designation, I developed an ear for choosing items for my several ambient playlists that I hope would please the ear, the heightened sensibilities, and the well-traveled soul of the psychedelic listener.

Some creators of ambient music are genuine composers, people who know music deeply, artists with a refined instinct for the psychological effects of various sound textures (since melody, as such, usually doesn't play a prominent role in ambient). A surprising number of ambient composers are "classically trained." Among myriad examples, I offer the following select list of track titles that provide a clear indication of the intentions and obsessions of many ambient artists.[1]

Mycelium Dawn
Kaleidoscopic Mind
Utopian Moon Garden
Ethereal Dreams
Untold Depths
Unconditional Love
Healing Earth
A Sacred Mind
Samadhi
Tree Spirits
Electric Dreams
Waves of Light
Moonlit Flowers
Enchanting Forest
Shower of Love and Light
Spacetime Curvature
Planetary Consciousness
Prismatic Sky
Time Tunnel
Death Is Eternal Bliss

The themes suggested are clear: portals and doorways to other worlds, the infinitude and unlimited wonders of the cosmos, the intoxicating and multidimensional beauties of nature, the oceanic depths of the mind, wide-open and extended senses, hallucinatory visions, aesthetic awe, mystic light, dream states, visionary states, enlightened states, invisible worlds, spiritual emotions, the sacred.

Even if you, the lover of classical music, cherish and feel content listening to classical pieces on psychedelics, there are times when the mind is so "full," so saturated or oversaturated with visual and emotional input/output, that even a gentle classical piece may feel like too much to process. The words "too much" always set off in my mind the rhythmic chanting of those words in George Harrison's obvious paean to tripping "It's All Too Much," which speaks of that sense of being overwhelmed by the sheer quantity and intensity of inner experience. When that happens, you may find that a minimalistic piece of ambient is the perfect sound-cloud on which to rest a weary psyche. Most ambient music has a spacious, flowing, timeless quality that is less likely to add significant experiential "mass" to a psychedelic state. Most of it is soothing, while still possessing aesthetic interest and a subtle multidimensionality.

There are also times, while listening to classical during a trip, that the music itself may lose its magical edge or even take a dark turn. In an experiential realm in which the mind is vulnerable and changeable, a classical piece may unexpectedly turn sour and unpleasant. When that happens, a gentle, flowing, high-vibe piece of ambient may become a saving grace. We've discussed in some depth the power of music to embody and evoke emotion and how that manifests in psychedelic states. Sometimes, however, emotion—however deep, meaningful, and revelatory—may itself become "too much"—may begin to feel overbearing or suffocating. Then too, ambient may be the perfect alternative, in part because it tends to be emotionally undemanding. That is not to say that ambient is in any sense merely "intellectual" or devoid of feeling, but rather that its inherent beauty and mystery does not depend on evoking an emotional response. Of course in a psychedelic state one can pile emotion onto anything, but it is rather less likely when the music lacks emotional specificity or dynamic range.

The experience, while tripping, of unexpected changes in the sound or "personality" even of beloved classical pieces is well documented: "It was a symphony of Brahms, and despite the fact he had long been one of my favorite composers, the music seemed heavy, earth-bound, and so discordantly ugly I called Dr. Davidson to shut it off."[2] "I remember particularly with some humor when a religious hymn turned into the sound of nagging voices."[3] A final example, this one involving music not becoming ponderous or discordant but lightweight and insubstantial: "S now reported 'a strange alteration of the emotional tone of the experience.' The lute music now seemed 'much too innocuous' and the *Brandenburg No. 4* was played—this being the same concerto to which S had responded so powerfully the previous week. Now, however, S reported that the concerto 'sounds very simple this time. Almost a simple little "pop" tune. Yet always before Bach's music has seemed to me almost as complicated as the God-Idea. This is amazing!'"[4]

The value of ambient music for psychedelic states is discussed by science writer Zoe Cormier, who cites neuroscientist (and musician) Christopher Timmermann of Imperial College London's Center for Psychedelic Research, who, she explains, "thinks the current trend for calm, quiet, ambient music serves psychedelic therapy best." Quoting Timmermann:

> From a neuroscientific perspective, there's only so much sonically that you can take in. When music is too disorganized, busy, and chaotic, it's not typically conducive to emotional breakthroughs. What most people need is music that is spacious: Abrasive and imposing music doesn't give enough space—enough sensory space, cognitive space, or emotional space for people to put their own stories and thoughts at the forefront of their experience and organize their minds. I also think the ambient genre is helpful because it is "decontextualized"—you don't have issues with locality, cultural appropriation, or triggering.[5]

The takeaway, here, is not the literal or obvious point that ambient music is superior to music that is inherently "disorganized, busy, and chaotic," but rather that under certain subjective circumstances, any music, even the most sublime, may be experienced as busy, chaotic, abrasive, imposing—sonically overwhelming—in which case ambient music is a valuable alternative.

As many different styles of music fall under the heading "classical," so does ambient music encompass different styles and sound qualities. And as not all classical is psychedelic-friendly, so it is with ambient. Similar to working with classical and other genres in the curation process, I have devoted much time and my best intuition in choosing the most felicitous ambient pieces for inclusion in my several ambient playlists on Spotify.

The primary ambient playlist that I compiled is titled simply "Psychedelic Ambient." The necessarily brief description on Spotify reads: "Expanses of free-form (beat-free) trippy electronica—immersive sound universes within which to dream and have visions and awakenings. Curated for psychedelic flavors of bliss-filled awe and wonder." https://open.spotify.com/playlist/450hrPZ6dYB1osiP4D3mYF?si=55c3a45d269e4853

Besides that principal or "best-of" list, there are five additional ambient (or mostly ambient) playlists, each constructed around a common sound-theme:

1. "Spacious/Ethereal"

Smooth, flowing, diaphanous, gently supportive sound textures that are like a big soft cloud for the soul to lay back upon while calmly beholding wonders. Shimmering, nearly empty sound canvases ready to receive and mirror the subtle movements of consciousness and being.

https://open.spotify.com/playlist/0jSfXDL1minqrXOrlxaURA?si=6b63b35c90ce4831

2. "Interstellar/Cosmic"

Spacious ambient pieces that may suggest endless journeys through infinite—interior or exterior—space. Some items feature a sci-fi vibe or a light-industrial texture that may evoke images and sensations of technological space-flight.

https://open.spotify.com/playlist/73gxiXU3JgGUJOnQSMZZeR?si=2172d77841e84751

3. "Alien, Otherworldly, Other-dimensional"

Like the previous playlist "Interstellar," but with an extra infusion of trippy "alien" weirdness, suggesting encounters with alien worlds, other-dimensional beings, inscrutable cosmic mysteries: sonic intuitions of the sheer, mind-blowing strangeness of antipodal otherness.

https://open.spotify.com/playlist/1zvLGS1Z3IN2VWpjcbkOvB?si=0c24375f53ce4252

4. "Emptiness/Oblivion"

Minimal tones and textures that flow on endlessly with little change or variation, drone-like—invoking, perhaps, a sense of eternity, oneness, emptiness, or sweet oblivion. These pieces offer the subtle sonic vibrations of a sublime transcendence, a shimmering within a vast ocean of cosmic wisdom and bliss.

https://open.spotify.com/playlist/4tN8LsJQkolEQS5AMD6fYj?si=381284dc12dd4203

5. "Primordial Depths"

(1) Oceanic, sub-marine, deep-sea, whale-song; (2) Subterranean, caves/caverns, earth tremors; (3) Prenatal, womb, heartbeat; (4) Cosmic origins, primordial soup. "Primordial Depths" includes, besides ambient pieces, recordings from nature such as deep ocean currents, whale and dolphin songs, womb sounds, heartbeat, as well as deep-pitched electronic tones and white noise.

https://open.spotify.com/playlist/1Kamlij9UORfWwrtSxovwa?si=e3db6c143dda4805

Two related lists are:

1. "Electronic Music for Altered States"

Difficult to define, but less minimal than "ambient," but far less insistently rhythmic than Techno/Rave. Compared to ambient, this intelligently composed electronic music displays more complex musical structures, rhythms, and forward movement. A few items are more experimental and difficult to categorize.

https://open.spotify.com/playlist/3R9B8Ciazh7tzp67YbMmFG?si=a7edd2ea17974536

2. "Neo-Classical for Psychonauts"

Contemporary composers engaging with electronica, minimalism, ambience, cinematic styles, and other experimental forms. May serve as "classical-lite" for some, yet here you'll find no lack of beauty, mystery, aesthetic depth, or visionary inspiration.

https://open.spotify.com/playlist/16yPohEXBCdDbxxXIe7Plg?si=-58893c27a67b4fb5

Note that much neo- (or post-) classical music contains ambient qualities, often blending the two, with some or many of its composers working in both genres. Many psychonauts who avoid "standard" classical are quite enamored of this genre, and no doubt lovers of classical will find much appeal in these more ethereal, abstract interpretations of that genre. One may think of neo-classical, generally speaking, as a friendly, fruitful marriage between classical and ambient.

12

"World Music" and the Collective Unconscious

There is an infinite abundance of music coming to us from every corner of the earth, more than any one person can digest in several lifetimes. While curating my Spotify playlist "World Music," I indeed explored the *world* of music, covering as much territory as possible, seeking as broad a representation of cultural sources as possible, without sacrificing the core curatorial intention of providing music supportive of psychedelic states. Though unavoidably far from exhaustive, my search did yield music of many different shapes, colors, and frequencies. In my brief (limited by Spotify to 300 taps of the keyboard) description of that playlist, I describe it as "Music from 'other' places and cultures, from otherly cultured minds, other music modalities. Entheogens facilitate a profound 'feeling into' unfamiliar territory through deep, intuitive, empathic openness. What formerly may have seemed alien may now glow with intense beauty and universal meaning."[1] Perhaps you'll find that to be true when you sample some of these recordings, especially in a heightened state. Because music so effectively expresses the subtleties of culture, consciousness, and emotion, this playlist is intended to introduce the sensitized listener to a wide spectrum of flavors of consciousness, ways of being, and alternative feeling-states. Listening to these sounds in a state of unconditional receptivity and unconditioned awareness provides rare access to the inner spirit, and perhaps the living spirits, of many a culture and religious tradition.

While soaking in the delicious multitoned music of distant cultures, even in a deeply receptive and empathetic state, we still need to acknowledge that fundamental cultural differences may prevent us from experiencing a full revelation of how the sounds are heard and mentally/emotionally processed by members of those cultures. Oxford professor of music psychology and aesthetics Eric Clarke explains why that is:

> Musical listening and musical consciousness are profoundly culturally and historically specific, and any attempts to generalize about music perception and musical consciousness come up against the unassailable otherness of different times and places. . . . The range of factors that might need to be considered is indeed overwhelming, encompassing aesthetic attitudes, the physical circumstances of musical events, people's memory skills and associative networks, the "cognitive style" of orality and of literacy, the impact of different kinds of representations of music (scores, paintings and other depictions, recordings), aesthetic ideologies, religious beliefs, conceptual and perceptual categories, relationships between music, dance, and drama—a panoply of biosocial factors as they might relate not only to music, but beyond that to the whole auditory and corporeal context of a historical subject.[2]

We can understand, therefore, that although psychedelics may greatly augment our receptivity and sensitivity to unfamiliar cultural forms, our innate conditioned subjectivity and lack of cultural omniscience may limit the possibility of unfettered experiential immersion in "foreign" sounds. Nevertheless, one is likely to be amazed, when listening to music from Bali, Tuva, India, or Armenia, that "what formerly may have seemed alien may now glow with intense beauty and universal meaning."

Many of the items you'll find in the World Music playlist are carefully chosen examples of the sacred music of a wide variety of religious and spiritual traditions. As musicologist and religion scholar Guy L. Beck explains, sacred music is a prime communicator of the religious and spiritual traditions from which they emerge, providing closer and deeper access to the inner mysteries of those traditions than that which can be offered by any purely intellectual or academic approach:

> Music and chant can no longer be viewed as marginal to religious experience or as gratuitous to some kind of theoretical religious enterprise, but must be seen as integrated into deep primary levels of religious meaning throughout world

history. . . . Accordingly, religious music often unveils the core or mystery of a faith tradition in ways that elude theology, philosophy, linguistics, historiography, literary criticism, or the social sciences. Enlarging upon Rudolf Otto's notion of the holy or "numinous" as beyond the scope of reason and morality . . . the holy or "sacred," as a category of practical human experience does not truly exist in a vacuum, nor solely in the intellect or merely in silence, but as consistently bound up with vocal and musical expression.[3]

Beck points to several different religious traditions, including Sufism, Hasidism, Hindu Bhakti, and "some Buddhist sects," noting that the music produced by explicitly mystical traditions "is employed to achieve particular states of ecstasy and bliss, termed *exstasis* in the texts of ancient mystery religions."[4] It is not difficult to imagine that when such sounds enter the ears of one already deeply sensitized to sound and to the sacred, the effects can be quite transformative.

Claudio Naranjo explains how psychedelics make us more "permeable" to these and other spiritual influences, and to great musicians from various religious cultures whose music transmits qualities like compassion, joy, ecstasy, and serenity:

> In the same way that psychedelic experience makes us more permeable to the direct spiritual influence of shamans or people more advanced than ourselves in our spiritual development, it also makes us more permeable to the spiritual wealth of music, be it religious music, the Western classics, or classical Hindu, Arabic, Turkish, or Chinese music—and no doubt the psychedelic experience of many in the sixties explains why such a great deal of ethnic music from all over the world has come into our culture. . . . [M]ore important than the emphasis on the repertoire seems to me the notion that the great musicians, both from the East and the West, have been transmitters of experiences that belong to that higher stratum of the mind to which also belong compassion, true joy and ecstasy, kindness, and detached serenity.[5]

Musician, composer. and musicologist Peter Michael Hamel reminds us that many psychedelic pioneers, drawn to the traditional musical forms of Asia, Africa, and elsewhere, traveled to and explored the music of those lands and then brought those influences back to the West, with the effect, significantly, of providing "access to the collective unconscious via music":

> Many [of these pioneers] . . . learnt exotic instruments, Indian chants or African rhythms—not so as to escape from incompatibility with present reality, but in order consciously to re-encounter the submerged magical mythical level of their own consciousness. . . . More and more young people from America and Europe were following the newly-discovered routes, returning in exotic clothes and bringing back with them Arabic, Indian, Javanese, Japanese, African or South American music as evidence of having undertaken the Great Journey. Accidentally or otherwise they had encountered cultures that were magically and mythically aware. . . . The very thing which most threatens to disappear from these ancient cultures is being impressed upon them as being of quintessential importance—their access to the collective unconscious via music.[6]

Hamel explains that this musical encounter serves to remind us of the "magical power" of music and, again, how music functions as a repository of the collective unconscious:

> Through the encounter with the non-European cultures a rediscovery of the suggestive effects of music has become possible for us in our present over-rationalised age. The knowledge of the magical power of music, for millennia an essential part of cultures the world over, is starting to figure prominently in the interests of many contemporary composers and music groups. Prolonged chants, ecstatic rhythms and ancient melodic patterns can carry present-day Westerners into states of consciousness that bring about a momentary release from the subjective personality and permit experience of the collective unconscious within the human psyche.[7]

Returning to the musical present, Stanislav Grof offers a rich array of suggestions for world music to be relished while tripping. His recommendations, particularly for "end-of-session relaxing music," include Ravi Shankar, music for Zen meditation, and Japanese music for the bamboo flute. He also speaks generally of ethnic music that is *"specifically designed as techniques for altering consciousness"* [emphasis added], offering these examples:

> Among the most powerful recordings in this category are the multivocal chanting of the Tantric Buddhist tradition in Tibet; the Hindu kirtans; the monkey chant, or ketjak, and other trance-inducing music from Bali; shamanic music from various parts of Asia, North America and South America; the hocketing of the Congolese Pygmies; trance music of the Kung! Bushmen of the Kalahari desert; and chants from the Sufi ceremonies. Similarly, Greek sirtak dances, flute music from the Andes, recordings of the African oud, songs of the Bauls of Bengal, Armenian liturgical chants, Spanish flamenco guitar music, and other interesting ethnic pieces are useful for psychedelic sessions.[8]

William Richards, from whom we've heard much with regard to Western classical music, offers these recommendations in world music:

> Some intricate percussive music, such as the trance music of Abdelmadjid Guemguem, known as Guem, has been reported to catalyze profoundly spiritual states of awareness for some listeners. Also the use of psychedelic substances for many has triggered a newfound appreciation for classical Indian ragas, such as the Carnatic compositions of Tyagaraja (1767–1847), with their repetitive rhythms and quarter-tone pitches. Even solemn Gregorian chants, mantras that often catalyze the progressive deepening of meditative forms of awareness, have been found uniquely effective by some people.[9]

Luis Eduardo Luna, an anthropologist who studies traditional Indigenous use of ayahuasca, suggests "tribal ethnic music," which he describes as "especially evocative; it may allow for experiencing the extraordinary cultural diversity still existing in the world."[10] It came somewhat as a surprise to me that my Spotify playlist bearing the broad title "Tribal, Trance, Drums, Shamanic, Ayahuasca" has attracted the greatest number of listeners. It's an eclectic collection, to be sure, including field recordings of remote African tribes, Shipibo shamans, ayahuasca ritual music, didjeridoo meditations, and percussive and ritual music from Africa, Indonesia, and the Middle East, along with contemporary studio recordings of modern performers exploring and interpreting the trance/tribal genre. My accompanying description reads: "Multi-cultural and cross-genre drumming, rhythm-making, ritual chant and dance (sacred and profane, raw & cooked, field & studio), expressing or suggesting group ritual, communal trance, shared ecstasy, shamanic healing, and music itself as a pathway to other worlds. Exotic, rare and unexpected gems."[11]

For a final reflection on the use of "sacred music" in psychedelic sessions: Jonathan Goldman, prominent composer of ambient and meditation music, offers an appropriate bit of wisdom. When asked by an interviewer to comment on where to find "sacred sounds," he responds:

> Anything can be a sacred sound, depending upon the intention we put into the sound. . . . It is very necessary for us not to get judgmental about what is and what is not a sacred sound. . . . Each one of us is such a unique vibratory being, all at different stages of physical, emotional, mental, spiritual and evolutionary development. . . . [H]ealing is such an individual thing. . . . Since we are all at such different levels of evolution, what works for me, may not have any effect on somebody else.[12]

In our choices of "sacred" or any other music for psychedelic purposes, let us be that broadminded and flexible in our definitions.

Close Up: Indian Classical Music

Ravi Shankar describes his music as a path, a spiritual discipline:

> Our tradition teaches us that sound is God—Nada Brahma. That is, musical sound and the musical experience are steps to the realization of the self. We view music as a kind of spiritual discipline that raises one's inner being to divine peacefulness and bliss. . . . The highest aim of our music is to reveal the essence of the universe it reflects, and the ragas are among the means by which this essence can be apprehended. Thus, through music, one can reach God.[13]

Shankar goes on to describe the essential difference between Indian and Western music: "Whereas a Western composition may be based on many moods and tonal colors, often sharply contrasting, the Indian melody concentrates on only one principal mood or emotion throughout, dwelling on it, expanding, elaborating. Thus, the effect becomes intense and hypnotic and often magical."[14]

Yehudi Menuhin, a classical violinist and towering figure in twentieth-century music, studied both yoga and Indian music in depth and collaborated with Ravi Shankar in a series of historic recordings blending the Western and Indian classical genres. Here he advises how best to approach Indian classical music:

> To appreciate Indian music one has to adopt a completely different sense of values . . . one must orientate oneself and, at least for the period concerned, forget there is a time-clock ticking away, and merely sink into a kind of subjective, almost hypnotic, trance. In that condition the repetitive features of Indian music, both rhythmic and melodic, acquire an extraordinary fascination and charm . . . despite the domination of this hypnotic mood, a characteristic of Indian music is that far from deadening the intellect, it actively liberates the mind.[15]

No wonder, then, that Indian classical music often strongly appeals to a meditative or spiritual sensibility. What through impatient ears may sound monotonous or boring will often sound entirely different, even magical or sublime, when distracted, ego-centric attention subsides while in a heightened state.

In a recent, definitive biography of Ravi Shankar, Oliver Craske describes the rise of interest in Indian music in the West during the 1960s:

> To many of the new hippies India represented an ancient, more enlightened culture . . . and Indian music was rising up through this efflorescence. Ravi found himself at the center of a psychedelically hued sunburst. . . .
>
> By the spring of 1967 Indian music was playing a ritual role for many of the new psychedelic explorers. When the writer Joan Didion sat in to observe a group of friends taking an LSD trip, she noted that four hours passed with no sound except

for the sitar music on the stereo. Many of the very musicians so attracted by Indian music were using the drug, including members of the Beatles,[16] as Paul McCartney revealed to *Life* magazine in June, and the Doors, who took their name from Aldous Huxley's book *The Doors of Perception*, his own ode to mescaline.[17]

Craske quotes author Jon Savage, who writes that Indian classical music became "*the central aural metaphor for LSD and the wider hallucinogenic experience*" [emphasis added].[18] Elaborating on this theme, author David Reck comments, "The sounds of Hindusthani instrumental music . . . became associated in the collective mind of the counterculture, European and American . . . with the spaced-out alternative consciousness state induced by drugs, ranging from marijuana to LSD, peyote and other hallucinogens. North Indian classical music, with its expanded timesense, perceived repetitiveness and hypnotic harmonics of the tambura drone . . . became a code for 'trippiness.'"[19]

In his book *Through Music to the Self*, Peter Michael Hamel chronicles the popularity of Indian classical music during the psychedelic 1960s and beyond. He begins by quoting from an early (1921) reaction to Indian music by Hermann Keyserlingk, an appreciative, metaphysically minded German traveler in India. Keyserlingk's romantic description provides an interesting foretaste of how this music would be received several decades later during the countercultural era:

> This music could neither be reduced to the framework of a melody, nor be related to particular harmonies, nor analysed in terms of a straightforward rhythm; even single notes varied in shape. . . . It is not easy to explain in words what Indian music means, for it has so little in common with ours: . . . it is a rushing and surging of the ever-flowing stream of life. Hence a like effect on the listener: it does not tire one, could go on forever, for nobody ever has enough of life . . . In no way does it reflect Time, but the circumstances of life, projected against the background of Eternity . . .
>
> A French artist once remarked of Indian music: "C'est la musique du corps astral" ["It is the music of the astral body."]. That is precisely what it is (in so far as there is an astral realm corresponding to the traditional concepts): a vast, unmeasurable

world in which states take the place of circumstances. One experiences nothing definite, nothing tangible while listening to it, and yet one feels most intensely alive. While following the cadences of the notes one is in reality listening to one's own self . . .

The quintessential point about Indian music is that it lies in a different dimension to ours. . . . The essence of this music lies elsewhere; in the dimension of pure intensity; there it needs no broad surface layer.[20]

Writing in the late 1970s, Hamel explains how the combination of psychedelics and Indian music opened many an inner ear, inspiring an "awakening through the medium of sound":

Concerts involving Indian musicians . . . have opened the inner ear of many people both young and old and set in train, so to speak, a spiritual awakening through the medium of sound. This had more than a little to do, in those days, with the psychedelic drugs, which encouraged an abandoned, relaxed form of listening: soon it became fashionable to listen to Indian music while "high." In the "Underground," the many new spiritual communities that have grown up in Europe and America over the years, Indian music is enjoying an ever-growing popularity. For those people who are involved in yoga or meditation . . . or in some other way gradually learning to increase their awareness of their own inner selves, Classical Indian music—the southern, *Karnatic* form just as much as the *Hindustani* music of the north—can prove itself a marvelous vehicle for the journey into the sub- and superconscious.[21]

Hamel, reflecting Yehudi Menuhin's words quoted earlier, offers some sage advice on the art of listening to Indian music, emphasizing that to get "the feel" of it, to penetrate its seemingly monotonous and alien surface, one must surrender and listen at a deep heart level:

An essential precondition [to hearing/understanding Indian music] is a willingness and surrender on the part of the listener . . . The sound of a single, prolonged note, or of a continually recurring sequence of notes, is more likely to make an exclusively mentally-oriented person edgy and irritable than

> to exert a calming or pleasant influence on him. Indian music, which springs directly from the mythical consciousness, requires a relaxed letting-go of oneself, an expectationless perseverance, the ability passively to penetrate those levels where unceasing thought and reasoning have no more power. . . .
>
> For Indian music, as for the performer himself, it is much more important that the public should be able to listen with the heart, rather than observe the musical development or "appreciate" the music critically and dispassionately. . . . This "listening with the heart" is . . . a very aware condition requiring both receptivity and the faculty of conscious, discriminating perception. Once one has "got the feel of" Indian music, its monotony suddenly becomes so colourful and full of nuances that its riches start to spill over into deeper dimensions.[22]

Hamel closes his meditation on psychedelics and traditional Indian music with this description of a 1970 sitar concert in Berlin by the master Imrat Khan:

> [T]he legend that this sitar-player could send one "on a trip," even without drugs, preceded him to the sold-out concert. . . . Many of those present at the evening concert underwent a magical sensation such as they had never before experienced. . . . Imrat Khan's music was at once urgent, hesitant and flowing, now robust and austere, now innocently merry, and finally sweetly romantic. At certain moments I found myself trembling, and it was as though gold-dust were trickling over me—an image that others present were to confirm. In the end the playing of Imrat's sitar became so moving that many began to weep. Imrat Khan himself was weeping too, and he told us later that these powers had been summoned up not by himself but by his School [musical lineage], his guru and his teachers' teachers. He saw himself merely as the medium of this music.[23]

Close-Up: Tibetan Ritual Music and Chant

Perhaps you've heard a recording of chants by the Gyuto monks of Tibet. Their highly distinctive, acoustically complex multiphonic vocal style was essentially "discovered" and brought to the West by Professor Huston Smith, mentioned earlier as a renowned religion scholar who has written a number of important essays on the religious significance of psychedelics.[24] More than once, Smith referred, with a note of irony, to his serendipitous encounter with and wide disclosure of Tibetan multiphonic music as "the one empirical discovery of my career."[25]

> If there is one thing I would like to be remembered for, it is not that I wrote *The World's Religions*, which has become a standard textbook for introductory courses. Rather, it is that mine were the first Western ears on which the chanting of the Gyuto monks comprehendingly fell. This made me the conduit through which this astounding vocal phenomenon was transmitted to Europe and America. Though I published the first recording of the Gyuto multiphonic chanting, it is Mickey Hart's indefatigable labors . . . that have brought the Gyuto monks into the spotlight of world acclaim.[26]

The following account of the "discovery" is blended from several sources:

> It was 3 o'clock one morning in 1964, on the eve of the highest holiday in the Tibetan calendar, when renowned religion scholar Huston Smith awoke in a monastery in the Himalayas to experience something transcendent. "There fell upon my ear the holiest sound I have ever heard."[27] "I was teaching at MIT then, and my first thought was 'They'll never believe me. I've got to get some proof at MIT.'"[28] Smith made a recording of the chanting, eventually bringing it back to the Massachusetts Institute of Technology. "There, he played it for a colleague [an acoustics specialist], who was similarly flabbergasted"[29] and with whom he later co-authored an article in the *Journal of the Acoustical Society of America*.[30] "Had I not possessed, first, a musical ear which alerted me immediately to the fact that in the Gyuto (Tibetan) chanting I was in the presence of something subtly astonishing; and second, a musical temperament which required that I get to the bottom of what had so moved me, the 'important landmark in the study of music' which *Ethnomusicology* (January 1972) credited the find, would not have been forthcoming."[31]

Since that time, other recordings of Tibetan monastic chant have appeared, along with other forms of Tibetan religious and ritual music.

Jonathan Goldman interestingly compares the multiphonic sound of Tibetan chanting with the sound of the Australian didjeridu, suggesting that both create "interdimensional windows":

> The Tibetan voice is a multi-dimensional sound. It's a sound that is also found in the didjeridu, an instrument played by the Australian Aboriginal people. I wonder how these two traditions, so totally different, created a sound so similar.
>
> The didjeridu is a blown instrument, found by the Aborigines in Dreamtime. The legend of the Wandjina, the Dreamtime people, is that they gave the didjeridu to the Aboriginal people, after they had created everything through sound. This was done so that when the Aborigines blew the didjeridu, they could contact the Wandjina, who would then come down to them. This is the same thing that happens with the Tibetans. They do an extraordinary visualization while they do this deep bass, guttural harmonic chant, with the intention to bring down their particular Tibetan deities. It may be that, in terms of their thoughtform consciousness, the way they manifest interdimensional, extraterrestrial, or stellar consciousness is through the Tibetan Deity forms. It's a different form and shape and belief system than the Aboriginal people have, but both these sounds create interdimensional windows. I'm quite interested in exploring this.[32]

A general sense of the metaphysical and cosmological significance of Tibetan Buddhist ritual music is provided by Lama Anagarika Govinda, who explains:

> Tibetan Buddhism regards man not as a solitary figure but always in connection with and against a universal background. In the same way Tibetan ritual music is not concerned with the emotions of temporal individuality, but with the ever-present, timeless qualities of universal life, in which our personal joys and sorrows do not exist, so that we feel in communion with the very sources of reality in the deepest core of our being. To bring us in touch with this realm is the purpose of meditation as well as of Tibetan ritual music, which is built upon the deepest

vibrations that an instrument or a human voice can produce: sounds that seem to come from the womb of the earth or from the depth of space like rolling thunder, the mantric sound of nature, which symbolize the creative vibrations of the universe, the origin of all things. They form the foundation as well as the background from which the modulations of the higher voices and the plaintive notes of the reed instruments rise like the forms of sentient life from the elementary forces of nature.[33]

Putting a fine spin on this discussion of Tibetan music, we have William Richards describing an unexpected, paradoxical exchange with a Tibetan religious leader:

> I vividly recall an evening in the mountainous terrain of Northern India, when I had been graciously invited to dinner in the home of Tendon Choegyal and his wife, Rinchen Khandro. . . . He is the youngest brother of Tenzin Gyatso, His Holiness, the 14th Dalai Lama.
> . . . Feeling honored to be in the presence of these auspicious Tibetan leaders for a few precious hours, I asked myself what I most wanted to discuss with them. One topic my mind seized upon was Tibetan music with its orchestration of unique horns, drums, cymbals, and gongs. I had heard of theories that different piercing or reverberating frequencies of sound might evoke various discrete phenomena within human consciousness and had listened to monks gutturally chanting "om mani padme hum" (roughly, "homage to the jewel in the center of the lotus") in the temple of the Dalai Lama with occasional bursts of instrumental accompaniment. "Tendzin," I said, "I'd be interested to learn something from you about Tibetan music and its relationship to consciousness." After a calming pause, he smiled and answered, "Bill, if you want to know the music that moves me most deeply spiritually, it is Beethoven's Pathetique Symphony."[34]

My World Music Spotify Playlists

I encourage readers to explore the riches of music from throughout the world, whether or not any particular piece of music is formally religious, the expression of some specific tradition. In many cultures we do not encounter the strong conceptual demarcation between religious and secular that we find in the modern West. Whether or not driven by some specific spiritual orientation, a human being who is using a musical instrument, or their voice, to express authentic love or longing or wonder, or any namable or unnamable human feeling, is music for the soul, an aid to expanding or refining consciousness.

Though I deeply appreciate and relish music from various regions of the world, I cannot possibly do justice here, in writing, to all of them. My personal favorite regional music happens to be that of India, not only Indian classical music but also various forms of devotional, ceremonial, folk, and secular. Most of this music can be discovered in these Spotify playlists:

1. "World Music"

Music from "other" places and cultures, from otherly-cultured minds, other music modalities. Entheogens facilitate a profound "feeling into" unfamiliar territory through deep, intuitive, empathic openness. What formerly may have seemed alien may now glow with intense beauty and universal meaning.

https://open.spotify.com/playlist/4g3FIjgzXB5oxkDzgHmTgv?si=33b33fcb2ab849eb.

2. "Tribal, Trance, Drums, Shamanic, Ayahuasca"

Multi-cultural and cross-genre drumming, rhythm-making, ritual chant and dance (sacred and profane, raw and cooked, field and studio), expressing or suggesting group ritual, communal trance, shared ecstasy, shamanic healing, and music itself as a pathway to other worlds. Exotic, rare and unexpected gems.

https://open.spotify.com/playlist/1q1S47ltVdq32KznkAeoxH?si=909d843f8072483b.

3. "Earth Women Sing"

Beautiful, powerful, poignant, mysterious, meditative, ecstatic—with every color and nuance of human feeling and emotion—sourced from many cultures and languages (lyrics rarely English). Drawn from several of my other playlists, and then some.

https://open.spotify.com/playlist/4pJEYzOhKNNqkNqNYd6N3A?si=4b5fee9de6454a1d

4. "Indian Classical Music"

Instrumental and vocal performances by Indian musicians of both the Northern (Hindustani) and Southern (Karnatic) traditions. With ancient spiritual roots, this music is, for many, uncannily "psychedelic." Instruments include sitar, vina, sarod, sarangi, bansuri flute, violin, shehnai, and tabla.

https://open.spotify.com/playlist/7KMTOeSTcHQeb4Qikb9uyc?si=96d80e81aa2747fc

5. "Hindu Prayers, Meditations, Devotions"

My choices are guided by subjective criteria including musicality, authenticity of expression, depth and nuance of emotion, and mystical suggestiveness: a hint, a hue, an echo of the eternal sublime. Includes both traditional and modern interpreters and performers. Strong in Krishna-bhakti.

https://open.spotify.com/playlist/7luVv1s2W9j6stFFgObAaZ?si=5d1c93c83852440b

6. "Tamboura Drones"

The unfretted four-stringed Indian tamboura, whose sound-resonator is a massive gourd, produces a deeply hypnotic harmonic drone awash in overtones: the sweet hum of eternity. A wonderful sonic meditation in any state of mind.

https://open.spotify.com/playlist/4NJhxhdmCHe1rne2m2F6RJ?si=85e6d6ced6cb4e6d

7. "Psychedelica Indica"

Multi-genre music blending Indian and psychedelic flavors.

https://open.spotify.com/playlist/217VPYwe90xI9AlCSRLjkO?si=98790730bb374fc0.

13

Sound Alternatives to Music

The Music of Nature and "White Noise"

The Music of Nature

A beautiful quote usually attributed to Shakespeare (but belonging, instead, to the poem "The Magic of Sound" by an obscure poet named Reginald Holmes) says that "The earth has its music for those who will listen." Many sensitive souls can hear that music. Ravi Shankar, for one, was quoted as saying, "I hear music in the waves, the breeze, the rain and even in the rustle of the leaves."[1] In the course of research for this book, I have not made a separate, focused study of the psychological effects of listening to the sounds of nature, whether on psychedelics or otherwise, whether out in nature or listening to a recording. I will say that I have found the experience of listening to a good field recording of nature sounds through headphones while on a psychedelic (rain, flowing water, ocean waves, forest sounds, wind, thunderstorms, birdsong, whale song, etc.) to be indescribably beautiful, inspiring, and deeply meaningful. Stanislav Grof supports this practice: "Occasionally, recordings of natural sounds might be very effective. Here belong, for example, the intra-abdominal sounds of a pregnant woman . . . , songs of the humpback whales, voices of the wolves, noises of insects, such as chirping of crickets or humming of the bees, singing of passerine birds, rushing of creeks and rivers, the rhythms of the splashing waves approaching the ocean shore." [2]

There may be times while tripping when music of any kind, however apparently unobtrusive, may begin to feel like an imposition, either because its presence somehow feels inorganic or "unnatural" (as a human creation), overbearing (too directive or manipulative), or simply that the mysterious richness of silence is preferred. Because we ourselves are part of the physical universe, our bodies made of organic matter, the sounds of nature, the songs of the Earth, can feel very reassuring, embracing, calming, and inspiring.

Human imagination, being the incredibly powerful and protean force that it is, particularly under the influence of a psychedelic, can transform a light rain (or any sound from nature) into ineffably beautiful music. Charles Baudelaire writes of the "alarming seductiveness" of the sound of water while under the influence of hashish:

> I have noticed that water assumes an alarming seductiveness for all artistically inclined minds when they are illuminated by hashish. Flowing water, fountains, rippling cascades, the blue immensity of the sea, roll along, sleeping and singing in the depths of your mind. It might perhaps not be a good idea to leave a man in this state next to a stretch of limpid water; like the fisherman in the ballad, he might perhaps allow himself to be dragged down by Undine.[3]

A less foreboding take on the mystical suggestiveness of water is beautifully expressed in a song by the psychedelically oriented Scottish folk group the Incredible String Band, aptly titled "The Water Song":

> God made a song when the world was new,
> Water's laughter sings it through.
> Oh, wizard of changes, teach me the lesson of flowing.[4]

It is only natural that a psychedelic state amplifies the beauties and mysteries of nature and its music. Michael Pollan writes of Alexander von Humboldt, the early nineteenth-century German scientist, "who revolutionized our understanding of the natural world" by citing human imagination and subjectivity as the best means for understanding nature's mysteries:

> Humboldt believed it is only with our feelings, our senses, and our imaginations—that is, with the faculties of human subjectivity—that we can ever penetrate nature's secrets. "Nature everywhere speaks to man in a voice" that is "familiar to his

soul." There is an order and beauty organizing the system of nature—a system that Humboldt, after briefly considering the name "Gaia," chose to call "Cosmos"—but it would never have revealed itself to us if not for the human imagination, which is itself of course a product of nature, of the very system it allows us to comprehend. The modern conceit of the scientist attempting to observe nature with perfect objectivity, as if from a vantage located outside it, would have been anathema to Humboldt. "I myself am identical with nature."[5]

Immersion in recorded sounds of nature can inspire elaborate visions of the natural world in all its cosmic complexity and profundity. Even through headphones, nature can speak to us "in a voice familiar to our soul" when our senses and imagination have been made porous and acutely sensitive. Here Pollan describes his own experience of nature manifesting through a musical recording:

> Around eleven, I told Fritz I was starting to feel wobbly. He suggested I lie down on the mattress and put on my eyeshades. As soon as he started the music—something Amazonian in flavor, gently rhythmic with traditional instruments but also nature sounds (rain showers and crickets) that created a vivid dimensional sense of outdoor space—I was off, traveling somewhere in my mind, in a fully realized forest landscape that the music had somehow summoned into being. It made me realize what a powerful little technology a pair of eyeshades could be, at least in this context: it was like donning a pair of virtual reality goggles, allowing me immediately to take leave of this place and time.[6]

In *The Antipodes of the Mind*, Benny Shanon describes how, on ayahuasca, even the usually annoying sound of a mosquito was transformed into something unexpectedly sublime. While lying on the grass in a meadow:

> I found that a mosquito was sitting on the tip of my nose. I was about to brush it off, but . . . I changed my mind and decided I might as well let it be and observe. I did just this, and thus I heard the mosquito sing Mozart. Having been frequently

> disturbed by mosquitoes both in my home country, Israel, and even more so during my travels throughout the Amazonian regions, I often wondered what justification there might be for the existence of these annoying creatures. After all, their only contribution was, I surmised, negative. And here, I found out, here was an answer. What generally sounds irritating and monotonous is, in fact, on another scale, wonderfully musical.[7]

In another passage, Shanon speaks more generally about the experience of nature while on a psychedelic, describing an emotionally tinged spiritual vision of the natural world. Intriguingly, he offers at best a vague distinction between the visionary and the visual: apprehending nature in the mind's eye versus physically encountering its beauty. In either case, the effect is the same:

> While not having a specific thematic content as such, many visions of nature impress viewers in their portrayal of its majesty. A common feature in these visions is the viewing of all of reality as a great, wonderfully harmonious symphony. Such visions can have a deep impact upon their viewers. Typically, these visions induce a feeling of awe that is coupled with a new, more humbling, perspective by which people better measure their own value and place in the universe. These usually induce sentiments of profound appreciation and gratitude for all that nature offers. Panoramic scenes of open landscapes are especially conducive in this regard. The viewer looks forward, to the distant horizon, and in a direct, non-mediated manner, senses how immense and eternal the world is. . . .
>
> Experiences of the kind described here are often coupled with religious sentiments and ideations. [Ayahuasca drinkers] feel that the whole of Existence is God's wondrous doing and that it is all there by virtue of its being permanently sustained by the Divine.[8]

While it's wonderful to experience nature when in its immediate physical embrace, a good field recording from forest or meadow heard while on a psychedelic can effectively "take you there." When a master creator of sacred and meditative music, Jonathan Goldman, was asked by an interviewer, "Where do you go to find sacred sounds besides chanting?," he answered, "The birds, the trees, the sounds of nature." Asked then "Do you think that's why there are so many tapes on the market with environmental sounds?," he answers, "Oh yes. The sound of nature is as sacred as it gets."[9]

While discussing Albert Hofmann's "deep connection with the Creation, with nature, with animals," one writer reported that "Just two weeks before his death he went to the ear doctor—not because it was hard for him to understand conversations, but because he could not hear the singing of the birds in all its nuances anymore."[10]

Devoting careful attention to the quality and variety of numerous recordings, I assembled a playlist on Spotify titled "Nature's Own Music," which I describe as "Good field recordings of the sounds of nature: rivers, streams, rainfall, wind, ocean/surf, thunder, forest/jungle ambience. And critters: whales, dolphins, birds, frogs, crickets, loons, a purring cat. For some, a sacred journey into the heart of Gaia. For others, pure sonic data seeding visions."[11] An accompanying playlist, "Nature Sounds Plus," is described as "Sounds of nature blended with soft, minimal ambient textures or with meditation tones and drones. Sometimes nature may be in the foreground, sometimes the music or tones are, but they blend into a beautiful flow of jeweled sound, projecting visual wonders in the theater of the mind.[12]

White Noise

Stanislav Grof recommends another possible alternative to music if and when, for any reason, music should begin to feel burdensome: "white noise." The term refers to "random acoustic patterns" generated either electronically or mechanically (e.g., the sound of a fan). White noise may serve as an unobtrusive, colorless neutral background, providing a reassuring, soothing, textured "hum." In a seemingly magical display, in psychedelic states the supercharged imagination may actually transform such tonally neutral "noise" into inner music, a rather mysterious but fascinating phenomenon.

> The ideal solution [when music feels too structured, complex, overly determinative of mood/emotion, or simply overwhelming] seems to be to play a tape of "white noise"—a sequence of random acoustic patterns produced by a sound generator.

> Listening to intense white noise through headphones, LSD subjects usually create their own inner music which seems to fit the nature and content of the experience perfectly, since it is coming from the same source. Thus, only non-specific acoustic stimulation is provided, which is then illusively transformed by the subject into music. Monotonous sounds, noises coming from various electric appliances, or recordings of the ocean tide can play a similar role.[13]

Notice in the last sentence that Grof adds "recordings of the ocean tide" as a possible alternative to mechanical or electronic white noise. Certain nature recordings possess a particularly minimalist, nearly featureless quality: reducing rain or flowing water to a silky sheet of homogenous, lightly textured sound, effectively obscuring the origin of the sound and rendering it indistinguishable (or nearly so) from inorganic white noise. Soundscape ecologist Bernie Krause, whose life is dedicated to exploring "the incomparable value of our natural sonic resources,"[14] writes about the significance of natural white noise in a book subtitled *Finding the Origins of Music in the World's Wild Places*:

> Ocean and lakeside waves, the effects of wind, and the sound of streams contain elements of white noise. Analogous to white light, this class of sound is made up of an infinite number of audible frequencies that are distributed over the entire audio spectrum. Each frequency appears at random and, over time, has equal power. Naturally generated white noise provides a number of positive effects and is, more often than not, pleasant to our ears and relaxing to the psyche.[15]

Krause also describes the incredibly subtle differences in sound frequencies to be found in nature, even between, for example, the shorelines of different beaches:

> Soundscape ecologists who have recorded shorelines on different continents and dozens of ocean beaches of the world frequently remark on the subtleties of sound that we've easily overlooked.... The water sounds at each beach have their own acoustic signatures as a result of the beaches' rakes, offshore and shoreline depths, currents, composite materials,

weather patterns, salinity, water temperature, climate, season, surrounding terrestrial environment, geological features, and a range of other dynamic components. . . . Until I heard side-by-side recordings made at the waterline of various beaches at slack-water high or low tide, it would never have occurred to me that ocean-shore ambiences could sound so different from one another. Wild terrestrial habitats, yes. But the sandy beaches at the shore?[16]

I discovered this for myself particularly while compiling my playlist "Nature's Own Music," in the course of which I "auditioned" scores of different recordings of rainfall and was amazed by the seemingly limitless variations of sound textures to be found therein. As psychedelics dramatically increase our sensitivity to sound, it is these remarkable subtleties that become not only apparent, but also a source of aesthetic wonder, not to mention enhanced appreciation for the natural music emanating from the vast biosphere in which we live.

Samples of "organic" white noise are collected in the playlist "White Noise: Organic/Natural," which I describe as "Smooth, uniform sheets of sound from nature that serve as a kind of blank screen upon which consciousness may project its own inner music. Serves as a good alternative to electronic or mechanical 'white noise' when one desires a more organic form of 'neutral' sound."[17]

Epilogue

> Whither is fled the visionary gleam?
> Where is it now, the glory and the dream?—
>
> —William Wordsworth, "Ode: Intimations of Immortality"

> The music in my heart I bore
> Long after it was heard no more.—
>
> —Wordsworth, "The Solitary Reaper"

Because this book was never intended as a general guide or survey on the use of psychedelics—focused, as it is, on the experience of music in psychedelic states—the subject of post-trip "integration" of the experience was never on the agenda. That said, we know, whether from reading or firsthand experience, that revisiting music heard during a trip can stimulate memories, emotions, and sensations from the experience, and that, of course, is quite relevant. In his magisterial work *LSD and the Mind of the Universe*, a psychedelic *Pilgrim's Progress* through the inner cosmos, Christopher Bache documents a series of deeply focused, intentional experiments with high-dose LSD over an extended period of time. Here he describes how revisiting music experienced during a trip can retrieve not only memories but even revivify the experience:

> Preserving an accurate memory of our psychedelic experience completes the circle of learning and lays a strong foundation for our next session. Part of my protocol, therefore, included writing a phenomenologically complete account of each session within twenty-four hours. This often required writing at the

very limits of my understanding as I struggled to describe experience that were deeply mysterious to me at the time. To help with this, I developed a strategy.

When I would write up a session, I would listen to the music used in the session in the same order it had been played inside the session. I played each piece over and over until I felt I had captured the essence of the experience I had had with this music; then I moved on to the next segment. The day after a session, you are still porous around the edges. I found that by listening to the music in this porous state with my verbal functions restored, I was able to reenter the edges of my psychedelic experience and get it down on paper more effectively. I called it "standing at the edge of the well."[1]

Whether one revisits music heard during a trip to aid the creation of a "trip report" or simply to remember, or partially relive, or to "integrate" the experience, such re-exposure may be quite impactful. Music heard under a psychedelic is received and internalized far more deeply than music heard under usual circumstances. Having entered our consciousness wrapped in a luminous glow of overwhelming beauty, profound emotions, and otherworldly visions, that piece of music is forever transformed, carrying within it, now, reverberations of mystical beauty and existential revelation. We might say that that particular music has become "psychedelicized." As a transformative psychedelic experience "fades into the light of common day" [William Blake], it is encouraging to discover that within your consciousness are stored sonic echoes of that numinous realm.

This phenomenon was affirmed in a talk by Johns Hopkins neuroscientist and psilocybin researcher Frederick Barrett:

> I began to learn how deeply most music seems to impact most people during psychedelic experiences. . . . After these sessions our volunteers practically beg us for the playlists, and some of them report returning to the songs that were most impactful to them during their psychedelic experience weeks, months and even many years after the experience. Somehow, these songs can turn into touchstones that can rekindle the most powerful, impactful and insightful experiences that people encountered during their psychedelic sessions.[2]

I have experienced this many times over the years. One particularly vivid memory is that of having listened, while tripping, to Jonathan Goldman's recording "Crystal Bowls Chakra Chants," in particular the two tracks "Heart Chakra—Rose of Compassion" and "3rd Eye Chakra—Indigo Vision." Listening to those pieces again, intermittently, during the following days was magical, filling the room and my mind with an uncanny sense—how else can I say it—of the *psychedelic*.

Much of the rich, illustrative, experiential testimony that you've encountered in these pages derive from trip reports culled from published sources. Given more time, energy, money, and assistance (and perhaps a diagnosis of OCD), I might have traveled the globe visiting various institutional and personal archives where old trip reports, from the living and the dead, fill boxes or files, probably gathering much dust. There I might have gathered hundreds (thousands?) of additional accounts of the magic of music experienced on psychedelics. Let someone out there take that as a hint, a whisper from their inner guide, a firm nudge from a guardian spirit or the Muse of Music herself, to attempt such a project, which would provide a beautiful gift not only to the international psychedelic community, but enrich and expand a growing psychedelic literature within the humanities. I'm reminded, once again, of Terence McKenna's emphasis on the importance, at this point in history, of gathering experiential reports from "intelligent, thoughtful people" concerning their psychedelic experiences. "It's too early for a science. What we need now are the diaries of explorers. We need many diaries of many explorers so we can begin to get a feeling for the territory."[3]

True, there is a world of difference between the psychedelic experience itself and any language employed to describe, explain, or analyze it. But just as psychedelics expand consciousness, a psychedelically inspired person can stretch language, if not enough to fully accommodate the ineffable, then at least to provide it temporary quarters. In his comments above, Christopher Bache describes having to write "at the very limits" of his understanding while still "porous around the edges" the day following a trip, a state he describes as "standing at the edge of the well." One can at least attempt that much. As someone who has taken on this subject with focused intention and dedication, I would love for you, the psychonautic reader, to try, if possible, to write about your own experiences with music while on psychedelics. Whether your writing is in a raw or polished state, I would love to read what you've written. I believe that the synergy between psychedelics and music is a subject that will attract increasing attention in the coming years, and it would be beneficial to have an abundant archive of these types of experiences.

Before saying adieu, I'd like to raise a point that needs attention. It concerns a subject I've all but avoided in this book: "popular" music. Other than a few offhand references to 1960s psychedelically infused rock, in this book I've said almost nothing about popular genres of music. The reason is simple: lyrics. As a general principle (there are of course exceptions), it is nearly universally accepted that instrumental music, music without lyrics, is ideal for psychedelic settings because words communicate thoughts and thoughts generate further thoughts and draw one back into a cerebral mode, away from that of pure, spontaneous experience. The commonly acknowledged exception to that guideline refers to the latter portion of a trip, during reentry or reorientation, when almost any kind of music can be appreciated, though still at a deeper level. To give a personal example, once while coming down off a trip at a friend's house, I put on some early Bob Dylan—Dylan as political and metaphysical poet: "A Hard Rain's A-Gonna Fall," "Mr. Tamborine Man," "Masters of War," and so on. Although I'd listened to these pieces numerous times in the past (mostly, at that point, a distant past), they came alive with an unexpected potency and poignancy, inspiring a deep inner meditation not only on Dylan's literary genius (for which he later was awarded the Nobel Prize), but on the unique effect he had had on a new generation just beginning to wake up from the sleep of postwar political apathy and social conformity. Rather than a random string of inner thoughts, vague musings, or mere nostalgia, this meditation expanded into an almost cinematic or novelistic revelation of what had been a significant cultural phenomenon.

Another important point to make about popular music is that when it tries to sound "psychedelic" it has a tendency, sometimes, to turn dark and disturbing. In his book *American Trip*, Ido Hartogsohn speaks of two opposing historical tendencies (from the 1960s onward) involving both psychedelic art and music: the psychotomimetic versus the psychedelic. "Psychotomimetic" was the term applied to LSD by some early (1950s) psychiatric researchers who defined the LSD state as one mimicking psychosis (and thus potentially providing a breakthrough in the study of schizophrenia). Dissolving the wall between the ego and the unconscious can unleash an overwhelming flood of subconscious materials into the conscious mind, overriding the mind's capacity to digest or "make sense" of the experience. If one is unable to "let go," to "go with the flow," the resistance itself can generate fear and paranoia that may lead to a nightmarish state, something akin to the psychotomimetic state hypothesized by those early researchers. That darker quality of experience may then come to define the psychedelic state for the experiencer and consequently impart a negative coloring to any artistic expression of the experience. Here is how Hartogsohn describes this phenomenon:

> While psychotomimetic experimenters and artists conceptualized the drug experience as one of psychotic, even demonic-like, possession, psychedelic artists and investigators conceived of the same experience as one of liberation. . . . In works inspired by hallucinogenic experiences but produced after the fact, both psychotomimetic and psychedelic art often tend to be colorful, elaborate, and meticulous in style, albeit with distinct stylistic features and widely dissimilar thematic orientations—the first reflecting themes of insanity and disorganization, the second featuring themes of natural flow, harmony, and order.[4]

Certain musical works presenting themselves as "psychedelic" that are offered to psychonauts as sonic food for tripping are, in fact, more expressive of the psychotomimetic tendency, expressing themes of insanity, chaos, breakdown, even of the demonic. That approach may represent, to some, a kind of "dark sublime," a fetishization of the weird and the nightmarish, but it isn't likely to inspire a positive mindset. One is, of course, free to listen to anything one wishes. I'm simply pointing out that it's better to trust one's own instincts, to rely on one's own felt sense of the spirit and flavor of a piece of music before unreflectively adding it to one's psychedelic playlist because someone, somewhere, promoted it as "psychedelic." The same holds true for the visual arts, particularly ostensive representations of psychedelic visionary states. One Facebook group that features mostly AI-generated "art for psychonauts" specifies in its rules, and occasionally has to remind posters "No demonic/Satanism" because of the tendency, among some, to equate "psychedelic" with hellish scenes of otherworldly terror—as if exposing oneself to such imagery represents a demonstration of macho courage. Despite the rule and the reminders, much of what is posted on that page still tends toward the nightmarish, with creators and consumers of these images resembling children watching horror movies for the sheer thrill of self-imposed terror.

Music in a Dark Time

As we discussed in the section "Letting Go" in chapter 3, "set and setting," in the broadest sense, refers not only to the immediate inner state and external physical environment of the psychedelic experiencer, but to the wider world, which inevitably, though sometimes imperceptibly, resounds within our consciousness. Hartogsohn speaks of *collective set and setting*: "the idea that sociocultural conditions determine the types of set and setting available in a given society." These external conditions "shape the mindscapes of individuals," thereby "creating a framework that structures the drug experiences of its members."[5] With that in mind, he offers some historical perspective on how that collective set/setting has influenced generations of psychonauts since the 1960s, when

> the visionary, euphoric and empathogenic qualities of psychedelic experiences . . . support[ed] the emergence of utopian and universalist modes of thinking, of the type that was strikingly common in the idealistic counterculture of the 1960s.[6] . . . The 1960s were an energetic and singular historical moment. The decade was a particularly permissive time to experiment with psychedelics. . . . At a time when society was undergoing a process of thorough and intensive self-reflection, the utopian potential of psychedelics manifested spectacularly.[7]

During that era, despite a fearful, reactionary society expressing its disapproval of psychedelics through sensational media accounts, and despite disapproving parents and other authority figures, a young psychonaut felt embraced and encouraged by a vital, inspired, and exuberant counterculture. That supportive social milieu consisted of peers in quest of similar utopian ideals, including transforming a society that, compared with the utopian psychedelic vision, appeared robotic, violent, even insane. With whatever acerbic eye one may now feel entitled to glance back on that period of extreme idealism—however anachronistic or naive the counterculture may appear in retrospect—to have been in the midst of it, to have been a young seeker there and then, was to have had the rare experience of participating in a unique historical moment of widespread idealistic and reformist zeal that, in the end, succeeded in leaving a strong mark on society and on history, with continuing repercussions.

Continuing his account, Hartogsohn relates that by the late 1960s, a conservative backlash against LSD began intentionally promoting disinformation (later discredited) about the dangers of psychedelics, effectively poisoning the social atmosphere and contaminating the "collective set and setting":

> Back in the late 1960s, evidence showed a sharp increase in the rate of bad LSD experiences. . . . It is worth remembering that this was a period during which public media dedicated its full attention to particularly grim assertions about psychedelics and their effects. News items at the time claimed that LSD users commonly suffered from flashbacks and spread the belief that LSD destroyed the brain and caused irreversible chromosome damage. Such claims were later refuted, but in the late 1960s they were accepted as fact by many, including countercultural users of psychedelics themselves. . . . In the climate of paranoia that developed, LSD experiences took a turn for the worse and the percentage of bad LSD trips rose sharply.[8]

That paranoia was fortified, explains Alan Watts, by "systematic persecution" by legal authorities—itself a response, and a contributor, to the proliferation of misleading information: "In the early days when LSD, psilocybin, and mescaline were used more or less legitimately among reasonably mature people, there was little trouble with 'bum trips,' and episodes of anxiety were usually turned into occasions for insight. But when federal and state authorities began their systematic persecution, the fears invoked to justify it became self-fulfilling prophecies, and there was now real reason for a paranoid atmosphere in all experiments conducted outside the sterile and clinical surroundings of psychiatric hospitals."[9] However, Hartogsohn continues, "by the mid-1970s, when the political controversy and moral panic surrounding LSD abated, the rate of occurrence of bad trips dropped by a dramatic 45 percent . . . leading to a corresponding improvement in set and setting conditions and a concomitant reduction of instances of harm caused by psychedelic drugs." At the same time, however, the fading of the counterculture greatly altered the cultural environment within which people pursued psychedelics:

> As the 1970s began and the ideals and dreams of the counterculture revolution started to wither away, psychedelics lost many of their countercultural symbolic connotations. The increasingly cynical generation of 1970s youth was less inclined to let their defenses down in pursuit of grand spiritual revelations or a rosy utopian future. A new world was emerging, in which psychedelics slowly but surely shed their revolutionary implications and became a normalized part of everyday existence. While psychedelics did not disappear from the scene, their use was no longer habitually linked to spiritual or revolutionary causes but rather increasingly seen within a framework of recreational drug use.[10]

There is, of course, much more to this evolving history of psychedelic use and societal responses over the following decades, including, most notably, the so-called "War on Drugs." That malicious militancy relied on scare tactics to "educate" middle- and high-schoolers about the evils of drugs, creating an atmosphere of fear and paranoia that presumably tainted, if not undermined, many a psychedelic trip.

But here we are, in the present, where new factors are acting to reshape the collective consciousness surrounding psychedelics, particularly the rebirth and vigorous growth of psychedelic research under the rubric of "Psychedelic Science" and the "Psychedelic Renaissance." As valuable as that is, Hartgsohn warns of the "commercialization and commodification" of psychedelics, leading to a "banalization and trivialization of the psychedelic experience." Aldous Huxley noticed the same phenomenon taking form even at the embryonic stage of psychedelic therapy. In a 1959 letter to pioneering psychedelic psychiatrist Humphry Osmond, Huxley wrote,

> Incidentally, what frightful people there are in your profession! We met two Beverly Hills psychiatrists the other day, who specialize in LSD therapy at $100 a shot [$1000 in today's terms]—and, really, I have seldom met people of lower sensitivity, more vulgar mind! To think of people made vulnerable by LSD being exposed to such people is profoundly disturbing. But what can one do about the problem? Psychiatry is an art based on a still imperfect science—and as in all the arts there are more bad and indifferent practitioners than good ones. How can one keep the bad artists out? Bad artists don't matter in

painting or literature—but they matter enormously in therapy and education; for whole lives and destinies may be affected by their shortcomings. But one doesn't see any practical way in which the ungifted and the unpleasant can be filtered out and only the gifted and good let through.[11]

Osmond's response:

I agree with you . . . It is very unfortunate. I only hope that some of our newer developments will make it less profitable for the incompetent and crooked. Many psychiatrists are either unsuited or insufficiently trained for the work. The trouble is that the demand is considerable and the less able or more unscrupulous can make much money. Medicine has a long and depressing history of substandard professional work about which we have been incredibly slow about doing very much.[12]

An atmosphere of rampant psychedelic "commercialization and commodification," accompanied by a proliferation of poorly trained and financially motivated "therapists" and "guides" responding to "considerable demand," can only muddy the waters and cause confusion for anyone seeking psychedelically-assisted therapy.

In a revealing and insightful article, "The Hidden Harms within the Psychedelic Renaissance,"[13] psychotherapist Tara Rae Behr laments the entrance into the field of psychedelic-assisted therapy of persons who are credentialed but often lack the kinds of sensitivity, wisdom, and careful training critical to this field. She writes, "There is much hype within the psychedelic movement right now. Starry-eyed weekend retreat shamans are emerging left and right, often with guides who have only been trained for a few months. In ancient and more mature cultures, shamans train for an entire lifetime to understand the nuances and depths of consciousness." She speaks of the dangers found in submitting to therapy with persons for whom "a short encounter with the mystical power found in psychedelics often inflates their core wounds, accentuating grandiosity and savior complexes"—therapists "who grasp for psychedelic fame" and whose "ego-driven agendas . . . flourish in the guise of wellness retreat centers, weekend spiritual experiences, and ketamine centers, with consequences both severe and unknown."

Related to the issue of commercialization and commodification, insisting that the use of psychedelics remain secured behind the walls of institutional psychology and psychiatry represents an extraordinary affront to human freedom. The focus on psychedelics as clinical tools for the exclusive use of medical and mental-health professionals both obscures their value as tools for personal growth, creativity, and problem-solving and keeps them out of the hands of those who seek to use them for these legitimate purposes.

Hartogsohn raises another critical point regarding the current societal atmosphere enveloping psychedelia. Despite the improving public attitudes about psychoactive substances, he reminds us that today's collective atmosphere for psychedelic experimentation is heavily colored by the state of a world in dangerous decline:

> The collective set and setting of the twenty-first century seems to have developed in an alarming and menacing manner. Fifty years after the Summer of Love, the utopian ideals of the 1960s seem light-years away. Recent years have been characterized by growing recognition of the daunting challenges faced by humanity in the twenty-first century: an unprecedented ecological crisis, the tightening grip of trans-national corporations, the rise of a new wave of nationalism and authoritarianism, and new state and corporate apparatuses of surveillance. In times of growing uncertainty and concerns about the future, psychedelic experimentation may have become an increasingly dicey business. The psychedelic amplification of meaning might become a liability in a new era of anxiety, when excessive ruminations about the planet's many woes and sorrows might lead one on the path to deeply unwholesome states of mind. Thus, while some might argue that psychedelics are direly needed at a time when new pathways and alternatives are demanded, new cultural risk factors on the horizon have the potential to mar many a good set and setting by emphasizing the social, cultural, and ecological concerns of the age.[14]

There is no way around the fact that these are dark and dangerous times. One barely needs to be reminded of a growing ecological crisis that is looming not in a distant future, or even the near-future, but that is ravishing parts of the planet at this moment. Extreme weather events are bringing record-breaking heat, massive fires, droughts, floods, and rising ocean levels that threaten coastal areas, likely leading, eventually, to the displacement of large populations. These conditions are expected only to worsen over time. To put it more bluntly and depressingly, we appear to be living on a dying planet. Rather than the hysterical cry of an end-times fanatic, this is the sober estimation of the overwhelming majority of the international scientific community.

Another evolving dystopian characteristic of our times is the rise and spread of authoritarian regimes throughout the world, with the United States itself teetering, as I write, on a fragile precipice. Those of us who are living in democratic or quasi-democratic nations and who lack a solid sense of history can barely imagine the nightmare of living within authoritarian and fascistic systems. Though our minds may instinctively resist contemplating the unthinkable, this may indeed be our fate. If you devote even a sliver of your attention to national and international affairs, you already know this. Even in the absence of a full-on authoritarian state, the public consciousness has already been poisoned by pervasive political lies and toxic conspiracy theories.

To add one more tragedy to the list, we're in the midst of a profound mental-health crisis, exacerbated by COVID-19 and a generally darkening mood nationally and internationally. Depression and suicide rates among the young are unprecedented. One can only imagine how a general atmosphere of fear and insecurity impacts the state of mind of those who might pursue psychedelic experiences. Despite desperate hopes that "psychedelics can save the world," the evidence is not compelling.

I wanted to state these things bluntly, because it is so easy (for many of us) to shield our awareness from these hellish realities. Civilizations come and go, species go extinct, planets die. What benefit is there in hiding these facts? However, we can derive more than a little solace, strength, and even optimism from spiritual convictions about the nature of consciousness beyond brain and body, along with a sense of the ongoing journey of the soul, if you will, within an infinite and multidimensional universe. For me, psychedelics undoubtedly have contributed substantially to these kinds of existence-affirming convictions, that *sense of the eternal* that can be a sanity saver. Personally, I also benefit from an inner residue of wisdom derived from a profound immersion, during early adulthood, in Eastern philosophical ideas, the kind that provide a healthy cosmic perspective.

While you and I are still here, in this darkening time and place, there are still wonderful, soul-elevating experiences to be had, including those found in the life-giving embrace of Mother Nature, as well as in the creative arts, including, of course, music: not as mere entertainment and distraction, but as a source of deep aesthetic and spiritual nourishment. I know this may sound, to some ears, naive or sentimental. It isn't. If one can, as William Blake declared, discover a world in a grain of sand or eternity in an hour, one can certainly find beauty, wisdom, comfort, and joy in certain brilliant configurations of composed sound. Since the most ancient of times, human beings have found inspiration and metaphysical sustenance in various musical forms. They are there to be heard, in innumerable varieties, with the click of a mouse or a swipe of a finger or the gliding of a tonearm across vinyl (accompanied, ideally, by a decent set of headphones or, as some prefer, a high-quality surround sound speaker system). The particular gift of psychedelics (including, for present purposes, the sacred cannabis plant) that I have tried to address in this book is their extraordinary power to usher us into the inner sanctum of music, to enable us to experience beauty, psychological healing, and spiritual wisdom there. Escapism? Sometimes escape is a reasonable strategy, even a saving grace, if one should find oneself in chains, in a conflagration, or in illusions.

Throughout this entire project, my one consistent motivation and inspiration has flowed from a simple mental image: that of one person—somewhere, anywhere—on a psychedelic voyage, tuned in to any one of the numerous pieces of music I happened to have discovered within a vast sea of possibilities and offered for psychedelic delectation in a carefully curated playlist. That one person, having that one utterly unique, unrepeatable, ineffable experience borne from music. Maybe that person is you. For all of us who have heard the music, who have participated in one or more magical mystery tours, we might wish to ask ourselves the cryptic question posed by John Lennon in the song "Baby You're a Rich Man": "Now that you've found another key, what are you going to play?"

Appendix I

Spotify Playlists for Psychedelic Sessions

Over the last decade I have been continually creating, editing, and refining a number of playlists on Spotify as resources for psychedelic sessions. As I stated earlier, these are not playlists in the usual sense, by which I mean planned, often timed musical itineraries, curated "soundtracks" engineered to provide a consistent tone or an experiential narrative, or, especially in psychotherapeutic settings, to encourage or impose a particular emotional trajectory. Rather, each playlist is a carefully selected but loose collection of items brought together under a particular category, the main types being (1) single genre ("Classical Music for Psychedelic States," "Psychedelic Ambient"); (2) sub-genre themes ("Classical: Fantastic Journeys," "Ambient: Alien/Otherworldly"); (3) cross-genre independent themes ("Faerie Realms," "Tribal"); and (4) extra-musical recordings ("Nature's Own Music," "White Noise"). Each playlist offers a generous selection of items to sample and choose from in creating your own personalized playlists. I'm just too much of a believer in the subjectivity of musical experience to presume that I or anyone else is qualified to create standardized, one-size-fits-all playlists, as if music consisted of a reliable "catalog of triggers" (see chapter 9). Altogether, my playlists represent a painstakingly, lovingly assembled library of music covering a fairly wide swath of the musical landscape, conscientiously pre-screened for psychedelic use. It is up to the reader, and listener, to decide whether or not I am a worthy guide in these matters. I leave it to you to dive into these reservoirs of music and find your own treasures.

The following link will take you to my Spotify profile where all my public lists can be accessed: https://open.spotify.com/user/stevengelberg?si=e5da925441e3486f. Alternatively, simply search on Spotify for "stevengelberg."

A number of my playlists have already been introduced and briefly described in this book, generally at the close of chapters. Here is a guide:

- Classical (12 playlists): chapter 10
- Ambient (5 playlists): chapter 11
- World Music (7 playlists): chapter 12
- Nature's Own Music and Nature Sounds Plus: chapter 13
- White Noise: Mechanical/Electronic: chapter 13
- White Noise: Organic/Natural: chapter 13

ADDITIONAL SPOTIFY PLAYLISTS:

"Sound Meditation for Psychedelic States"
A careful selection of meditation and healing music/sounds/drones/mantras that invite deep dives. In expanded states, these rich sound-flows may take on greater dimensionality, beauty, and existential/spiritual significance. Turn off your mind, relax, open your ears, and let the sounds take you.
https://open.spotify.com/playlist/1yLavHv9Ryhp99P07nKqj9?si=4673b85bb50747c0

"Hi-Vibes"
Ambient, meditation, and other music with sound textures and energies that feel (to me) positive, peaceful, elevated, spiritual. These sonorous/sonic high-vibes may calm and center a frazzled mind, ease a heavy heart, fill an inner eye with awesome visions, or bathe a soul in beauty and grace.
https://open.spotify.com/playlist/0nxRUb91BwWJQxZNLfmmfh?si=15e8caea024f4049

"Faerie Realms"
Classical (and other) pieces that suggest enchantment, fantasy, forest magic, hidden faerie worlds alight with music, dance, and play—worlds of infinite delicacy, charm, and beauty. A handful of items are from early church and monastic music, repurposed (and reclaimed herewith) for the forest faeries.

https://open.spotify.com/playlist/3ohyn3pN3RlabgEKSRXL2M?si=4ee5aa1e30a24502

"Sacred Singing Bowls"

For meditation, inner healing, aesthetic exploration, altered states. Sound and Silence exploring their exquisitely subtle relationship, testing boundaries, learning to dance together. [includes chimes, bells, etc.]

https://open.spotify.com/playlist/2Rz8nXVTonu7wF2ggdkTWo?si=a87aaf0f2d7645fa

"Mystical Flutes"

Smooth, spacious, ethereal, translucent, crystalline, luminous, angelic. Flutes (and related) from various cultural sources including Native American, Tibetan, Indian classical, Japanese, Zen, Middle Eastern and Sufi.

https://open.spotify.com/playlist/1YLorCkgyNepjoxsrVhKa6?si=bfc2dd217c794716

"The Healing Female Voice"

https://open.spotify.com/playlist/1d8zhPoJfqAFkfzyqCdr9n?si=b-363872d77ab4346

"Expanded Jazz for Altered States"

"Jazz" conceived liberally, flowing out into electronica, techno, ethnic and beyond—offering some fascinatin' fusions. A generous interpretation of the genre opening up worlds of sound worthy of psychedelic delectation.

https://open.spotify.com/playlist/5zap6IYIYVyeupRNARtuIu?si=86925bb6312c4c2b

"Electronic Music for Altered States"

Electronic music closer to the softer, meditative end of the spectrum, but with more complex musical structures, rhythms, and forward movement than "Ambient." A few items are more experimental and difficult to categorize. Curated for psychedelic flavors.

https://open.spotify.com/playlist/3R9B8Ciazh7tzp67YbMmFG?si=a7edd2ea17974536

[**Note**: Most items in these final two lists include lyrics (in English) and therefore may not be appropriate for use until late in a trip (for reasons explained in chapter 8).]

"1960s Psychedelic Rock"
Conveys, in myriad ways, the psycho-spiritual zeitgeist of the 1960s counterculture, threaded through with the sound textures—and the surreality and spirituality—of Psychedelia. Well-known and rarer items. [See also "Neo-Psychedelic" playlist.]
https://open.spotify.com/playlist/1q4kHMF3BA7sAINyoasX4t?si=e6ac06f8dd704895

"Neo-Psychedelic (Rock/Pop/Electronica)"
Post hippie-era psychedelic flavors in popular music (atmospheric, drony, shoe-gazey, dream-poppy, surreal, flower-power, Beatle-esque, etc.).
https://open.spotify.com/playlist/7LdqzFzqDU62kHqH5j8uKw?si=8a540788979b408e

Appendix II

Abbreviated Versions of Select Spotify Playlists

For those without access to Spotify, or in the event that Spotify itself should become unavailable for any reason, what follows are carefully chosen selections from nine particular Spotify playlists of mine, constituting a substantial, self-contained library of music for psychedelic use. If necessary, these items can be accessed via other streaming services, original recording media, or from alternative sources.

1. CLASSICAL

Hugo Alfvén—Uppenbarelsekantat (Revelation Cantata), Op. 31: Andante religioso. Royal Stockholm Philharmonic Orchestra/Neeme Jarvi [4:04]
Anonymous—O monialis. Theatre of Voices/Paul Hiller (album: *Monastic Song—12th Century Monophonic Chant*) [3:41]
Anonymous—Sia laudato San Francesco. The Rose Ensemble/Carrie Henneman Shaw, Kim Sueoka, Jordan Sramek (album: *Il Poverello: Medieval and Renaissance Music for Saint Francis of Assisi*) [6:43]
Johann Sebastian Bach—Concerto for 2 Violins, Strings, and Continuo in D Minor, BWV 1043: 2. Largo ma non tanto. Pinchas Zukerman, Midori, Saint Paul Chamber Orchestra [7:09]
Alex Baranowski—Wiosna (album: *Angele Dubeau: Portrait. Alex Baranowski*) [8:59]
Ludwig van Beethoven—Symphony No. 6 in F Major, Op. 68, "Pastoral": I. Pleasant, cheerful feelings aroused on approaching the countryside: Allegro ma non troppo. Bratislava CSR Symphony Orchestra/Michael Halasz [9:27]

Ludwig van Beethoven—Symphony No. 6 in F Major, Op. 68, "Pastoral": II. Scene by the brook: Andante molto mosso. Bratislava CSR Symphony Orchestra/Michael Halasz [12:55]

Ludwig van Beethoven—Violin Concerto in D Major, Op. 61: II. Larghetto. Lisa Petrova, Sinfonia Varsovia/Jean-Jacques Kantorow [9:52]

Ludwig van Beethoven—Piano Concerto No. 5 in E-Flat Major, Op. 73 "Emperor": II. Adagio un poco mosso. Inon Barnatan, Academy of St. Martin in the Fields/Alan Gilbert (album: *Beethoven Piano Concertos, Part 2*) [7:42]

Ernest Bloch—Concerto Grosso No. 2: II. Andante. Amadeus Chamber Orchestra/Agnieszka Duczmal [3:45]

Johannes Brahms—4 Gesange, Op. 17: No. 4. Gesang aus Fingal. Kodály Zoltán Female Choir [7:07]

Max Bruch—Violin Concerto No. 1 in G Minor, Op. 26: II. Adagio. Midori, Berliner Philharmoniker/Mariss Jansons [9:18]

Jean Coulthard—Introduction and 3 Folksongs (after Canada Mosaic): I. Lullaby on a Snowy Night. CBC Vancouver Orchestra/Mario Bernardi [3:01]

Jean Coulthard—Introduction and 3 Folksongs (after Canada Mosaic): IV. Billowing Fields of Golden Wheat. CBC Vancouver Orchestra/Mario Bernardi [2:50]

Claude Debussy—Suite bergamasque: III. Clair de lune. San Francisco Ballet Orchestra/Emil de Cou (album: *Debussy Rediscovered*) [5:28]

Claude Debussy—Prelude a l'apres-midi d'un faune, CD 87. Royal Concertgebouw Orchestra/Bernard Haitink [11:11]

Claude Debussy—Nocturnes, L.91: III. Sirenes. Cleveland Orchestra/Pierre Boulez, Ladies of the Cleveland Orchestra Chorus [9:40]

Frederick Delius—2 Pieces for Small Orchestra: No. 1, On Hearing the First Cuckoo in Spring. Royal Philharmonic Orchestra/Sir Thomas Beecham [7:01]

Antonin Dvorak—Romance for Violin and Orchestra in F Minor, Op. 11. Dani Kim, Slovak Philharmonic Orchestra/Damian Iorio [13:08]

Antonin Dvorak—Czech Suite, Op. 39 B.93: 4. Romanza (Andante con moto). Detroit Symphony Orchestra/Antal Dorati [5:21]

Gabriel Fauré—Requiem, Op. 48: 4. Pie Jesu. Jonathon Bond, Stephen Cleobury, Academy of St. Martin in the Fields/George Guest [3:32]

Gabriel Fauré—Requiem, Op. 48: 7. In paradisum. Choir of St. John's College, Cambridge/Stephen Cleobury, Academy of St. Martin in the Fields/George Guest [3:41]

Philip Glass—Prophecies (*Koyaanisqatsi* soundtrack) [10:34]
Christoph Willibald Gluck—Orphée et Eurydice, Wq. 41, Act 2: Dance des ombres heureuses (Dance of the Blessed Spirits). Academy of St. Martin-in-the-Fields/Sir Neville Marriner, Paul Davies (album: *Baroque Masterpieces*) [6:04]
Edvard Grieg—2 Lyric Pieces, Op. 68 (version for orchestra): V. Badnlat (At the cradle). CBC Vancouver Orchestra/Mario Bernardi (album: *Northern Landscapes*) [4:15]
George Frideric Handel—Messiah: Pastoral Symphony. Royal Philharmonic Orchestra/Sir Thomas Beecham [4:40]
Hildegard von Bingen—Symphonia virginum: O dulcissime amator, La Reverdie (album: *Sponsa Regis*) [9:15]
Gustav Holst—The Planets, Op. 32: VII. Neptune, the Mystic. The Georgian Festival Orchestra/Jahni Mardjani (album: *Holst, The Planets*) [8:33]
Erich Wolfgang Korngold—Violin Concerto in D Major, Op. 35: II. Romanze: Andante.Ulrike-Anima Mathe, Dallas Symphony Orchestra/ Andrew Litton [9:01]
Orlando de Lassus—Domini est terra. Sabine Lutzenberger, Per-Sonat (album: *Bis an der Welt ihr Ende*) [3:39]
Franz Liszt—A Dante Symphony, S.109:—Magnificat, Staatskapelle Dresden/Giuseppe Sinopoli. Dresden State Opera Chorus/Matthias Brauer [7:56]
Anatoly Lyadov—The Enchanted Lake, Op. 62. New York Philharmonic/ Alan Gilbert [6:54]
Bohuslav Martinů—Violin Concerto No. 2, H. 293: II. Andante moderato. Lorenzo Gatto, National Orchestra of Belgium/Walter Weller [8:15]
Felix Mendelssohn—Calm Sea and Prosperous Voyage, Op. 27 (Excerpt). Adelaide Symphony Orchestra/David Stanhope (album: *Very Best of Mendelssohn*) [3:58]
Wolfgang Amadeus Mozart—Violin Concerto No. 3 in G Major, K. 216: II. Adagio. Itzhak Perlman, Berliner Philharmoniker [8:11]
Wolfgang Amadeus Mozart—Clarinet Concerto in A Major, K. 622: II. Adagio. Sabine Meyer, Staatskapelle Dresdon/Hans Vonk [6:39]
Wolfgang Amadeus Mozart—Così fan tutte, K. 588: "Soave sia il vento" (Orchestral version). London Philharmonic Orchestra/Charles Gerhardt (album: *The Insomniac's Dream*) [3:21]
Wolfgang Amadeus Mozart—Piano Concerto No. 21 in C Major, K. 467: II: Andante. Geza Anda, Camerata Salzburg [7:15]

Modest Mussorgsky—Khovanshchina (arr. N. Rimsky-Korsakov): Act 1: Prelude: Dawn over the Moscow River. Royal Philharmonic Orchestra/Grzegorz Nowak [6:08]
Andrzej Panufnik—Concerto Festivo: II. Lirico. Berlin Konzerthaus Orchestra/Lukasz Borowicz (album: *Andrzej Panufnik – Votiva*) [7:49]
Andrzej Panufnik—Jagiellonian Triptych: II. Cantio: Adagietto. Polish Chamber Orchestra/Mariusz Smolij (album: *Panufnik—Homage to Polish Music*) [3:24]
Arvo Pärt—Spiegel im Spiegel. Vadim Gluzman, Angela Yoffe [8:30]
Pérotin—Beata viscera. Mikk Uleoja, Tõnis Kaumann, Vox Clamantis/Jaan-Eik Tulve (album: *Filia Sion*) [8:20]
Giacomo Puccini—Madame Butterfly, 1. Akt: Vogliatemi bene (Mona Lisa): Act II Part I: "Humming Chorus." Hungarian State Opera Chorus and Orchestra [3:15]
Jean-Philippe Rameau—Castor et Pollux: Scène funèbre. Les Musiciens du Louvre/Marc Minkowski (album: *Rameau—Une Symphonie Imaginaire*) [3:25]
Einojuhani Rautavaara—Cantus arcticus, Op. 61, "Concerto for Birds and Orchestra": I. The Bog. Helsinki Philharmonic Orchestra/Leif Segerstam (album: *Apotheosis: The Best of Einojuhani Rautavaara*) [6:51]
[Maurice Ravel]—Vocalise En Forme De Habanera. Mélanie Thiébaut, Orchestra Manifesto/Fleur Grüneissen (album: *La Magie des Plus Beaux Adagios, Vol. 3*) Bayard Musique [2:56]
Joaquin Rodrigo—Canconeta for Violin and String Orchestra. Mikhail Ovrutsky, Orquesta Sinfónica de Castilla y León/Max Darman Bragado (album: *Rodrigo: Complete Orchestral Works, 3*) [3:39]
Joseph Boulogne Chevalier de Saint-Georges—Violin Concerto in D Major, Op. 3, No. 1: Adagio. Zhou Qian, Toronto Camerata/Kevin Mallon (album: *Saint-Georges Violin Concertos*) [4:38]
Camille Saint-Saëns—Le Carnaval des animaux: VII. Aquarium. Concentus Bestiales, Julian Reynolds, Peter Lockwood [2:41]
Robert Schumann—Symphony No. 4 in D Minor Op. 120: II. Romanze. Bamberg Symphony Orchestra/Christoph Eschenbach (album: *Schumann Symphonies 1–4*) [4:37]
Igor Stravinsky—Suite from the Firebird: III. Khorovod. Round Dance of the Princesses (1919 Version). Chicago Symphony Orchestra/Carlo Maria Giulini [5:46]
Josef Suk—Zrani (Ripening), Op. 34: VI. Self-Moderation. Berlin Comic Opera Orchestra/Kirill Petrenko [4:40]

Pyotr Ilyich Tchaikovsky—Violin Concerto In D Major, Op. 35, TH. 59: II. Canzonetta (Andante). Hilary Hahn, Royal Liverpool Philharmonic Orchestra/Vasily Petrenko [6:23]

Pyotr Ilyich Tchaikovsky—The Snow Maiden, Op. 12: XII. Girls' Round Dance (Khovorod). Moscow Capella, Moscow Symphony Orchestra/ Igor Golovschin (album: *Tchaikovsky – The Snow Maiden, Op. 12*) [3:27]

Pyotr Ilyich Tchaikovsky—Andante cantabile (Arr. for Cello and Orchestra from String Quartet No. 1 in D Major, Op. 11). Sol Gabetta, Muncher Rundfunkorchester/Ari Rasilainen [6:33]

Mieczyslaw Weinberg—Violin Concertino, Op. 42: I. Allegretto cantabile. Ewelina Nowicka, Amadeus Chamber Orchestra of Polish Radio/ Agnieszka Duczmal [8:14]

Ralph Vaughan Williams—The Lark Ascending. Hilary Hahn, London Symphony Orchestra/Sir Colin Davis [16:19]

Takashi Yoshimatsu—White Landscapes, Op. 47a: II. Stillness in Snow. Moderato. Manchester Camarata/Sachio Fujioka, John Barrow, Kate Wilson, Jonathan Price [3:15]

Domenico Zipoli—Elevazione for Solo Oboe, Solo Cello, Strings and Organ (arr. V. Hunt). Gordon Hunt, Norrköping Symphony Orchestra/ Antoni Wit (album: *Elevazione, The magic of the oboe*) [8:20]

2. Neo-Classical for Psychonauts

Lennart Altgenug / "Epilogue" / *Neo-Classical Essentials, Vol. 1* / 1:51
Olafur Arnalds, Nils Frahm / "23:17" / *Trance Frendz* / 5:20

Mason Bates / "Anthology of Fantastic Zoology: Nymphs" / *Mason Bates: Anthology of Fantastic Zoology* / 2:48
Ken Benshoof/Kronos Quartet / "When" / *In Formation* / 2:24
Petra Birgisdóttir / "Akureyi" / *Akureyi* / 1:59
Brendan Eder Ensemble / "Ending" / *Therapy* / 8:19
Tracey Chattaway / "Holding On" / *Nightsky* / 4:46
Julie Cooper / "Earth To Infinity" / *Symphonic Skies* / 2:51
Jane Antonia Cornish / "Drift" / *Seascapes* / 9:22
Darker in Vine / "Deux Pensées" / *Deux Pensées* / 2:49
Ross Edwards et al. / "Dawn Mantras" / *Eternity: The Timeless Music of Australia's Composers* / 7:20
Ensemble Rivr Dane / "Foveaux Strait" / *Foveaux Strait* / 3:44

Joel Christian Goffin / "Waterfelt" / *Waterfelt* / 3:43
Hildur Guðnadóttir / "Heyr Himnasmiður"/ *Saman* / 3:09
Irena and Vojtech Havlovi / "Velvetly" / *Light Circles* / 4:40
Jon Hopkins / "Cold Out There" / *Opalescent* / 3:54
Luke Howard / "A Softer World" / *Sun, Cloud* / 6:30
Jóhann Jóhannsson / "Ég heyrði allt án þess að hlusta" / *Englabörn & Variations* / 2:05
Jóhann Jóhannsson / "Form" / *Jóhannsson: 12 Conversations with Thilo Heinzmann* / 2:46
Jónsi, Alex Somers / "Boy 1904" / *Riceboy Sleeps* / 5:03
Zoë Keating / "Zinc (after T. Riley's In C)" / *Riley, T.: In C Remixed* / 5:21
Keith Kenniff / "Grace" / *Branches* / 3:35
Aaron Martin/Christoph Berg / "Pillows" / *Day Has Ended* / 2:19
Danny Mulhern / "Flow State Vestida 4" / *Flow States* / 3:49
Anne Müller / "For Leah" / *Martyrs Lane* / 3:13
Thomas Newman / "Brooks Was Here" / *The Shawshank Redemption* / 5:06
Pauline Oliveros / "Grains" / *The Roots of the Moment* / 6:21
Hannah Peel / "Horizon" / *Horizon* / 4:56
Camille Pépin/Orchestre De Picardie / "The Sound of Trees: Apaisé, boisé" / *The Sound of Trees* / 3:27
Barry Phillips Cello Ensemble / "Tomorrow Never Knows" / *Summer of Cello* / 4:33
Max Richter / "Psychogeography" / *Voices 2* / 6:53
Sigur Rós, Dmitri Ensemble / "Fljótavik" (Arr. for Violin and String Orchestra) / *Iceland—The Eternal Music* / 4:20
Felix Rösch, Modena quartet / "Humming Bird Rework" / *Humming Bird Rework* / 3:22
Homay Schmitz / "Brolly Weather" / *Spitfire: Down in the Dumps* / 2:34
Stars of the Lid / "Requiem for Dying Mothers, Pt. 2" / *The Tired Sounds of Stars of the Lid* / 7:39
[Yann Tiersen] / "Comptine d'un autre été, l/après-Midi" (Arr. for Violin, Harp, and Orchestra by David Le Page) / *Labyrinths*, Orchestra of the Swan / 2:29
Charley van Veldhoven, Turion, Henrik Meierkord / "Hemellichaam IV—Henrik Meierkord Recycle" / *Hemellichaam IV—Henrik Meierkord Recycle* / 6:24
Chris Warner / "Whirlpool Galaxy" / *Wonders of the Cosmos* / 3:13

A Winged Victory for the Sullen / "Steep Hills of Vicodin Tears" / *A Winged Victory for the Sullen* / 4:27
Hans Zimmer / "Day One" / *Interstellar* (soundtrack) / 3:19

3. PSYCHEDELIC AMBIENT

Rudy Adrian / "Desert Realms" / *Desert Realms* / 8:02
Alio Die / "Honey Mushroom IV" / *Rêverie* / 11:21
Alio Die, Sylvi Alli / "Across a Splendid Vista" / *Amidst the Circling Spires* / 8:07
Michael Brant DeMaria / "Turiya" / *Bindu* / 6:39
Michael DeMaria / "Moonlight" / *The River* / 8:22
Federico Durand / "Lluvia de estrellas" / *La Niña Junco* / 7:33
Canada Effervescent / "Brume De Surface" / *Crystalline* / 8:18
Elve / "Mycelium Dawn" / *Infinite Garden* / 5:32
Brian Eno / "Thursday Afternoon"—2005 Digital Remaster / *Thursday Afternoon* / 1:00:51
Entheo / "Beauty & Truth" / *Lucid Surrender* / 13:00
J. S. Epperson / "417 Hz Undo" / *Solfeggio Suite with Binaural Beats* / 8:24
Jonathan Goldman / "3rd Eye Chakra—Indigo Vision" / *Crystal Bowls Chakra Chants* / 6:06
Jonathan Goldman, Laraaji, Sarah Benson, Andi Goldman / "Angel Dreams" / *De-Stress* / 22:04
Chloe Goodchild / "Eternal A—Pt. 10" / *Eternal A* / 11:11
Hollan Holmes / "The Arrival" / *A Distant Light* / 6:56
Jon Hopkins, 7RAYS / "Ascending, Dawn Sky" / *Music for Psychedelic Therapy* / 9:22
Kelly Howell / "Deep Sleep" / *Deep Sleep* / 28:59
Ishq / "Leaf" / *And Awake* / 14:34
Ishq / "Aurora" / *Sunflower* / 21:07
Jon Jenkins / "Breathing in the Deep" / *Flow* / 10:48
Jeffrey Koepper / "Light and Truth" / *Luminosity* / 9:54
John Lyell / "Eternity" / *Eternity* / 6:32
Matthewdavid's Mindflight / "Ode To Flora" / *Spaciousness (Music without Horizons)* / 10:23
Coyote Oldman / "Tear of the Moon" / *Tear of the Moon* / 10:06
Otoaoustic Emissions / "Sun 126, 22Hz—Real Holophonic Planet Frequencies" / *Holophonic: Space Brainwaves* / 6:38

Otoaoustic Emissions / "Venus 221, 23Hz—Real Holophonic Planet Frequencies" / *Holophonic: Space Brainwaves* / 6:38
David Parsons / "The Valley Below" / *Jyoti* / 9:36
David Parsons / "Dance of the Tree Spirits" / *Rainforest Dreaming* / 10:25
Steve Roach, Dirk Serries / "Here" / *Low Volume Music* / 8:02
Don Slepian / "Sea of Bliss" / *Sea of Bliss* / 29:33
Sound Healing Center / "Sparkling Flicker Tone for Yoga Concentration" / *Relaxing Tones and Drones* / 5:25
Source Vibrations / "741 Hz Consciousness Expansion" / *Solfeggio Harmonics, Vol. 1* / 9:22
Starseed / "Shower of Love and Light" / *Ocean of Eternity* / 13:24
Juta Takahashi / "Moonlit Flowers" / *Moonlit Flowers* / 17:20
Dr. Jeffrey Thompson / "Ethereal Dreams" / *Ambient Music for Sleep* / 30:23
Gus Till / "Sayan" / *Aquana Volume 1: Stillness* / 7:39
Phillip Wilkerson / "Unseen Unnoticed" / *Swiftly the Sun* / 4:44
Phillip Wilkerson / "Pt. 4: Walking Across the River" / *Walking Across the River* / 31:45
Erik Wallo / "Ody At Sea" / *Sources (Early Works 1986-1992)* / 3:38
Zen Hanami / "Just Like Sunlight Through the Trees" / *Reflection 1* / 4:33

4. SOUND MEDITATION FOR PSYCHEDELIC STATES

Vidura Barrios / "Chanting Om with Harmonics" / *Chanting Om with Overtones* / 33:42
Binaural Beats / "For Dreaming—Theta Binaural Beats" / *Binaural Beats* / 20:00
Brainwave-Sync / "Om Mani Padme Hum" / *Spiritual Chanting—Sacred Sounds* / 19:48
Mirabai Ceiba / "Chattr Chattr Deep Relaxation" / *Sevati* / 11:17
Sheila Chandra, The Ganges Orchestra / "Pure Drone 2" / *Pure Drones, Vol. 1* / 7:00
Christopher Lloyd Clarke / "Om Mantra" / *Om Mantra* / 1:00:00
Phil Cory / "Balance and Strength" / *Insomnia Therapy—Deep Waves and Crystal Bowls* / 11:59
Crystal Tones / "Rose Quartz" / *Crystal Tones Chakra Resonance Series, Vol. 1 "Heart Chakra"* / 19:28
Ash Dargan / "Kendi" / *Demurru Meditation* / 5:43
Dreamflute Dorothée Fröller / "528 Hz Solfeggio Love Frequency" / *Love Frequency 528 Hz—Solfeggio Sound Meditation* / 12:03

Electric Dreams / "Low Frequency White Noise" / *Low Frequency White Noise* / 1:00:00
Robert Gass and On Wings of Song / "Kyrie" / *Alleluia to the Pachelbel Canon in D/Kyrie* / 29:16
Ananda Giri / "The Oneness Om" / *The Oneness Om* / 50:40
Jonathan Goldman / "Heart Chakra—Rose of Compassion" / *Crystal Bowls Chakra Chants* / 10:03
Inlakesh / "The Between" / *Didjeridoo Meditation* / 8:00
Inner Splendor Meditation Music and Yoga Project / "Tamboura with Deep Healing Synth Drone for Meditation" / *Deep Relaxation with the Celestial Sound of the Tamboura* / 37:45
Annie Jameson / "Deep Gentle Calm" / *Deep Gentle Calm (Extended Version)* / 1:04:30
Annie Jameson / "Ripples of Light" / *Rain Blessings* / 30:30
Music for Deep Meditation / "Singing Bowl Meditation" / *Tibetan Singing Bowl* / 31:31
Musica Para Meditación Profunda / "Tamboura Para Meditación" / *Viaje Mistico: Mantras Sagrados Para Los 7 Chakras ...* / 10:28
Natura Sound Therapy / "THETA 6hz—Deep Meditation 3" / *Relaxing and Inspiring Sound Therapy Theta 2* / 30:01
Layne Redmond / "Elements into Light" / *Chanting the Chakras* / 8:35
Robbins Island Music Group / "Deep Sustained Major Fifth Chord" / *Single Tones for Meditation* / 7:32
Singers of the Art of Living / "Om Nama Shivaya" / *Sacred Chants of Shiva* / 31:34
The Solfeggio Peace Orchestra / "Meditation on 528 Hz Healing Cycles" / *Meditation on Healing Cycles* / 45:17
Sonic Yogi / "Tibetan Singing Bowls—A# Third Eye Chakra (936hz)" / *Tibetan Singing Bowls ...* / 27:55
Splendor of Meditation / "Tibetan Singing Bowl with Soothing Sound of Rain" / *The Healing Sounds of Tibetan Singing Bowls...* / 31:41
Dr. Jeffrey Thompson / "Centered Presence" / *Gamma Meditation System 2.0* / 30:38
Solala Towler / "Eternal Om" / *Sacred Soundings* / 20:05
White Sun / "Eka Mai Recitation" / *Eka Mai Recitation* / 35:06

5. WORLD MUSIC

Amma / "Radha Ramana (Vintage Version)" / *Amritanjali, Vol. 6 (Remastered)* / 6:34

Emilia Amper / "Trueman" / *Lux* / 4:53
Paban Das Baul / "Kaliya" / *Music of the Honey Gatherers* / 3:17
Kristen Bråten Berg / "Heiemo Og Nykkjen" / *Nordisk Sang* / 4:57
Bulgarian State Television Female Choir / "Mir Stanke le (Harvest Song from Thrace)" / *Le Mystery Des Voix Bulgares* / 3:10
Danit / "Cuatro Vientos" / *Aliento* / 7:27
Erdal Erzincan / "İlahi Dostun Bağına" / *Al Mendil* / 3:39
Gamelan Semara Pegulingan / "Bepong" / *Music of Bali* / 4:37
Divan Gasparyan / "I Will Not Be Sad in This World" / *I Will Not Be Sad in This World* / 6:18
Huun-Huur-Tu / "Highland Tune" / *Where Young Grass Grows* / 6:07
Inlakesh / "The Between" / *Didgeridoo Meditation* / 8:00
Weishan Liu / "Moonlight Over Spring River" / *Great Ocean* / 10:03
Malicorne / "La mule" / *Le bestiaire* / 3:49
Muzsikás (w/Márta Sebestyén) / "Szerelem, szerelem (Love, Love)" / *Prisoners' Songs* / 4:37
Myrkur / "Två Konungabarn" (Single) / *Två Konungabarn* / 3:36
Sainkho Namtchylak / "Dance of Eagle" / *Stepmother City* / 4:36
Ayub Ogada / "Obiera" / *En Mana Kuoyo* / 5:40
Rustavi Folk Choir, Anzor Erkomaishvili / "Chonguro" / *Georgian Lyric Songs* / 4:13
Shruti Sadolikar / "Beet Gaye Din—Raag Hari Kauns" / *Bhakti Varsha—Bhajans* / 4:10
Aruna Sairam, Gayatri Sriram / "Berceuse (Malarum Malarada)" / *Sources—Devotional Chants of Southern India and Medieval Europe* / 4:32
Oumou Sangaré / "Mogoya" / *Mogoya* / 3:31
Rajalakshmee Sanjay / "Annapoorna Stotram" / *Annapoorna Stotram* / 12:09
Raghunath Seth, Chris Hinze / "Christi (Creation), Based on Raga Hansadhwani" / *Cosmic Energy Collection 1: Sun* / 7:33
Shu-de / "Durgen Chugaa" / *Voices from the Distant Steppe* / 3:58
Idrissa Soumaoro, Ali Farka Touré / "Bèrèbèrè "/ *Djitoumou* / 5:19
Tibetan Monks / "Dinchen Lama" / *Tibet Is Calling* / 2:35
Ali Farka Touré, Toumani Diabaté / "Ruby" / *Ali & Toumani* / 5:55
Nezih Uzel, Kudsi Erguner / "Taksim Makam Nihavend, Ney" / *Turkey, Sufi Music* / 4:58
Satish Vyas / "Raga Salang—Alap" / *Cutting Edge* / 3:05
Zhang Weiliang / "Song of a Warm Southerly Breeze" / *Riverside Scenes on a Bright Day* / 5:35

Werdi Sentana / "Tabuh Pengalus" / *Jegog: The Bamboo Gamelan of Bali* / 3:21

6. Indian Classical Music

Ashwini Bhide-Deshpande / "Raga Bageshri: Madhya Bandish" / *Sandhya* / 5:56
Hariprasad Chaurasia / "Alap" / *Sans Breath* / 11:22
S. Gayathri / "Enadhu Manam" / *S. Gayathri and Sugandha Kalamegham* / 5:07
Zakir Hussain, Fazal Qureshi, Sultan Khan / "Taal Pancham Sawari, Raga Asha Mand (Naghma) on Sarangi" / *Essence of Rhythm* / 14:37
Doraiswamy Iyengar / "Raga Ratnamalikache—Raga Riti Gaula" / *Thyagaraja Masterpieces, Vol. 1* / 15:10
Alam Khan / "Pahari Jhinjhoti" / *Solace* / 10:00
Bismillah Khan / "Mishra Mel Ki Malhar" / *The Rain Raga* / 15:02
Bismillah Khan / "Raga Purbi: Alap in Rupaktaal" / *Ustad Bismillah Khan and Party: Shehnai* / 9:40
Shafaat Ahmed Khan, Shivkumar Sharma / "Raga Pahadi-Thumri in Kaharva Tal" / *Mountain Breeze* / 13:58
Tejendra Majumdar, Swapan Chaudhuri / "Dhun in Madhyam se Gara" / *Silken Strings* / 6:00
Ram Narayan / "Raga Baïragi—Bhaïrav" / *North India: The Art of the Sarangi* / 10:48
Ram Narayan / "Mishra Des" / *Sarangi* / 15:44
Ranganayaki Rajagopalan / "Kriti: "cakkanirāja"—Pallavi" / *South India: Ranganayaki Rajagopalan* / 6:05
N. Ramani / "Ragam Tanam: Ranjani Raga" / *Classical Karnatic Flute* / 10:09
Kala Ramnath / "Raag Rageshri Jhaptal" / *Nectar* / 12:39
Kala Ramnath / "Vilambit Ektaal Composition (p1)" / *Touching Air* / 18:09
Ranjani-Gayatri / "Jagadhodharana-Pilu—Adi" / *Soundaryam* / 6:43
G. S. Sachdev / "Rag Chandrakauns—Full Moon" / *Goddess: Divine Energy* / 5:29
Shruti Sadolikar / "Hamsakankini—Khyal in Jhaptaal" / *Women Through the Ages Series* / 21:31
Veena Sahasrabuddhe / "Raga Madhmad Sarang" / *Raga Madhmad Sarang & Bhajan* / 18:59
Raghunath Seth / "Raag Schuddh Sarang—Alap" / *Pandit Raghunath Seth* / 6:32

Anoushka Shankar / "Bhairavi" / *Traveller* / 10:26
Ravi Shankar / "Living Room Session 2: Raga Khamaj" / *The Living Room Sessions Part 1* / 18:57
Ravi Shankar / "Living Room Session 5: Raga Mishra Kafi" / *The Living Room Sessions Part 2* / 18:13
Ravi Shankar / "Raga Bairaga—Remastered" / *The Ravi Shankar Collection: In New York* / 5:37
Ravi Shankar / "Raga Malkauns (Alap)—Remastered" / *The Ravi Shankar Collection: Sound of the Sitar* / 10:03
Sikkil Sisters / "Entha Muddo" / *Venu Gaanaamrutham (Flute)* / 5:02
S. Sowmya / "Gajavadhana—Sri Ranjani—Adi" / *S. Sowmya—Classical Vocal* / 5:35
L. Subramaniam / "Raga Sarasvatipriya" / *Three Ragas for Solo Violin* / 24:53
Satish Vyas / "Raga Jhinjhoti—Alap" / *Cutting Edge* / 5:58

7. Tribal, Trance, Drums, Shamanic, Ayahuasca

Acid Arab, Les Filles de Illighadad / "Soulan" / *Jdid* / 4:58
Aphex Twin / "#17" / *Selected Ambient Works, Vol. II* / 7:17
Ayahuasca Icaros / "Medicine (Cures for All)" / *Icaros for Ceremony (Vol. 1)* / 8:14
Bahramji, Mashti / "Being With You" / *Sufiyan* / 7:04
Chris Berry & The Bayaka of Yandoumbe / "Younga" / *Oka!* / 3:23
Deya Dova / "Birthplace of the Sun" / *Birthplace of the Sun* / 5:14
Deya Dova / "Song For Charli" / *The Jasmani Garden* / 4:34
Michael Drake / "15 Minute Didgeridoo with Rattle" / *Didgeridoo for the Shamanic Journey* / 15:40
Lisa Gerrard / "The Rite" / *The Mirror Pool* / 3:22
The HU / "The Legend of Mother Swan" / *The Gereg* / 5:25
Inlakesh / "Navigator" / *The Dreaming Gate* / 6:19
Brent Lewis / "Ode to Mesmera" / *The Primitive Truth* / 5:00
Liquid Bloom / "Fire Gathering" / *Shaman's Eye* / 14:46
Manish de Moor / "Dragonfly Realm" / *Icaro* / 4:14
Master Minded / "Shaman's Dream 936hz" / *Heart and Soul* / 5:45
Byron Metcalf, Rob Thomas, Inlakesh / "A Deeper Descent" / *Medicine Work* / 15:20
Nomad / "Trading Ground" / *Nomad* / 5:24
Babatunde Olatunji / "Stepping (Isise)" / *Circle of Drums* / 5:42
Outersect / "Light Universe" / *Caldera* / 6:56

Poranguí / "Ayahuasca" / *Ayahuasca (Original Motion Picture Soundtrack)* / 7:25
Hossam Ramzy / "Arabian Knights" / *Baladi Plus* / 8:33
Ray&Kjavik / "Nahimana" / *Mountiri* / 7:57
Layne Redmond / "Breath of the Chakras: Instrumental Version" / *Chakra Breathing Meditations* / 21:14
Istvan Sky / "Impossible Shamanic Voice" / *Voice of Avatar* / 16:31
Stag Hare / "A Rose for the White Witch" / *Spirit Canoes* / 11:20
Shiuli Subaya / "Shiva Gayatri Mantra" / *Raa Maa* / 5:53
Tarshito / "Triaging Tonga" / *African Drum Grooves* / 5:29
Phil Thornton / "Meditation" / *Tibetan Meditation* / 4:58
Werdi Sentana / "Tabuh Pengawit: Gending Truntungan" / *Jegog—The Bamboo Gamelan of Bali* / 7:15
Woomera / "Arrinyenin Apurta—Stone Circle" / *Traditional Aboriginal Music* / 5:04

8. THE HEALING FEMALE VOICE

Anonymous, La Reverdie/Roberto Spremulli / "Resectum ergo—Exaudivit Dominus—Hue Pastor" / *Historia Sancti Eadmundi* / 3:40
Aphir / "Melting Cups" / *Plasticchoir* / 3:11
Ashana / "Soulmerge" / *Jewels of Silence* / 9:36
N'Gou Bagayoko / "Kulu" / *Kulu* / 3:45
Julianna Barwick / "Healing Is a Miracle" / *Healing Is a Miracle* / 4:11
Catherine Braslavsky / "Le bon Pasteur" / *Un jour d'entre les jours* / 3:36
Sheila Chandra / ABoneCroneDrone 1 / *ABoneCroneDrone* / 7:27
Beautiful Chorus / "Faith's Hymn" / *Hymns of Spirit* / 6:20
Deya Dova / "Bloom" / *The Jasmani Garden* / 4:04
Choying Drolma, Steve Tibbetts / "Ney Ogmin Chöying Podrang," 2016 Remaster / *Chö* (Remastered) / 2:28
Enya / "Aníron" / *The Very Best of Enya (Deluxe Edition)* / 2:45
Hildegaard von Bingen, Stevie Wishart, Sinfonye / "O Successores Alio Modo" / *Hildegard* / 2:30
Hildegaard von Bingen, La Reverdie / "Nunc gaudeant maternal viscera ecclesia (Song to Ecclesia)" / *Sponsa Régis la victoire de la vierge dans l'oeuvre d'Hildegard von Bingen* / 4:20
Sona Jobarteh / "Mamaké" / *Fasiya* / 5:08
Karnamrita / "Gopi Gita" / *Dasi—Prayers by Women* / 9:33
Jaya Lakshmi / "Sri Vrndavan" / *Sublime* / 5:49

Yungchen Lhamo / "Mani" / *Gifted—Women of the World* / 5:24
Bliss Looper, Claire Michelle, Ayaharmony / "Aquamarine" / *Aquamarine* / 3:18
Manose, Choying Drolma / "Eternal Chant" / *Dhyana Aman—Meditation of No Mind* / 6:01
Maarja Nuut, Ruum / "Une meeles" / *Muunduja* / 5:27
Niccolo da Perugia, Palatino87 / "Dio mi guardi" / *La Bella Mandorla: Madrigals from the Codex Squarcialupi* / 3:11
Craig Pruess and Ananda / "Devi Prayer" / *108 Sacred Names of Mother Divine* / 21:24
[Radha], Mooji Mala / "Shivoham" / *Sahaja Samadhi* / 9:27
Robbie Robertson, The Red Road Ensemble, Ulali / "Mahk Jchi (Heartbeat Drum Song)" / *Music for "The Native Americans"* / 4:18
The Rose Ensemble / "Alme presul et beate" / *Slavic Holiday: Legends from Ancient Bohemia and Poland* / 4:56
Dechen Shak-Dagsay / "Om Mani Padme Hum – Chenresi" / *Spirit of Compassion* / 9:15
Thorkell Sigurbjörnsson / "Heyr, himna smiour" / *Vökuro* / 2:42
Atli Heimir Sveinsson, Graduale Nobili / "Haustvísur til Máríu" / *In Paradisum: Icelandic Music for Women's Choir* / 3:17
Ananda Vdovic / "Om Shanti: Mantra for Peace" / *Mantras for a Happy Life* / 3:01
Mel Zeki / "Medicine Buddha Mantra" / *Heart Caravan* / 3:11

9. Nature's Own Music

Atmosphere Asmr / "Night Time Forest" / *Relaxing Nature Soundscapes* / 10:00
Gordon Hampton / "Atlantic Sunrise" / *Atlantic Sunrise* / 1:00:37
Doug Kilgore / "Wind and Rustling Leaves" / *Wind and Rustling Leaves* / 9:59
Nature Sound Series / "Lake Waves Lapping at the Cottage Dock..." / *50 Shades of Nature Sounds* / 6:00
Nature Sounds / "Soothing Loon Calls Across a Northern Lake" / *Loons—Sounds of Nature* / 9:30
Nature Sounds / "Soothing Evening Cricket Chorus" / *Nature Sounds for Relaxing Meditation...* / 1:10:01
Nature Sounds / "Birdsong in the Spring Sunshine" / *Nature Sounds: Total Relaxation* / 9:59

Renewing Vibrations / "Mystical Whale Songs" / *Mystical Whale Songs…* / 42:52

Frauke Rotwein / "Talking Brook" / *Sounds of Nature Volume II* / 17:19

Perry Rotwein / "Rambling Stream" / *Watersounds* / 16:26

Sound Healing Center / "Babbling Brook in the Forest" / *Babbling Brook in the Forest…* / 1:00:07

Sounds of Nature White Noise… / "Peace of Mind: Distant Storm Clouds and Thunder" / *Thunder* / 8:00

Dr. Jeffrey Thompson / "Meditative Stream" / *Meditative Stream* / 1:00:00

Dr. Jeffrey Thompson / "Sleepy Ocean" / *Music to Change Your Brain: Deep Sleep* / 1:00:00

Tmsoft's White Noise Sleep Sounds / "Fallingwater Waterfall" / *Natural Water Sounds for Sleep and Relaxation, Volume 2* / 30:00

Tmsoft's White Noise Sleep Sounds / Churning Winter Creek / *Natural Water Sounds for Sleep and Relaxation, Volume 2* / 30:00

Tmsoft's White Noise Sleep Sounds / "Amazon Jungle" / *Amazon Jungle* / 9:50

Tmsoft's White Noise Sleep Sounds / "Crickets Chirping" / *Crickets Chirping* / 9:50

Tmsoft's White Noise Sleep Sounds / "Forest Rain Sound" / *Forest Rain Sound* / 9:50

Tmsoft's White Noise Sleep Sounds / "Frogs at Night" / *Frogs at Night* / 9:50

Tmsoft's White Noise Sleep Sounds / "Lake Rain" / *Lake Rain* / 9:50

Tmsoft's White Noise Sleep Sounds / "Purring Cat Sound" / *Purring Cat Sound* / 9:50

Tmsoft's White Noise Sleep Sounds / "Rain Storm Sound" / *Rain Storm Sound* / 9:50

Tmsoft's White Noise Sleep Sounds / "Tent Rain" / *Tent Rain* / 9:50

Tmsoft's White Noise Sleep Sounds / "Trickling Falls Sound" / *Trickling Falls Sound* / 9:50

Tmsoft's White Noise Sleep Sounds / "Tropical Rain Sound" / *Tropical Rain Sound* / 9:50

Tmsoft's White Noise Sleep Sounds / "Volcanic Springs" / *Volcanic Springs* / 9:50

Tmsoft's White Noise Sleep Sounds / "Wind Blowing" / *Wind Blowing* / 9:50

Whale Song / "Humpback Whale Sounds" / *Humpback Whale Sounds* / 8:00

Wild Eden Nature Sounds / "Jahanjang Central Kalimantan Primary Rainforest" / *Magic of Borneo* / 14:30

Notes

Preface

1. "The world is holy! The soul is holy! The skin is holy! . . . Everything is holy! everybody's holy! everywhere is holy! everyday is in eternity! Everyman's an angel!" Allen Ginsberg, *Howl and Other Poems* (San Francisco: City Lights Books, 1956), 27.

2. "It was at the Magh Mela (Kumbha Mela) at Allahabad . . . that I heard a Nepalese lady singing 'Hare Krishna Hare Rama,' and the melody was so beautiful that it stuck in my head and I took it home to America in 1962 and began singing it at poetry parties, after poetry readings with finger cymbals first and later the harmonium." Debayudh Chatterjee, "Following Inner Moonlight: Ginsberg's Involvement with the Haré Krishna Movement," *JUSAS Online—The web log of the Jadavpur University Society for American Studies*, August 31, 2013, https://jusasonline.wordpress.com/2013/08/31/following-inner-moonlight-ginsbergs-involvement-with-the-hare-krishna-movement/.

3. "The Mantra-Rock Dance," https://back2godhead.com/biography-pure-devotee-11/. We also have an account, from Diane Di Prima's *Memoirs of a Beatnik*, of Ginsberg chanting the Krishna mantra at Timothy Leary's Millbrook estate in 1966. *Sisters of the Extreme: Women Writing on the Drug Experience*, ed. Cynthia Palmer and Michael Horowitz (Rochester, VT: Park Street Press, 2000), 197, 198–99.

4. Though Ginsberg admired Bhaktivedanta's sincerity and deep devotion for Krishna, the Swami's penchant for denouncing other spiritual teachers (particularly Sri Ramakrishna, whom Ginsberg admired) was disillusioning for the poet, who eventually came to view the Swami as a sectarian and fundamentalist, comparing him to a "Hard Shell Baptist" [unpublished interview with Allen Ginsberg by the author, 1978].

5. As Theodore Roszak wrote in 1976, "To a very great extent, these [new religious] movements are functioning as drug rehabilitation programs for their youthful members: the shelter of an orderly life after the chaos of too many bad, bewildering trips. They are last-ditch sanity savers and, to that degree, a welcome mercy to their adherents." However, "We have good reason to fear the need for

absolute meaning where that need strays from the visionary powers which can alone keep it sane and kindly." Well said. The Krishna movement did quickly evolve into a dogmatic cult. Psychedelics, and all "intoxicants," even coffee and tea, were banned from the movement's inception. *Unfinished Animal: The Aquarian Frontier and the Evolution of Consciousness* (London: Faber and Faber, 1976), 70–71, 225.

6. Elcock, *Psychedelic New York*, 167. More on this subject can be found in J. Stillson Judah, *Hare Krishna and the Counterculture* (New York: John Wiley & Sons, 1975).

7. Steven J. Gelberg, *India in a Mind's Eye: Travels and Ruminations of an Ambivalent Pilgrim*, 2nd ed. (San Francisco: Spiraleye Press, 2024), 10.

8. One example: Steven J. Gelberg, "The Call of the Lotus-Eyed Lord: The Fate of Krishna Consciousness in the West," in *When Prophets Die: The Postcharismatic Fate of New Religious Movements*, ed. Timothy Miller (Albany: State University of New York Press, 1991).

9. Steven J. Gelberg, *Hare Krishna, Hare Krishna: Five Distinguished Scholars on the Krishna Movement in the West* (New York: Grove Press, 1983). Among those interviewed was the noted British Indologist Prof. A. L. Basham, author of the classic *The Wonder That Was India*, and the well-known Harvard theologian Dr. Harvey Cox.

10. I described our (my wife's and my) gradual disillusionment in a journal I kept during a longer-than-usual stay in India in 1986. I later self-published an edited version of the journal as *India in a Mind's Eye*, 2nd ed. (San Francisco: Spiraleye Press, 2024). A more concise expression of that disillusionment can be found in the online essay "On Leaving ISKCON" (https://surrealist.org/cults/gelberg1.html), republished in *The Hare Krishna Movement: The Postcharismatic Fate of a Religious Transplant*, ed. Edwin F. Bryant and Maria L. Ekstrand (New York: Columbia University Press, 2004).

11. http://www.stevengelberg.com/.

12. Specific playlists with links are included in various chapters herein and in Appendix I, "Spotify Playlists for Psychedelic Sessions." Note that these links are current as of completion of the manuscript for this book.

Introduction

1. William James, *The Will to Believe*. Quoted in Marcus Boon, *The Road of Excess: A History of Writers on Drugs* (Cambridge, MA: Harvard University Press, 2002), 109–10.

2. R. G. Watson, "The Hallucinogenic Fungi of Mexico: An Inquiry into the Origins of the Religious Idea among Primitive Peoples," 1961. Quoted in Ann and Alexander Shulgin, "A New Vocabulary," in *Entheogens and the Future of Religion*, ed. Robert Forte (1997; repr., Rochester, VT: Park Street Press, 2012), 54.

3. Along with Aldous Huxley, Alan Watts is one of the great articulators of psychedelic experience. In their foreword to Watts's seminal book *The Joyous Cosmology,* Leary and Alpert describe it as "a brilliant arrangement of words describing experiences for which our language has no vocabulary." Alan W. Watts, *The Joyous Cosmology: Adventures in the Chemistry of Consciousness* (New York: Vintage Books, 1962), ix.

4. Alf Gabrielsson, *Strong Experiences with Music* (Oxford: Oxford University Press, 2011), 3.

5. Myron J. Stolaroff, *The Secret Chief Revealed: Conversations with Leo Zeff, Pioneer in the Underground Psychedelic Therapy Movement*, rev. ed. (Sarasota, FL: MAPS, 2004), 157.

6. G. William Barnard, *Liquid Light: Ayahuasca Spirituality and the Santo Daime Tradition* (New York: Columbia University Press, 2022), 50.

7. Rousseau, *Essay on the Origin of Languages* [written in 1754 but published posthmously in 1781]. Quoted in Gilbert Rouget, *Music and Trance: A Theory of the Relations between Music and Possession*, trans. and rev. Brunhilde Biebuych (Chicago: University of Chicago Press, 1985), xxi.

8. Terrence McKenna, *The Archaic Revival* (San Francisco: Harper San Francisco, 1991), 68, 69.

9. Clare O'Callaghan, Daniel J. Hubik, Justin Dwyer, Martin Williams, and Margaret Ross, "Experience of Music Used with Psychedelic Therapy: A Rapid Review and Implications," *Journal of Music Therapy*, vol. 57, no. 3 (2020): 283.

The remaining findings describe music therapists' important potential contribution to the "psychedelic therapy research renaissance" through "assisting with research to optimize music-based protocols used. If psychedelics become approved medicines, music therapists may be involved in offering psychedelic therapy as part of therapeutic teams."

10. O'Callaghan et al., "Experience of Music Used With Psychedelic Therapy," 293.

11. Mike Jay, *Emperors of Dreams: Drugs in the Nineteenth Century* (Cambridge, UK: Dedalus, 2000), 221.

12. Thomas Bradford Roberts, "New Learning," in *Psychedelic Reflections*, ed. Lester Grinspoon and James Bakalar (New York: Human Sciences Press, 1983), 236–37.

13. June McDaniel, *Lost Ecstasy—Its Decline and Transformation in Religion* (London: Palgrave Macmillan, 2018), 1, 12.

14. McDaniel, *Lost Ecstasy*, 2.

15. An enlightening introduction to psychedelic humanism, especially in literary terms, can be found in R. A. Durr's *Poetic Vision and the Psychedelic Experience* (Syracuse, NY: Syracuse University Press, 1970). Though currently out of print, the full text can be accessed online at https://arena-attachments.s3.amazonaws.com/10152370/d62bd438207b36329cdcc9080b92ffb6.pdf?16100777.

16. James Fadiman, *The Psychedelic Explorer's Guide: Safe, Therapeutic, and Sacred Journeys* (Rochester, VT: Park Street Press, 2011), 25–26. The millennia-old role of music in religious ritual (whether or not psychoactive substances are involved) is a complex subject, debated by historians, cultural anthropologists, musicologists, religious studies scholars, and others. Aside from a lack of scholarly consensus concerning the precise types of psychoactives used in various traditional societies, and/or the nature of the music employed, a deep dive into the subject would take us too far afield from our primary concern, which is with contemporary psychedelic practice. For some guidance on the topic, one might consult Gilbert Rouget's classic study *Music and Trance* (see bibliography).

17. Defining "set," William Richards writes, "Above all it reflects qualities such as trust, honesty, courage, humility, reverence, and also a sense of adventure and a willingness to receive and learn, even if it should entail some degree of suffering." "Here and Now: Discovering the Sacred with Entheogens," *Zygon*, vol. 49, no. 3 (September 2014): 658.

18. Stanislav Grof, *Realms of the Human Unconscious: Observations from LSD Research* (New York: Viking Press, 1975), 40. Likewise, from James Fadiman: "The most common comment we hear is, 'I never knew music could be so beautiful and so intricate.'" Richard Louis Miller, *Psychedelic Medicine* (Rochester, VT: Park Street Press, 2017), 62.

19. Discussing similar themes, author Nick Bromell speaks of "the closely related phenomenologies of music and psychedelics" in *Tomorrow Never Knows: Rock and Psychedelics in the 1960s* (Chicago: University of Chicago Press, 2000), 72–73.

20. I should make clear that I am a lover, but not a scholar, of music. My grasp of music theory is that of a layman, not an expert. So, should any reader with expertise in these matters encounter a technical imperfection or questionable interpretation in my ruminations, I beg their indulgence.

21. In Albert Hofmann's words, "Like colours, sounds do not exist objectively. What is objectively present in the hearing process are waves, wavelike compressions and rarefactions of air which register on the eardrum in the ear and become the *psychic* perception of sound in the acoustical centre of the brain." Albert Hofmann, "Science and the Mystico-Religious Experience of the World: The Sender-Receiver Model of Reality, in *Hofmann's Elixir: LSD and the New Eleusis*, ed. Amanda Feilding, trans. Jonathan Ott (Oxford: Beckley Foundation Press, 2008), 39.

22. Marlene Dobkin de Rios and Oscar Janiger, *LSD, Spirituality, and the Creative Process* (Rochester, VT: Park Street Press, 2003), 161.

23. "A recent survey by two Norwegian researchers, Teri Krebs and Pal-Orjan Johansen, based on 2010 data, estimated thirty-two million current residents of the United States alone who have used psilocybin, LSD, or mescaline. The Drug Policy Alliance in 2014 estimated the number of citizens who have used psychedelics in the United States at thirty-four million." William A. Richards,

Sacred Knowledge: Psychedelics and Religious Experiences (New York: Columbia University Press, 2016), 7.

24. DIY home cultivation of "magic mushrooms" is a growing trend.

25. As Thomas B. Roberts reminds us, though psychedelics "commonly produce states that enhance our ability to have spiritual experiences," they are not "always ecstatic, beautiful, or pleasurable," but may in fact produce "hellish emotions, terrible thoughts, and psychological suffering." Thomas B. Roberts, ed., *Psychoactive Sacramentals: Essays on Entheogens and Religion* (San Francisco, CA: Council of Spiritual Practices, 2001), 236, 237.

26. I'll never forget that day, many years ago at the Metropolitan Museum of Art in New York, visually absorbing, alongside an artist friend, an exhibit of old Indian miniature paintings on ivory (perhaps the Eilenberg Collection?). One soul could barely accommodate such a mind-blowing aesthetic feast. Unforgettable. For an account of one man's experiences tripping in art museums, see Daniel Tumbleweed, *The Museum Dose: 12 Experiments in Pharmacologically Mediated Aesthetics* (Phoropter Press, 2015).

27. Significantly, Hofmann himself clearly disputed the assumed notion that LSD, unlike organic plant-based psychedelics, is merely "synthetic": "LSD is not just a synthetic substance from the laboratory. After the discovery of lysergic acid amide and lysergic acid hydroxyethylamide (very closely related to lysergic acid diethylamide) as the entheogenic principles of *Ololiuqui*, an ancient sacred plant of Mexican Indians, LSD ha[s] to be regarded as belonging to the group of natural entheogenic drugs of Mesoamerica. These two characteristics of LSD legitimate its use in a religious framework." Albert Hofmann, "LSD as a Spiritual Aid," in *Psychoactive Sacramentals*, ed. Thomas B. Roberts (San Francisco: Council on Spiritual Practices, 2001), 121.

28. Hofmann, "LSD as a Spiritual Aid," 121.

29. Nancy H. Frankenberry, ed., *The Faith of Scientists in Their Own Words* (Princeton: Princeton University Press, 2008), 157. Quoted in June McDaniel, *Lost Ecstasy*, 12.

30. William James, *The Varieties of Religious Experience*. Quoted in Marcus Boon, *The Road of Excess: A History of Writers on Drugs* (Cambridge, MA: Harvard University Press, 2002), 109.

31. Letter to Humphry Osmond, August 3, 1957, Betty Grover Eisner, *Remembrances of LSD Therapy Past* (2002), 59, http://www.erowid.org/culture/characters/eisner_betty/remembrances_lsd_therapy.pdf.

Chapter 1

1. Lester Grinspoon and James Bakalar, eds., *Psychedelic Reflections* (New York: Human Sciences Press, 1983), 13.

Notes to Chapter 1

2. Michael Pollan, *How to Change Your Mind* (New York: Penguin Press, 2018), 162.

3. Michael Pollan, *This Is Your Mind on Plants* (New York: Penguin Books, 2022), 168.

4. R. E. L. Masters and Jean Houston, *The Varieties of Psychedelic Experience* (New York: Holt, Rinehart and Winston, 1966), 323–24.

5. Aldous Huxley, *The Doors of Perception* and *Heaven and Hell* (1954; repr., New York: Harper Colophon Books, 1963), 23–24.

6. Quoted in G. William Barnard, *Liquid Light: Ayahuasca Spirituality and the Santo Daime Tradition* (New York: Columbia University Press, 2022), 57. [William James, "Confidences of a 'Psychical Researcher,'" in *Essays in Psychical Research* (Cambridge, MA: Harvard University Press, 1986), 374.]

7. Aldous Huxley, "Culture and the Individual," in *LSD: The Consciousness-Expanding Drug*, ed. David Solomon (New York: G. P. Putnam's Sons, 1964), 36.

8. Rupert Sheldrake, Terence McKenna, and Ralph Abraham, *Chaos, Creativity and Cosmic Consciousness* (Rochester, VT: Park Street Press, 2001), 17.

9. Grof goes further, stating, "I have not been able to find a single phenomenon that could be considered an invariant product of the chemical action of [LSD] in any of the areas studies—perceptual, emotional, ideational and physical." Quoted in Huston Smith, *Cleansing the Doors of Perception*, 81.

10. Charles Tart, *On Being Stoned—A Psychological Study of Marijuana Intoxication* (Palo Alto, CA: Science and Behavior Books, 1971), 13.

11. Stanislav Grof, *LSD Psychotherapy* (1980; repr., Ben Lomond, CA: Multidisciplinary Association for Psychedelic Studies, 2008), 11–12.

12. Grof, *LSD Psychotherapy*, 12.

13. Pollan, *How to Change Your Mind*, 352.

14. Pollan, *How to Change Your Mind*, 388.

15. R. A. Durr, *Poetic Vision and the Psychedelic Experience* (Syracuse, NY: Syracuse University Press, 1970), 91–92. [Quoted from E. D. McDonald, ed., *Phoenix: The Posthumous Papers of D. H. Lawrence* (London: Viking, 1961), 379–80.]

16. Alan Watts, *The Joyous Cosmology: Adventures in the Chemistry of Consciousness* (New York: Vintage Books, 1962), 72.

17. Huston Smith, "Introduction," in Aldous Huxley, *The Divine Within: Selected Writings on Enlightenment*, ed. Jacqueline Hazard Bridgeman (1992; repr., New York: Harper Perennial, 2013), 4.

18. For a comparison of divergent views within psychedelic neuroscience, viewing the brain either as source or receiver of consciousness, see Ron Cole-Turner, "Entheogens, Mysticism, and Neuroscience," *Zygon*, vol. 49, no. 3 (September 2014): 642–51.

19. Albert Hofmann, *Insight/Outlook*, ed. Robert Grayson Hall (Atlanta: Humanics New Age: 1989), 25–26.

20. Marlene Dobkin de Rios and Oscar Janiger, *LSD, Spirituality, and the Creative Process* (Rochester, VT: Park Street Press, 2003), 109–10.

21. Masters and Houston, *The Varieties of Psychedelic Experience,* 5–6.

22. C. Savage, J. Fadiman, R. E. Mogar, and M. Allen, "The Effects of Psychedelic (LSD) Therapy on Values, Personality, and Behavior," *International Journal of Neuropsychiatry,* vol. 2, no. 3 (1966): 241–54.

23. Christopher Partridge, *High Culture: Drugs, Mysticism, and the Pursuit of Transcendence in the Modern World* (Oxford: Oxford University Press, 2018), 245.

24. Ido Hartogsohn, *American Trip: Set, Setting, and the Psychedelic Experience in the Twentieth Century* (Cambridge, MA: MIT Press, 2020), 12, 13.

25. Hartogsohn, *American Trip,* 210, 211.

26. Hartogsohn, *American Trip,* 209–10.

27. Hartogsohn, *American Trip,* 209.

28. William A. Richards, "The Phenomenology and Potential Religious Import of States of Consciousness Facilitated by Psilocybin," *Archive for the Psychology of Religion* 30 (2008): 189–99, 190.

29. Pollan, *How to Change Your Mind,* 374–75.

30. Stanislav Grof, *Realms of the Human Unconscious: Observations from LSD Research* (New York: Viking Press, 1975), 139–40.

31. Grof, *LSD Psychotherapy,* 11.

32. Grof, *Realms of the Human Unconscious,* 139.

33. Richard Maurice Bucke, *Cosmic Consciousness* (1901; repr., New York: E. P. Dutton, 1969), 358–59.

34. Grof, *Realms of the Human Unconscious,* vii.

35. Grof, *Realms of the Human Unconscious,* xiii.

36. Theodore Roszak, *Unfinished Animal—The Aquarian Frontier and the Evolution of Consciousness* (London: Faber and Faber, 1976), 17–18, 19.

37. Stanislav Grof, "Beyond the Brain: New Dimensions in Psychology and Psychotherapy," in *Gateway to Inner Space: Sacred Plants, Mysticism and Psychotherapy,* ed. Christian Ratsch (Dorset, UK: Prism Press, 1989), 57–58. In his latest work, *The Way of the Psychonaut* (vol. 2, 23), Grof seems to put a premium on higher-dose (*psychedelic*) therapy because of its greater ability to break through defense mechanisms and thus effect a "cleaner resolution."

38. Stanislav Grof, "The Potential of Entheogens as Catalysts of Spiritual Development," in *Psychoactive Sacramentals: Essays on Entheogens and Religion,* ed. Thomas B. Roberts (San Francisco: Council on Spiritual Practices, 2001), 45. Some authors have criticized what they view as a tendency to over-idealize psychedelic effects, as if they automatically bestow upon their users a kind of provisional sainthood, pointing to the fact that psychedelics have been embraced and cynically employed by more than a few unsavory characters, ideologies or institutions. Their reservations are well-founded. In defense of Grof's seemingly unreserved endorsement of psychedelics as spiritual agents, I can only underscore his critical modifying clause: "used responsibly and in a mature way."

39. Betty Grover Eisner, *Remembrances of LSD Therapy Past* (2002), 21, http://www.erowid.org/culture/characters/eisner_betty/remembrances_lsd_therapy.pdf.

40. Eisner, *Remembrances of LSD Therapy Past,* 129.

41. Huston Smith, *Cleansing the Doors of Perception: The Religious Significance of Entheogenic Plants and Chemicals* (New York: Jeremy P. Tarcher/Putnam, 2000), 10–11.

42. Huston Smith, "Do Drugs Have Religious Import? A Thirty-Five Year Retrospect," in *Psychoactive Sacramentals: Essays on Entheogens and Religion,* ed. Thomas B. Roberts (San Francisco: Council of Spiritual Practices, 2001), 15.

43. Smith, "The Sacred Unconscious," in *Cleansing the Doors of Perception,* 76.

44. See beginning of introduction.

Chapter 2

1. David Aldridge, "Music Therapy and Spirituality (A Transcendental Understanding of Suffering)," in *Music and Altered States: Consciousness, Transcendence, Therapy and Addiction,* ed. David Aldridge and Jorg Fachner (London: Jessica Kingsley, 2006), 109.

2. Aldous Huxley, "The Rest Is Silence," in *Music at Night and Other Essays* (London: Flamings/HarperCollins, 1994 [1931]), 12.

3. Stefan Lorenz Sorgner and Oliver Furbeth, eds., *Music in German Philosophy—An Introduction* (Chicago: University of Chicago Press, 2010), 12.

4. Sorgner and Furbeth, eds., *Music in German Philosophy,* 137.

5. Sorgner and Furbeth, eds., *Music in German Philosophy,* 128–29.

6. John Tavener, *The Music of Silence—A Composer's Testament,* ed. Brian Keeble (London: Faber & Faber, 1999), 163.

7. Benny Shanon, "Music and Ayahuasca," in *Music and Consciousness—Philosophical, Psychological, and Cultural Perspectives,* ed. David Clarke and Eric Clarke (Oxford: Oxford University Press, 2011), 291.

8. Louise Bachelder, ed., *The Gift of Music* (Mount Vernon, NY: Peter Pauper Press, 1975), 61.

9. Bachelder, 61–62.

10. Al-Gazzali, in Judith Becker, *Deep Listeners: Music, Emotion, and Trancing* (Bloomington: Indiana University Press, 2004), 28.

11. Jonathan Harvey, *Music and Inspiration* (London: Faber and Faber, 1999), 127, 145, 151, 154.

12. Michael Tippett, "Art, Judgment and Belief: Towards the Condition of Music," in *The Symbolic Order,* ed. Peter Abbs (London: Falmer Press, 1989), 47. Quoted in Anthony Storr, *Music and the Mind* (New York: Free Press, 1992), 146–47.

13. "Listening to Philip Glass—The Composer Speaks with Tricycle," *Tricycle—The Buddhist Review,* vol. IX, no. 1 (Fall 1999): 40–42.

14. Rudolf Otto, *The Idea of the Holy* (1923; repr., Oxford: Oxford University Press, 1958), 47–49.

15. Marcel Proust, *Remembrance of Things Past,* quoted in Anthony Storr, *Music and the Mind* (New York: Free Press, 1992), 70–71. How apropos, here, is

Aldous Huxley's observation that "Language is a device for taking the mystery out of reality." Cited in Huston Smith, "Introduction," in Aldous Huxley, *The Divine Within: Selected Writings on Enlightenment*, ed. Jacqueline Hazard Bridgeman (1992; repr., New York: Harper Perennial, 2013), 4.

16. William James, *The Varieties of Religious Experience* (New York: Penguin, 1982), 380–81.

17. Benny Shanon, *The Antipodes of the Mind: Charting the Phenomenology of the Ayahuasca Experience* (Oxford: Oxford University Press, 2010), 176–77.

Note that aside from quoting Prof. Shanon from time to time concerning musical aesthetics vis-à-vis ayahuasca, where his insights apply equally to other psychedelics, I have avoided, herein, addressing the use of music in ayahuasca rituals as a separate subject because of its unique and distinctive attributes: primarily (1) the use of "live" vocal and percussive music, (2) guided by a shaman representing a particular cultural and musical metaphysic, (3) meant to "[induce] stereotypic visions to achieve predetermined goals" (Dobkin de Rios, 2003, 161). This cultic, ritual use of music in ayahuasca settings differs, obviously, from the kinds of settings and experiences addressed in the present work. As a unique, more esoteric area of study, I simply lack the expertise to deal with it adequately. For an authoritative academic and experiential treatment of the subject, see, for example, G. William Barnard, *Liquid Light: Ayahuasca Spirituality and the Santo Daime Tradition* (New York: Columbia University Press, 2022) and Beatriz Caluby Labate and Gustavo Pacheco, *Opening the Portals of Heaven: Brazilian Ayahuasca Music*, trans. Matthew Meyer (Berlin: LIT Verlag, 2010).

18. Shanon, *The Antipodes of the Mind*, 312–13.

19. Shanon, "Music and Ayahuasca," 291.

20. William A. Richards, *Sacred Knowledge: Psychedelics and Religious Experiences* (New York: Columbia University Press, 2016), 155, 156–57.

21. Claudio Naranjo, *My Psychedelic Explorations* (Rochester, VT: Park Street Press, 2020), 332.

22. Naranjo, *My Psychedelic Explorations*, 331–32.

23. Claude Levi-Strauss, *The Raw and the Cooked*, quoted in Anthony Storr, *Music and the Mind* (New York: Free Press, 1992), xi.

24. Leo Tolstoy, *The Kreutzer Sonata* (New York: Modern Library, 2003), 60.

25. Aldous Huxley, *Island* (New York: Harper & Row, 1962), 274.

26. Huxley to Osmond, 23 December 1955, *Psychedelic Prophets: The Letters of Aldous Huxley and Humphrey Osmond*, ed. Cynthia Carson Bisbee et al. (Montreal: McGill-Queen's University Press, 2018), 238.

27. Michael Pollan, *How to Change Your Mind* (New York: Penguin Press, 2018), 268.

28. Walter Houston Clark, *Chemical Ecstasy: Psychedelic Drugs and Religion* (New York: Sheed and Ward, 1969), 29.

29. R. E. L. Masters and Jean Houston, *The Varieties of Psychedelic Experience* (New York: Dell, 1966), 182.

30. Ido Hartogsohn, *American Trip: Set, Setting, and the Psychedelic Experience in the Twentieth Century* (Cambridge, MA: MIT Press, 2020), 212–13.

31. Naranjo, *My Psychedelic Explorations,* 59–60.

Chapter 3

1. R. A. Durr, *Poetic Vision and the Psychedelic Experience* (Syracuse, NY: Syracuse University Press, 1970), 29.

2. Humphry Osmond, "A Review of the Clinical Effects of Psychotomimetic Agents," in *LSD; The Consciousness-Expanding Drug,* ed. David Solomon (New York: G. P. Putnam's Sons, 1964), 146.

3. Marlene Dobkin de Rios and Oscar Janiger, *LSD, Spirituality, and the Creative Process* (Rochester, VT: Park Street Press, 2003), 110.

4. Alan W. Watts, *The Joyous Cosmology: Adventures in the Chemistry of Consciousness* (New York: Vintage Books, 1962), 6–7.

5. Oliver Sacks, *Musicophilia: Tales of Music and the Brain* (New York: Knopf, 2007), 148.

6. Sacks, *Musicophilia*, 73.

7. Sacks, *Musicophilia*, 148.

8. Julie Holland, "An Interview with Michael Pollan," in *The Pot Book: A Complete Guide to Cannabis—Its Role in Medicine, Politics, Science, and Culture,* ed. Julie Holland (Santa Cruz, CA: Multidisciplinary Association for Psychedelic Studies, 2010), 375–76.

9. Allen Ginsberg, "The Great Marijuana Hoax: First Manifesto to End the Bringdown," in Allen Ginsberg, *Deliberate Prose—Selected Essays 1952-1995,* ed. Bill Morgan (New York: HarperCollins, 2000), 87, 88.

10. Anthony Storr, *Music and the Mind* (New York: Free Press, 1992), 136.

11. Letter to Humphry Osmond, 24 October 1955, *Psychedelic Prophets: The Letters of Aldous Huxley and Humphrey Osmond,* ed. Cynthia Carson Bisbee et al. (Montreal: McGill-Queen's University Press, 2018), 217.

12. R. E. L. Masters and Jean Houston, *The Varieties of Psychedelic Experience* (New York: Dell, 1966), 155.

13. Alan Watts, "A Psychedelic Experience: Fact or Fantasy?," in *LSD: The Consciousness-Expanding Drug,* ed. David Solomon (New York: G. P. Putnam's Sons, 1964), 125.

14. Durr, *Poetic Vision and the Psychedelic Experience,* 26.

15. Durr, *Poetic Vision and the Psychedelic Experience,* 38.

16. Vladimir Jankelevitch, *Music and the Ineffable,* trans. Carolyn Abbate (1961; repr., Princeton: Princeton University Press, 2003), 101, 102.

17. *Collected Works of J. Krishnamurti,* vol. VII, 1952–1953: *Tradition and Creativity* (Ojai, CA: Krishnamurti Foundation America, 2012), 213.

18. Judith Becker, *Deep Listeners: Music, Emotion, and Trancing* (Bloomington: Indiana University Press, 2004), 57.

19. Aldous Huxley, *Island* (New York: Harper & Row, 1962), 274–75.

20. Huxley, *Island*, 274–75. Commenting on this episode in Huxley's *Island*, Albert Hofmann wrote, "The more than 20-page account of the *moksha*-night . . . is the best description I know of the difficult-to-detail experience of entheogenic states of consciousness." Albert Hofmann, "A.H., A.H. and LSD," in *Hofmann's Elixir: LSD and the New Eleusis*, ed. Amanda Feilding and trans. Jonathan Ott (Oxford: Beckley Foundation Press, 2008), 86.

21. Raphaël Millière, Robin L. Carhart-Harris, Leor Roseman, Fynn-Mathis Trautwein, and Aviva Berkovich-Ohana, "Psychedelics, Meditation, and Self-Consciousness," *Frontiers in Psychology*, vol. 9 (2018): 1475.

22. William A. Richards, "The Phenomenology and Potential Religious Import of States of Consciousness Facilitated by Psilocybin," *Archive for the Psychology of Religion* 30 (2008): 189–99, 195–96.

23. Recommended playlists: "Peace & Serenity" (Classical), https://open.spotify.com/playlist/2v1W31awEzwzJ0nYhWjiwV?si=1e758b0dc2d94386 / "Spacious/Ethereal" (Ambient), https://open.spotify.com/playlist/0jSfXDL1minqrXOrlxaURA?si=0290f69cebba4445.

24. Ram Dass, "A Roundtable with Ram Dass, Robert Aitken Roshi, Richard Baker Roshi, and Joan Halifax Roshi," in *Zig Zag Zen: Buddhism and Psychedelics*, ed. Allan Hunt Badiner (San Francisco: Chronicle Books, 2002), 221.

25. R. E. L. Masters and Jean Houston, *The Varieties of Psychedelic Experience* (New York: Dell, 1966), 143.

26. Stanislav Grof, *LSD Psychotherapy* (1980; repr., Ben Lomond, CA: Multidisciplinary Association for Psychedelic Studies, 2008), 141, 142.

27. James Fadiman, *The Psychedelic Explorer's Guide: Safe, Therapeutic, and Sacred Journeys* (Rochester, VT: Park Street Press, 2011), 26.

28. Helen Bonny and Walter N. Pahnke, "The Use of Music in Psychedelic (LSD) Psychotherapy," in *Music Consciousness: The Evolution of Guided Imagery and Music*, ed. Helen Bonny (Lower Village Gilsum, NH: Barcelona Publishers, 2002), 22.

29. Ruth Fox, MD, "Is LSD of Value in Treating Alcoholics?," in *The Use of LSD in Psychotherapy and Alcoholism,* ed. Harold A. Abramson (Indianapolis: Bobbs-Merrill, 1967), 479.

30. Christopher M. Bache, *LSD and the Mind of the Universe* (Rochester, VT: Park Street Press, 2019), 47.

31. Mark Evan Bonds, *Absolute Music—The History of an Idea* (Oxford: Oxford University Press, 2014), 106.

32. Betty Eisner, "Set, Setting, and Matrix," *Journal of Psychoactive Drugs*, vol. 29, no. 2 (1997): 214.

33. Logan Neitzke-Spruill and Carol Glasser, "A Gratuitous Grace: The Influence of Religious Set and Intent on the Psychedelic Experience," *Journal of Psychoactive Drugs*, vol. 50, no. 4 (2018): 314–21 (cited in Ron Cole-Turner, 2022).

34. John J. Pilch, "Music and Trance," in *Music and Altered States: Consciousness, Transcendence, Therapy and Addiction,* ed. David Aldridge and Jorg Fachner (London: Jessica Kingsley Publishers, 2006), 43.

35. Pilch, "Music and Trance," 43–44. [A. Kleinman, *Rethinking Psychiatry* (New York: Free Press and Collier Macmillan, 1988).]

36. Théophile Gautier, "Hashish," trans. Maurice Stang, in Charles Baudelaire/Théophile Gautier, *Hashish, Wine, Opium* (1843; repr., Surrey, UK: Alma Classics, 2009), 60.

37. Aldous Huxley, *The Doors of Perception* and *Heaven and Hell* (1954; repr., New York: Harper Colophon Books, 1963), 53.

38. Pilch, "Music and Trance," 44.

39. Judith Becker, *Deep Listeners: Music, Emotion, and Trancing* (Bloomington: Indiana University Press, 2004), 11, 13.

40. Becker, *Deep Listeners,* 29.

41. Gilbert Rouget, *Music and Trance: A Theory of the Relations between Music and Possession,* trans. and rev. Brunhilde Biebuych (Chicago: University of Chicago Press, 1985), xvii.

42. Marghanita Laski, *Ecstasy* (Los Angeles: Jeremy P. Tarcher, 1961), 190.

43. Claudio Naranjo, *My Psychedelic Explorations* (Rochester, VT: Park Street Press, 2020), 48.

44. Marlene Dobkin de Rios and Oscar Janiger, *LSD, Spirituality, and the Creative Process* (Rochester, VT: Park Street Press, 2003), 161.

45. J. Ross MacLean, D. C. MacDonald, F. Ogden, and E. Wilby, "LSD 25 and Mescaline as Therapeutic Adjuvants," in *The Use of LSD in Psychotherapy and Alcoholism,* ed. Harold A. Abramson (Indianapolis: Bobbs-Merrill, 1967), 419.

46. Benny Shanon, "Music and Ayahuasca," in *Music and Consciousness—Philosophical, Psychological, and Cultural Perspectives,* ed. David Clarke and Eric Clarke (Oxford: Oxford University Press, 2011), 290.

47. Jane Dunlap, *Exploring Inner Space: Personal Experiences under LSD-25* (New York: Harcourt, Brace & World, 1961), 155.

48. Stanislav Grof, *Psychology of the Future: Lessons from Modern Consciousness Research* (Albany: State University of New York Press, 2000), 186–87.

49. Daniel Pinchbeck, *Breaking Open the Head: A Psychedelic Journey into the Heart of Contemporary Shamanism* (New York: Broadway Books, 2002), 267. (The subject was on DPT, a chemical cousin of DMT.)

Chapter 4

1. Edgar Z. Friedenberg et al., eds., *The Cosmos Reader* (New York: Harcourt Brace Jovanovich, 1971), 650–60. [Reprinted from the *California Law Review,* vol. 56, no. 100, 1968.]

2. Alan Watts, *In My Own Way: An Autobiography* (New York: Vintage Books, 1973), 397–98.
3. Watts, *In My Own Way*, 399.
4. Friedenberg et al., *The Cosmos Reader*, 652–53.
5. Alan Watts, "The New Alchemy," in *This is It (and Other Essays on Zen and Spiritual Experience)* (New York: Collier Books, 1967), 134.
6. Quoted in Rasa Gustaitis, *Turning On* (New York: Macmillan, 1969), xix.
7. LSD Journal, n.d., edited.
8. Watts, "The New Alchemy," 135.
9. Watts, "The New Alchemy," 135.
10. Charles Tart, *On Being Stoned—A Psychological Study of Marijuana Intoxication* (Palo Alto, CA: Science and Behavior Books, 1971), 71, 287–88.
11. Jorg Fachner, "Music and Drug-Induced Altered States of Consciousness," in *Music and Altered States: Consciousness, Transcendence, Therapy and Addictions*, ed. David Aldridge and Jorg Fachner (London: Jessica Kingsley Publishers, 2006), 90.
12. Jorg Fachner, "Drugs, Altered States, and Musical Consciousness: Reframing Time and Space," in *Music and Consciousness—Philosophical, Psychological, and Cultural Perspectives*, ed. David Clarke and Eric Clarke (Oxford: Oxford University Press, 2011), 275.
13. Fachner, "Music and Drug-Induced Altered States of Consciousness," 93.
14. Jacques-Joseph Moreau, *Hashish and Mental Illness*, trans. Gordon J. Barnett (1845; repr., New York: Raven Press, 1973), 42.
15. See chap. 5 herein, "Music, Emotion and Aesthetic Ecstasy."
16. Paul Moser, in *The Drug Experience: First-Person Accounts of Addicts, Writers, Scientists and Others*, ed. David Ebin (New York: Orion Press, 1961), 359.
17. Helen Bonny and Walter N. Pahnke, "The Use of Music in Psychedelic (LSD) Psychotherapy," in *Music Consciousness: The Evolution of Guided Imagery and Music*, ed. Helen Bonny (Lower Village Gilsum, NH: Barcelona Publishers, 2002), 27–28.
18. Gaston Bachelard, *The Poetics of Reverie: Childhood, Language, and the Cosmos*, trans. Daniel Russell (1960; repr., Boston: Beacon Press, 1969), 173, 174–75.
19. Gerald Heard, "Can This Drug Enlarge Man's Mind?" in *The Psychedelic Reader*, ed. Gunther M Weil, Ralph Metzner, and Timothy Leary (New Hyde Park, NY: University Books, 1965), 3, 5–6. [Note: Opus 135 is Beethoven's String Quartet No. 16. I suspect the "searing" emotions may refer to the third or, more likely, fourth movement, portions of which are, indeed, rather intense and not to be recommended for psychedelic use.]
20. Michael Pollan, *How to Change Your Mind* (New York: Penguin Press, 2018), 310.
21. Peter Michael Hamel, *Through Music to the Self* (Boulder: Shambhala, 1979), 39.

22. Malden Grange Bishop, *The Discovery of Love: A Psychedelic Experience with LSD-25* (New York: Torquil/Dodd, Mead, 1963), 172.

23. Lester Grinspoon, *Marihuana Reconsidered* (Cambridge, MA: Harvard University Press, 1971), 110.

24. Ward, R. H., *A Drug-Taker's Notes*, 168–69.

25. Ward, R. H., *A Drug-Taker's Notes*, 170.

26. *Cinerama* was a novel, trademarked, wide-screen movie projection system introduced in the 1950s that "projected images simultaneously from three synchronized 35mm projectors onto a huge, deeply curved screen" having an arc of 146 degrees. See https://en.wikipedia.org/wiki/Cinerama.

27. Charles Bush, "The Psychedelic Cinerama," in *Psychedelic Wisdom: The Astonishing Rewards of Mind-Altering Substances*, ed. Richard Louis Miller (Rochester, VT: Park Street Press, 2022), 335–36.

28. Benny Shanon, "Music and Ayahuasca," in *Music and Consciousness—Philosophical, Psychological, and Cultural Perspectives*, ed. David Clarke and Eric Clarke (Oxford: Oxford University Press, 2011), 284.

29. Shanon, "Music and Ayahuasca," 285.

30. Robert S. DeRopp, *The Master Game: Pathways to Higher Consciousness Beyond the Drug Experience* (New York: Delta, 1968), 39.

31. Marlene Dobkin de Rios and Oscar Janiger, *LSD, Spirituality, and the Creative Process* (Rochester, VT: Park Street Press, 2003), 128–29.

32. Bonny and Pahnke, "The Use of Music in Psychedelic (LSD) Psychotherapy," 39.

33. *Hallucinogenic Drugs and Their Psychotherapeutic Use*—The Proceedings of the Quarterly Meeting of the Royal Medico-Psychological Association in London, February 1961, ed. Richard Crocket, R. A. Sandison, and Alexander Walk (London: H. K. Lewis, 1963), 176.

34. Pollan, *How to Change Your Mind*, 268.

35. R. A. Durr, *Poetic Vision and the Psychedelic Experience* (Syracuse, NY: Syracuse University Press, 1970), 6.

36. Sidney Cohen, *The Beyond Within: The L.S.D. Story* (New York: Atheneum, 1965), 160.

37. John Robertson, "Uncontainable Joy," in *The Ecstatic Adventure*, ed. Ralph Metzner (New York: Macmillan, 1968), 88. "John Robertson" is a pseudonym for William A. Richards (as revealed to me by Dr. Richards).

38. Jerry Richardson, "Who Am I, and So What if I Am?," in *Psychedelics—The Uses and Implications of Hallucinogenic Drugs*, ed. Bernard Aaronson and Humphry Osmond (Garden City, NY: Anchor Books/Doubleday, 1970), 53.

39. Stanislav Grof, *Realms of the Human Unconscious: Observations from LSD Research* (New York: Viking Press, 1975), 40. The same concept is stated by Sufi mystic Hazrat Inayat Khan in his book *The Music of Life*: "There is no greater and more living resonator of sound than the human body. Sound has an effect on each atom of the body, for each atom resounds."

40. Marlene Dobkin de Rios and Oscar Janiger, *LSD, Spirituality, and the Creative Process* (Rochester, VT: Park Street Press, 2003), 127.
41. Dobkin de Rios and Janiger, *LSD, Spirituality, and the Creative Process*, 129.
42. Linda Sontag, "The Eyes of the Child-Corpse Were Open Wide," in *The Ecstatic Adventure*, ed. Ralph Metzner (New York: Macmillan, 1968), 180.

Chapter 5

1. Quoted in R. A. Durr, *Poetic Vision and the Psychedelic Experience* (Syracuse, NY: Syracuse University Press, 1970), 100.
2. Walter N. Pahnke et al., "The Experimental Use of Psychedelic (LSD) Psychotherapy," *Journal of the American Medical Association*, vol. 212, no. 11 (1970), reprinted in *Hallucinogenic Drug Research: Impact on Science and Society*, ed. James R. Gamage and Edmund L. Zerkin (Beloit, WI: Stash Press, 1970), 52.
3. Benny Shanon, "Music and Ayahuasca," in *Music and Consciousness—Philosophical, Psychological, and Cultural Perspectives*, ed. David Clarke and Eric Clarke (Oxford: Oxford University Press, 2011), 291.
4. Jenefer Robinson, *Deeper Than Reason: Emotion and Its Role in Literature, Music, and Art* (Oxford: Oxford University Press, 2005), 380–81.
5. Lawrence Kramer, *Why Classical Music Still Matters* (Berkeley: University of California Press, 2007), 213.
6. Roseman, Leor, David J. Nutt, and Robin L. Carhart-Harris, "Quality of Acute Psychedelic Experience Predicts Therapeutic Efficacy of Psilocybin for Treatment-Resistant Depression," *Frontiers in Pharmacology*, vol. 8 (2018): 974.
7. Betty Grover Eisner, *Remembrances of LSD Therapy Past* (2002), 19, https://www.erowid.org/culture/characters/eisner_betty/remembrances_lsd_therapy.pdf.
8. BBC Radio, "Beyond Belief: Faith in the Psychedelic Renaissance," January 8, 2024, https://www.bbc.co.uk/sounds/play/m001v3g3.
9. See Roman Palitsky et al., "Importance of Integrating Spiritual, Existential, Religious, and Theological Components in Psychedelic-Assisted Therapies," *JAMA Psychiatry*, vol. 80, no. 7 (2023): 743–49. https://doi.org/10.1001/jamapsychiatry.2023.1554.
10. Christopher Partridge, *High Culture: Drugs, Mysticism, and the Pursuit of Transcendence in the Modern World* (Oxford: Oxford University Press, 2018), 117.
11. Huston Smith, *Cleansing the Doors of Perception: The Religious Significance of Entheogenic Plants and Chemicals* (New York: Jeremy P. Tarcher/Putnam, 2000), 15.
12. Concerning music's ineffable inner *charm*, Benny Shanon concurs, "Music has the special quality of being able to create an ambiance of enchantment—a property that is reflected in the close relationship between the English words chant and enchant, as also between *canto* (song) and *encanto* (charm), and

between *cantar/e* (to sing) and *encantar/e* (to enchant)." Benny Shanon, "Music and Ayahuasca," in Clark and Clark, *Music and Consciousness—Philosophical, Psychological, and Cultural Perspectives*, 290.

13. Vladimir Jankelevitch, *Music and the Ineffable*, trans. Carolyn Abbate (1961; repr, Princeton: Princeton University Press, 2003), 102. Closely related is this comment from respected music scholar Mark Evan Bonds: "In the end, any attempt to explain music's power is driven by a desire to assert control over it, overcome its danger, and quell our anxiety that we are in fact not so great as we might be." Mark Evan Bonds, *Absolute Music—The History of an Idea* (Oxford: Oxford University Press, 2014), 36–37.

14. Leo Tolstoy's Diary, January 20, 1905 [the quote is often wrongly attributed to his novella *The Kreutzer Sonata*].

15. Diane Ackerman, *A Natural History of the Senses* (New York: Vintage Books, 1990), 213.

16. Jankelevitch, *Music and the Ineffable*, 128–29.

17. Anthony Storr, *Music and the Mind* (New York: Free Press, 1992), 144. [Source: *The World as Will and Representation*, vol. 1 (trans. by E. F. J. Payne) (New York: Dover, 1966), 261.]

18. Paul Elmer More, "Lafcadio Hearn," *Shelburne Essays*, Second Series (New York: G. P. Putnam's Sons, 1905), 64–65.

19. G. William Barnard, *Exploring Unseen Worlds: William James and the Philosophy of Mysticism* (Albany: State University of New York Press, 1997), 193. More recently Prof. Barnard has written a book on ayahuasca spirituality (see bibliography).

20. Barnard, *Exploring Unseen Worlds,* 205. [The reference is to Eugene Fontinell, *Self, God, and Immortality* (Philadelphia: Temple University Press, 1986), 27, 154.]

21. Jerry Richardson, "Who Am I, and So What if I Am?" in *Psychedelics—The Uses and Implications of Hallucinogenic Drugs*, ed. Bernard Aaronson and Humphry Osmond (Garden City, NY: Anchor Books/Doubleday, 1970), 53.

22. Jane Dunlap, *Exploring Inner Space: Personal Experiences under LSD-25* (New York: Harcourt, Brace & World, 1961), 155–56.

23. Eugene Seaich, *The Far-Off Land—An Attempt at a Philosophical Evaluation of the Hallucinogenic Drug-Experience* (Xlibris Corporation, 2012). [Written in 1959 and published by his grandson, Eric Hendrickson, in 2012 via print-on-demand, 62.]

24. Huston Smith, "The Good Friday Experiment," in *Cleansing the Doors of Perception: The Religious Significance of Entheogenic Plants and Chemicals* (New York: Jeremy P. Tarcher/Putnam, 2000), 101.

25. Harvey Cox, *Turning East: The Promise and Peril of the New Orientalism* (New York: Simon and Schuster, 1977), 47.

26. Bo Holmstedt, "Introduction to Moreau de Tours," in Jacques-Joseph Moreau, *Hashish and Mental Illness*, trans. Gordon J. Barnett (1845; repr., New York: Raven Press, 1973), xiv.

27. Jacques-Joseph Moreau, *Hashish and Mental Illness*, trans. Gordon J Barnett (1845; repr., New York: Raven Press, 1973), 1.

28. Moreau, *Hashish and Mental Illness*, 38–39.

29. Aaron Copland, *Music and Imagination: The Charles Eliot Norton Lectures, 1951–1952* (Cambridge, MA: Harvard University Press, 1952), 14.

30. https://open.spotify.com/playlist/1cIlMlQu7LaCMeGMc6UvCo?si=81879796f08249cf.

31. Author, reflections after a trip, n.d.

Chapter 6

1. https://www.psychologytoday.com/us/basics/synesthesia.

2. https://en.wikipedia.org/wiki/Mary_Whiton_Calkins.

3. Described in *Mescal: A New Artificial Paradise*, 1898.

4. In *Les Paradis Artificiels (Artificial Paradises)*, 1860.

5. Note that in these settings hashish was consumed in doses that made it an "intensely powerful hallucinogen." Mike Jay, *Emperors of Dreams: Drugs in the Nineteenth Century* (Cambridge: Daedalus, 2000), 91.

6. Mike Jay, *Psychonauts: Drugs and the Making of the Modern Mind* (New Haven: Yale University Press, 2023), 228–29.

7. Jay, *Psychonauts*, 197

8. Jay, *Psychonauts*, 196.

9. Jay, *Psychonauts*, 197.

10. Christopher Partridge, *High Culture: Drugs, Mysticism, and the Pursuit of Transcendence in the Modern World* (Oxford: Oxford University Press, 2018), 154. [Helena P. Blavatsky, *Collected Writings*, ed. Boris de Zirkoff (Wheaton: Theosophical Publishing House, 1956), 7:58.]

11. One's innate capacity for visualization may influence the degree of its activation in psychedelic states.

12. Benny Shanon, "Music and Ayahuasca," in *Music and Consciousness—Philosophical, Psychological, and Cultural Perspectives*, ed. David Clarke and Eric Clarke (Oxford: Oxford University Press, 2011), 290.

13. Nick Bromell, *Tomorrow Never Knows: Rock and Psychedelics in the 1960s* (Chicago: University of Chicago Press, 2000), 72–73.

14. Mark Evan Bonds, *Absolute Music—The History of an Idea* (Oxford: Oxford University Press, 2014), 30.

15. Becker, *Deep Listeners*, 27.

16. Lawrence E. Sullivan, ed., *Enchanting Powers—Music in the World's Religions* (Cambridge, MA: Harvard University Press, 1997), 3–4. For a discussion

and anthology of music as a stimulus for human imagination under "normal" (non-psychedelic) circumstances (including practical exercises), see Helen L. Bonny and Louis M. Savary, *Music & Your Mind: Listening with a New Consciousness* (Barrytown, NY: Station Hill Press, 1990).

17. Benny Shanon, "Music and Ayahuasca," 286.

18. Blake, A *Descriptive Catalog*, Number IV. Alexander Gilchrist, *The Life of William Blake* (1863; repr., Mineola, NY: Dover Publications, 1998), 513.

19. Quoted in Michael Pollan, *How to Change Your Mind* (New York: Penguin Press, 2018), 111.

20. V. P. Wasson and R. G. Wasson, *Mushrooms, Russia and History* (New York: Pantheon Books, 1957), 294. Quoted in Robert Forte, *Entheogens and the Future of Religion* (Rochester, VT: Park Street Press), 147.

21. Joan Watts and Anne Watts, *The Collected Letters of Alan Watts* (Novato, CA: New World Library, 2017), 520. I would venture to say that here Watts is referring to the color landscape work of Eliot Porter when reproduced in books with high-quality glossy stock, where the images indeed possess a beautiful crystalline quality, with every twig and leaf a visual statement of great clarity and delicacy.

22. Marlene Dobkin de Rios and Oscar Janiger, *LSD, Spirituality, and the Creative Process* (Rochester, VT: Park Street Press, 2003), 129.

23. Alan Watts, "The New Alchemy," in *This is It (and Other Essays on Zen and Spiritual Experience)* (New York: Collier Books, 1967), 132.

24. Mark Seelig, "Communion with the Goddess: Three Weeks of Ayahuasca in Brazil," in *The Divine Spark: Psychedelics, Consciousness, and the Birth of Civilization*, ed. Graham Hancock (San Francisco: Disinformation Books, 2015), 185.

25. Christopher Partridge, "Psychedelic Music," in *The Bloomsbury Handbook of Religion and Popular Music*, ed. Christopher Partridge and Marcus Moberg (London: Bloomsbury, 2018), 297.

26. Robert Graves, *On Poetry: Collected Talks and Essays* (Garden City, NY: Doubleday, 1969), 378–79.

27. Sidney Cohen, *The Beyond Within: The L.S.D. Story* (New York: Atheneum, 1965), 160–62.

28. Pollan, *How to Change Your Mind,* 247–49.

29. R. E. L. Masters and Jean Houston, *The Varieties of Psychedelic Experience* (New York: Dell, 1966), 19–20. The "female twenty-four-year-old university instructor [on] 225 micrograms of LSD" turns out to be coauthor Jean Houston herself, who repeats the scene nearly verbatim in her later autobiographical work *A Mythic Life* (New York: HarperCollins, 1996), 173–74.

30. Huxley to Osmond, December 23, 1955, *Psychedelic Prophets: The Letters of Aldous Huxley and Humphrey Osmond,* ed. Cynthia Carson Bisbee et al. (Montreal: McGill-Queen's University Press, 2018), 237.

31. Huxley to Osmond, January 21, 1956, *Psychedelic Prophets*, 245. In a later letter to Osmond (July 17, 1960), Huxley mentions that even 100 micrograms of

LSD "doesn't make me see things with my eyes shut," and asks, "Have you any idea why some people visualize and others don't? I don't . . ." *Psychedelic Prophets*, 452.

Chapter 7

1. Terence McKenna, *Food of the Gods* (New York: Bantam Books, 1992), 161, 162. Quote is from an early account of a hashish experience by an American traveler, Bayard Taylor, in *The Lands of the Saracen (or Pictures of Palestine, Asia Minor, Sicily and Spain) & Travels in Arabia* [1854] (Prince Classics, 2020), 104, 106.

2. Helen Bonny and Walter N. Pahnke, "The Use of Music in Psychedelic (LSD) Psychotherapy," in *Music Consciousness: The Evolution of Guided Imagery and Music*, ed. Helen Bonny (Lower Village Gilsum, NH: Barcelona Publishers, 2002), 35. "Minimal auditory stimulus" can refer to "white noise," as discussed in chapter 13, "Sound Alternatives to Music."

3. Jane Dunlap, *Exploring Inner Space: Personal Experiences under LSD-25* (New York: Harcourt, Brace & World, 1961), 61.

4. Oliver Sacks, *Musicophilia: Tales of Music and the Brain* (New York: Alfred A. Knopf, 2007), 52.

5. Sacks, *Musicophilia*, 31–32.

6. Sacks, *Musicophilia*, 51 (footnote 1).

7. Sacks, *Musicophilia*, 51 (footnote 1).

8. Robert Jourdain, *Music, the Brain, and Ecstasy (How Music Captures Our Imagination)* (New York: HarperCollins/Quill, 2002), 188. I do not know whether Tchaikovsky's case qualifies as "neuropathological." I tentatively place him in this category only because (1) his story complements that of Schumann's, and (2) his distressed reaction *may* imply as much.

9. Jacques-Joseph Moreau, *Hashish and Mental Illness*, trans. Gordon J. Barnett (1845; repr., New York: Raven Press, 1973), 184.

10. https://www.catholic.org/saints/saint.php?saint_id=34.

11. Joscelyn Godwin, *Music, Mysticism and Magic—A Sourcebook* (London: Arkana, 1987), 111–12.

12. Richard Maurice Bucke, *Cosmic Consciousness* (1901; repr., New York: E. P. Dutton, 1969), 183.

13. Sir Francis Younghusband, *Modern Mystics* (1935; repr., New Hyde Park, NY: University Books, 1970), 174.

14. Mircea Eliade, *Yoga: Immortality and Freedom*, trans. Willard R. Trask (Princeton, NJ: Princeton University Press, Bollingen Series LVI, 2nd ed., 1969), 132–33. *Theophany: A visible manifestation of a deity; God revealed to human senses.

15. D. Scott Rogo, *A Casebook of Otherworldly Music* (vol. 1 of *Paranormal Music Experiences*) (1970; repr., San Antonio: Anomalist Books, 2005), 5.

16. D. Scott Rogo, *Beyond Reality* (Northants: Aquarian Press, 1990), 104–5.

17. D. Scott Rogo, *A Psychic Study of the Music of the Spheres* (vol. 2 of *Paranormal Music Experiences*) (1972; repr., San Antonio: Anomalist Books, 2005), 69.

18. Rogo, *A Psychic Study of the Music of the Spheres*, 123.

19. London: Psychic Book Club, 1941, no author listed.

20. Rogo, *A Psychic Study of the Music of the Spheres*, 123–24.

21. Mike Jay, *Emperors of Dreams: Drugs in the Nineteenth Century* (Cambridge: Dedalus, 2000), 91.

22. Mike Jay, *Psychonauts: Drugs and the Making of the Modern Mind* (New Haven: Yale University Press, 2023), 170.

23. Victor Robinson, *An Essay on Hasheesh, Including Observations and Experiments* (New York: Medical Review of Reviews, 1912), 65–68. Nabu Public Domain Reprint (n.d.).

24. Timothy Leary, *Flashbacks: A Personal and Cultural History of an Era—An Autobiography* (Los Angeles: Jeremy P. Tarcher, 1990), 398.

25. Anaïs Nin, *The Diary of Anaïs Nin (Volume Five, 1947-1955)*, ed. Gunther Stuhlmann (New York: Harcourt Brace Jovanovich, 1974), 256–58.

26. A different aspect of this event was described earlier, in chapter 5.

27. Harvey Cox, *Turning East: The Promise and Peril of the New Orientalism* (New York: Simon and Schuster, 1977), 46–48. For more on this episode, focusing on Cox's emotional response to the experience, see chapter 5.

28. Benny Shanon, *The Antipodes of the Mind: Charting the Phenomenology of the Ayahuasca Experience* (Oxford: Oxford University Press, 2010), 185.

29. Shanon, *The Antipodes of the Mind*, 152–53.

30. Shanon, *The Antipodes of the Mind*, 184.

31. Myron J. Stolaroff, *The Secret Chief Revealed: Conversations with Leo Zeff, Pioneer in the Underground Psychedelic Therapy Movement*, rev. ed. (Sarasota, FL: MAPS, 2004), 162.

32. Dunlap, *Exploring Inner* Space, 59–60.

33. Dunlap, *Exploring Inner* Space, 61–62.

34. Dunlap, *Exploring Inner* Space, 62.

35. Dunlap, *Exploring Inner* Space, 155–56.

36. Dunlap, *Exploring Inner* Space, 168–69.

37. Dunlap, *Exploring Inner* Space, 200.

Chapter 8

1. For an excellent, detailed survey and analysis, see Mike Jay, *Psychonauts: Drugs and the Making of the Modern Mind* (New Haven: Yale University Press, 2023). It should go without saying that the use of psychoactive substances, often

for healing purposes as variously conceived, goes back millennia. This chapter, and book, clearly focuses on the modern era, during which psychoactive substances or psychedelics become an object of study and experimentation by institutional science, psychiatry, and psychology.

2. I am omitting from this discussion the darkest, most shameful—some might even say demonic—episode in psychedelic research: that conducted by the US military, the CIA, and other government agencies in pursuit of potential tools for interrogation, mind control, and psychological torture. This abuse included, most prominently, the generously funded, wide-ranging, highly secretive Project MK-Ultra that operated from 1953 to 1973, at which time most of its records were destroyed. See, for example, John Marks, *The Search for the Manchurian Candidate: The CIA and Mind Control* (1979; repr., New York: W. W. Norton, 1991) and Stephen Kinzer, *Poisoner in Chief: Sidney Gottlieb and the CIA Search for Mind Control* (New York: St. Martin's Griffin, 2020). For a more concise account, see Chapter 1, "In the Beginning There Was Madness…" in Lee and Shlain, *Acid Dreams: The CIA, LSD and the Sixties Rebellion* (New York: Grove Press, 1985).

A close contender in the "therapeutic" realm, with LSD employed essentially as a form of "shock" therapy, is documented in the disturbing article by Zoë Dubus, "Women, Mental Illness, and Psychedelic Therapy in Postwar France," in *Expanding Mindscapes: A Global History of Psychedelics*, ed. Erika Dyck and Chris Elcock (Cambridge, MA: MIT Press, 2023), 76–98.

3. Harold A. Abramson, ed., *The Use of LSD in Psychotherapy: Transactions of a Conference on d-Lysergic Acid Diethylamide (LSD-25), Princeton, NJ, April 22–24, 1959* (New York: Josiah Macy Jr. Foundation, 1960), 20–21. Eisner herself writes in a 1957 letter: "Thursday I took LSD with a therapeutic orientation with a friend of mine . . . and Sid [Dr. Sidney Cohen] present. The equivalent of four years of analysis in six hours. And it's still coming" ("Remembrances of LSD Therapy Past," 19).

4. Abramson, *The Use of LSD in Psychotherapy*, 11.

5. Abramson, *The Use of LSD in Psychotherapy*, 225–26. It should be noted that this conference, along with many similar ones, were secretly funded by the CIA, which sought thereby: (1) to keep abreast of studies that might provide scientific data useful to MK-ULTRA mind-control experiments and espionage applications (both foreign and domestic), and (2) to actively promote, for their own purposes, the psychotomimetic (psychosis mimicking) model of psychedelics within the "above-ground" professional research community. Consequently, Dr. Paul Hoch, a longtime CIA consultant who chaired the conference, "was incredulous when other participants in the Macy conference reported that their patients found their LSD sessions beneficial and personally rewarding and were usually eager to take the drug again (Lee and Shlain, *Acid Dreams*, 69).

6. Miriam Siegler and Humphrey Osmond, *Models of Madness, Models of Medicine* (New York: Macmillan, 1974), 1.

7. Abramson, *The Use of LSD in Psychotherapy*, 104, 106.
8. Abramson, *The Use of LSD in Psychotherapy*, 107.
9. Abramson, *The Use of LSD in Psychotherapy*, 90.
10. Abramson, *The Use of LSD in Psychotherapy*, 91.
11. Erika Dyck, *Psychedelic Psychiatry—LSD from Clinic to Campus* (Baltimore: Johns Hopkins University Press, 2008), 98–99. The Hubbard quote is from a letter (October 11, 1957) to Canadian psychiatrist and early psychedelic researcher Dr. Abram Hoffer.
12. Patrick Lundborg, *Psychedelia: An Ancient Culture, A Modern Way of Life* (Stockholm: Lysergia, 2012), 17, 25.
13. R. E. L. Masters and Jean Houston, *The Varieties of Psychedelic Experience* (New York: Holt, Rinehart and Winston, 1966), 35.
14. Alan W. Watts, *The Joyous Cosmology: Adventures in the Chemistry of Consciousness* (New York: Vintage Books, 1962), 23.
15. Psychedelic Conference at Chapman University, April 28, 1994, https://www.ramdass.org/consciousness-psychedelics/.
16. This conference was described by participant Betty Grover Eisner as "The last important conference for those of us who had worked with LSD," even if "at times the Conference seemed somewhat redundant since by that time virtually all LSD for clinical work had been withdrawn." Nevertheless, she describes the resulting published volume as containing "the distilled knowledge from lifetimes of work with psychedelics. When once again society sees fit to use psychedelics for healing and for knowledge, this book might well serve as an operational text, written by people who were there and who lived and worked [with] it, themselves, to achieve the outstanding results described." That description is well deserved. Betty Grover Eisner, *Remembrances of LSD Therapy Past* (2002), 132, 136, http://www.erowid.org/culture/characters/eisner_betty/remembrances_lsd_therapy.pdf.

The conference proceedings, in their entirety, may be accessed here: https://www.samorini.it/doc1/alt_aut/ad/abramson-the-use-of-lsd-in-psychotherapy-and-alcoholism.pdf.

17. Abram Hoffer, "A Program for the Treatment of Alcoholism: LSD, Malvaria and Nicotinic Acid," in *The Use of LSD in Psychotherapy and Alcoholism*, ed. Harold A. Abramson (Indianapolis: Bobbs-Merrill, 1967), 362. The quoted article by Humphrey Osmond: "A Review of the Clinical Effects of Psychotomimetic Agents," *Annals of the New York Academy of Science*, vol. 66, no. 3 (1957): 418–34.
18. Betty Grover Eisner, "The Importance of the Non-Verbal," in *The Use of LSD in Psychotherapy and Alcoholism*, ed. Harold A. Abramson (Indianapolis: Bobbs-Merrill, 1967), 557.
19. Victor Frankl, *Der Unbewusste Gott* (*The Unconscious God*).
20. G. W. Arendsen Hein, "Dimensions in Psychotherapy," in Abramson, *The Use of LSD in Psychotherapy and Alcoholism*, 572–73.
21. Mike Jay, *Emperors of Dreams: Drugs in the Nineteenth Century* (Cambridge: Dedalus, 2000), 221. Neuropsychopharmacologist Dr. David Nutt offers important

insights into the human cost of the suppression of psychedelics and psychedelic therapy in a revealing interview, "The Rise of Psychedelic Therapies," available on YouTube: https://www.google.com/search?client=firefox-b-1-e&q=the+rise+of+-psychedelic+therapies+youtube+video#fpstate=ive&vld=cid:59fa16b0,vid:Nah1u6 EjNY0,st:0.

22. William A. Richards, *Sacred Knowledge: Psychedelics and Religious Experiences* (New York: Columbia University Press, 2016), 158.

23. Helen Bonny and Walter N. Pahnke, "The Use of Music in Psychedelic (LSD) Psychotherapy," in *Music Consciousness: The Evolution of Guided Imagery and Music*, ed. Helen Bonny (Lower Village Gilsum, NH: Barcelona Publishers, 2002), 22.

24. Bonny and Pahnke, "The Use of Music in Psychedelic (LSD) Psychotherapy," 23–24. (On the theory of "depth provocation," they cite I. A. Taylor and F. Paperte, "Current Theory and Research in the Effects of Music on Human Behavior," *Journal of Aesthetics and Art Criticism*, 17 [1958], 251.)

25. Stanislav Grof, *Psychology of the Future: Lessons from Modern Consciousness Research* (Albany: State University of New York Press, 2000), 186–87.

26. Grof, *Psychology of the Future*, 187.

27. Stanislav Grof, *LSD Psychotherapy* (1980; repr., Ben Lomond, CA: Multidisciplinary Association for Psychedelic Studies, 2008), 141.

28. Eisner, "The Importance of the Non-Verbal," 543–44, 552–53.

29. Myron J. Stolaroff, "A Protocol for a Sacramental Service," in *Psychoactive Sacramentals: Essays on Entheogens and Religion*, ed. Thomas B. Roberts (San Francisco: Council on Spiritual Practices, 2001), 159.

30. Myron J. Stolaroff, *The Secret Chief Revealed: Conversations with Leo Zeff, Pioneer in the Underground Psychedelic Therapy Movement*, rev. ed. (Sarasota, FL: MAPS, 2004), 80, 81, 82.

31. Stolaroff, *The Secret Chief Revealed*, 73.

32. James Fadiman, *The Psychedelic Explorer's Guide: Safe, Therapeutic, and Sacred Journeys* (Rochester, VT: Park Street Press, 2011), 27.

33. Stanislav Grof, *The Way of the Psychonaut*, vol. 2 (Santa Cruz, CA: Multidisciplinary Association for Psychedelic Studies [MAPS], 2019), 23.

34. Bonny and Pahnke, "The Use of Music in Psychedelic (LSD) Psychotherapy," 31.

35. Grof, *LSD Psychotherapy*, 141.

36. Bonny and Pahnke, "The Use of Music in Psychedelic (LSD) Psychotherapy," 39.

37. Grof, *LSD Psychotherapy*, 142.

38. Walter N. Pahnke, "The Contribution of the Psychology of Religion to the Therapeutic Use of the Psychedelic Substances," in Abramson, *The Use of LSD in Psychotherapy and Alcoholism*, 639–40.

39. Claudio Naranjo, *My Psychedelic Explorations* (Rochester, VT: Park Street Press, 2020), 330.

40. Grof, *LSD Psychotherapy*, 142.
41. Eisner, *Remembrances of LSD Therapy Past*, 49.
42. Grof, *LSD Psychotherapy*, 142.
43. Stolaroff, "A Protocol for a Sacramental Service," 159.
44. Bonny and Pahnke, "The Use of Music in Psychedelic (LSD) Psychotherapy," 33.
45. Grof, *LSD Psychotherapy*, 142.
46. Eisner, *Remembrances of LSD Therapy Past*, 49.
47. Bonny and Pahnke, "The Use of Music in Psychedelic (LSD) Psychotherapy," 33–34.
48. Grof, *LSD Psychotherapy*, 142.
49. Stolaroff, "A Protocol for a Sacramental Service," 159.
50. Bonny and Pahnke, "The Use of Music in Psychedelic (LSD) Psychotherapy," 34–35. Regarding the use of "powerful," "overwhelming" or "dramatic" music, please note my comments under "In Praise of Quietude and Subtlety" near the end of chapter 12.
51. Grof, *LSD Psychotherapy*, 142.
52. Bonny and Pahnke, "The Use of Music in Psychedelic (LSD) Psychotherapy," 36.
53. Stolaroff, "A Protocol for a Sacramental Service," 159.
54. Grof, *LSD Psychotherapy*, 142.
55. William A. Richards, *Sacred Knowledge: Psychedelics and Religious Experiences* (New York: Columbia University Press, 2016), 190.
56. Bonny and Pahnke, "The Use of Music in Psychedelic (LSD) Psychotherapy," 36.
57. Humphry Osmond et al., "Some Problems in the Use of LSD 25 in the Treatment of Alcoholism," in Abramson, *The Use of LSD in Psychotherapy and Alcoholism*, 437.
58. Rick Strassman, "Preparation for the Journey," in *Inner Paths to Outer Space: Journeys to Alien Worlds through Psychedelics and Other Spiritual Technologies*, ed. Rick Strassman et al. (Rochester, VT: Park Street Press, 2008), 285.
59. Bonny and Pahnke, "The Use of Music in Psychedelic (LSD) Psychotherapy," 34.
60. Grof, *LSD Psychotherapy*, 141–42.
61. Friederike Meckel Fisher, *Therapy with Substance: Psycholytic Psychotherapy in the Twenty-First Century* (London: Mussel Hill Press, 2015), 115.
62. Bonny and Pahnke, "The Use of Music in Psychedelic (LSD) Psychotherapy," 35.
63. Strassman, "Preparation for the Journey," 285.
64. Stolaroff, *The Secret Chief*, 73.
65. Personal communication, September 27, 2023.

66. Grof, *LSD Psychotherapy*, 141.

67. Bonny and Pahnke, "The Use of Music in Psychedelic (LSD) Psychotherapy," 27.

68. Andrew Feldmár, "On the Therapeutic Stance during Psychedelic Psychotherapy," in *Psychedelics & Psychotherapy: The Healing Potential of Expanded States*, ed. Tim Read and Maria Papaspyrou (Rochester, VT: Park Street Press, 2021), 7, 8.

Chapter 9

1. Andy Mitchell, *Ten Trips—The New Reality of Psychedelics* (London: Bodley Head/Penguin, 2023), 155–56.

2. Humphry Osmond, "A Comment on Some Uses of Psychotomimetics in Psychiatry," in *The Use of LSD in Psychotherapy and Alcoholism*, ed. Harold A. Abramson (Indianapolis: Bobbs-Merrill, 1967), 433.

3. Judith Becker, *Deep Listeners: Music, Emotion, and Trancing* (Bloomington: Indiana University Press, 2004), 111, 112.

4. Albert Hofmann, "Natural Science and the Mystical Worldview," in Robert Forte, *Entheogens and the Future of Religion* (Rochester, VT: Park Street Press, 2012), 72.

5. Walter Freeman, "Happiness Doesn't Come in Bottles," *Journal of Consciousness Studies*, vol. 4, no. 1 (1997): 69.

6. Walter Freeman, "A Neurobiological Role of Music in Social Bonding," in *The Origins of Music*, ed. Nils L. Wallin, Bjorn Merker, and Steven Brown (Cambridge, MA: MIT Press, 2000), 411–24, 414.

7. Becker, *Deep Listeners*, 115.

8. Oliver Sacks, *Musicophilia: Tales of Music and the Brain* (New York: Knopf, 2007), 148.

9. Anthony Storr, *Music and the Mind* (New York: Free Press, 1992), 70.

10. Helen Bonny and Walter N. Pahnke, "The Use of Music in Psychedelic (LSD) Psychotherapy," in *Music Consciousness: The Evolution of Guided Imagery and Music*, ed. Helen Bonny (Lower Village Gilsum, NH: Barcelona Publishers, 2002), 23–24.

11. Vladimir Jankelevitch, *Music and the Ineffable*, trans. Carolyn Abbate (1961; repr., Princeton: Princeton University Press, 2003), 73–75.

12. Sidney Cohen, *The Beyond Within: The L.S.D. Story* (New York: Atheneum, 1965), 170.

13. Betty Grover Eisner, *Remembrances of LSD Therapy Past* (2002), 30–31, http://www.erowid.org/culture/characters/eisner_betty/remembrances_lsd_therapy.pdf.

14. Peter Michael Hamel, *Through Music to the Self* (Boulder: Shambhala, 1979), 39–40.

15. Huxley to Osmond, December 23, 1955, *Psychedelic Prophets: The Letters of Aldous Huxley and Humphrey Osmond*, ed. Cynthia Carson Bisbee et al. (Montreal: McGill-Queen's University Press, 2018), 239.

16. Friedrich Schleiermacher, *On Religion: Speeches to Its Cultured Despisers*, 2nd ed., trans. Richard Crouter (Cambridge: Cambridge University Press, 1996), 39. Quoted in Christopher Partridge, *High Culture: Drugs, Mysticism, and the Pursuit of Transcendence in the Modern World* (Oxford: Oxford University Press, 2018), 44.

17. Allen Ginsberg, "The Great Marijuana Hoax: First Manifesto to End the Bringdown," in *Deliberate Prose—Selected Essays 1952-1995*, ed. Bill Morgan (New York: HarperCollins, 2000), 87.

Chapter 10

1. Claudio Naranjo, *My Psychedelic Exploration*s (Rochester, VT: Park Street Press, 2020), 332.

2. Albert Hofmann, "LSD: Quite Personal," in *Hofmann's Elixir: LSD and the New Eleusis*, ed. Amanda Feilding, trans. Jonathan Ott (Oxford: Beckley Foundation Press, 2008), 57, 58.

3. Terrence McKenna, *The Archaic Revival* (San Francisco: HarperSanFrancisco, 1991), 68, 69.

4. Of course outside the realm of academic and clinical investigation, the music of choice among psychonauts of the 1960s and afterward (as burned into my own memory) was predominantly rock, later to be joined by various forms of electronica/techno. Popular (and a few academic) studies abound that focus exclusively on "psychedelic rock," techno, and rave.

5. Jack S. Margolis and Richard Clorfene, *A Child's Garden of Grass* (North Hollywood, CA: Contact Books, 1969), 41–42.

6. Lawrence Kramer, *Why Classical Music Still Matters* (Berkeley: University of California Press, 2007), 225–26.

7. Myron J. Stolaroff, "A Protocol for a Sacramental Service," in *Psychoactive Sacramentals: Essays on Entheogens and Religion*, ed. Thomas B. Roberts (San Francisco: Council on Spiritual Practices, 2001), 159.

8. Myron Stolaroff, "How Much Can People Change?," in *Higher Wisdom: Eminent Elders Explore the Continuing Impact of Psychedelics,* ed. Roger Walsh and Charles S. Grob (Albany: State University of New York Press, 2005), 62–63.

9. Stanislav Grof, *LSD Psychotherapy* (1980; repr., Ben Lomond, CA: Multidisciplinary Association for Psychedelic Studies, 2008), 266.

10. William A. Richards, *Sacred Knowledge: Psychedelics and Religious Experiences* (New York: Columbia University Press, 2016), 190.

11. Christopher Gray, *The Acid Diaries: A Psychonaut's Guide to the History and Use of LSD* (Rochester, VT: Park Street Press, 2010), 117–18, 120. Many examples of Medieval and Renaissance music can be found in my playlist "Christian Mystical Music" (cited at end of this chapter).

12. Paul Morely, *A Sound Mind: How I Fell in Love with Classical Music (and Decided to Rewrite Its Entire History)* (New York: Bloomsbury Publishing, 2020), 41, 52–53, 299.

13. Robert Jourdain, *Music, the Brain, and Ecstasy (How Music Captures Our Imagination)* (1997; repr., New York: HarperCollins/Quill, 2002), 261.

14. Harvey Cox, *Turning East: The Promise and Peril of the New Orientalism* (New York: Simon and Schuster, 1977), 43–44, 45.

15. On this question, psychedelic activist and a founder of the Women's Visionary Council Mariavittoria Mangini comments in an interview, "This is one of the reasons that I have such an affection for LSD, because I feel like it's one of the areas in which I don't have to fear that I'm trespassing into somebody else's sacred lineage or history. If there is a cultural container for LSD, I'm it." "Psychedelics and the Social Matrix," in Richard Louis Miller, *Psychedelic Wisdom: The Astonishing Rewards of Mind-Altering Substances* (Rochester, VT: Park Street Press, 2022), 222.

16. Arthur M. Abell, *Talks with Great Composers* (New York: Philosophical Library, 1987), 5.

17. Patrick Lundborg, *Psychedelia: An Ancient Culture, A Modern Way of Life* (Stockholm: Lysergia, 2012), 113–15.

18. Havelock Ellis, "Mescal: A New Artificial Paradise," in *Wildest Dreams: An Anthology of Drug-Related Literature*, ed. Richard Rudgley (1898; repr., London: Little, Brown, 1999), 285–86.

19. Jourdain, *Music, the Brain, and Ecstasy,* 314.

20. Stanislav Grof, *The Adventure of Self-Discovery* (Albany: State University of New York Press, 1988), 186.

21. Grof, *LSD Psychotherapy,* 142–43.

22. Grof, *The Adventure of Self-Discovery,* 190–91.

23. Richards, *Sacred Knowledge,* 157.

24. Richards, *Sacred Knowledge,* 156.

25. Richards, *Sacred Knowledge,* 157.

26. Claudio Naranjo, *My Psychedelic Explorations* (Rochester, VT: Park Street Press, 2020), 328–30.

27. Helen Bonny and Walter N. Pahnke, "The Use of Music in Psychedelic (LSD) Psychotherapy," in *Music Consciousness: The Evolution of Guided Imagery and Music*, ed. Helen Bonny (Lower Village Gilsum, NH: Barcelona Publishers, 2002). 24. In this regard, see my playlist "Healing Female Voices," https://open.spotify.com/playlist/1d8zhPoJfqAFkfzyqCdr9n?si=b363872d77ab4346.

28. Walter N. Pahnke, "The Contribution of the Psychology of Religion to the Therapeutic Use of the Psychedelic Substances," in *The Use of LSD in Psycho-*

therapy and Alcoholism, ed. Harold A. Abramson (Indianapolis: Bobbs-Merrill, 1967), 639–40.

29. Ido Hartogsohn, *American Trip: Set, Setting, and the Psychedelic Experience in the Twentieth Century* (Cambridge, MA: MIT Press, 2020), 84.

30. Betty Grover Eisner, *Remembrances of LSD Therapy Past* (2002), 49, http://www.erowid.org/culture/characters/eisner_betty/remembrances_lsd_therapy.pdf.

31. Eisner, *Remembrances of LSD Therapy Past*, 151–52.

32. Betty Eisner, "Set, Setting, and Matrix," *Journal of Psychoactive Drugs*, vol. 29, no. 2 (1997): 215.

33. James Fadiman, *The Psychedelic Explorer's Guide: Safe, Therapeutic, and Sacred Journeys* (Rochester, VT: Park Street Press, 2011), 26. In a footnote Fadiman cites another (unnamed) guide's choices: Brahms Requiem, Barber's *Adagio for Strings*, Goreki's Third Symphony, and Brahms Violin Concerto—Adagio.

34. Stolaroff, "A Protocol for a Sacramental Service," 159.

35. David King Dunaway, *Huxley in Hollywood* (New York: Harper & Row, 1989), 354.

36. Jourdain, *Music, the Brain, and Ecstasy*, 195.

37. Jankelevitch, *Music and the Ineffable*, 151.

38. Lester Grinspoon and James B. Bakalar, *Psychedelic Drugs Reconsidered* (1979; repr., New York: Lindesmith Center, 1997), 106.

39. Elena Mannes, *The Power of Music: Pioneering Discoveries in the New Science of Song* (New York: Walker, 2011), 215–16.

Chapter 11

1. Some of the titles in the list come from one of the premier creators of ambient music known as "Pearl of Tranquillity," which for some unknown (at least to me) reason has disappeared from Spotify and most of whose exceptional CDs are no longer available. A real loss, in my opinion.

2. Jane Dunlap, *Exploring Inner Space: Personal Experiences under LSD-25* (New York: Harcourt, Brace & World, 1961), 91.

3. Helen Bonny and Walter N. Pahnke, "The Use of Music in Psychedelic (LSD) Psychotherapy," in *Music Consciousness: The Evolution of Guided Imagery and Music*, ed. Helen Bonny (Lower Village Gilsum, NH: Barcelona Publishers, 2002), 25.

4. R. E. L. Masters and Jean Houston, *The Varieties of Psychedelic Experience* (New York: Dell, 1966), 284.

5. Zoe Cormier, "Music As Medicine," March 17, 2022. Proto.life, https://neo.life/2022/03/music-as-medicine/.

Chapter 12

1. https://open.spotify.com/playlist/4g3FIjgzXB5oxkDzgHmTgv?si=33b33fcb2ab849eb.

2. Eric Clarke, "Music Perception and Musical Consciousness," in *Music and Consciousness—Philosophical, Psychological, and Cultural Perspectives*, ed. David Clarke and Eric Clarke (Oxford: Oxford University Press, 2011), 202–3.

3. Guy Beck, *Sacred Sound: Experiencing Music in World* Religions (Waterloo, Ontario: Wilfrid Laurier University Press, 2006), 9–10.

4. Beck, *Sacred Sound: Experiencing Music in World* Religions, 17.

5. Claudio Naranjo, *My Psychedelic Exploration*s (Rochester, VT: Park Street Press, 2020), 332.

6. Peter Michael Hamel, *Through Music to the Self* (Boulder: Shambhala, 1979), 42, 43, 44.

7. Hamel, *Through Music to the Self*, 92.

8. Stanislav Grof, *LSD Psychotherapy* (1980; repr., Ben Lomond, CA: Multidisciplinary Association for Psychedelic Studies, 2008), 143. Nearly all these examples can be found in my "World Music" playlist.

9. William A. Richards, *Sacred Knowledge: Psychedelics and Religious Experiences* (New York: Columbia University Press, 2016), 157.

10. Luis Eduardo Luna, "The Varieties of the Ayahuasca Experience," in Rick Strassman et al., *Inner Paths to Outer Space: Journeys to Alien Worlds through Psychedelics and Other Spiritual Technologies* (Rochester, VT: Park Street Press, 2008), 130.

11. https://open.spotify.com/playlist/1q1S47ltVdq32KznkAeoxH?si=909d843f8072483b.

12. Joshua Leeds, *Sonic Alchemy: Conversations with Leading Sound Practitioners* (Sausalito, CA: InnerSong Press, 1999), 210–12.

13. Ravi Shankar, *My Music, My Life* (1968; repr., San Rafael, CA: Mandala Publishing, 2007), 24.

14. Shankar, *My Music, My Life*, 26.

15. Peggy Holroyde, *The Music of India* (New York: Praeger, 1972), 185.

16. George Harrison studied sitar seriously with Ravi Shankar for several years and brought the Indian influence into many so-called "raga-rock" creations (with and without sitar): *Within You and Without You, Love You Too, The Inner Light, Blue Jay Way, It's All Too Much,* among others—inspiring a cottage industry of bad imitations.

17. Oliver Craske, *Indian Sun: The Life and Music of Ravi Shankar* (New York: Hachette Books, 2020), 278, 335.

18. John Savage, *1966: The Year the Decade Exploded* (London: Faber, 2015), 125.

19. D. Reck, "The Beatles and Indian Music," in *Sgt. Pepper and the Beatles: It Was Forty Years Ago Today*, ed. O. Julien (Aldershot, UK: Ashgate, 2008). Quoted in Christopher Partridge, "Psychedelic Music," in *The Bloomsbury Handbook of Religion and Popular Music*, ed. Christopher Partridge and Marcus Moberg (London: Bloomsbury Academic, 2018), 295.

20. Graf Hermann Keyserlingk, *Das Reisetagebuch einer Philosophen* (Darmstadt, 1921). Quoted in Peter Michael Hamel, *Through Music to the Self* (Boulder: Shambhala, 1979), 46-47.

21. Hamel, *Through Music to the Self*, 50.

22. Hamel, *Through Music to the Self*, 50, 52–54.

23. Hamel, *Through Music to the Self*, 50.

24. Huston Smith, *Cleansing the Doors of Perception: The Religious Significance of Entheogenic Plants and Chemicals* (New York: Jeremy P. Tarcher/Putnam, 2000).

25. Smith, *Cleansing the Doors of Perception*, 51.

26. "The Gyuto Monks—In Search of the Sound of Life," June 22, 2015, https://www.mickeyhart.net/news/the-gyuto-monks-in-search-for-the-sound-of-life-4961.

27. NPR website, Morning Edition: "Gyuto Monks: Ancient Practice, Modern Sound," March 24, 2009, https://www.npr.org/2009/03/24/102234687/gyuto-monks-ancient-practice-modern-sound.

28. YouTube: "Huston Smith about his Recording of the Gyuto Monks and the Music of Tibet," https://www.google.com/search?client=firefox-b-1-e&q=YouTube+Huston+Smith+tibetan+chanting#fpstate=ive&vld=cid:bc1bcebf,vid:OJ_J4OZQruY.

29. NPR website, Morning Edition: Gyoto Monks.

30. Huston Smith, Kenneth N. Stevens, and Raymond S. Tomlinson, "On an Unusual Mode of Chanting by Certain Tibetan Lamas," *Journal of the Acoustical Society of America*, vol. 41 (1967): 1262–64, https://asa.scitation.org/doi/10.1121/1.1910466.

31. Smith, *Cleansing the Doors of Perception*, 51.

32. Quoted in Joshua Leeds, *Sonic Alchemy*, 213.

33. Lama Anagarika Govinda, *The Way of the White Clouds: A Buddhist Pilgrim in Tibet* (Berkeley: Shambala, 1971), 29–30.

34. William A. Richards, *Sacred Knowledge: Psychedelics and Religious Experiences* (New York: Columbia University Press, 2016), 157, 158. Note: Dr. Richards informs me that the musical work cited should have been Beethoven's *Pastoral* Symphony (#6).

Chapter 13

1. Dolly Rizvi, "Pandit Ravi Shankar: Behind the Screen," *Filmfare*, May 4, 1962 (quoted in Oliver Craske, *Indian Sun: The Life and Music of Ravi Shankar*, 136).

2. Stanislav Grof, *The Adventure of Self-Discovery* (Albany: State University of New York Press, 1988), 187.

3. Charles Baudelaire, *On Wine and Hashish*, trans. Andrew Brown (London: Hesperus Press, 2002), 23.

4. From the album "The Hangman's Beautiful Daughter" (Elektra Records, 1968).

5. Michael Pollan, *How to Change Your Mind* (New York: Penguin Press, 2018), 126–27.

6. Pollan, *How to Change Your Mind*, 247.

7. Benny Shanon, *The Antipodes of the Mind: Charting the Phenomenology of the Ayahuasca Experience* (Oxford: Oxford University Press, 2010), 184.

8. Shanon, *The Antipodes of the Mind*, 149.

9. *Sonic Alchemy: Conversations with Leading Sound Practitioners* (Sausalito, CA: InnerSong Press, 1999), 210–12.

10. Albert Hofmann, *LSD and the Divine Scientist: The Final Thoughts and Reflections of Albert Hofmann* (Rochester, VT: Park Street Press, 2013), 93. This quote first appeared in an obituary by Roger Liggenstorfer in the May 2, 2008 issue of the *Tages Anzeiger* newspaper (Zurich, Switzerland).

11. https://open.spotify.com/playlist/48OkR7p1MRVl7f4OCOTp78?si=d2cb38c97c604804.

12. https://open.spotify.com/playlist/6YppF7fuW7iIxH2zoFSy1I?si=0cd08c9cc191422f.

13. Stanislav Grof, *LSD Psychotherapy* (1980; repr., Ben Lomond, CA: Multidisciplinary Association for Psychedelic Studies, 2008), 142. See Spotify playlist "White Noise: Mechanical/Electronic": https://open.spotify.com/playlist/35bKK9MkqQqdlnxsqHliMC?si=c2eb94c2091d4351.

14. Bernie Krause, *The Great Animal Orchestra—Finding the Origins of Music in the World's Wild Places* (New York: Back Bay Books/Little, Brown and Company, 2012), 226.

15. Krause, *The Great Animal Orchestra*, 164–65.

16. Krause, *The Great Animal Orchestra*, 41–42.

17. https://open.spotify.com/playlist/6DAj00r9QpYOeeyP7MuJZ5?si=187321ef21bf4f79.

Epilogue

1. Christopher Bache, "The Challenges of Integrating an Extreme Psychedelic Journey," in *Psychedelics & Psychotherapy: The Healing Potential of Expanded States*, ed. Tim Read and Maria Papaspyrou (Rochester, VT: Park Street Press, 2021), 304. This version is nearly identical to that found in the book.

2. Frederick Streeter Barrett, "The Neuroscience of Psychedelic Drugs, Music and Nostalgia," TEDMED talk, 2020, https://www.tedmed.com/talks/show?id=770763.

3. Terrence McKenna, *The Archaic Revival* (San Francisco: HarperSanFrancisco, 1991), 68, 69.

4. Ido Hartogsohn, *American Trip: Set, Setting, and the Psychedelic Experience in the Twentieth Century* (Cambridge, MA: MIT Press, 2020), 142–45.

5. Hartogsohn, *American Trip*, 189–90.

6. Hartogsohn, *American Trip*, 180–81.

7. Hartogsohn, *American Trip*, 255.

8. Hartogsohn, *American Trip*, 281.

9. Alan Watts, *In My Own Way: An Autobiography* (New York: Vintage Books, 1973), 408–9.

10. Hartogsohn, *American Trip*, 255–56.

11. Huxley to Osmond, November 29, 1959, *Psychedelic Prophets—The Letters of Aldous Huxley and Humphrey Osmond*, ed. Cynthia Carson Bisbee et al. (Montreal: McGill-Queen's University Press, 2018), 433.

12. Osmond to Huxley, December 9, 1959, *Psychedelic Prophets*, 435.

13. Tara Rae Behr, "The Hidden Harms within the Psychedelic Renaissance," *Mad in America—Science, Psychiatry and Social Justice*, July 7, 2023, https://www.madinamerica.com/2023/07/hidden-harms-psychedelic-renaissance/.

14. Ido Hartogsohn, *American Trip*, 265–66.

Bibliography

Aaronson, Bernard, and Humphry Osmond. *Psychedelics—The Uses and Implications of Hallucinogenic Drugs.* Garden City, NY: Anchor Books/Doubleday, 1970.

Abell, Arthur M. *Talks with Great Composers.* New York: Philosophical Library, 1987.

Abramson, Harold A., ed. *The Use of LSD in Psychotherapy and Alcoholism.* Indianapolis, IN: Bobbs-Merrill, 1967.

Abramson, Harold A., ed. *The Use of LSD in Psychotherapy: Transactions of a Conference on d-Lysergic Acid Diethylamide (LSD-25), Princeton, NJ, April 22–24, 1959.* New York: Josiah Macy Jr. Foundation, 1960.

Ackerman, Diane. *A Natural History of the Senses.* New York: Vintage Books, 1990.

Aldridge, David. "Music Therapy and Spirituality (A Transcendent Understanding of Suffering)." In *Music and Altered States: Consciousness, Transcendence, Therapy and Addiction*, edited by David Aldridge and Jorg Fachner. London: Jessica Kingsley Publishers, 2006.

Aldridge, David, and Jorg Fachner, eds. *Music and Altered States: Consciousness, Transcendence, Therapy and Addiction.* London: Jessica Kingsley Publishers, 2006.

Bache, Christopher M. "The Challenges of Integrating an Extreme Psychedelic Journey." In *Psychedelics & Psychotherapy: The Healing Potential of Expanded States*, edited by Tim Read and Maria Papaspyrou. Rochester, VT: Park Street Press, 2021.

Bache, Christopher M. *LSD and the Mind of the Universe.* Rochester, VT: Park Street Press, 2019.

Bachelard, Gaston. *The Poetics of Reverie: Childhood, Language, and the Cosmos.* Translated by Daniel Russell. 1960. Reprint, Boston: Beacon Press, 1969.

Bachelder, Louise, ed. *The Gift of Music.* Mount Vernon, NY: Peter Pauper Press, 1975.

Badiner, Allan Hunt, ed. *Zig Zag Zen: Buddhism and Psychedelics.* San Francisco: Chronicle Books, 2002.

Barnard, G. William. *Exploring Unseen Worlds: William James and the Philosophy of Mysticism*. Albany: State University of New York Press, 1997.

Barnard, G. William. *Liquid Light: Ayahuasca Spirituality and the Santo Daime Tradition*. New York: Columbia University Press, 2022.

Barrett, Frederick Streeter. "The Neuroscience of Psychedelic Drugs, Music and Nostalgia." TEDMED talk, 2020. https://www.tedmed.com/talks/show?id=770763.

Baudelaire, Charles. *Artificial Paradises*. Translated by Stacy Diamond. 1860. Reprint, New York: Citadel Press, 1996.

Baudelaire, Charles. *On Wine and Hashish*. Translated by Andrew Brown. 1851. Reprint, London: Hesperus Press, 2002.

Beck, Guy L., ed. *Sacred Sound: Experiencing Music in World Religions*. Waterloo, Ontario: Wilfrid Laurier University Press, 2006.

Becker, Judith. *Deep Listeners: Music, Emotion, and Trancing*. Bloomington: Indiana University Press, 2004.

Behr, Tara Rae. "The Hidden Harms Within the Psychedelic Renaissance." *Mad in America—Science, Psychiatry and Social Justice*, July 7, 2023. https://www.madinamerica.com/2023/07/hidden-harms-psychedelic-renaissance/.

Bisbee, Cynthia Carson, Paul Bisbee, Erika Dyck, and Patrick Farrell, eds. *Psychedelic Prophets—The Letters of Aldous Huxley and Humphry Osmond*. Montreal: McGill-Queen's University Press, 2018.

Bishop, Malden Grange. *The Discovery of Love: A Psychedelic Experience with LSD-25*. New York: Torquil/Dodd, Mead, 1963.

Bonds, Mark Evan. *Absolute Music—The History of an Idea*. Oxford: Oxford University Press, 2014.

Bonny, Helen, and Walter N. Pahnke. "The Use of Music in Psychedelic (LSD) Psychotherapy." In *Music Consciousness: The Evolution of Guided Imagery and Music*, edited by Helen Bonny. Lower Village Gilsum, NH: Barcelona Publishers, 2002.

Bonny, Helen L, and Louis M. Savary. *Music & Your Mind: Listening with a New Consciousness*. Barrytown, NY: Station Hill Press, 1990.

Boon, Marcus. *The Road of Excess: A History of Writers on Drugs*. Cambridge, MA: Harvard University Press, 2002.

Bromell, Nick. *Tomorrow Never Knows: Rock and Psychedelics in the 1960s*. Chicago: University of Chicago Press, 2000.

Bucke, Richard Maurice. *Cosmic Consciousness*. 1901. Reprint, New York: E. P. Dutton, 1969.

Bush, Charles. "The Psychedelic Cinerama." In *Psychedelic Wisdom: The Astonishing Rewards of Mind-Altering Substances*, edited by Richard Louis Miller. Rochester, VT: Park Street Press, 2022.

Clarke, David. "Music, Phenomenology, Time Consciousness: Meditations after Husserl." In *Music and Consciousness—Philosophical, Psychological, and Cultural Perspectives*, edited by David Clarke and Eric Clarke. Oxford: Oxford University Press, 2011.

Clarke, David, and Eric Clarke, eds., *Music and Consciousness—Philosophical, Psychological, and Cultural Perspectives.* Oxford: Oxford University Press, 2011.

Clarke, Eric. "Music Perception and Musical Consciousness." In Clark and Clark, *Music and Consciousness—Philosophical, Psychological, and Cultural Perspectives.*

Clark, Walter Houston. *Chemical Ecstasy: Psychedelic Drugs and Religion.* New York: Sheed and Ward, 1969.

Cohen, Sidney. *The Beyond Within: The L.S.D. Story.* New York: Atheneum, 1965.

Cole-Turner, Ron. "Entheogens, Mysticism, and Neuroscience." *Zygon*, vol. 49, no. 3 (September 2014), 642–51.

Cole-Turner, Ron. "Psychedelic Mystical Experience: A New Agenda for Theology." *Religions*, vol. 13, no. 5 (2022): 385. https://doi.org/10.3390/rel13050385.

Copland, Aaron. *Music and Imagination: The Charles Eliot Norton Lectures, 1951–1952.* Cambridge, MA: Harvard University Press, 1952.

Cormier, Zoe, "Music as Medicine." March 17, 2022. *Proto.life*. https://neo.life/2022/03/music-as-medicine/.

Cox, Harvey. *Turning East: The Promise and Peril of the New Orientalism.* New York: Simon and Schuster, 1977.

Craske, Oliver. *Indian Sun: The Life and Music of Ravi Shankar.* New York: Hachette Books, 2020.

Crocket, Richard, R. A. Sandison, and Alexander Walk, eds. *Hallucinogenic Drugs and Their Psychotherapeutic Use—*The Proceedings of the Quarterly Meeting of the Royal Medico-Psychological Association in London, February 1961. London: H. K. Lewis, 1963.

DeRopp, Robert S. *The Master Game: Pathways to Higher Consciousness Beyond the Drug Experience.* New York: Delta, 1968.

Dobkin de Rios, Marlene. *Visionary Vine: Psychedelic Healing in the Peruvian Amazon.* San Francisco: Chandler, 1972.

Dobkin de Rios, Marlene, and Oscar Janiger. *LSD, Spirituality, and the Creative Process.* Rochester, VT: Park Street Press, 2003.

Dubus, Zoë. "Women, Mental Illness, and Psychedelic Therapy in Postwar France." In *Expanding Mindscapes: A Global History of Psychedelics*, edited by Erika Dyck and Chris Elcock. Cambridge, MA: MIT Press, 2023.

Dunaway, David King. *Huxley in Hollywood.* New York: Harper & Row, 1989.

Dunlap, Jane. *Exploring Inner Space: Personal Experiences under LSD-25.* New York: Harcourt, Brace & World, 1961.

Durr, R. A. *Poetic Vision and the Psychedelic Experience.* Syracuse, NY: Syracuse University Press, 1970. Accessible at https://arena-attachments.s3.amazonaws.com/10152370/d62bd438207b36329cdcc9080b92ffb6.pdf?16100777.

Dyck, Erika. *Psychedelic Psychiatry—LSD from Clinic to Campus.* Baltimore: Johns Hopkins University Press, 2008.

Dyck, Erika, and Chris Elcock, eds. *Expanding Mindscapes: A Global History of Psychedelics.* Cambridge, MA: MIT Press, 2023.

Ebin, David, ed. *The Drug Experience: First-Person Accounts of Addicts, Writers, Scientists and Others*. New York: Orion Press, 1961.

Eisner, Betty Grover. "The Importance of the Non-Verbal." In Abramson, *The Use of LSD in Psychotherapy and Alcoholism*.

Eisner, Betty Grover. *Remembrances of LSD Therapy Past*. 2002. http://www.erowid.org/culture/characters/eisner_betty/remembrances_lsd_therapy.pdf.

Eisner, Betty. "Set, Setting, and Matrix." *Journal of Psychoactive Drugs*, vol. 29, no. 2 (April–June 1997): 213–16.

Elcock, Chris. *Psychedelic New York: A History of LSD in the City*. Montreal: McGill-Queen's University Press, 2023.

Eliade, Mircea. *Yoga: Immortality and Freedom*. Translated by Willard R. Trask. Bollingen Series LVI, 2nd ed. Princeton, NJ: Princeton University Press, 1969.

Ellis, Havelock. "Mescal: A New Artificial Paradise." In *Wildest Dreams: An Anthology of Drug-Related Literature*, edited by Richard Rudgley. 1898. Reprint, London: Little, Brown, 1999.

Fachner, Jorg. "Drugs, Altered States, and Musical Consciousness: Reframing Time and Space." In Clark and Clark, *Music and Consciousness—Philosophical, Psychological, and Cultural Perspectives*.

Fachner, Jorg. "Music and Drug-Induced Altered States of Consciousness." In *Music and Altered States: Consciousness, Transcendence, Therapy and Addiction*, edited by David Aldridge and Jorg Fachner. London: Jessica Kingsley Publishers, 2006.

Fadiman, James. *The Psychedelic Explorer's Guide: Safe, Therapeutic, and Sacred Journeys*. Rochester, VT: Park Street Press, 2011.

Feilding, Amanda, ed. *Hofmann's Elixir: LSD and the New Eleusis*. Translated by Jonathan Ott. Oxford: Beckley Foundation Press, 2008.

Feldmár, Andrew. "On the Therapeutic Stance during Psychedelic Psychotherapy." In *Psychedelics & Psychotherapy: The Healing Potential of Expanded States*, edited by Tim Read and Maria Papaspyrou. Rochester, VT: Park Street Press, 2021.

Fisher, Friederike Meckel. *Therapy with Substance: Psycholytic Psychotherapy in the Twenty First Century*. London: Mussel Hill Press, 2015.

Forte, Robert, ed. *Entheogens and the Future of Religion*. Rochester, VT: Park Street Press, 2012.

Fox, Ruth. "Is LSD of Value in Treating Alcoholics?" In Abramson, *The Use of LSD in Psychotherapy and Alcoholism*.

Frankl, Victor. *The Unconscious God*. New York: Simon & Schuster, 1975.

Gabrielsson, Alf. *Strong Experiences with Music*. Oxford: Oxford University Press, 2011.

Gamage, James R., and Edmund L. Zerkin, eds. *Hallucinogenic Drug Research: Impact on Science and Society*. Beloit, WI: Stash Press, 1970.

Gautier, Théophile. "Hashish." Translated by Maurice Stang. In Charles Baudelaire/Théophile Gautier, *Hashish, Wine, Opium*. 1843. Reprint, Surrey, UK: Alma Classics, 2009.

Gelberg, Steven J. "The Call of the Lotus-Eyed Lord: The Fate of Krishna Consciousness in the West." In *When Prophets Die: The Postcharismatic Fate of New Religious Movements*, edited by Timothy Miller. Albany: State University of New York Press, 1991.

Gelberg, Steven J. *India in a Mind's Eye: Travels and Ruminations of an Ambivalent Pilgrim*. 2nd ed. San Francisco: Spiraleye Press, 2024. https://www.blurb.com/b/12042672-india-in-a-mind-s-eye

Gelberg, Steven J. Unpublished interview with Allen Ginsberg, 1978.

Gilchrist, Alexander. *The Life of William Blake*. Mineola, NY: Dover Publications, 1998.

Ginsberg, Allen. "The Great Marijuana Hoax: First Manifesto to End the Bringdown." In Allen Ginsberg, *Deliberate Prose—Selected Essays 1952-1995*, edited by Bill Morgan. New York: HarperCollins, 2000.

Ginsberg, Allen. *Howl and Other Poems*. San Francisco: City Lights Books, 1956.

Glass, Philip. "Listening to Philip Glass—The Composer Speaks with Tricycle." *Tricycle—The Buddhist Review*, vol. IX, no. 1 (Fall 1999).

Godwin, Joscelyn. *Music, Mysticism and Magic—A Sourcebook*. London: Arkana, 1987.

Goldman, Jonathan. *Healing Sounds: The Power of Harmonics*. 1992. Reprint, Rochester, VT: Healing Arts Press, 2002.

Govinda, Lama Anagarika. *The Way of the White Clouds: A Buddhist Pilgrim in Tibet*. Berkeley: Shambhala, 1971.

Graves, Robert. "The Poet's Paradise." In *Wildest Dreams: An Anthology of Drug-Related Literature*, edited by Richard Rudgley. London: Little, Brown, 1999.

Gray, Christopher Gray. *The Acid Diaries: A Psychonaut's Guide to the History and Use of LSD*. Rochester, VT: Park Street Press, 2010.

Grinspoon, Lester. *Marihuana Reconsidered*. Cambridge, MA: Harvard University Press, 1971.

Grinspoon, Lester, and James B. Bakalar. *Psychedelic Drugs Reconsidered*. 1979. Reprint, New York: Lindesmith Center, 1997.

Grinspoon, Lester, and James B. Bakalar, eds. *Psychedelic Reflections*. New York: HumanSciences Press, 1983.

Grof, Stanislav. *Realms of the Human Unconscious: Observations from LSD Research*. New York: Viking Press, 1975.

Grof, Stanislav. *The Adventure of Self-Discovery*. Albany, NY: State University of New York Press, 1988.

Grof, Stanislav. "Beyond the Brain: New Dimensions in Psychology and Psychotherapy." In *Gateway to Inner Space: Sacred Plants, Mysticism and Psychotherapy*, edited by Christian Ratsch. Dorset, UK: Prism Press, 1989.

Grof, Stanislav. *LSD Psychotherapy*. 1980. Reprint, Ben Lomond, CA: Multidisciplinary Association for Psychedelic Studies, 2008.

Grof, Stanislav. "The Potential of Entheogens as Catalysts of Spiritual Development." In *Psychoactive Sacramentals: Essays on Entheogens and Religion*, edited by Thomas B. Roberts. San Francisco: Council on Spiritual Practices, 2001.

Grof, Stanislav. *Psychology of the Future: Lessons from Modern Consciousness Research* Albany. NY: State University of New York Press, 2000.

Grof, Stanislav. *The Way of the Psychonaut*. Santa Cruz, CA: Multidisciplinary Association for Psychedelic Studies [MAPS], 2019.

Gustaitis, Rasa. *Turning On*. New York: Macmillan, 1969.

Hamel, Peter Michael. *Through Music to the Self*. Boulder: Shambhala, 1979.

Hancock, Graham. *The Divine Spark: Psychedelics, Consciousness, and the Birth of Civilization*. San Francisco: Disinformation Books, 2015.

Hartogsohn, Ido. *American Trip: Set, Setting, and the Psychedelic Experience in the Twentieth Century*. Cambridge, MA: MIT Press, 2020.

Harvey, Jonathan. *Music and Inspiration*, edited by Michael Downes. London: Faber and Faber, 1999.

Hayter, Alethea. *Opium and the Romantic Imagination*. Berkeley, CA: University of California Press, 1968.

Heard, Gerald. "Can This Drug Enlarge Man's Mind?" In *The Psychedelic Reader* [Selected from the *Psychedelic Review*], edited by Gunther M Weil, Ralph Metzner, and Timothy Leary. New Hyde Park, NY: University Books, 1965.

Hein, G. W. Arendsen. "Dimensions in Psychotherapy." In Abramson, *The Use of LSD in Psychotherapy and Alcoholism*.

Hendrickson, Eric. [see Eugene Seaich, *The Far-Off Land*].

Hoffer, Abram. "A Program for the Treatment of Alcoholism: LSD, Malvaria and Nicotinic Acid." In Abramson, *The Use of LSD in Psychotherapy and Alcoholism*.

Hofmann, Albert. "A.H., A.H. and LSD." In Feilding, *Hofmann's Elixir: LSD and the New Eleusis*.

Hofmann, Albert. *Insight/Outlook*. Edited by Robert Grayson Hall. Atlanta, GA: Humanics New Age, 1989.

Hofmann, Albert. *LSD and the Divine Scientist: The Final Thoughts and Reflections of Albert Hofmann*. Rochester, VT: Park Street Press, 2013.

Hofmann, Albert. "LSD as a Spiritual Aid." In *Psychoactive Sacramentals*, edited by Thomas B. Roberts. San Francisco: Council on Spiritual Practices, 2001.

Hofmann, Albert. "LSD: Quite Personal." In Feilding, *Hofmann's Elixir: LSD and the New Eleusis*.

Hofmann, Albert. "Natural Science and the Mystical Worldview." In Robert Forte, *Entheogens and the Future of Religion*. Rochester, VT: Park Street Press, 2012.

Hofmann, Albert. "Science and the Mystico-Religious Experience of the World: The Sender-Receiver Model of Reality." In Feilding, *Hofmann's Elixir: LSD and the New Eleusis,*.

Holland, Julie." An Interview with Michael Pollan." In *The Pot Book: A Complete Guide to Cannabis—Its Role in Medicine, Politics, Science, and Culture*, edited by Julie Holland. Santa Cruz, CA: Multidisciplinary Association for Psychedelic Studies, 2010.

Holroyde, Peggy. *The Music of India*. New York: Praeger, 1972.

Huxley, Aldous. "Culture and the Individual." In *LSD: The Consciousness-Expanding Drug*, edited by David Solomon. New York: G. P. Putnam's Sons, 1964.

Huxley, Aldous. *The Divine Within: Selected Writings on Enlightenment*. Edited by Jacqueline Hazard Bridgeman. 1992. Reprint, New York: Harper Perennial, 2013.

Huxley, Aldous. *The Doors of Perception* and *Heaven and Hell*. 1954. Reprint, New York: Harper Colophon Books, 1963.

Huxley, Aldous. *Island*. New York: Harper & Row, 1962.

Huxley, Aldous. *Moksha—Writings on Psychedelics and the Visionary Experience* (1931–1963), edited by Michael Horowitz and Cynthia Palmer. New York: Stonehill, 1977.

Huxley, Aldous. "The Rest Is Silence." In *Music at Night and Other Essays*. 1931. Reprint, London: Flamingo/HarperCollins, 1994.

James, William. *The Varieties of Religious Experience*. 1902. Reprint, New York: Penguin, 1982.

Jankelevitch, Vladimir. *Music and the Ineffable*. Translated by Carolyn Abbate. 1961. Reprint, Princeton: Princeton University Press, 2003.

Jay, Mike. *Emperors of Dreams: Drugs in the Nineteenth Century*. Cambridge: Dedalus, 2000.

Jay, Mike. *Psychonauts: Drugs and the Making of the Modern Mind*. New Haven: Yale University Press, 2023.

Johnson, Raynor C. *Watcher on the Hills*. 1959. Reprint, Hove, UK: White Crow Books, 2016.

Jourdain, Robert. *Music, the Brain, and Ecstasy (How Music Captures our Imagination)*. 1997. Reprint, New York: Harper Collins/Quill, 2002.

Kramer, Lawrence. *Why Classical Music Still Matters*. Berkeley: University of California Press, 2007.

Krause, Bernie Krause. *The Great Animal Orchestra—Finding the Origins of Music in the World's Wild Places*. New York: Back Bay Books/Little, Brown, 2012.

Krishnamurti, J. *The Collected Works of J. Krishnamurti*. Vol. VII, 1952–1953: *Tradition and Creativity*. Ojai, CA: Krishnamurti Foundation America, 2012.

Laski, Marghanita. *Ecstasy*. Los Angeles: Jeremy P. Tarcher, 1961.

Leary, Timothy. *Flashbacks: A Personal and Cultural History of an Era—An Autobiography*. Los Angeles: Jeremy P. Tarcher, 1990.

Lee, Martin A., and Bruce Shlain. *Acid Dreams—The CIA, LSD and the Sixties Rebellion*. New York: Grove Press, 1985.

Leeds, Joshua. *Sonic Alchemy: Conversations with Leading Sound Practitioners*. Sausalito, CA: InnerSong Press, 1999.

Leventhal, Sallye, ed., *Notations—Quotations on Music*. New York: Barnes & Noble, 2003.

Luna, Luis Eduardo. "The Varieties of the Ayahuasca Experience." In Rick Strassman et al., *Inner Paths to Outer Space: Journeys to Alien Worlds through Psychedelics and Other Spiritual Technologies.* Rochester, VT: Park Street Press, 2008.

Lundborg, Patrick. *Psychedelia: An Ancient Culture, A Modern Way of Life.* Stockholm: Lysergia, 2012.

MacLean, J. Ross, D. C. MacDonald, F. Ogden, and E. Wilby. "LSD 25 and Mescaline as Therapeutic Adjuvants." In Abramson, *The Use of LSD in Psychotherapy and Alcoholism.*

Maeterlinck, Maurice. *The Treasure of the Humble.* Translated by Alfred Sutro. London: George Allen, 1897.

Mangini, Mariavittoria. "Psychedelics and the Social Matrix" [interview]. In *Psychedelic Wisdom: The Astonishing Rewards of Mind-Altering Substances*, edited by Richard Louis Miller. Rochester, VT: Park Street Press, 2022.

Mannes, Elena. *The Power of Music: Pioneering Discoveries in the New Science of Song.* New York: Walker, 2011.

Margolis, Jack S., and Richard Clorfene. *A Child's Garden of Grass.* North Hollywood, CA: Contact Books, 1969.

Masters, R. E. L., and Jean Houston, *The Varieties of Psychedelic Experience.* New York: Dell, 1966.

McDaniel, June. *Lost Ecstasy—Its Decline and Transformation in Religion.* London: Palgrave Macmillan, 2018.

McKellar, Peter. "Mescaline and Human Thinking." In *Hallucinogenic Drugs and Their Psychotherapeutic Use*—The Proceedings of the Quarterly Meeting of the Royal Medico-Psychological Association in London, February 1961, edited by Richard Crocket, R. A. Sandison, and Alexander Walk. London: H. K. Lewis, 1963.

McKenna, Terrence. *The Archaic Revival.* San Francisco: HarperSanFrancisco, 1991.

McKenna, Terrence. *Food of the Gods.* New York: Bantam Books, 1992.

Metzner, Ralph, ed. *The Ecstatic Adventure.* New York: Macmillan, 1968.

Miller, Richard Louis, ed. *Psychedelic Medicine: The Healing Powers of LSD, MDMA, Psilocybin and Ayahuasca.* Rochester, VT: Park Street Press, 2017.

Miller, Richard Louis, ed. *Psychedelic Wisdom: The Astonishing Rewards of Mind-Altering Substances.* Rochester, VT: Park Street Press, 2022.

Raphaël, Millière, Robin L. Carhart-Harris, Leor Roseman, Fynn-Mathis Trautwein, and Aviva Berkovich-Ohana. "Psychedelics, Meditation, and Self-Consciousness." *Frontiers in Psychology*, vol. 9 (2018). https://doi.org/10.3389/fpsyg.2018.01475.

Mitchell, Andy. *Ten Trips—The New Reality of Psychedelics.* London: Bodley Head/Penguin, 2023.

More, Paul Elmer. "Lafcadio Hearn." *Shelburne Essays.* 2nd Series. New York: G. P. Putnam's Sons, 1905.

Moreau, Jacques-Joseph. *Hashish and Mental Illness*. Translated by Gordon J. Barnett. 1845. Reprint, New York: Raven Press, 1973.

Morely, Paul Morely. *A Sound Mind: How I Fell in Love with Classical Music (and Decided to Rewrite Its Entire History)*. New York: Bloomsbury, 2020.

Naranjo, Claudio. *My Psychedelic Explorations*. Rochester, VT: Park Street Press, 2020.

Neitzke-Spruill, Logan, and Carol Glasser. "A Gratuitous Grace: The Influence of Religious Set and Intent on the Psychedelic Experience." *Journal of Psychoactive Drugs*, vol. 50, no. 4 (2018): 314–21.

Nin, Anaïs. *The Diary of Anaïs Nin (Volume Five, 1947-1955)*. Edited by Gunther Stuhlmann. New York: Harcourt Brace Jovanovich, 1974.

O'Callaghan, Clare, Daniel J. Hubik, Justin Dwyer, Martin Williams, and Margaret Ross. "Experience of Music Used with Psychedelic Therapy: A Rapid Review and Implications." *Journal of Music Therapy*, vol. 57, no. 3 (2020): 282–314.

Osmond, Humphry. "A Comment on Some Uses of Psychotomimetics in Psychiatry." In Abramson, *The Use of LSD in Psychotherapy and Alcoholism*.

Osmond, Humphry. "A Review of the Clinical Effects of Psychotomimetic Agents." In Solomon, *LSD: The Consciousness-Expanding Drug*.

Osmond, Humphry, Frances Cheek, Robert Albahary, and Mary Sarett. "Some Problems in the Use of LSD 25 in the Treatment of Alcoholism." In Abramson, *The Use of LSD in Psychotherapy and Alcoholism*.

Otto, Rudolf. *The Idea of the Holy*. Translated by John W. Harvey. 1923. Reprint, London: Oxford University Press, 1980.

Pahnke, Walter N. "The Contribution of the Psychology of Religion to the Therapeutic Use of the Psychedelic Substances." In Abramson, *The Use of LSD in Psychotherapy and Alcoholism*.

Pahnke, Walter N., Albert A. Kurland, Sanford Unger, Charles Savage, and Stanislav Grof. "The Experimental Use of Psychedelic (LSD) Psychotherapy." In *Hallucinogenic Drug Research: Impact on Science and Society*, edited by James R. Gamage and Edmund L. Zerkin. Beloit, WI: Stash Press, 1970.

Palitsky, Roman, Deanna M. Kaplan, Caroline Peacock, Ali John Zarrabi, Jessica L. Maples-Keller, George H. Grant, Boadie W. Dunlop, and Charles L. Raison. "Importance of Integrating Spiritual, Existential, Religious, and Theological Components in Psychedelic-Assisted Therapies." *JAMA Psychiatry*, vol. 80, no. 7 (2023): 743–49. https://doi.org/10.1001/jamapsychiatry.2023.1554.

Palmer, Cynthia, and Michael Horowitz, eds. *Sisters of the Extreme: Women Writing on the Drug Experience*. Rochester, VT: Park Street Press, 2000.

Partridge, Christopher. *High Culture: Drugs, Mysticism, and the Pursuit of Transcendence in the Modern World*. Oxford: Oxford University Press, 2018.

Partridge, Christopher. "Psychedelic Music." In *The Bloomsbury Handbook of Religion and Popular Music*, edited by Christopher Partridge and Marcus Moberg. London: Bloomsbury, 2018.

Pilch, John J. "Music and Trance." In *Music and Altered States: Consciousness, Transcendence, Therapy and Addiction*, edited by David Aldridge and Jorg Fachner. London: Jessica Kingsley Publishers, 2006.

Pinchbeck, Daniel. *Breaking Open the Head: A Psychedelic Journey into the Heart of Contemporary Shamanism*. New York: Broadway Books, 2002.

Pollan, Michael. *How to Change Your Mind*. New York: Penguin Press, 2018.

Pollan, Michael. *This Is Your Mind on Plants*. New York: Penguin Books, 2022.

Ram Dass. Psychedelic Conference at Chapman University, April 28, 1994. https://www.ramdass.org/consciousness-psychedelics/.

Ram Dass. "A Roundtable with Ram Dass, Robert Aitken Roshi, Richard Baker Roshi, and Joan Halifax Roshi." In *Zig Zag Zen: Buddhism and Psychedelics*, edited by Allan Hunt Badiner. San Francisco, CA: Chronicle Books, 2002.

Reck, D. "The Beatles and Indian Music." In *Sgt. Pepper and the Beatles: It Was Forty Years Ago Today*, edited by Olivier Julien. Aldershot, UK: Ashgate, 2008.

Richards, William A. "Here and Now: Discovering the Sacred with Entheogens." *Zygon*, vol. 49, no. 3 (September 2014).

Richards, William A. "The Phenomenology and Potential Religious Import of States of Consciousness Facilitated by Psilocybin." *Archive for the Psychology of Religion*, vol. 30 (2008): 189–99.

Richards, William A. *Sacred Knowledge: Psychedelics and Religious Experiences*. New York: Columbia University Press, 2016.

Richardson, Jerry. "Who Am I, and So What If I Am?" In *Psychedelics—The Uses and Implications of Hallucinogenic Drugs*, edited by Bernard Aaronson and Humphrey Osmond. Garden City, NY: Anchor Books/Doubleday, 1970.

Roberts, Thomas B. "An Entheogen Idea-Map—Further Explorations." In *Psychoactive Sacramentals*, edited by Thomas B. Roberts. San Francisco: Council on Spiritual Practices, 2001.

Roberts, Thomas Bradford. "New Learning." In Grinspoon and Bakalar, *Psychedelic Reflections*.

Roberts, Thomas B., ed. *Psychoactive Sacramentals: Essays on Entheogens and Religion*. San Francisco, CA: Council of Spiritual Practices, 2001. [Note that the third and latest edition of this book is re-titled *Psychedelics and Spirituality: The Sacred Use of LSD, Psilocybin, and MDMA for Human Transformation*. Rochester, VT: Park Street Press, 2020.]

Robertson, John. "Uncontainable Joy." In *The Ecstatic Adventure*, edited by Ralph Metzner. New York: Macmillan, 1968.

Robinson, Victor. *An Essay on Hasheesh, Including Observations and Experiments*. New York: Medical Review of Reviews, 1912. [Nabu Public Domain Reprint (n.d.)]

Robinson, Jenefer. *Deeper Than Reason: Emotion and Its Role in Literature, Music, and Art*. Oxford: Oxford University Press, 2005.

Rogo, D. Scott. *A Casebook of Otherworldly Music*. Vol. 1 of *Paranormal Music Experiences*. 1970. Reprint, San Antonio, TX: Anomalist Books, 2005.

Rogo, D. Scott. *A Psychic Study of the Music of the Spheres*. Vol. 2 of *Paranormal Music Experiences*. 1972. Reprint, San Antonio, TX: Anomalist Books, 2005.

Rogo, D. Scott. *Beyond Reality*. Wellingborough, Northamptonshire, UK: Aquarian Press, 1990.

Roseman, Leor, David J. Nutt, and Robin L. Carhart-Harris. "Quality of Acute Psychedelic Experience Predicts Therapeutic Efficacy of Psilocybin for Treatment-Resistant Depression." *Frontiers in Pharmacology*, vol. 8 (2017).

Roszak, Theodore. *Unfinished Animal: The Aquarian Frontier and the Evolution of Consciousness*. London: Faber and Faber, 1976.

Rouget, Gilbert. *Music and Trance: A Theory of the Relations between Music and Possession*. Translated and revised by Brunhilde Biebuych. Chicago: University of Chicago Press, 1985.

Rudgley, Richard. *Wildest Dreams: An Anthology of Drug-Related Literature*. London: Little, Brown, 1999.

Sacks, Oliver. *Musicophilia: Tales of Music and the Brain*. New York: Knopf, 2007.

Savage, C., J. Fadiman, R. E. Mogar, and M. Allen. "The Effects of Psychedelic (LSD) Therapy on Values, Personality, and Behavior." *International Journal of Neuropsychiatry*, vol. 2 (1966): 241–54.

Savage, John. *1966: The Year the Decade Exploded*. London: Faber, 2015.

Schleiermacher, Friedrich. *On Religion: Speeches to Its Cultured Despisers*. 2nd ed. Translated by Richard Crouter. Cambridge: Cambridge University Press, 1996.

Seaich, Eugene. *The Far-Off Land—An Attempt at a Philosophical Evaluation of the Hallucinogenic Drug-Experience*. 1959. Reprint, Xlibris Corporation, 2012.

Seelig, Mark. "Communion with the Goddess: Three Weeks of Ayahuasca in Brazil." In *The Divine Spark: Psychedelics, Consciousness, and the Birth of Civilization*, edited by Graham Hancock. San Francisco: Disinformation Books, 2015.

Shankar, Ravi. *My Music, My Life*. San Rafael, CA: Mandala Publishing, 2007.

Shanon, Benny. *The Antipodes of the Mind: Charting the Phenomenology of the Ayahuasca Experience*. Oxford: Oxford University Press, 2010.

Shanon, Benny. "Music and Ayahuasca." In Clark and Clark, *Music and Consciousness—Philosophical, Psychological, and Cultural Perspectives*.

Sheldrake, Rupert, Terence McKenna, and Ralph Abraham. *Chaos, Creativity and Cosmic Consciousness*. Rochester, VT: Park Street Press, 2001.

Shulgin, Ann, and Alexander Shulgin. "A New Vocabulary." In *Entheogens and the Future of Religion*, edited by Robert Forte. Rochester, VT: Park Street Press, 2012.

Siegler, Miriam, and Humphrey Osmond. *Models of Madness, Models of Medicine*. New York: Macmillan, 1974.

Smith, Huston. *Cleansing the Doors of Perception: The Religious Significance of Entheogenic Plants and Chemicals*. New York: Jeremy P. Tarcher/Putnam, 2000.

Smith, Huston. "Do Drugs Have Religious Import? A Thirty-Five Year Retrospect." In *Psychoactive Sacramentals: Essays on Entheogens and Religion*, edited by Thomas B. Roberts. San Francisco, CA: Council of Spiritual Practices, 2001.

Smith, Huston. "Introduction." In Huxley, *The Divine Within*.
Solomon, David, ed. *LSD: The Consciousness-Expanding Drug*. New York: G. P. Putnam's Sons, 1964.
Sontag, Linda. "The Eyes of the Child-Corpse Were Open Wide." In *The Ecstatic Adventure*, edited by Ralph Metzner. New York: Macmillan, 1968.
Sorgner, Stefan Lorenz, and Oliver Furbeth, eds. *Music in German Philosophy—An Introduction*. Chicago: University of Chicago Press, 2010.
Stolaroff, Myron J. "A Protocol for a Sacramental Service." In *Psychoactive Sacramentals: Essays on Entheogens and Religion*, edited by Thomas B. Roberts. San Francisco: Council on Spiritual Practices, 2001.
Stolaroff, Myron J. "How Much Can People Change?" In *Higher Wisdom: Eminent Elders Explore the Continuing Impact of Psychedelics*, edited by Roger Walsh and Charles S. Grob. Albany, NY: State University of New York Press, 2005.
Stolaroff, Myron J. *The Secret Chief Revealed: Conversations with Leo Zeff, Pioneer in the Underground Psychedelic Therapy Movement*. Rev. ed. Sarasota, FL: MAPS, 2004.
Storr, Anthony. *Music and the Mind*. New York: Free Press, 1992.
Strassman, Rick. "Preparation for the Journey." In Strassman et al., *Inner Paths to Outer Space*.
Strassman, Rick, Slawek Wojtowicz, Luis Eduardo Luna, and Ede Frecska. *Inner Paths to Outer Space: Journeys to Alien Worlds through Psychedelics and Other Spiritual Technologies*. Rochester, VT: Park Street Press, 2008.
Sullivan, Lawrence E., ed. *Enchanting Powers—Music in the World's Religions*. Cambridge, MA: Harvard University Press, 1997.
Tart, Charles. *On Being Stoned—A Psychological Study of Marijuana Intoxication*. Palo Alto, CA: Science and Behavior Books, 1971.
Tavener, John. *The Music of Silence—A Composer's Testament*. Edited by Brian Keeble. London: Faber & Faber, 1999.
Tippett, Michael. "Art, Judgment and Belief: Towards the Condition of Music." In *The Symbolic Order*, edited by Peter Abbs. London: Falmer Press, 1989.
Tolstoy, Leo. *The Kreutzer Sonata*. 1889. Reprint, New York: Modern Library, 2003.
Tumbleweed, Daniel. *The Museum Dose: 12 Experiments in Pharmacologically Mediated Aesthetics*. Phoropter Press, 2015.
Walsh, Roger, and Charles S. Grob, eds. *Higher Wisdom: Eminent Elders Explore the Continuing Impact of Psychedelics*. Albany, NY: State University of New York Press, 2005.
Ward, R. H. *A Drug-Taker's Notes*. London: Victor Gollancz, 1957.
Wasson, R. Gordon. "The Hallucinogenic Fungi of Mexico: An Inquiry into the Origins of the Religious Idea Among Primitive Peoples." In *The Psychedelic Reader* [Selections from the *Psychedelic Review*], edited by Gunther M. Weil, Ralph Metzner, and Timothy Leary. New Hyde Park, NY: University Books, 1965.

Watts, Alan. "A Psychedelic Experience: Fact or Fantasy?" In Solomon, *LSD: The Consciousness-Expanding Drug.*
Watts, Alan. *In My Own Way: An Autobiography.* New York: Vintage Books, 1973.
Watts, Alan. *The Joyous Cosmology: Adventures in the Chemistry of Consciousness.* New York: Vintage Books, 1962.
Watts, Alan. "The New Alchemy." In *This is It (and Other Essays on Zen and Spiritual Experience).* New York: Collier Books, 1967.
Watts, Alan. "Psychedelics and Religious Experience." In *The Cosmos Reader*, edited by Edgar Z. Friedenberg et al. New York: Harcourt Brace Jovanovich, 1971. [Reprinted from *California Law Review*, vol. 56, no. 100 (1968).]
Watts, Joan, and Anne Watts, *The Collected Letters of Alan Watts.* Novato, CA: New World Library, 2017.
Weil, Gunther M., Ralph Metzner, and Timothy Leary, eds. *The Psychedelic Reader* [Selected from the *Psychedelic Review*]. New Hyde Park, NY: University Books, 1965.
Younghusband, Sir Francis, *Modern Mystics.* 1935. Reprint, New Hyde Park, NY: University Books, 1970.

Index

Ackerman, Diane, 90
African music, 79, 193–94, 195–96
Al-Gazzali, 38–39
Aldridge, David, 35
Alpert, Richard. *See* Ram Dass
ambient/electronica, 162, 185–90
   common themes/visions/messages embodied by, 186
   compared to Neo-classical genre, 190
   contrasted with "New Age" music, 185–86
   playlists, 188–90, 237–38
   situational alternative to classical, as 187–88
American Trip. See Ido Hartogsohn
Antipodes of the Mind, The, 209. *See also* Shanon, Benny
Archaic Revival, The (Terence McKenna), 4
ayahuasca, 3, 101, 121–23, 195, 255n17, 262n19
   aesthetic experience under, 38, 42–44, 74
   music and, 43, 74
   nature, mystical visions of, under, 210
   synesthesia/visionary experience with, 102, 104

Bach, Johann Sebastian, 168–69, 174–78 passim, 231
   "supremely psychedelic," as, 175
   synesthetic/eidetic vision featuring, 107–108
   works by, experienced under psychedelics: Aldous Huxley, 45–46, 54–55; Michael Pollan, 46, 71, 76–77; William Richards, 77–78; various others, 63, 107–108, 156–57, 187–88
Bache, Christopher M., 58, 215–16, 217
Bachelard, Gaston, 70
Balinese music, 120–21, 192, 195, 240, 241, 243
Barber, Samuel, 175–76
Barnard, G. William, 3–4, 91–92, 99, 255n17
Barrett, Frederick, 216
Baudelaire, Charles, 2, 74–75, 100, 118, 208
Beatles, xii, xiii, 56, 198, 276n19
   Harrison, George, xii, xiv, 187, 275n16
   Lennon, John, 226
Beck, Guy L., 192–93
Becker, Judith, 53–54, 60–61, 101–102, 155

Beecham, Sir Thomas, 157
Beethoven, Ludwig van, 71 (*see also* 259n19), 111, 149, 170, 171, 177, 178, 203, 231–32
   Ninth Symphony, 169, 175, 176
   Pastoral Symphony (#6) as ideal psychedelic "score," 171
   works by, experienced under psychedelics, 71, 106, 168–69
Behr, Tara Rae, 223
Bergson, Henri, 18, 33, 82
Bhaktivedanta, Swami, xv, 247n4
Bizet, Georges, 75, 149, 173 (Scheherazade)
Blake, William, xi, 103, 155, 216, 226
Bloch, Ernest, 172, 232
Boehme, Jacob, 114
Bonds, Mark Evan, 101, 262n13
Bonny, Helen, 139–40, 144, 178, 263–64n16
Bonny, Helen and Walter Pahnke (as co-authors), 75, 148–49, 149
   female voice (in music), as therapeutically beneficial, 177 (*See also* "The Healing Female Voice")
   music, on choice of in therapy, 143–44, 177; role of in psychedelic therapy, 58, 140
   phases of therapeutic session and appropriate music, on 146–48
   silences, on need to avoid, 150–51
   spontaneously produced (hallucinated) music, on, 112
Brahms, Johannes, 165, 170–71, 175, 176, 177, 187, 232, 274n33
   "very particular therapeutic power" of (Naranjo), 177
Bromell, Nick, 101, 250n19
Bruch, Max, 178, 232
Bucke, Richard Maurice, 29–30, 114

Buddhism, 53, 104; Tibetan, xv, 202–203; Zen, 28, 194

Calkins, Mary Whiton, 99–100
cannabis/marijuana, 13, 51–52, 68–69, 158, 163, 165–66, 226. *See also* hashish
Cecilia, Saint, 113–14
Chopin, Frédéric, 176, 178
Christian themes, 93–94, 94–95, 113–14, 121, 125, 182, 273n11
CIA. *See* MK-ULTRA
Clarke, Eric, 192
classical music, 161–83
   Bach, Brahms and Mozart, works by as "supremely psychedelic," 175
   Baroque, 173–74, 176
   composers as conduits of higher wisdom, 36–37, 44–45, 161, 169–71
   Havelock Ellis's synesthetic experiment with, 172–73
   Hoffman, Albert, on Mozart's "heavenly music," 161
   "intense" or "overwhelming" pieces, use of questioned, 178–80
   "language of the gods," as 44
   "liberated sound existing in a pure metaphysical space," as, 167
   narrative and "impressionist" styles as psychedelic-friendly, 171–73
   playlists, 180–83, 231–35
   prominence in psychedelic therapy, reasons for, 161–62
   psychedelic, as inherently, 167–68
   stereotypes and resistance to, overcoming, 162, 163–68
   works recommended by "psychedelic" authors, 174–78
   See also names of individual composers

Cohen, Sidney, 32, 106, 119, 130, 132, 267n3
Cole-Turner, Ron, 252n18
Coleridge, Samuel Taylor, 50
Copland, Aaron, 97–98
cosmic consciousness, 19–20, 24, 30, 127
Cosmic Consciousness (Bucke), 29, 114
counterculture/hippies, xi–xvi, 6, 87–88, 136, 197–98, 199–200, 220–22, 230, 248n6
Cox, Harvey, 94–95, 121, 168–69, 248n9
Craske, Oliver, 197–98

Davy, Humphry, 139
Debussy, Claude, 55, 171–72, 177, 232
"deep listening," 60–61, 98
Delius, Frederick, 172, 232
Diary of Anaïs Nin, The, 1947–1955. See Nin, Anaïs
didgeridoo, 107, 195–96, 202, 240, 242
Dobkin de Rios, Marlene, 11, 25, 50, 61–62, 255n17
Donovan, xiii, 104
Doors of Perception, The, (Huxley), xi, 18–19, 198
drums, 79, 125, 178, 195–96, 203, 204
Dubus, Zoë, 267n2
Dunlop, Jane, 63, 112, 121, 123–27
Durr, R. A., 52, 249n15
Dylan, Bob, xi, 218

eidetic/eidetic imagery, 12, 42, 47, 101, 102–103. See also psychedelics and psychedelic experience: synesthesia/eidetic vision
Einstein, Albert, 15

Eisner, Betty Grover, 16, 32, 59, 85, 130, 132, 137, 141, 146, 157, 178, 267n3, 268n16
Elgar, Edward, 177
Eliade, Mircea, 114–15
Eliot, T. S., 76
Ellis, Havelock, 47, 100, 139, 172–73
Emerson, Ralph Waldo, xi, 52, 77
emotion
    blunting of, 81, 83–84
    broader definition proposed, 89
    See also under Music II; psychedelics and psychedelic experience: emotion
Exploring Inner Space: Personal Experiences under LSD-25. See Dunlop, Jane

Fachner, Jorg, 68–69
Fadiman, James, 7–8, 58, 143, 157, 178
Fauré, Gabriel, 177, 178, 232
Feldmár, Andrew, 151
flute/flute music, 115, 121, 125, 161, 169, 178, 194–95, 205, 229, 241, 242
Fox, Ruth, 58
Frankl, Victor, 137–38
Freeman, Walter, 155
Fremont-Smith, Frank, 131
Fromm, Erich, xiii

Gabrielsson, Alf, 3
Gautier, Théophile, 60, 100
Ginsberg, Allen, xi (*see also* 247n1), xiii, xiv–xv (*see also* 247n2, n3, n4), 52, 158
Glass, Philip, 39–40, 49, 233
Goldman, Jonathan, 196, 202, 210–11, 217, 237, 239
Gounod, Charles, 114, 175, 177

Govinda, Lama Anagarika, 202–203
Graves, Robert, 2, 104–105
Gray, Christopher, 165–66
Griffes, Charles, 172
Grinspoon, Lester, 17, 72, 179
Grof, Stanislav, 8, 22, 78, 143, 164, 207, 252n9, 253n37
   "carrier wave," music functions as, 11, 63, 140–41
   LSD peak experience described, 27–29
   music, general guidelines, 144–50 passim, 174
   musical choices, personal, 175, 194–95
   music's value for psychedelic therapy, 58, 140
   "non-specific catalyst of the psyche" (LSD), 21–22
   "non-specific catalyst" vs. "a higher universal order," 29–32
   psychedelic and *psycholytic* therapies compared, 31–32
   white noise, on 211–12
Gyuto (Tibetan) monks, 200–201

hallucinated music, 111–27
Hamel, Peter Michael, 71–72, 193–94, 198–200
Handel, George Frideric, 174, 175, 176, 233
Hanslick, Eduard, 82
harm reduction, 13–14
Harrison, George. *See* Beatles
Hare Krishna (Krishna Consciousness, ISKCON), xv–xvii, 115, 247–48n5, 248n6, 248n9
Hartogsohn, Ido, 26–27, 47, 178, 218–22, 224
Harvard Divinity School, xvii
Harvey, Jonathan, 39

hashish, 1, 60, 68–69, 72, 74–75, 95–97, 100, 118–19, 208, 265n1
Hashish Eater, The (Fitz Hugh Ludlow), 72
Haweis, Hugh R., 38
"Healing Female Voice, The" (playlist), 243–44
Heard, Gerald, 71
Hein, G. W. Arendsen, 137–38
Hesse, Hermann, xi
Hildegard of Bingen, 165, 233, 243
Hindu/Hinduism/India, xiv, xvii, 48, 53, 114–15, 120, 156, 193, 203, 248n10, 251n26
Hindu/Indian music, xii, 193–94, 195, 196–200, 204, 205, 229, 241–42, 275n16
   "became the central aural metaphor for [the] hallucinogenic experience," 198
   playlists, 205, 241–42
   psychedelic counterculture, importance in, xiii, 79, 104, 162, 176, 178, 194, 197–98, 199–200
   See also Shankar, Ravi; sitar
Hoffer, Abram, 137, 268n11
Hoffman, E. T. A., 38
Hofmann, Albert, 15, 24–25, 155, 161, 211, 250n21, 251n27, 257n20
Holland, Julie, 51
Holotropic Breathwork, 150, 175
Houston, Jean. *See Varieties of Psychedelic Experience, The*
Hovhanness, Alan, 175, 178
Hubbard, Al, 134, 146
Huichol, 94, 168–69
Humboldt, Alexander von, 208–209
Huxley, Aldous, vii, xi, xiii, 15, 24, 47, 52, 60, 109, 157, 254–55n15, 257n20
   criticizes unqualified psychedelic therapists, 222–23

experiencing/responding to music, 35, 45–46, 54–55, 178
"reducing-valve" model of brain, on 18–20, 82
See also *Doors of Perception*; *Island*
Huxley, Francis, 76
Huxley, T. H., 50

Ibert, Jacques, 178
icaros, 105, 242
Idea of the Holy, The (Otto), 40–41
Incredible String Band, xii, 208
India in a Mind's Eye (Gelberg), 115, 248n10
Island (Aldous Huxley), 54–55, 257n20

James, William, 1–2, 15–16, 19–20, 42, 91–92
Janiger, Oscar, 25, 78, 119, 123
Jankelevitch, Vladimir, 53, 88, 156, 179
Jay, Mike, 6, 99–100, 118–19, 138–39
jazz, 162, 167, 229
Josiah Macy, Jr. Foundation, 131, 267n5
Jourdain, Robert, 113, 167–68, 173, 179
Journal of Music Therapy, 5
Joyous Cosmology, The (Watts), vii, xi, 249n3
"jungle gym within consciousness," 11, 61–62

ketamine, 178, 223
Khan, Hazrat Inayat, 260n39
Khan, Imrat, 200
Kleinman, Arthur, 60
Kramer, Lawrence, 83–84, 163–64
Krause, Bernie, 212–13
Krishnamurti, J., 53

Labate, Beatriz Caluby, 255n17
Laing, R. D., xi
Lanier, Jaron, 154
Laski, Marghanita, 61
Lassus, Orlando de, 166, 233
Lawrence, D. H., 24, 81
Leary, Timothy, xiii, xv, 32, 178, 247n3, 249n3
Les Paradis Artificiels (*Artificial Paradises*) (Baudelaire), 75, 100
Leuner, Hanscarl, 139–40, 157
Levi-Strauss, Claude, 45
Liszt, Franz, 149, 233
LSD
[Note: Qualities and experiences shared with other psychedelics can mostly be found under "psychedelics and psychedelic experience." Related musical themes can be found in "Music II" and in "psychedelic therapy, role of music in."]
abuses of, in early research, 131–34, 267n2
aesthetic vs. mystical, 65–66
author's experiences with, xi, 34, 67, 251n26
backlash against, 220–22
banning of, 13
counterculture and, xiii–xiv
cultural context, independence from any particular, 273n15
dosages, 22, 31, 45, 65, 107, 109, 132, 133, 143, 264–65n31
Eisner, Betty Grover, and, 32, 130, 141, 157, 267n3, 268n16
equivalent to years of therapy, 130, 267n3
experience with compared to liberal education, 6
experiences with as widely variable, 21–22

LSD *(continued)*
    Ginsberg, Allen, and, xv
    Heard, Gerald, and, 71
    Hoffman, Albert, and, 15, 24–25, 161, 251n27
    Houston, Jean, vision experienced on, 107–108, 264n29
    Huxley, Aldous, and, 45–46, 54–55, 109, 222–23
    Huxley, Francis, and, 76
    Indian classical music and, 197–98
    Luce, Henry and Clare, and, 119
    Nin, Anaïs and, 119–21
    Osmond, Humphrey, and, 109, 222–23
    pioneering psychedelic research, as prime focus of, 129–34, 268n16
    playing music on, 71–72
    spiritual value of, 15, 32
    value of in psychedelic therapy, 58
    Watts, Alan, and, 65–66, 104, 249n3
    See also: Bache, Christopher; Cohen, Sidney; Dunlop, Jane; Grof, Stanislav
LSD—The Consciousness-Expanding Drug, xii
Luce, Henry and Clare, 119
Ludlow, Fitz Hugh, 72, 118
Luna, Luis Eduardo, 195–96
Lundborg, Patrick, 134–35, 171–72
Lyadov, Anatoly, 172, 233

Maeterlinck, Maurice, 1, 34
magic mushrooms. *See* psilocybin
Mangini, Mariavittoria, 273n15
Mannes, Elena, 179
"Mantra-Rock Dance," xv
marijuana. *See* cannabis
Maryland Psychiatric Research Center (MPRC), 31, 140, 150
Maslow, Abraham, 29

Masters, R.E.L., see *Varieties of Psychedelic Experience, The*
McDaniel, June, 6–7
McFerrin, Bobby, 179
McKenna, Terence, 4, 20, 162, 217
Meister Eckhart, 77
Mendelssohn, Felix, 149, 233
Menuhin, Yehudi, 197, 199
Mescal: A New Artificial Paradise (Havelock Ellis), 172–73, 263n3
mescaline, 21, 32–33, 45, 47, 60, 109, 135, 172–73, 198, 221, 250–51n23. *See also* peyote
metaself, 60
Mira, 115–16
Mitchell, Andy, 153–54
MK-ULTRA, 267n2, 267n5
More, Paul Elmer, 90–91
Moreau, Jacques-Joseph, 69, 95–97, 113
Morely, Paul, 166–67
Mozart, Wolfgang Amadeus, 157, 168–69, 175, 178, 233
    "communicate tenderness and the spirit of play" (Naranjo), 177
    sung by a mosquito (ayahuasca hallucination), 209–10
    "supremely psychedelic" (Richards), 175
    understood for first time on LSD, 93
    works of heard under psychedelics, 78–79, 93, 103–104, 106, 161, 169, 178
Music I [general and universal characteristics]
    aesthetic responsiveness to, 37
    Al-Gazzali on, 38–39
    arouses feelings of the numinous (Rudolf Otto), 40–41
    axis-mundi—link to higher worlds, as, 43

brain-mediated (second-hand) hearing of, 50–51
"charm" as ineffable quality of, 88–89, 261–62n12
communicates more deeply than language, 36–37, 41, 43–44
composer as transmitter of higher wisdom, 36–37, 39, 44–45, 161, 169–71
defies rational analysis, 9–10, 37
ecstatic experience, "best door way to" (Naranjo), 47–48
emotion and, 10, 11, 39, 40–41, 44, 82, 89–91; emotional nuance and, 97–98
faulty and limited hearing of, 49, 50–51, 53, 54, 83–84
gives form to our inner experience, voice to our deepest instincts, 38, 39, 44
hallucinated, 112–18
Hoffman, E. T. A. on, 38
inexpressible, expresses the, 35, 38, 44
"liquid metaphysics," as (Tavener), 37
"meaning" of resides in the emotions it conveys or invokes, 43–44
multi-dimensional or transpersonal, as, 39–40, 90–92
mystical properties and functions of, 35–41
ontology of, similar to that of psychedelics, 8–10
other worlds and higher realms, as portal to, 38–39, 43, 101
Proust on, 41
Pythagorean notions of, 101, 117
Romanticism and, 36–37
Schopenhauer on, 36–37, 90, 170
subconscious and transpersonal realms, invoked by, 90–91
subjective nature of experience of, 154–56
"supreme mystery of the science of man," as (Claude Levi-Strauss), 45
trance states, conducive to, 60–61, 101–102
transcendence, expresses a longing for, 38–40
Wordsworth on, 215
"world-creating power" of, 10
Music II [in psychedelic states]
aesthetics and mysticism of, 41–48, 54–55, 71
"becoming the music" (via dissolution of ego), 13, 21, 44, 45, 48, 76–79
cannabis/hashish and, 68–69, 72, 74–75, 95–97, 118–19, 163, 165–66
choral/chorus, 72, 117–18, 121, 125, 161, 169, 175, 176, 177
composer, insights into or communion with, 13, 44–45, 74–75, 158, 163
delightful even to the nonmusical, 71
dosage, intensity of experience of influenced by, 21
emotion and, 10, 43–44, 63, 71, 78, 81–82, 92–98, 140
experiencer testimonies: Donovan, 104; Robert Graves, 105; Aldous Huxley, 45–46, 54–55; Michael Pollan, 46, 71, 76–77, 106–107, 209; William Richards, 77–78; Huston Smith, 93–94; select others, 46–47, 69, 73, 75, 77, 78, 78–79, 79, 93, 106
eyes, should be closed while listening, 31, 61, 104, 107, 109, 142, 143, 146, 172, 209

Music I *(continued)*
  focus on any one instrument in an orchestra, ability to, 13, 71, 72, 75
  "food and fuel" for psychedelic states, as 42
  Gregorian chant experienced under, 157, 169, 178, 195
  hallucinated/imagined, 111–12, 118–27
  heard as if for the first time, 8, 72, 77, 140, 250n18
  hearer should avoid distanced, intellectual, critical attitude, 174
  hearing as composer heard the music, 45, 74
  "hyperreal," experienced as, 47–48
  hypersensitivity to, 12–13, 70–75
  integration (post trip), use of music in, 164–65, 215–17
  "jungle gym" analogy for consciousness-stabilizing function of, 11, 61–62
  "letting go"/surrendering, music as aide to, 55–61
  nature sounds ("music of nature") as alternative to, 207–11
    playlists, 244–45, 277n11, 277n12
  negative experiences with, 71 (*see also* 259n19), 149–50, 156–57, 158, 179–80, 187–88
  overtones and microintervals, more acute perception of, 71
  "penetrates to inaccessible realms of consciousness," 91–92
  performance of, under psychedelic, 43, 71–72
  "placeholder" for deconstructed inner psychic structure, as, 61–62
  playlists, 7, 8, 153–54, 216;
    abbreviated, select playlists (Appendix II), 231–45; curation of author's, xviii, 97–98, 158–59, 162–63, 179–80, 185–86, 195–96, 227; titles, descriptions, and links to, 180–83, 188–90, 203–205, 211 (*see also* 277n11/12), 212 (*see also* 277n13), 213 (*see also* 277n17), 228–30
  popular, classical preferred over, by patients (Leo Zeff), 164
  Rock, music of choice among 1960s psychonauts, 272n4; psychedelic (playlist), 230; psychotomimetic (dark/disturbing) forms of, popular with some psychonauts, 218–20
  set and setting, critical role of in, 42
  "smooth, peaceful, and majestic music is best" (Pahnke), 177
  subjectivity/variability of experience, 144–45, 153–54, 156–57
  timbre (as conveyor of emotion), more nuanced processing of, 71
  timelessness and, 12–13, 62–63, 65–70, 73
  "vehicle that takes you to all the different places you go on your trip," the (Stolaroff), 142
  visionary states via, *see* psychedelics and psychedelic experience: synesthesia/eidetic vision
  white noise as alternative to, 211–13, 265n2
    playlists, 245, 277n13, 277n17
  women's voices, 177, 243–44
  See also ambient/electronica; classical music; names of individual composers; psychedelics and psychedelic experience: synesthesia/eidetic

vision; psychedelic therapy, role of music in
Music and the Ineffable. *See* Jankelevitch, Vladimir
"music of the spheres," 117, 123
Music, the Brain, and Ecstasy. *See* Jourdain, Robert
Musicophilia: Tales of Music and the Brain. *See* Sacks, Oliver
Mussorgsky, Modest, 75, 234
mysticism, 6–7, 8, 35, 40, 42, 53, 66, 84–85, 91, 104

Nada Brahman, Sabda Brahman ("sound is God"), x, 48, 116, 196
Naranjo, Claudio, 44–45, 47–48, 61, 145, 161, 176–77, 193
nature, "music" of, 207–11, 244–45
near-death experience, 116, 117
Neo-classical, 190, 235–37
Nin, Anaïs, 2, 119–21
"Norwegian Wood" (Beatles), xii
Nutt, David, 268–69n21

Ockeghem, Johannes, 165, 166
Olatunji, Babatunde, 79, 242
opium, 1
Osmond, Humphry, 16, 50, 109, 131, 137, 148, 155, 222–23
Otto, Rudolf, 40–41, 193

Pachelbel, 175
Pahnke, Walter N., 81–82, 93, 145, 177. *See also* Bonny and Pahnke
paranormal, 92, 116–18. *See also* hallucinated music
Parrish, Maxfield, 67
perception, 12, 18–20, 24–25, 28, 50–54, 65, 70, 137, 155, 172, 250n21
peyote, 94, 100, 121, 168–69, 198. *See also* mescaline

pharmaceuticals, 21, 30, 157
Phenomenology, 2, 23, 27, 49, 52, 172, 215
piano, 157, 172–73, 177, 178, 232, 233
Pilch, John J., 60
Plato, 33, 43, 103
playlists. *See under* Music II
Plotinus, 20
Poetic Vision and the Psychedelic Experience (Durr), 52, 249n15
Pollan, Michael, 18, 22–24, 27, 51–52, 208–209
    psilocybin experiences of, 46, 71, 76–77, 106–107, 209
Poulenc, Francis, 175
Proust, Marcel, 41
psilocybin/magic mushrooms, 15, 24, 71, 77, 93–94, 178, 216, 221, 250–51n23, 253n28, 261n6. *See also* Pollan, Michael, psilocybin experiences of
Psychedelia—An Ancient Culture, A Modern Way of Life, 134–35, 171–72
Psychedelic Psychotherapy. *See* Grof, Stanislav
psychedelic renaissance, 13, 14, 151, 222–24, 261n8
psychedelic science, xix, 6, 15, 85–86, 151, 153–54, 222–24
psychedelics and psychedelic experience
    aesthetic sensitivity and awareness enhanced by, 12–13, 25–27, 37–38, 42–43, 52, 53–54, 65, 71, 74
    awe, as key aspect of phenomenology of, 27, 33, 51, 158, 181, 210
    "bad trip," 57, 218–19, 221, 222, 251n25
    "cerebral reducing-valve" model of, 18–20, 33, 82

psychedelics and psychedelic
    experience *(continued)*
  "cosmic consciousness," compared
    to, 29–30
  de-habituation as effect of, 13,
    49–54, 60–61
  dosage, 21–22, 27. *See also* LSD,
    dosage
  early research in, 129–34; animal
    experimentation, 131–32;
    children as patients and
    experimental subjects, 132–34;
    conferences and conference
    proceedings, 129–34, 136–38;
    confusion and conflict within,
    129–31, 134; dissenters to the
    psychiatric/medical model,
    134–36; funding by CIA
    (MK-ULTRA), 267n5; humanistic
    and existential approaches, 136–
    39; self-dosing by researchers,
    130, 267n3
  Eastern religions/philosophies and,
    xiii–xvi, 28, 53–54, 193
  effects of as highly variable, 17,
    20–22
  ego/egotism/egoic: basic functions
    of, 22–23; as controlling,
    censorious, 24, 52, 56, 60, 81,
    82, 92; defenses of, 57, 60, 85,
    87; dissolving of ("ego-loss"),
    22–25, 26, 27, 31–32, 66, 76,
    218–19; divides conscious from
    subconscious, 22–23; divides self
    and other, 22–23, 24–25; Albert
    Hoffman on, 24–25; inflation
    of, 15, 85, 223; insubstantiality
    of, 24; interior and exterior,
    57; D. H. Lawrence on, 24;
    mental and societal construct,
    as, 22, 60; music and art, in
    (egotism), 75; music "detours,"
    140; music's effect on, 11,
    57–58, 62; Michael Pollan on
    importance in psychedelic theory,
    22–24; surrendering of, 56, 59;
    transcendence of, 137–38, 197;
    Alan Watts on, 24
  emotion: intensification of, 25, 81–84,
    92–97; subject of, disarming to
    researchers, 84–86, 87–88. *See
    also* Music II: emotion and
  excessive use of, 15
  five phases/stages of, 145–48
  "gratuitous grace" or spiritual gift,
    as, 15, 257n33
  humanistic/experiential vs.
    scientific/medical approaches to,
    xix, 2–7, 84–87, 129–39, 151,
    153–54, 249n15
  integration (post-trip), use of music
    in, 165, 215–17
  language, limitations of in
    describing, xix, 1–2, 32–33, 41,
    54, 106, 217, 249n3, 254–55n15
  legality/illegality of, 13–14, 84, 129,
    221
  "letting go"/surrender, as key to
    the experience (and resistance
    against), 55–61
  meaning/meaningfulness,
    intensification of, 26–27, 47
  museum, visiting while on, 15, 251n26
  music. *See* Music II; psychedelic
    therapy, role of music in
  mystical/spiritual aspects of, 15,
    23–24, 24–25, 28–29, 30–34, 42,
    65–66, 86–87, 104
  nature/natural beauty, appreciation
    enhanced by, 28, 208–209, 210
  "non-specific catalysts" of psyche,
    as, 21–22
  "non-specific catalyst" vs. spiritual/
    metaphysical experience, 29–32

ontology of, similar to that of music, 8–10
overviews/inventories of general effects on consciousness, 25–27
"peak" experience described, 27–29
pharmaceuticals, contrasted with standard, 20–22
psyche: authentic expressions of, facilitated by, 21–22; intrinsic wisdom and healing powers of, stimulated by, 27
psychedelic vs. *psycholytic* therapy, 31–32
psychiatry, critical tools for (as are microscope and telescope for science), 22
"psychotomimetic": tendencies in the arts, 218–20; model promoted by CIA, 267n5
set and setting, 8, 17, 59, 250n17; "collective," 220–25
"stunning synergy" of, with music, 101
subconscious/buried memories, provide access to, 25, 91–92
synesthesia/eidetic vision, 10, 12, 73, 78, 99–110, 171; with hallucinated music, 119–27
time (slowing of); timelessness, 7, 12–13, 25, 62–63, 65–70, 73, 140
"too early for a science of" (McKenna), 4, 162, 217
widespread use of, 13, 250–51n23
See also LSD; other psychoactive substances; Music II; psychedelic therapy, role of music in
psychedelic therapy, role of music in, 139–51
aids initial ascent and soothes difficulties thereafter, 11, 56, 57–59, 141, 146
assists patients in surrendering to the experience, 58, 140
choices and practices to avoid, 148–51, 158
"detours the ego and intellectual controls," 140
emotions, facilitates access to and release of deep, 5, 81–82, 140, 141, 147
group sessions, music in, 141–43, 145
moves patients from intellectual to emotional level, 141
peak experience, facilitates, 140
"potentiates" the drug, 141
projection screen for consciousness and emotions, serves as, 11, 155–56
selection of, guidelines for therapists, 143–48
"sincerity" of music, clients sensitive to, 74–75, 144
stimulates patient's imagination. *See* psychedelics and psychedelic experience: synesthesia/eidetic vision
structure/stabilization, provides, 5, 11, 61–63, 140–41, 141, 147
subconscious, facilitates access to, 11, 91, 140
See also Music II
psychiatry/psychiatrists, 14, 22, 31, 129–30, 134, 135, 154, 222–24
Psychology Today, 99

Rago, D. Scott, 116–18
Ram Dass (Richard Alpert), xiii, xiv, 15, 57, 136
Ravel, Maurice, 177, 234
Realms of the Human Unconscious (Grof), 29–30, 32
Respighi, Ottorino, 178

Richards, William A., vii, ix–x, 27, 44, 56, 139, 148, 150, 164–65, 175–76, 195, 203, 250n17
Roberts, Thomas Bradford, 6, 251n25
Robinson, Victor, 119
Romanticism, 36–37, 38, 50, 52, 171
Roszak, Theodore, 31, 247–48n5
Rouget, Gilbert, 61, 250n16
Rousseau, Jean-Jacques, 4, 28
Roussel, Albert, 156
Rubber Soul (Beatles), xii

Sabina, Maria, 105, 178
Sacks, Oliver, 50–51, 112–13, 155
Sacred Knowledge: Psychedelics and Religious Experience. *See* William Richards
sacred sound/music, 47–48, 175, 176, 193, 196, 210–11, 275n3. *See also* *Nada Brahman*
Schleiermacher, Friedrich, 158
Schopenhauer, Arthur, 36–37, 44, 52, 90, 170
Schubert, Franz, 112, 177
Schumann, Robert, 39, 113, 173, 234
Scriabin, Alexander, 175
Segovia, Andrés, 157
Shakespeare, William, 108, 207
shaman/shamanic, 62, 94, 179, 193, 195–96, 204, 223, 242–43, 255n17
Shankar, Ravi, xii, xiii, 79, 104, 162, 176, 178, 194, 196–97, 207, 242, 275n16. *See also* Hindu/Indian music: importance in psychedelic counterculture
Shanon, Benny, 37–38, 42–44, 62–63, 74, 82, 101, 102, 121–23, 209–10, 255n17, 261–62n12
Shipibo (Shipibo-Conibo), 195
silence, 35, 112, 142, 150–51, 193, 208, 229
Simmel, Georg, 83–84

sitar, xii, 79, 162, 197–98, 200, 205, 242, 275n16
Smetana, Bedřich, 177
Smith, Huston, 32, 86–87, 93–94, 200–201
"Sound Meditation for Psychedelic States" playlist, 238–39
Stanley, Owsley, xv
Steindl-Rast, David, 7
Stolaroff, Myron J., 3, 123, 141–42, 146, 147, 147–48, 164, 178
Storr, Anthony, 155–56
Strassman, Rick, 148, 150
Strauss, Richard, 75
Stravinsky, Igor, 177, 234
Sufi/Sufism, 193, 195, 229, 240, 260n39
Sullivan, Lawrence E., 102
Suso, Henry, 114
synesthesia. *See under* psychedelics and psychedelic experience

tamboura, xiv, 79, 205, 239
Taoism/Taoist, 28, 53, 66
Tart, Charles, 20–21, 68
Tavener, John, 37
Tchaikovsky, Pyotr Ilyich, 46–47, 113 (*see also* 265n8), 124, 235
Thérèse of Lisieux, Saint, 114
Thoreau, Henry David, xi
Tibetan ritual music, 195, 200–203
Tibetan Book of the Dead, 56
time perception, timelessness. *See under* psychedelics and psychedelic experience
Timmermann, Christopher, 188
Tippett, Michael, 39
Tolstoy, Leo, 45, 89–90
Traherne, Thomas, 50, 105
trance, 60–61, 101–102, 115–16, 195–96, 197, 204, 242–43, 250n16. *See also* "deep listening"

"Tribal, Trance, Drums, Shamanic, Ayahuasca" playlist, 195–96, 204, 242–43
trip-reports (general comments), xix, 2, 5, 8, 161, 162, 216, 217
Tumbleweed, Daniel, 251n26

Use of LSD in Psychotherapy and Alcoholism, The, 136–38, 268n16

Varieties of Psychedelic Experience, The, xii, 57, 135, 264n29
Varieties of Religious Experience, The. *See* William James
Vaughan Williams, Ralph, 172, 235
Verdi, Giuseppe, 157, 175
violin, 46, 70, 72, 114, 125, 197, 205, 231–36 passim, 242, 274n33
Vivaldi, Antonio, 174

Wagner, Richard, 149
Wasson, R. Gordon, 2, 103, 105
Watts, Alan, vii, xi, xiii, 2, 24, 50, 52, 65–66, 68, 103, 104, 136, 221, 249n3
Wilber, Ken, 3

Wittgenstein, Ludwig, 66–67
Wordsworth, William, 51, 52, 181, 215
world/ethnic music, 191–205
 entheogens deepen openness and insight into, 191
 introduced to the West by returning hippie travelers, 193–94
 playlists, 204–205, 239–41
 provides access to the world's collective unconscious, 194
 recommendations in by various "psychedelic" writers, 194–96
 sacred forms of, open the listener to other religious and spiritual forms, 192–93
 See also Hindu/Indian music; Shankar, Ravi; sitar; Tibetan ritual music

Yo-Yo Ma, 179
Yoshimatu, Takashi, 172
Younghusband, Sir Francis, 114

Zeff, Leo, 142–43, 150, 176